History of Rock and Roll

Thomas E. Larson
University of Nebraska

KENDALL/HUNT PUBLISHING COMPANY
4050 Westmark Drive   Dubuque, Iowa 52002

Book Team
Chairman and Chief Executive Officer   Mark C. Falb
Senior Vice President, College Division   Thomas W. Gantz
Director of National Book Program   Paul B. Carty
Editorial Development Manager   Georgia Botsford
Developmental Editor   Lynne Rogers
Vice President, Production and Manufacturing   Alfred C. Grisanti
Assistant Vice President, Production Services   Christine E. O'Brien
Project Coordinator   Kimberly Terry
Permissions Editor   Colleen Zelinsky
Designer   Jodi Splinter
Managing Editor, College Field   David L. Tart
Associate Managing Editor, College Field   W. Ray Wood
Acquisitions Editor, College Field   Eric Klosterman

Cover Images © Digital Vision
Copyright © 2004 by Kendall/Hunt Publishing Company

ISBN 0-7872-9969-3

Printed in the United States of America
10 9 8 7 6 5 4 3

ABOUT THE AUTHOR

Tom Larson teaches the History of Rock Music, History of American Jazz and jazz piano at the University of Nebraska-Lincoln School of Music. He received a Bachelor of Music Degree from Berklee College of Music in Boston, Massachusetts in 1977 and a Master of Music in Composition from the University of Nebraska in 1985. He has composed the scores for numerous documentary films, including *In the White Man's Image, Around the World in 72 Days* and *Monkey Trial* for WGBH-TV's *The American Experience, In Search of the Oregon Trail* for the Public Broadcasting System, and *Ashes From the Dust* for NOVA. Larson has played in numerous rock, jazz and jazz/rock bands over the years, and in 2003 released his first CD of original compositions entitled *Flashback.* He is also the author of *History and Tradition of Jazz,* also published by Kendall/Hunt.

CONTENTS

CHAPTER 7
1960S BLUES AND PSYCHEDELIA
135

CHAPTER 8
CHANGING DIRECTIONS   159

PREFACE

Rock and roll is the music of America, of youth, of rebellion, and of the common spirit that ties all that together. It has also, since its birth nearly fifty years ago, spread throughout the entire world. Its history is a compelling story of musical and cultural changes that like a tidal wave changed the existing mores and conventions of life in the 20th century. Rock and roll's history is the story of controversy, tragedy and self-indulgence; and also of love, peace and the triumph of the human spirit. The history of rock and roll also encompasses the stories of some of the most interesting and creative people of the last half-century.

The History of Rock and Roll is designed for the college non-music major, but is also useful and interesting reading for anyone. Although at the current time there are not an abundance of college level rock history courses offered, it is the author's belief that in time this will change as the cultural impact of rock and roll becomes more self evident. This book is a resource for any rock music class whose intent is to make the connections between the music and the culture in which it interacted.

Included with *The History of Rock and Roll* is an audio CD that contains twenty-two important recordings that are described in short synopses at the conclusion of the text. These recordings are in no way a complete anthology (most of the important recordings from the sixties forward are simply to expensive to license at this time), but they are worthy of further study. The synopses that accompany each recording provide interesting insights and information that can assist in the understanding of the music and the recording artists. Obviously, this CD will need to be augmented with other recordings for a complete study of rock and roll.

The History of Rock and Roll also details the most important rock styles, how they evolved, and their important artists, as well as a listing of key recordings in each. The text also contains biographical information on recording artists, composers, producers, DJ's, record executives, and other figures relevant to the history of the music. It is my hope that any interested student of the music will find the text to provide a wealth of information that will nurture an understanding of the music and its place in our cultural fabric.

Thomas E. Larson

ACKNOWLEDGMENTS

I would like to gratefully thank the following people who have assisted in some way with the completion of this book:

Kendall/Hunt Publishing, and especially Development Editors Liz Recker and Angela Willenbring for your help, guidance and enthusiasm.

Tom Laskey at Sony Music for helping secure music permissions.

Carolyn McMahon of the Associated Press and Casey Coleman of the Lincoln Journal Star for help in securing photo permissions.

Dr. Scott Anderson for countless stimulating discussions on the subject of rock history and for the loaning of a ton of valuable books and CDs.

Dr. Randall Snyder for being an inspiration and a source of wisdom.

All the rock musicians who I have rehearsed with, hung out and listened to records with, played gigs and had a ton of fun with since 1970.

James Pelter and Jim Koudelka for additional assistance and information.

Thomas Irvin for proofreading and editing.

Lastly, thanks to those with whom I am closest for your support and general willingness to put up with me while I was writing: my daughter Kalie and son Will (thanks to both of you for your thoughtful insights and opinions); Carolyn and Kim Collier; and especially my parents, who back in my garage band days managed to survive countless hours of bone rattling basement rehearsals, kids coming and going at all hours of the day and night, and the fear of not knowing where it was all leading to while still remaining supportive.

Tom Larson

The Roots of Rock and Roll

Rock and Roll: The Music That Changed the World

When rock and roll exploded onto the American landscape in the mid 1950s, it marked nothing less than a defining moment in our history. Rock and roll represented the beginnings of a seismic shift in our cultural fabric: from an elitist to a working class ethos; from an adult-oriented society to one that was youth oriented; and from one where art was defined by European standards to one where art was defined in purely American terms. The birth of rock and roll came about from the convergence of musical parents that included the blues, jazz, rhythm and blues, gospel, hillbilly, country, folk, and honky tonk music. However, almost from the beginning, rock embraced a wide variety of influences, from new technologies, changing social conditions, and interpretations by British imitators. As a result, it evolved very quickly: within ten years or so there were already a number of styles that fit under the rock umbrella. To demonstrate how remarkable that is, consider that jazz and the blues both evolved in a sort of one-style-at-a-time fashion for nearly fifty years before they started the natural process of diversification.

The emergence of rock and roll also signaled a major shift in the nature of our popular music. Unlike the pop music of the first half of the 20th century, which was largely conceived by an industry based in New York and watered down to appeal to the largest audience possible—in other words, white, middle class America—rock and roll was from the south and middle states, and was decidedly rural, lower class, and dynamic. It was also dramatically more African American. This shift underscores one of the central themes that runs throughout the music's history: the virus-like resistance that rock has shown to meddling by the pop music industry. Every time the industry appears to have harnessed the music's power for its own self-interest, rock and roll seems to take an unpredictable turn and reinvent itself. Like the musicians who create it, rock in this sense is rebellious and independent, resentful of authority, and defies subordination.

Rock and roll is, simply stated, the music of the people. During the mid-1950s, it exploded onto the American cultural landscape through the insistence of small independent record labels, renegade radio DJs, and a teen audience that wouldn't take the watered-down industry product any more. For the first time in our history, the music of the streets and cities, of the underprivileged and disaffected, the angry and rebellious became America's popular music. As rock and roll took its place on center stage, it changed our society, and in turn reflected those changes within itself. In a sense, it changed America and the world.

This chapter will look into American music as it evolved in the first half of the 20th century and how it laid the groundwork for the rock and roll revolution, examining the different styles that emerged and the people who made them happen. Subsequent chapters will look at the evolutionary stages of rock music, and the important people and events that have shaped the course of the most important and influential music in history.

The Early Years of American Pop Music

TIN PAN ALLEY

America's pop music industry was created in the late 1800s when the publishers and songwriters of Tin Pan Alley began to supply vaudeville and Broadway shows with popular songs. These songs were also made available in written form to the general public through the sale of **sheet music.** Tin Pan Alley was originally an actual place, on 28th Street between Broadway and 6th Avenue in New York, where many of the earliest publishing companies set up shop. Although most eventually moved uptown, the name stuck and today is generally used to describe the music publishing industry as it operated in the first half of the 20th century. The music of the Tin Pan Alley composers defined much of our popular song catalogue of the era, and was eventually used not only for theatrical shows but also for popular songs, Hollywood movies, and jazz standards. Among the greatest Tin Pan Alley composers were **Irving Berlin** ("God Bless America," "White Christmas"); **George and Ira Gershwin** ("I Got Rhythm," "'S Wonderful"); **Richard Rodgers,** teaming with lyricists **Lorenz Hart** ("My Funny Valentine") and **Oscar Hammerstein II** (Broadway musicals *South Pacific, Oklahoma, The Sound of Music*); and **Cole Porter** ("I've Got You Under My Skin").

THE FIRST POP SINGERS

One of the first important pop singers in 20th century America was **Al Jolson,** who, singing in blackface as minstrel singers had done in the mid-1800s, became Broadway's biggest star in the early 1900s. In 1927 Jolson also starred in the first successful talking picture, *The Jazz Singer.* As recordings and radio began to replace sheet music as the most popular medium by which to distribute pop music, the first true pop singers, known as crooners, emerged. **Rudy Vallee,** who used a megaphone to project his voice (before amplification was used), became one of the first entertainers to effectively use radio to reach stardom in the 1920s. **Bing Crosby** became the most influential crooner with his easy-going charm and witty style of singing ballads. Starting his career in 1926 making records with the Paul Whiteman Orchestra (with whom he had his first number 1 hit in 1928 with "Ol' Man River"), Crosby began working in network radio and film in 1931, eventually starring in more than sixty movies before his death in 1977. His recording of "White Christmas" from the 1942 movie *Holiday Inn* rose to the number 1 spot on the charts, won a Grammy Award for best song of 1942, and eventually sold over 30 million copies, making it the best selling single in history.

The first pop singer to create a unique personal style and image was **Frank Sinatra.** Influenced by jazz singers Louis Armstrong and Billy Holiday, Sinatra took liberties with melodies and interpreted songs in his

Sheet music is music that is notated and sold in a loose, unbound sheet format. From the late nineteenth century to the present, popular music had been sold in this fashion, with lyrics, melody, and piano accompaniment.

Tin Pan Alley Composers

- ❏ Irving Berlin
- ❏ George & Ira Gershwin
- ❏ Richard Rodgers
- ❏ Lorenz Hart
- ❏ Oscar Hammerstain II
- ❏ Cole Porter

See Appendix A, "The Way You Look Tonight" by Frank Sinatra. Track 1 on enclosed CD.

The first pop singer to create a unique personal style and image was Frank Sinatra.
AP/WIDE WORLD PHOTOS

own way. Starting as a big band singer with the Tommy Dorsey Orchestra, Sinatra became a solo artist and film star in the fifties, while developing a tough guy image that made him appear as both dangerous and admirable at the same time. Although he condemned rock and roll at first, Sinatra's public macho posturing, womanizing, and associations with shadowy figures in fact became a sort of blueprint for many rock stars that followed him. He also spawned a whole generation of dark and handsome Italian singers, such as Dean Martin, Tony Bennett and Vic Damone, who also had considerable pop success.

THE SWING ERA

During the Swing Era (1935-1946), big band jazz or swing music became the dominant form of pop music. Swing brought the recording industry back to life after it was almost killed by the Depression. It helped the country get through WWII, as many of the biggest Swing Era hits were sentimental in nature and reflected the mood of anxiety that accompanied the war. Swing also firmly established itself as music to dance to, and spawned several dance fads, such as the Fox Trot, Lindy Hop, Jitterbug, and Rumba. During the early years of the Swing Era, most of the hit records were of original material written and arranged by the bands themselves. After 1942, most of the hits were novelty and sing-along songs from Tin Pan Alley that featured the band vocalists. It was in this way that the careers of Frank Sinatra, Doris Day, Peggy Lee, and others were launched.

The first star of the Swing Era was the unassuming **Benny Goodman,** whose meteoric rise to fame started at the Palomar Ballroom in Los Angeles on August 21, 1935. Hundreds of teens showed up that night to hear and dance to the music they had been hearing on the NBC network radio program *Let's Dance.* One secret of Goodman's success was the arrangements he had bought from black musicians such as **Fletcher Henderson** and **Don Redman** which up to that point had rarely been heard outside of Harlem. By virtue of being white, Goodman was able to bring the music of African American culture to the mass white audience, in much the same way that Elvis Presley would do twenty years later. In his wake, hundreds of other bands that looked like Goodman's and sounded like pale imitations of the Harlem musicians who created the music provided the country with the soundtrack to an era.

Sinatra on Rock and Roll

Fank Sinatra, who was the object of shrieking female fans himself in the 1940s, originally dismissed rock and roll, commenting that "It is sung, played, and written for the most part by cretinous goons, and by means of its almost imbecilic reiteration and sly, lewd, in plain fact dirty, lyrics it manages to be the martial music of every side-burned delinquent on the face of the earth." However, his tune quickly changed, and by 1960 he co-hosted a network TV special with Elvis Presley on which the two sang each other's signature tunes, "Love Me Tender" and "Witchcraft."

THE POST-WAR YEARS

From 1946 to 1954, the pop music business was in transition—essentially the calm years before the storm hit that changed everything. **Race music** (later called rhythm and blues) and country western songs were becoming increasingly popular among a growing, albeit segmented, audience. In spite of this, the major labels pretty much ignored these styles and their audiences, as they had done since the 1920s, and continued to promote their mainstream pop artists such as **Patti Page, Perry Como, Rosemary Clooney,** and Sinatra. During this same time period, a number of small independent record labels began to spring up, eager to find any kind of niche in the marketplace; R&B and country music fit the bill for many. In spite of the fact that by 1952 there were around 100 independents, their mark on the industry was still negligible—only five of the 163 singles that were million sellers between 1946 and 1952 came from independent labels.

On the rare occasion that an R&B or country record did break through and become a hit, the strategy that major labels often employed was to quickly record a **cover** version by a pop singer that had a broad commercial appeal. Covers were usually stripped of anything that might be offensive to any segment of record buyers, including any traces of ethnic vocal delivery or off-color lyrics. As a result, most often ended up sounding sanitized and antiseptic, even laughable. The poster child for this tactic could have been **Pat Boone,** whose watered-down covers of Fats Domino's "Ain't That a Shame" in 1955 and Little Richard's "Tutti Frutti" in 1956 both outsold the original versions.

Covers were an effective strategy for the 1946–54 period, and as a result were an obstacle to commercial success for many R&B and country artists and their independent labels. However, once white teenagers started demanding the real thing, covers were no longer an effective marketing approach.

A **cover** is a new recording of a charting song that seeks to 'cover' up the original recording.

The Music Industry

RECORD SALES: 1920–1959

Although Victrola phonograph players had been around since the early 1900s, it took several years before they became popular with consumers and there were any significant record sales. Before 1920, two of the most popular artists were opera singer Enrico Caruso and concert bandleader John Phillip Sousa (composer of "The Stars and Stripes Forever"). The first jazz recording, "Livery Stable Blues" made in 1917 by the Original Dixieland Jazz Band was one of the first records to sell over one million copies. Throughout the 1920s, record sales were generally strong, hovering around $100 million a year. However, when radio first became popular in the mid-1920s and the Great Depression hit in 1929, record sales went into a tailspin, dropping to $6 million almost immediately, causing most of the smaller independent labels to go out of business.

Helped by the popularity of crooners like Bing Crosby and the big band music of the Swing Era, record sales rebounded throughout the thirties and forties. By 1945, sales were back up to $109 million; after wartime restrictions on shellac were lifted, sales soared to $218 million in 1946 where they leveled off for the next eight years. Helping the recovery was the introduction of the Duo Jr. in 1932, which, selling for $16.50, was the first affordable and portable electric turntable. In 1934 jukeboxes began popping up in thousands of restaurants and nightclubs around the country, which in some years accounted for as much as 40% of all record sales. Once rock and roll caught on with the nation's teenagers, record sales took off again and nearly tripled between 1954 and 1959, from $213 million to $613 million.

RECORDING TECHNOLOGY

There were vast improvements in the way recordings were made and sold throughout the first half of the 20th century. Before 1925, recordings were made using the **acoustical process,** in which an acoustical horn captured the sound of the musicians huddled in front of it and transferred the sound vibrations to a stylus that cut grooves onto a wax disc. Because the shellac records that resulted spun at 78 rpm, only three minutes of music could be recorded on a side. Because of the poor frequency response of the process, records also sounded tinny. In 1925, the **electrical process** was introduced, where microphones were used to transfer the sound waves to an electrical signal, greatly improving sound quality.

After World War II, magnetic tape recorders were increasingly used to record the master tapes from which records were pressed. Among the many advantages to tape recording to disc recording is the ability to edit the master tape. An engineer could now construct a new version of a song by splicing two or more separate takes (or versions) together, eliminating any mistakes that may have been present in the original takes. This was a giant leap forward for recording artists, who previously had to strive for cutting a perfect take to disc, or settle for an imperfect one. Tape is also cheap, and can be reused many times, allowing an engineer to simply record over a bad take to further cut costs. It also allowed for longer songs to be recorded, as tape reels could hold up to 30 minutes of music, eliminating the 3-minute limit of the 78-rpm disc.

Two back-to-back innovations in the late forties also had a dramatic impact on the record business. In 1948, Columbia introduced the 12-inch **33-1/3 LP** (long playing) format. In addition to an increased playing time of 23 minutes of music per side, LPs were made of vinylite (vinyl), which offered superior fidelity and made the records less breakable and easier to distribute. The next year, RCA Victor introduced a rival format, the 7-inch **45 rpm** format, also on vinyl (later on polystyrene). RCA also introduced a low cost portable turntable that included an attachment enabling several 45s to be stacked, allowing the listener a sequence of uninterrupted songs to play. Within a few years, all the major record labels were releasing product on both formats, with 45s becoming more popular with teens, LPs among adults. In 1958, the world standard for stereo was established and the first stereo LPs were sold soon after.

The **acoustical process,** used an accoustical horn to capture the sound of the musicians huddled in front of it and transferred the sound vibrations to a stylus that cut grooves onto a wax disc.

In the **electrical process,** microphones are used to transfer sound waves to an electrical signal.

The Black Roots of Rock and Roll

THE BLUES

The blues is a uniquely American musical form, born in the southern middle states sometime between the years 1880 and 1900. It evolved from the **work songs** and **field hollers** sung by slaves in plantation fields and prison camps. Songs sung to accompany various daily jobs and duties are a functional part of everyday life in Africa and a celebration of doing work to improve the quality of one's life. In the New World, however, the very nature of the work song began to change, as the singer was no longer doing work for himself but for someone else—and the work did not improve the quality of life. Over time, the songs sung in the fields, therefore, became personal expressions of pain and oppression. Work songs and field hollers became a catharsis for feelings of lost love, sexual frustration, poverty, jealousy, and hard times. It is from this context that the blues evolved.

After the Civil War, thousands of freed slaves began traveling through the South, looking for work, armed with no job skills to speak of other than as a common laborer. Once **Reconstruction** ended, life became increasingly bleak for many of them, as racial oppression became as commonplace as the hard work and poverty. Singing in work camps, street corners, and juke joints for food and tips was one of the few professions available to a black man in which he wasn't directly working for the white man (preaching was another, and in fact many of the first blues singers were former preachers). Today many scholars speculate that the blues incubated in the **Mississippi Delta,** a 250-mile oval of land stretching south from Memphis, Tennessee to Vicksburg, Mississippi. The characteristics of the blues are listed in Box 1–1.

The First Blues Singers

The first blues performers were solo singers who accompanied themselves on the guitar in a rambling and spontaneous fashion that became known as **country blues.** These performers worked out the basic standard blues formula: a three-phrase **AAB lyric form** of 12-bar length, with each phrase answered by the guitar in a call and response fashion. This evolution occurred in the backwoods away from almost everyone who might have been interested, and before there were any recording devices, so documentation of exactly how it happened is scarce. One of the first to archive the blues was **W. C. Handy,** a bandleader and former schoolteacher from Alabama, who in 1903 heard a man playing and singing at

Work Songs and **Field Hollers** were songs of African origin used to relieve the burden of working in southern work camps.

Reconstruction was the period following the Civil War from 1865–1877 when the Federal Government controlled social legislation in the South that was introduced to grant new rights to freed black citizens.

Country blues were the earliest form of the blues, performed by solo male singers accompanying themselves on guitar.

AAB lyric form is the format of most blues poetry, in which each verse is comprised of three lines, the second of which is a repeat of the first.

Box 1-1 Characteristics of the Blues

1. 12 bar musical form
2. Three phrase, AAB lyrical form
3. Emotional, personal lyrics convey feelings of lust, lost love, jealousy, suffering, hard times, etc.

the train station in Tutwiler, Mississippi. In his autobiography, Handy wrote: "As he played, he pressed a knife on the strings of the guitar in a manner popularized by Hawaiian guitarists who used steel bars. 'Goin' where the Southern cross' the Dog'. The singer repeated the line three times, accompanying himself on the guitar with the weirdest music I had ever heard. The tune stayed in my mind." Realizing the commercial potential of this new music, Handy became the first to publish blues songs, including "Memphis Blues" in 1912 and "St. Louis Blues" in 1914. Both were huge hits through the sale of sheet music, and earned Handy the title "Father of the Blues." The blues remained popular until 1917 when the first jazz recording became a hit and started the jazz craze.

The First Blues Recordings

Classic blues was an early form of the blues from the 1920s, sung by female vocalists with small group backing.

The blues regained its popularity in the twenties with the first commercially sold blues recordings by what became known as the **classic blues** singers. When "Crazy Blues" by Mamie Smith sold one million copies within a year of its 1920 release, record companies realized that there was a huge untapped black consumer market. Most of the classic blues recordings were released on small independent labels such as Vocalion, Black Swan, and Okeh that specialized in race music, a market that the major labels were largely unwilling to pursue. Although many of these female singers were merely singing pop tunes with a tragic delivery (nearly all the records had the word "blues" in the title), some of them such as **Bessie Smith** (the "Empress of the Blues") and **Ethel Waters** were outstanding blues singers. In 1929 the Depression almost killed the record industry, and did manage to finish off the classic blues era.

It wasn't until 1925 that the first country blues singers began to record. It was that year that **Blind Lemon Jefferson** recorded "Black Snake Moan" in Chicago, after having worked his way north through the Delta from his native Texas. Another Texan, Huddie Ledbetter, better known as **Leadbelly** surfaced in the 1940s New York City folk scene with Woody Guthrie and Pete Seeger after several troublesome years in and out of prison. But the most spine-tingling blues performances came from the haunting vocals and bottleneck guitars of the Delta bluesmen, such as **Charley Patton, Willie Brown, Son House,** and **Robert Johnson.** Although Johnson only recorded twenty-nine sides during his life, his songs are among the most influential in American history, including "Love in Vain," "Cross Road Blues," "Sweet Home Chicago," and "I Believe I'll Dust My Broom." Johnson's singing and guitar playing on these recordings is riveting even today. Unfortunately, his mythic life ended before he achieved any real national attention when a jealous husband poisoned him at a juke joint outside of Greenwood, Mississippi in 1938.

Delta Bluesmen

❏ Charley Patton
❏ Willie Brown
❏ Son House
❏ Robert Johnson

Chicago

Boogie woogie was a form of piano blues whose main characteristic is a left hand repeated pattern that imitates blues guitar.

By this time, millions of black folks were heading north to Chicago and other northern industrialized cities in search of a better life and to escape the poverty and racism of the South. The blues followed them and thrived in its new environment. The blues piano style known as **boogie woogie,** although actually born in Texas, was cultivated in Kansas City and Chicago and created a national fad after it was introduced to the rest of the country at John Hammond's "From Spirituals to Swing" concert at New York's Carnegie Hall in December 1938.

Chicago was also where the blues first went electric, when Delta bluesmen began amplifying their guitars to be heard over the din of the crowded clubs on the South Side. One of the first to define the new electric style known as **urban blues** or **Chicago blues** was a Delta transplant named McKinley Morganfield, who went by the name **Muddy Waters.** With menacing vocals and searing bottleneck playing, Waters began recording for Aristocrat Records (later known as Chess) in 1948. Among his classic records are "Rolling Stone," "I'm Your Hoochie Coochie Man," "I Just Want to Make Love to You," and "Got My Mojo Workin'." His songs were full of Delta imagery that evoked sweet memories for many of the southern immigrants who now called Chicago home.

Urban blues was the electrified version of the Delta blues that first appeared in Chicago in the 1940s.

Jazz

An improvisational art form of individual expression, **jazz** developed as a parallel universe alongside the blues throughout the first half of the 20th century. Originally evolving as an ensemble folk music in New Orleans and other southern locales around the turn of the century, like the blues it worked its way north to Chicago around 1920. It was in the twenties that its first true innovator, trumpeter **Louis Armstrong,** revolutionized jazz by turning it into a soloist's art form simply on the strength and drama of his virtuoso improvisations. The 65 sides that he recorded for Okeh as the leader of the Hot Five and Hot Seven between 1925 and 1928 are among the most important artifacts of American music. By the 1930s, the center of the jazz world had moved to New York, where composers and arrangers such as Fletcher Henderson and **Duke Ellington** helped develop the jazz big band that was to become the standard ensemble of the Swing Era. At the same time, bandleaders in Kansas City like **Count Basie** were developing an exciting riff-based boogie style that would further invigorate swing music with the blues.

Jazz is the music of individual expression whose main characteristics are improvisation and swing rhythm.

During the Swing Era, jazz essentially became pop music, and creative innovation and musical integrity suffered. But jazz began to reinvent itself around 1940 in the late night jam sessions at tiny nightclubs in Harlem such as Minton's Playhouse. Modern jazz, or **bebop,** was created by a small group of young musical revolutionaries as a reaction against the banalities of swing. Among the leaders were some of the most gifted musical talents America has ever produced:

❏ Alto saxophonist **Charlie Parker,**

❏ Trumpeter **Dizzy Gillespie,**

❏ Eccentric genius pianist **Thelonius Monk.**

Although bebop infused a fresh new vitality into jazz, it also made it impossible for most people to dance or even listen to. As the popularity of jazz began to diminish around 1946, rhythm and blues became increasingly popular. In the meantime, jazz musicians experimented with different stylistic approaches, including cool jazz, hard bop, and free jazz. In 1969 trumpeter Miles Davis, who had often been at the forefront of innovation throughout his music career, fused rock and jazz together with his seminal album *Bitches Brew.* Jazz continues to incorporate influences from rock and its offshoots to this day.

Gospel

Gospel is a highly emotional evangelical vocal music that emerged from spirituals and was highly influential to rhythm and blues.

Gospel emerged as a style in the early 1930s from the traditional spirituals that had been a part of black religious culture since the days of slavery. The man most responsible for commercializing gospel music was **Thomas A. Dorsey,** who is often called the "Father of Gospel Music." Ironically, before turning his attention to religious music, Dorsey was known as "Georgia Tom," the piano playing half (along with guitarist Tampa Red) of the Hokum Brothers. Their hit recording "It's Tight Like That" from 1928 contained lewd, off color, humorous lyrics that presaged similar songs by Louis Jordan, Little Richard, and Chuck Berry. In the thirties Dorsey started writing songs of good news and salvation with blues-influenced melodies that quickly became popular at church services in the black community. Among his many gospel standards are "Take My Hand, Precious Lord," written in 1932. Later gospel stars include Sister Rosetta Tharpe and Mahalia Jackson.

Melisma is the singing embellishment of a single syllable into several notes.

Gospel's influence on American popular music is immense. The **melismatic** singing of gospel can be heard throughout the entire history of rock music. Gospel backup bands often used the Hammond B3 organ, which became one of the most popular instruments in rock in the 1960s. Typically performed in church with large choirs, the male gospel quartets that started to become popular in the 1930s were ancestors to doo wop groups in the fifties. Many of the early crossover R&B stars of the fifties had gospel roots, including Little Richard and Sam Cooke, whose career took off when he joined the venerable gospel group the Soul Stirrers. Gospel is also one of the foundational blocks of soul music, and its influence can be heard in the voice of the first soul singer, Ray Charles, and in every sixties soul singer from James Brown to Otis Redding and Aretha Franklin.

Rhythm and Blues

Rhythm & blues was an evolution of the blues that was more dance and commercially oriented. R&B bands often included electric instruments, vocalists, and a horn section, often with a honking tenor saxophone soloist.

Once the blues went electric, it was a natural progression to speed it up, put in a heavier beat, and make it more danceable. Although the term **rhythm and blues** wasn't coined until 1949 (by **Jerry Wexler** of *Billboard Magazine*), it had been crystallizing throughout the forties as an alternative to jazz, which was becoming less dance-oriented and more intellectual. One type of early R&B, as defined by historian Charlie Gillett in his authoritative book *The Sound of the City: The Rise of Rock and Roll,* was the **dancehall band style,** which evolved from the Kansas City style swing bands such as the Count Basie Orchestra. Dancehall bands tended toward simpler arrangements and fewer soloists than their jazz counterparts, often featuring only a shouting lead vocalist and a honking, screeching tenor sax. These bands played loud, with fast, rocking tempos that generated great excitement for dancers.

Jazz veteran **Lionel Hampton** had one of the first dancehall R&B hits in 1942 with "Flying Home," and the biggest R&B hit of 1946, "Hey! Ba-Ba-Re-Bop." Omaha native **Wynonie Harris** had the number 1 R&B hit of 1947 with "Good Rocking Tonight," a song that Elvis Presley would later cover. Dancehall bands included those led by **Jackie Brenston,** whose "Rocket 88" from 1951 would be one of the first R&B tunes to inspire a pop cover (by Bill Haley) and **Joe Turner,** whose 1954 hit recording of "Shake Rattle and Roll" was also covered by Haley. Earl Bostic, and Ruth Brown were among other popular dancehall style performers.

Another type of early R&B was the **jump band style,** which sounded somewhat like boogie woogie orchestrated for piano, drums, bass, guitar, a small horn section, and vocalist. Jump bands were also more polished and jazz influenced than other types of R&B. The most popular jump band in the 1940s was **Louis Jordan's Tympani Five,** who had their first hit in 1942 with "Choo Choo Ch'Boogie." Jordan, who sang and played alto sax, had a huge crossover audience, due in part to his detached, humorous singing style and his innovative short movies of the Tympani Five in performance that were shown between feature films at theatres—predecessors to the contemporary music video. **Johnny Otis** and **T-Bone Walker** both led Los Angeles-based jump bands that rose to prominence in the 1940s. After fronting the house band at the Club Alabam on Central Avenue, Otis went on to score ten Top Ten R&B hits in 1949, and backed Big Mama Thornton on her 1953 hit "Hound Dog". Guitarist/vocalist Walker was a pioneer in his use of the guitar as a prop in his stage act, sometimes holding it in various sexual positions, playing it behind his back or doing the splits while playing.

A third type of R&B was found in the **bar blues band style** that emerged mainly in Chicago. This was a raunchier, louder, and more intense style of R&B that was most closely related to the Chicago urban blues. Muddy Waters was the leading transitional figure between the blues and the bar blues R&B style, but others included harmonica players **Little Walter** and **Sonny Boy Williamson,** guitarists **Elmore James** and **John Lee Hooker** and singer Chester Burnett, better known as **Howlin' Wolf.** All of these artists recorded for Chess Records in Chicago, where composer **Willie Dixon** was a session bass player. The bar blues R&B style is the most closely linked style to the soon to emerge rock and roll styles of Bo Diddley and Chuck Berry, and highly influential to many rock bands in the 1960s, especially the Rolling Stones, Cream, and others from Britain.

Rhythm and blues would become one of the most prevailing influences in popular music in the last half of the 20th century. In the mid-1950s its most commercially successful practitioners would play important roles in shaping the sound of early rock and roll. The lives and music of these men—Bo Diddley, Chuck Berry, Little Richard, Fats Domino, and others—will be discussed in the next chapter.

Doo Wop

In terms of record sales, **doo wop** was the most popular style of R&B in the fifties. Its origins go back as far as the 1930s and the popularity of

See Appendix A, "Hey! Ba-Ba-Re-Bop" by Lionel Hampton and His Orchestra. Track 2 on enclosed CD.

R&B Types

❑ Dancehall Band Style
❑ Jump Band Style
❑ Bar Blues Band Style

See Appendix A, "All Night Long" by Johnny Otis and His Orchestra. Track 3 on enclosed CD.

Doo wop was an a cappella group vocal style that incorporates high falsetto vocal leads, scat singing, rhythmic vocal backings and sometimes spoken verse by the bass singer. Most doo wop recordings added a rhythm section for more commercial dance appeal.

male gospel quartets and commercial vocal groups such as the Mills Brothers and the Ink Spots. The **Mills Brothers** (who were in fact four brothers from Ohio) prided themselves in creating a tightly woven cross between jazz and barbershop vocal harmonies with only guitar accompaniment. The **Ink Spots** were also influential to doo wop, featuring lead vocalist Bill Kenny singing in a melismatic, gospel-inspired high tenor voice that became a staple of doo wop. Both groups were immensely popular throughout the thirties and forties.

The Earliest Doo Wop Groups

During the late forties and early fifties, it became fashionable for amateur teenage vocal groups to perform a cappella on street corners and on the front steps of apartment buildings, especially in New York. This was usually just for fun, although the possibility of being discovered by a talent scout was never far from anyone's thoughts. The first of these groups to hit it big was the **Ravens** with their 1947 hits "Write Me a Letter" and "Old Man River." The latter song, which sold two million copies, was unusual in that bass singer Warren Suttles sang the vocal lead. This technique was to become one of the signature characteristics of the doo wop genre. The Ravens also featured choreography in their shows—another first that was to become a staple of later soul acts such as the Temptations and Supremes.

Other groups started to copy these innovations. The **Orioles'** (who, like the baseball team, were from Baltimore) first pop hit was "It's Too Soon to Know," which hit the Top Twenty in 1948. The song's huge crossover appeal was unprecedented for a race record and helped the group become regulars on the R&B charts over the next few years. Their biggest success came in 1953 with "Crying in the Chapel," which climbed to number 11. With the success of the Orioles and the Ravens, other "bird" groups appeared, including the Penguins, Flamingos, and Swallows. Later, "car" names became popular, with the Cadillacs, T-Birds, Fleetwoods, and Imperials to name just a few. A partial list of Doo Wop Groups from the fifties is listed in Box 1-2.

Another doo wop group that achieved notoriety of sorts was **Hank Ballard and the Midnighters.** In 1954 they had a series of "Annie"

Box 1-2 A Partial List of Doo Wop Groups from the Fifties

Bird Groups:	*Car Groups:*
Ravens	Cadillacs
Orioles	T-Birds
Penguins	Imperials
Flamingos	Fleetwoods
Swallows	Corvairs
Bluebirds	Galaxies
Crows	El Dorados
Robins	Impalas

records ("Work with Me Annie," "Annie Had a Baby," and "Annie's Aunt Fanny") that sold over a million copies each despite being widely banned from radio play. Each song contained sexually suggestive lyrics—the "work" in the first hit was a thinly disguised metaphor for sex—that were as funny as they were risqué. Ballard also wrote "The Twist" in 1958, which became a number 1 hit for Chubby Checker in 1960 and spawned the dance craze of the same name. In the context of the "Annie" records, one should reconsider what Ballard was writing about in the first line of "The Twist": "Well come on baby, *let's do the twist.*" It probably wasn't dancing he was singing about . . .

The Industry Moves In

Although doo wop originated as an a cappella style, recordings were most often made using instrumental accompaniment, as record labels tried to maximize the commercial appeal of the records and make them more danceable. Many labels also took advantage of the street singers, who most often had no business skills and were just happy to get a record contract. The classic example of this type of exploitation is the story of **Frankie Lymon and the Teenagers,** who rose to fame in 1956 with "Why Do Fools Fall in Love" (number 6) when Lymon was only 13 years old. Producer George Goldman paid Lymon a stipend of $25 a week with the rest of his earnings going into a "trust fund." When Lymon's voice changed a few years later and his career went in decline, he discovered that there was no trust fund. He turned to heroin and died from an overdose at twenty-six. Many other doo wop groups were "one hit wonders," as bad business deals, competing cover versions and instability of the small independent labels took their toll. One of the best examples of the one hit wonder was the **Chords,** whose only hit "Sh-Boom" in 1953 was quickly buried by the Crewcuts cover.

See Appendix A, "Why Do Fools Fall in Love" by Frankie Lymon and the Teenagers. Track 4 on enclosed CD.

One fledgling record company, Atlantic Records, had unusual success with doo wop. Although its primary focus was on jazz when it was founded in 1947, Atlantic signed **Clyde McPhatter** of the Dominos in 1953 and built a new group, the **Drifters,** around him. They were an instant smash, with five hits that went to number 1 or number 2 on the R&B charts within the next two years. McPhatter was drafted into the military in 1955, and was replaced by a succession of lead singers until **Ben E. King** took over in 1958. At around the same time, the young songwriting duo of **Jerry Leiber** and **Mike Stoller** were assigned to the group, and their first production, "There Goes My Baby" went to number 2 pop and stayed on the charts for fourteen weeks. Between 1957 and 1959, Leiber and Stoller also wrote five Top Ten hits for another doo wop group, the **Coasters.**

Doo Wop Matures, Fades Away

The most successful doo wop group was the **Platters,** who between 1955 and 1960 had eighteen Top Forty hits, four of them going to number 1 ("The Great Pretender," "My Prayer," "Twilight Time," and "Smoke Gets in Your Eyes"). The Platters were not a typical doo wop group, as they tended to use more complex jazz harmonies and stay away from the rhythmic use of scat syllables usually employed by doo wop groups.

The style and crossover appeal of the Platters was an important link to the smoother pop-oriented soul of the 1960s.

As rock entered the sixties, doo wop faded away, although there were still a few hits left in the genre: the Drifters had another Leiber and Stoller Top Ten hit in 1963 with "On Broadway," and neo-doo wop group Sha-Na-Na started a revival in 1969 when they appeared at Woodstock and performed a medley of doo wop tunes including "At the Hop." Doo wop's influence has remained palpable, extending to groups such as the Beach Boys, sixties Motown artists, and recent groups like Boyz II Men.

The White Roots of Rock and Roll

TRADITIONAL RURAL MUSIC

Traditional rural music in America evolved primarily from the folk music brought to the New World by British immigrants. The Appalachian region of Tennessee, Kentucky, Virginia and West Virginia were particularly fertile areas for the survival of this music tradition, as the rural and isolated mountainous settings hampered contact with the changing outside world. By the early 20ᵗʰ century, city dwellers began to mockingly call the poor white inhabitants of this region hillbillies, and the simple folk music they played **hillbilly music.**

The British folk tradition included:

- ❏ **Ballads,** which typically tell a story, some of them epic tales;
- ❏ **Lyric songs,** which are often songs of love;
- ❏ **Work songs.**

Unlike African work songs, British work songs often came in the form of sea chanteys, railroad songs, and lumber songs. At first, folk music in America was simply sung verbatim by the new colonists as it had been in England; over time songs often underwent subtle changes as their original meanings and purposes were forgotten and singers adapted them to their new environment. New songs in the same tradition were also written. A good example of a traditional English ballad that survived in America is "Barbara Allen," a timeless song about young lovers and death believed to be from the 17ᵗʰ century. Although it has evolved over the years, it is still a folk standard that has been performed by everyone from Joan Baez to the Everly Brothers to Bob Dylan. On the other hand, "Sweet Betsy from Pike," written around 1870 using a traditional English melody, is a uniquely American song about the hard journey West, with lyrics that invoke the imagery of the Platte River, Salt Lake City, and California.

Unlike blues and country musicians who embraced new technology such as electric instruments, rural and folk musicians continued to use the traditional instruments from the past, such as the fiddle, acoustic gui-

Hillbilly music was the traditional old time music of the rural southern United States, with origins in English folk tradition. Hillbilly music is the foundation of modern country music.

tar, and banjo. After 1900, other acoustic instruments such as the mandolin, string bass, autoharp, and Hawaiian steel guitar were also often included. To this day, many folk musicians typically use only these traditional instruments in their performances.

The First Country Recordings

Traditional rural music was first recorded in 1923 when Okeh Records recorded Atlanta favorite Fiddlin' John Carson at a local radio station. The records sold surprisingly well throughout the region, much to the amazement of company officials. Sensing a business opportunity, **Ralph Peer** of Victor Records went on a talent hunt for other rural musicians in August of 1927. Setting up his primitive mobile recording equipment in a warehouse in Bristol, Tennessee and offering $50 per song to anyone that would audition, Peer struck gold. Among the many who came down from the hills to record were both the Carter Family and Jimmie Rodgers, who would become the first commercially successful and important performers of country music, as it was starting to be labeled by the late twenties.

The **Carter Family,** led by A. P. Carter, his wife Sara, and their sister-in-law Maybelle, had learned hundreds of traditional songs and performed them putting emphasis on their strong vocals and a revolutionary boom-chuck guitar picking style that is still commonly used by folk guitarists. **Jimmie Rodgers,** known alternately as the "Father of Country Music," the "Mississippi Blue Yodeler," and the "Singing Brakeman," was indeed a railroad worker until his poor health forced him to quit and concentrate on music. Between 1927 and 1933 when he died from tuberculosis, Rodgers recorded over 100 songs, sold millions of records and became the first nationally-known country star. His song topics and vocal style (which included blues inflections and his signature yodeling) set the mold for later stars such as Ernest Tubb and Hank Williams. As one of the three original inductees into the Country Music Hall of Fame, Rodgers plaque identifies him as "the man who started it all."

Nashville and the Grand Ole Opry

Radio played an important role in popularizing country music. In 1923, the first "barn dance" program was broadcast on station WBAP in Dallas, featuring live performances by country artists. Other shows soon followed: in 1924 Chicago's WLS premiered its National Barn Dance program, and on November 28, 1925 the WSM Barn Dance began broadcasting in Nashville. In 1927 WSM changed the name of the program to the **Grand Ole Opry** and with the station's **clear channel** designation, the Opry became the most widely heard and influential radio show of its kind. Other "barn dance" programs included the Louisiana Hayride on KWKH in Shreveport, Louisiana, the Midwestern Hayride on WLW in Cincinnati, and the Big D Jamboree on KRLD in Dallas.

The Opry influenced the course of country music by putting an emphasis on programming pop-oriented and crooning country singers

Clear channel stations are radio stations that had a powerful signal of up to 50,000 watts that could be heard for hundreds of miles, depending on atmospheric conditions.

(and forbidding drums for many years). Careers were often made by a successful debut there. Because the Opry was a live broadcast, performers had to maintain a presence in Nashville at least one day each week, and throughout the forties and fifties, many moved there permanently. Songwriters, publishers, recording studios, and all the major record labels soon followed, and by the early 1950s, Nashville became the capital of the country music industry—in large part because of the Grand Ole Opry.

COWBOY MUSIC, WESTERN SWING AND BLUEGRASS

Cowboy songs were traditional country and hillbilly songs used in Hollywood films that were orchestrated to create a more commercial pop sound.

Western swing was a form of country music that incorporated jazz swing rhythm and instruments associated with a jazz swing band.

Bluegrass was a fast paced, acoustic music that incorporated virtuoso improvised solos similar to those found in jazz.

Honky tonk was the direct predecessor to country western that used a rhythm section, electric guitar and electric pedal steel guitar to create a louder and hard driving sound. Honky tonk lyrics often dealt with drinking, cheating, etc.

Around the same time that radio was starting to make country music more accessible, Hollywood filmmakers were popularizing **cowboy songs** in Westerns, and stars such as **Gene Autry** ("The Singing Cowboy") and **Roy Rogers** rose to fame. Cowboy songs were dressed up and orchestrated to give them a smoother and more commercial sound; the singing cowboys themselves were also dressed up in hats, boots, and ties to elevate them from the older and undesirable hillbilly image. Cowboy songs helped pave the way for other commercialized offshoots of country to emerge that would reinvent the genre. One of these was **western swing,** which became popular during the Swing Era, and whose biggest star was Texas fiddler **Bob Wills.** Wills began broadcasting on station KVOO in Tulsa, Oklahoma in 1934 with his band the Texas Playboys, which combined traditional country instruments with those found in a swing big band: trumpets, saxophones, and drums. Despite their tendencies toward jazz, the Playboys wore the traditional country attire of cowboy hats, boots, and string ties. Wills had his biggest hit in 1940 with "New San Antonio Rose," which went to number 11 on the charts.

Another stylistic development was **bluegrass,** which was invented and named by mandolin player **Bill Monroe.** With his band the Blue Grass Boys, which he formed in 1938, Monroe developed a unique genre that relied on faster tempos and jazz-like virtuoso solos that were spread evenly among mandolin, fiddle, and guitar. When guitarist and vocalist **Lester Flatt** and banjo wizard **Earl Scruggs** joined the band in 1944, the Blue Grass Boys were in their prime. Scruggs did nothing less than reinvent banjo playing with his amazing fast picking style. Flatt and Scruggs left in 1948 (due to Monroe's stubbornness and difficult personality) and started their own band, which in time became more popular than Monroe's.

HONKY TONK

Honky tonk grew out of the bars and roadhouses (called "honky tonks") of Texas and the South, where the patrons were rough and rowdy and hard drinkers. The music is characterized by songs of drinkin' and cheatin', loves gained and lost. To be heard above the din of the crowded saloons, the honky tonkers developed a louder, driving sound by adding drums, electric guitar, and electric pedal steel guitar that modernized country music and inched it closer in sound to the first rock and roll style, rockabilly. The first honky tonk artist was **Ernest Tubb,** who with his Texas Troubadours had been touring constantly and performing on radio since the early thirties, achieving national celebrity in the 1940s with movie roles and Opry appearances.

Another honky tonk artist, Texas born William **"Lefty" Frizzell,** is widely credited with creating a smoother singing style that became the blueprint for modern country singers. He as a regular on the country charts throughout the fifties and early sixties.

Although his recording career lasted only six years (1946–52), the man who most personified honky tonk was undoubtedly **Hank Williams,** the "Hillbilly Shakespeare." Williams was a master poet with a knack for catchy melodies who wrote some of the most enduring tunes in country music history, including "Hey Good Lookin'," "Jambalaya," "Cold, Cold Heart," and "Your Cheatin' Heart." Williams became so popular in the late forties and early fifties that he had eleven records that sold a million copies or more and his concerts often resembled the near riots that Elvis Presley would endure a few years later. Unfortunately, his growing drinking problem paralleled that of his rising fame, and his life began to fall apart. He died of alcohol intoxication in the back seat of a car on the way to a gig on January 1, 1953. The last single released in his lifetime was his prophetic composition "I'll Never Get Out of This World Alive."

See Appendix A, "Shine, Shave, Shower" by Lefty Frizzell. Track 5 on enclosed CD.

Chapter 1
Study Questions

1. Describe Frank Sinatra's relationship to rock and roll, both his reaction to it and his influence on it.

   _____

   _____

   _____

   _____

2. How did American pop music evolve from the late 1800s up to 1954?

   _____

   _____

   _____

   _____

3. Why were covers used in the forties and fifties?

   _____

   _____

   _____

4. Describe how the blues evolved from its beginning until the 1940s.

   _____

   _____

   _____

5. What are the differences between the dancehall band style and the jump band style?

   _____

   _____

   _____

6. Describe the music that influenced doo wop and how doo wop in turn influenced rock and roll.

_____

_____

_____

_____

_____

7. Describe how music from the British folk tradition changed after it was brought to America.

_____

_____

_____

_____

_____

8. Why is Nashville such an important music center?

_____

_____

_____

_____

9. What were the musical influences on western swing and how did they manifest themselves?

_____

_____

_____

_____

10. Why is honky tonk music so important to early rock and roll?

_____

_____

_____

_____

The Rock and Roll Explosion

Postwar America

CHANGE AND PROSPERITY

In the years after World War II, America found itself in a state of peace and prosperity for the first time since the late 1920s. Economic good times meant a dramatic expansion of the middle class. Household items and consumer goods like refrigerators and televisions changed from being luxuries to necessities: between the mid 1940s and the mid 1950s, the number of TV sets in the U.S. increased from less than 10,000 to 50 million. Technological and scientific change was progressing at a stunning pace: computers, although new at the time, were becoming faster and more portable. Medicine brought us the polio vaccine, and electrical engineering made the introduction of the transistor radio possible. Research into the safe use of nuclear power was underway, resulting in the first commercial plant in 1957. When the Soviet Union sent Sputnik into orbit that same year, the world was ushered into a futuristic "space age" where space travel to space colonies was envisioned.

One of the biggest changes in our society was the increased consumption and use of the automobile. By the mid 1950s, there were nearly 70 million privately owned cars in America, and they began to change our lifestyles in profound ways. Suburban living became possible—and popular—as a way to attain the American dream of owning a home. Shopping centers sprang up, interstate highways were built, and families took more and more road trips and vacations. Disneyland opened, as did the first Holiday Inn and the first McDonald's, all of which catered to our new and fast paced mobile life. Cars became a national obsession: faster, bigger, and shinier appealed to everyone, most of all teenagers.

TEENAGERS

Ah yes, teenagers—the word had been around since the 1940s, but teens in the fifties were a different breed than any that preceded them. They were the first in American history that didn't have to work to help support the family—they could now take after school jobs to earn and spend their own money. Add to this the advent of modern mass marketing on television and radio, and teens became a consumer entity with unprecedented buying power. They began to develop their own cultural values, social arrangements, fashions, and awareness of the world around them. Teenagers had become a class all unto themselves.

Parents were not oblivious to all this and many were none too happy, either. In an era where anxiety about The Bomb, Communism, and the Red Scare already had many feeling that they were heading straight for the apocalypse, there was a growing concern that teenagers might get them there even sooner. With their new class status and independence, adults sensed that teens were flouting authority. Many were critical of a generation that had too much money and too much free time—teens had it too easy. Adults pointed to the growing problems of juvenile delinquency (although statistically there was no increase over previous years) and sexual permissiveness as the basis for their distrust. There seemed to be bored teenagers hanging out everywhere, just waiting to get themselves into trouble. The growing disapproval of adults only served to fuel any rebellious feelings that already existed in teens. Welcome to the **Generation Gap.**

DISCONNECT

In fact, a lot of teens *were* bored. There were strong feelings of disconnect for many: from parents, from authority, from each other. Television and suburbia fueled this isolation and loneliness, as did the usual problem of parents that didn't listen or understand. Cars with radios became essential to stay connected. Many teens looked to new role models that characterized their same feelings of alienation, such as the sarcastic and cynical anti-hero Holden Caulfield from J. D. Salinger's *Catcher in the Rye.* Young charismatic movie stars such as **Marlon Brando** and **James Dean** wore leather jackets, sullen looks, and sneers while playing troubled youth in popular films such as 1954's *The Wild One,* starring Brando. Dean's portrayal of Jim Stark in *Rebel without a Cause* (released in 1955) made him a cult hero, and his death in a fiery auto accident before the movie even opened made him a legend. *Rebel* was one of the first movies to explore themes of alienation and despair from the vantagepoint of the teen rather than the adult. Many teens identified with Jim Stark, including a young wannabe singer living in Memphis named Presley.

As the 1950s unfolded, a new teenage nation had arrived. All it needed was its own music.

The Record Industry: Early 1950s

THE MAJORS AND THE INDEPENDENTS

Over the years, the major record labels (or simply majors) had built up well-established distribution networks and alliances with radio stations to distribute and promote their product. At the start of the rock and roll era, there were six labels that were large enough to be considered major. With near total control of the marketplace, they were able to prevent most records that they did not distribute from making an impact on the national charts. Even though most majors had a few race or R&B artists on their rosters, it was the numerous (there were hundreds by the mid fifties) small independent labels that historically had specialized in recording black, or race music. Although many of the top country artists were signed with majors, they were also regarded as having a specialty market, so it was common for country songs to also be covered by pop artists, as was the case with Patti Page's version of "Tennessee Waltz," a number 1 hit in 1950.

The typical major was headquartered in New York, Chicago, or Los Angeles with a team of producers, talent scouts, A&R (artist & repertoire) staff and advance men. Professional composers, arrangers, and recording studios were utilized to carefully craft the product. An independent label, on the other hand, could be found in any town, and might be operating out of the back room of a store, a basement, garage, or even the trunk of a car. The small staff (often less than five, usually just one or two) handled all details, from finding the talent to distributing the records in stores and meeting with disc jockeys to get airplay. Although some "indies" had their own small studios, often times storage rooms or garages were used as makeshift studios. With their low overhead and constant struggle for survival, indies were more willing to take risks and quickly change business tactics to keep up with emerging industry trends. Box 2-1 lists some early major and independent labels.

Despite their competitive disadvantages, the indie labels were perfectly positioned to grab a larger share of the record market as a growing number of white teenagers started to turn away from major label pop to listen to R&B. But to connect with this new audience they needed some help along the way, which they got from a group of renegade radio disc jockeys.

HOT 100S AND GOLD RECORDS

The most reliable source for charting record sales throughout the rock era has been *Billboard Magazine.* First published in 1894, *Billboard* began charting songs in 1940. In 1942 the magazine began to track the

---

Box 2-1   Early Major and Independent Labels

The Major Labels in the Early 1950s
Columbia—founded in 1885 in New York
RCA Victor—1901, New York
Decca—1934, New York
Capitol—1942, Los Angeles
Mercury—1946, Chicago
MGM—1946, Hollywood

Important Independent Labels from the Late 1940s and Early 1950s
King—founded in 1945 in Cincinnati by Syd Nathan
Specialty—1945, Los Angeles by Art Rupe
Modern—1945, Los Angeles by Jules and Saul Bihari
Imperial—1945, Los Angeles by Lew Chudd
Chess—1947, Chicago by Phil and Leonard Chess (originally named Aristocrat)
Atlantic—1948, New York by Ahmet Ertegun and Herb Abramson
Duke/Peacock—1949, Houston by Don Robey
Sun—1953, Memphis by Sam Phillips

emerging country and R&B styles under a single category "Western and Race," eventually splitting them into two separate charts, "Country and Western" and "Rhythm and Blues" in 1949. From 1955 until 1958, it published a number of separate charts, including the Top 100, Best Sellers in Stores, Most Played in Jukeboxes, and Most Played by Disc Jockeys, all of which were merged into the new Hot 100 in 1958. The chart listings used in this book for singles are from the Hot 100 (or the Top 100 chart that preceded it), unless otherwise noted.

The **Record Industry Association of America** (RIAA) began certifying albums with sales of 500,000 as gold in 1958, and albums with sales of one million as platinum in 1976. From 1958 through 1988, singles required sales of one million to be certified gold and two million to be platinum; however on January 1, 1989 the requirements were lowered to 500,000 and one million respectively. Please keep in mind as you read this book how much more difficult it was for a single to achieve gold status in the years before 1989.

Radio

RADIO AND DJs

The first commercial radio station in America, KDKA in Pittsburgh, began broadcasting in 1920. Throughout the early twenties, radio experienced explosive growth: by 1924 there were nearly 600 commercial stations broadcasting and three million receivers. However, as television appeared on the scene in the late forties and early fifties, many analysts were predicting radio's demise. Radio stations up to this point had programmed a variety of material, including live music, drama, variety shows, sporting events, and news. With TV's dramatic success, radio stations were forced into both concentrating their efforts on playing music and emphasizing local programming rather than the network feed. These trends led to the rise in popularity of the local **disc jockey.** DJs often had complete control of the style of their show and the records that they played. After a time, it was not enough just to have a unique show, and many DJs started developing flamboyant and eccentric on-air personalities. They became showmen; in fact, several early rock and roll artists actually began their careers as DJs, including one at WDIA in Memphis named Riley B. King. King was known on the air as the "Blues Boy"; he later adopted those initials and became known simply as B. B.

Like the nation itself, in the late forties and early fifties radio was segregated: black stations programmed jazz and R&B to black audiences, white stations played pop and country specifically aimed at white audiences. However, R&B was enjoying growing popularity during the transitional period between the Swing Era and the birth of rock and roll from 1946–54. Much of the increase came from white teenagers, who responded to the more emotional and exciting nature of R&B over conventional pop. To get their R&B fix, these teens were at first tuning in to the larger "Negro stations" around the country such as WDIA in Memphis ("America's Only 50,000 Watt Negro Radio Station"), WERD in Atlanta,

Although the term **Disc Jockey** was first used in a June 23, 1941 issue of *Variety,* the first DJ is believed to have been Al Jarvis of KFWB in Los Angeles, who was injecting his own personality into his show as early as 1932.

in KXLW in St. Louis. Among the most popular black DJs in R&B radio were "Yo' Ol' Swingmaster" Al Benson in Chicago, "Jockey Jack" Gibson in Atlanta, Tommy "Dr. Jive" Smalls in New York, and "Professor Bop" in Shreveport.

As the audience for R&B grew, the more attentive white DJs picked up on the trend and also began to play R&B records. Early white DJs who programmed R&B included Hunter Hancock *(Huntin' with Hunter)* at KFVD and KGFJ in Los Angeles, George "Cat Man" Stiles at WNJR in Newark, George "Hound Dog" Lorenz at WKBW in Buffalo, and "Symphony Sid" Torin at WBMS in Boston and later WOV in New York. By connecting the rapidly expanding needs of the teenage nation with R&B and rock and roll records, these renegade DJs, both black and white, essentially saved radio from television's onslaught. For all its strengths as a medium for family entertainment, TV could not connect with the young in the same direct way that radio could. By playing rock and roll records (which was also—conveniently—cheap programming), radio could pinpoint it's audience with deadly accuracy. It was also portable: teens could listen at home or at school on transistor radios, or in their cars while cruising at night.

ALAN FREED

The most famous and influential of all the white DJs was Alan Freed (1921–65). Freed was a former jazz musician from Pennsylvania who was entrepreneurial, flamboyant, a hard worker, and a hard drinker. In June 1951 he took over the late night *Record Rendezvous* show on Cleveland station WJW and turned it into an R&B program after seeing first-hand how white teenagers enthusiastically bought R&B records at a local store. Freed, who often drank while on the air, developed a wacky personality and renamed the show *The Moondog House Rock and Roll Party* (he sometimes howled like a dog during the show opening). Encouraged by the program's popularity, Freed's next move was to promote a dance that featured the same artists whose records he played.

Moondog

When Alan Freed moved to WINS in 1954, he was forced to change the name of his show from *The Moondog House Rock and Roll Party* to the *Rock and Roll Show* by a blind street musician who dressed up in a Viking costume. Thomas Louis Hardin claimed that he had, in fact, used the name Moondog for many years, and that by using the name for his radio show, Freed was infringing on Hardin's right to make a living. After Hardin filed suit, Judge Carroll Walter awarded him $7,500 and forbade Freed from using the name Moondog. Although Alan Freed did not coin the term Rock and Roll (it was a black euphemism for sexual intercourse that had been around for at least thirty years), he undoubtedly helped connect the label to the music for an ever-widening audience.

The *Moondog Coronation Ball* was set for the 10,000 seat Cleveland Arena in March 1952, but a near riot ensued as an overflow crowd of over 21,000 tried to get in, forcing the cancellation of the show. Later concert attempts proved successful, however, and Freed's growing popularity led to his being hired by WINS in New York in September 1954. Freed named his new program *The Rock and Roll Show,* and began calling himself "Mr. Rock and Roll," and quickly turned WINS into the number 1 station in the city.

The First Sounds

BILL HALEY

Other DJs around the country began programming R&B after hearing of Freed's success. Record distributors also caught wind of what was going on, and started putting R&B records in jukeboxes, giving teens even more access to the music. White bands started to respond to the demand for the music by including a few R&B-type songs into their repertoire. One of these was a country group called the Saddlemen, led by guitarist/vocalist Bill Haley (1925–1981). The Saddlemen in 1951 had recorded a cover of Jackie Brenston's "Rocket 88," giving it a slightly more country feel than the original. One of their next records was "Rock the Joint," which attracted the attention of Alan Freed, who started giving the song airplay. By 1952, with their popularity growing, Haley and the band (who were now all in their late 20s and early 30s, playing for teenagers at school dances) decided to scrap the cowboy image and adopt a wilder R&B-styled stage act. They also changed their name to Bill Haley and His Comets (a play on the Halley's Comet theme). When "Crazy Man Crazy" (a Haley original whose inspiration came from hearing teens talk at a dance) hit number 15 on the pop charts in 1953, they became the first white band to hit the Top Twenty with an R&B song. After signing with Decca Records in 1954, Haley recorded a cover of Joe Turner's "Shake, Rattle and Roll" (with cleaned up lyrics) that went to number 7 in late 1954 and early 1955 and sold over a million copies.

See Appendix A, "Crazy Man Crazy" by Bill Haley and His Comets. Track 6 on enclosed CD.

THE FIRST ROCK AND ROLL BAND

But Haley's biggest hit was yet to come. On April 12, 1954 the Comets recorded "Rock around the Clock," which hit number 23 and sold 75,000 copies before dropping off the charts. However, the song breathed new life when it was placed over the opening credits to the hit film *The Blackboard Jungle.* Decca re-released "Rock around the Clock," and in May 1955 it shot up to number 1 where it stayed for eight weeks, eventually selling over twenty million records. Haley went on to score two more Top Ten hits, "Burn That Candle" (number 9) in late 1955 and "See You Later, Alligator" (number 6) in early 1956. The band appeared on national television, and was featured in the fictionalized teen film *Rock around the Clock.* For a short while, they were not just the most popular white rock and roll band in the world, they were the *only* one.

Unfortunately, Haley was soon swept aside by Elvis Presley, who scored his first national hit in March 1956 ("Heartbreak Hotel"). Presley was ten years younger, leaner, surlier, and more aggressively sexual than the rather pudgy and balding Haley. Nonetheless, Haley's calculated fusion of country and R&B was the same formula that Presley and many other rock and roll stars would use. While Haley's music is often categorized with Presley and the other Sun Studio artists as rockabilly, his sound was slightly different than the Sun sound. The Comets included saxophone and drums, instruments that were often used in R&B groups but not present in the early rockabilly records from Sun. Haley also used group vocal chants, a technique often used by western swing bands but not typically used at Sun, where there was usually only one vocalist. Regardless, Bill Haley played an important role in pushing rock and roll up a notch in popularity.

THE INDIES TAKE OVER

Even though Bill Haley was signed to one of the industry majors (Decca), the prevailing industry thought was that rock and roll was a fad that would quickly burn itself out. In fact, Haley and Elvis Presley were the only important rock and roll stars of the fifties who were signed to major labels (Presley with RCA). By ignoring rock and roll, the majors inadvertently opened the door for the independents, which were quick to jump on the bandwagon and grab control of the new market. Sales figures confirm this, as Box 2-2 of *Billboard's* Top Ten rock and roll hits from 1955 to 1959 shows:

These impressive gains were made in a five-year period (1954–59) where total record sales nearly tripled, from $213 million to $613 million. One of the more aggressive independent labels was Memphis-based Sun Records, owned by **Sam Phillips.**

SUN RECORDS AND SAM PHILLIPS

Sam Phillips (1923–2003) was a true musical visionary, and tremendously influential to the birth of rock and roll. He started his career as a DJ, but the allure of R&B enticed him to start his own recording studio in 1949, the Memphis Recording Service in the vacant radiator shop at 706 Union Avenue. He had a great ear and an even better nose for talent,

Box 2-2 Billboard Top Ten Rock and Roll Hits from 1955 to 1959					
	1955	1956	1957	1958	1959
Top Ten major label rock and roll hits	3	9	14	11	9
Top Ten indie label rock and roll hits	5	10	29	28	29

and the Memphis area, strategically located at the northernmost edge of the Mississippi Delta, was loaded with it. Although anyone could plunk down $2 and make a record at the studio (which helped pay the rent in the early days), Phillips's primary interest was in making authentic recordings of the many blues and R&B singers in the area. One of his early recordings was 1951's "Rocket 88" by Jackie Brenston and the Kings of Rhythm, which, because of its theme (a hot Oldsmobile sports car with hints of sexual innuendo), its boogie beat, and distorted guitar is regarded by many to be the first rock and roll record. Initially, Phillips recorded singers such as Howlin' Wolf, B. B. King and Elmore James and leased the master tapes to the independent labels Chess and Modern; however, in 1953, he started his own label, Sun Records.

Phillips worked like a maniac to get his label off the ground. He not only owned the company, he served as engineer, producer, talent scout, and advance man. He spent days and weeks on the road, driving thousands of miles with boxes of 45s in the trunk of his car to distribute to record shops and radio stations. Phillips's studio was a small room, so he experimented with an innovative **tape-delay echo** to enhance and fatten up the sound, a technique that his Sun recordings would become famous for. More importantly, he was on a mission to capture the passion and raw energy of the Memphis blues scene. He often spent hours in the studio with unknown performers to that end, while most other labels were trying to come up with a smooth, commercial sound. "My feeling was that there was more talent, innately natural, in the people that I wanted to work with—Southern black, Southern country white—than there was in the people who wrote the arrangements." Among those he took chances on in the early days were Joe Louis Hill, a one-man band, and The Prisonaires, a vocal group comprised of inmates from a local prison.

Phillips's first Sun hit came quickly: "Bear Cat" by Rufus Thomas, the "answer" record to Big Mama Thornton's "Hound Dog" hit number 3 on the R&B chart in 1953. Although he was hit with a copyright infringement lawsuit over the song (which he lost), it gave Phillips his first taste of success and put him on the map. But he was still looking for something new and different—something that would reflect the honesty and personality of the common folk. Phillips's instincts told him that combining R&B and country music properly would have a huge **crossover**

Phillips created his **Tape-Delay Echo** by feeding a sound source, such as a vocal, into the record head of a separate tape machine and then back into the mix as it passes the playback head a split second later.

Crossover refers to a record or an artist who has appeal in more than one audience segment, such as some early R&B singers such as Fats Domino, whose fan base included both blacks and whites.

Rocket 88

Although Jackie Brenston is officially listed as the leader of the group that recorded "Rocket 88," it was really pianist and guitarist **Ike Turner** who led the Kings of Rhythm. Hailing from Clarksdale, Mississippi, the group ran into trouble on the drive north to Memphis on March 5, 1951: the guitar amp fell off the top of the car, tearing the speaker cone. The resourceful Phillips stuffed it with paper and actually featured the distorted sound in the record's mix. He later said, "It sounded like a saxophone." It stands today as one of the first examples of distorted guitar ever recorded. "Rocket 88" hit number 1 on the R&B charts in June, and was the second biggest R&B record of 1951.

Box 2-3 Rockabilly

Characteristics of Rockabilly

1. The earliest rock and roll style, heavily influenced by R&B and honky tonk
2. Fast tempos and jumping, nervous beat
3. Sparse instrumentation: electric and acoustic guitar, upright bass played in 'slap' fashion to achieve percussive effect, drums (not used in early Sun recordings)
4. Single vocalist using effects such as hiccuping and the use of heavy echo

Key Rockabilly Recordings

- "Rock around the Clock"—Bill Haley, 1954
- "That's All Right"/"Blue Moon of Kentucky"—Elvis, Scotty and Bill, 1954
- "Blue Suede Shoes"—Carl Perkins, 1955
- "Be-Bop-a-Lula"—Gene Vincent, 1956
- "That'll Be the Day"—Buddy Holly, 1957

appeal. Even though the early recordings of Bill Haley had done this to a certain degree, Phillips Sun recordings would codify what would eventually be known as rockabilly, the first style of rock and roll.

Phillips also knew that he needed a distinctive vocal stylist to crystallize the sound he was looking for, someone "you'd know the moment you heard him," as he often said in those days. "If I could find me a white man who sang with the Negro feel, I could make a million dollars." In August 1953, an 18-year-old truck driver walked in the front door of the Memphis Recording Service. Sam Phillips and Elvis Aron Presley were about to change the world.

Elvis Presley

THE CAT

Elvis Presley (1935–1977) was born in Tupelo, Mississippi to his parents Vernon and Gladys. The Presleys were dirt poor, moving frequently to stay a step ahead of missed rent payments. Vernon was even jailed for a brief time in 1938 for forgery. In 1948 the family moved to Memphis, living in various public housing tenements before finally renting a house of their own. By this time, Elvis was showing an interest in music, and his singing won a talent contest as a ten-year-old. For his 11th birthday, his parents bought him his first guitar. He was also absorbing music from a variety of influences: hearing country music from listening to the Grand Ole Opry on radio, singing gospel music at church, and from Memphis's black radio stations, R&B. One particular favorite R&B show was "Red, White, and Blue" on Memphis's WHBQ, hosted by "Daddy-O" Dewey Phillips (no relation to Sam). Of course, Elvis was also hanging out at the nightclubs along Beale Street in Memphis, where he heard artists like B. B. King and Wynonie Harris perform live.

Although he was painfully shy, by the time he had entered Humes High School, Elvis was becoming the personification of the Southern "cat": greasing his long hair back, wearing brightly colored jackets, pants, and two-toned shoes, which he bought at Lansky Brothers on Beale Street, a store which normally catered to black customers. He usually made an impression on those that met him, not only for his shyness and his clothes, but also for his sincere and burning desire to become somebody.

THE DISCOVERY

In August 1953, Presley recorded two songs at the Memphis Recording Service, ostensibly as a gift for his mother's birthday (which was actually in April). Although Sam Phillips was only mildly impressed ("We might give you a call sometime"), in the summer of 1954 he hooked Elvis up with guitarist **Scotty Moore** and bassist **Bill Black** of the Starlite Wranglers, a country group. At the trio's first recording session, on July 5, 1954, nothing was going particularly well. Finally they decided to take a break. Then, according to Scotty:

> "All of a sudden Elvis just started singing this song, jumping around and acting the fool, and then Bill picked up the bass and he started acting the fool, too, and I started playing with them. Sam, I think, had the door to the control booth open . . . and he stuck his head out and said, 'What are you doing?' And we said, 'We don't know.' 'Well, back up,' he said, 'try to find a place to start, and do it again.'"

The song was an R&B tune by Arthur "Big Boy" Crudup called "That's All Right," but Elvis had reinvented it as an electrifying cross between country western and R&B (they also recorded a Bill Monroe tune, "Blue Moon of Kentucky" in much the same way). The sound was different, yet puzzling—no one was quite sure how to categorize it. But the reaction

Elvis Presley at Sun Studios in 1954 with Bill Black, Scotty Moore, and Sam Phillips at the mixing console.
AP/WIDE WORLD PHOTOS

Key Elvis Presley Recordings

- ❏ "That's All Right"/"Blue Moon of Kentucky," 1954
- ❏ "Mystery Train," 1955
- ❏ "Don't Be Cruel"/"Hound Dog," 1956
- ❏ "Love Me Tender," 1956
- ❏ "Jailhouse Rock," 1957

was instantaneous: two nights later, when Dewey Phillips played it seven times in a row on his radio show, the phone lines lit up. Presley was literally an overnight sensation. Over the next several months, Elvis, Scotty, and Bill performed around the region, including appearances at the Grand Ole Opry and Louisiana Hayride (they bombed at the conservative Opry, but were a hit at the Hayride). They recorded a total of ten sides—five single releases—for Sun, and were getting noticed in *Billboard*.

Promoting Presley presented somewhat of a marketing problem for Phillips. Was he country or was he R&B? For many listeners, he was "too black" sounding. Phillips chose to market him as a country artist, and his early releases only appeared on the country charts (his first country number 1 hit was "Mystery Train," from July 1955). One thing that *was* for sure was the effect Presley had on audiences at his live shows. He brought a surliness and bad boy fierceness that defied his off stage shyness. He wiggled his hips and kicked his legs like jackknives, eliciting an explosive effect on the crowd. Often he was forced to flee as young women rushed the stage, attempting to tear his clothes off. Their jealous boyfriends were also chasing Elvis, but for different reasons.

RCA AND COL. PARKER

Despite Presley's stunning success, Sun Records neared bankruptcy as it got caught in a money squeeze between the up-front costs of pressing thousands of records, and the delayed collections from distributors. To raise sorely needed cash, near the end of 1955, Sam Phillips sold Elvis' contract and the master tapes to RCA for $35,000 (at the time an unheard of amount of money). Around the same time, **Col. Tom Parker** became Elvis' new manager. Parker, a crude and shrewd illegal immigrant from the Netherlands (his real name was Andreas Cornelius van Kujik), was a former carnival hawker who deftly went about turning Elvis into a mass-merchandised commodity. He quickly secured more lucrative gigs, getting national TV exposure, creating Elvis consumer products and getting him into Hollywood movies and Las Vegas. Over time, the Colonel took complete control of all business decisions while taking a 50% cut (as opposed to the usual 10%), all with Presley's blessing. Parker was also instrumental in shielding Elvis from the public, believing that whetting the public's appetite with only occasional appearances was a good marketing strategy. In reality, this tactic only contributed to isolating Elvis in his own private hell.

Presley's initial RCA recordings were done in Nashville and New York, and the change of locale coincided with some other subtle changes that began to take place. RCA was at first very nervous about their new investment, and to make the recordings more accessible to a wide audience, brought in veteran studio musicians such as Chet Atkins on guitar and Floyd Cramer on piano, as well as the Jordanaires, a gospel backup chorus. At first the musical changes were minimal, but over time Presley's recordings became slicker and more polished, and lost most of the raw energy that Sam Phillips had honed at Sun. Eventually Parker fired Scotty and Bill, leaving the two longtime sidemen bitter and Presley even more isolated and alone. Nonetheless, RCA produced stunning results for Presley. By April of 1956, Elvis had his first two number 1 hits,

"Heartbreak Hotel" and "I Want You, I Need You, I Love You." In August, the songs "Don't Be Cruel" and "Hound Dog" were released back-to-back on the same single, and stayed at the top of the charts for eleven weeks.

Elvis made his first national TV appearance on the *Dorsey Brothers Stage Show* on January 28, 1956. After several more appearances on it, the *Milton Berle Show*, and the *Steve Allen Show*, he made his first appearance on the *Ed Sullivan Show* on September 9, and drew an astonishing 83% of the viewing public—53 million viewers. His third and final appearance on the program, January 6, 1957 was the famous "above the waist" show, where the producers decided to show only Elvis' upper body because of the uproar over his suggestive hip movements.

Sgt. Presley

Presley made his first movie, *Love Me Tender*, in 1956, and the title song produced yet another number 1 hit. Eventually he made thirty-one films, and although many of them are of questionable value, the movies were commercially successful, and Elvis did a creditable job with sub par scripts. Since Presley did not tour in the sixties, it was mainly through his films that his fans were able to see him until the early 70s. In March 1957, he bought Graceland, one of the most prestigious properties in Memphis. It was here that Elvis lived with his parents (although his mother died soon after in 1958) until his death in 1977.

On March 24, 1958, Presley entered the army, where he served in Germany with no special privileges until March 1960, when he was discharged after working his way up to the rank of sergeant. In the less than four years prior to being called up, Elvis remarkably had scored ten number 1 hits and starred in four films. While in the service, Col. Parker continued to release Presley recordings, with ten hitting the Top Twenty-Five and two going to number 1 ("Hard Headed Woman" and "A Big Hunk O' Love"). Elvis continued to sell consistently well throughout the sixties, but under Parker's guidance, his material became increasingly pop oriented, and he fell out of touch with the younger rock audience. Although he staged a comeback on February 1, 1968 with the powerful live TV special *Elvis*, in the seventies, Presley was reduced to performing in Las Vegas in increasingly gaudy jump suits and flamboyant shows that cultivated a following of devoted mostly middle-aged female fans. Unbeknownst to the world, Elvis' life was becoming increasingly insular and depressing, and he began abusing prescription drugs such as barbiturates and tranquilizers. His weight ballooned as his health declined, all of which contributed to his death of a heart attack in his second floor bathroom at Graceland in the early morning hours of August 16, 1977. His last performance was in Indianapolis on June 25.

The Presley Legacy

Elvis Presley symbolized the American dream, growing up poor and becoming rich. He also symbolized a much darker side of life: of corruption, greed, isolation, and drug abuse. Elvis was at ground zero of the turf war between parents and teenagers, between country music and

R&B purists, and was a catalyst in bringing black culture and music to the attention of white America. He was the first personification of a rock star. Most importantly, Elvis turned rock and roll into a phenomenon that could no longer be ignored. He was, and will forever be, the King.

Elvis' sales figures dwarf everyone else's in the history of rock music, including the Beatles. Some facts and figures from the Elvis legacy:

❏ Over one billion records sold worldwide.

❏ In America alone, 131 different albums and singles that have been certified gold, platinum or multi-platinum by the Recording Industry Association of America.

❏ 149 songs on Billboard's Top 100 Pop Chart in America. Of these, 114 were in the Top Forty, thirty-eight were in the Top Ten and eighteen went to number 1. His number 1 singles spanned a total of 80 weeks at that position.

❏ Over 90 charted albums with nine reaching number 1 (this figure is for the American pop charts only), and sixteen reaching platinum or multi-platinum status. He was also a leading artist in the American country, R&B, and gospel fields, and his chart success in other countries was substantial.

❏ Eleven of his movie soundtrack albums went to the Top Ten, and of those, four went to number 1, and two, *Loving You* (1957), and *G.I. Blues* (1960) each stayed at the top for ten weeks. The album from *Blue Hawaii* was number 1 for twenty weeks in 1961 and was on the chart for 79 weeks.

The First Crossover Artists

ROCK AND ROLL EXPLODES

In the wake of Presley's success, record sales exploded and rock and roll became big business. The majors began to realize that they had misjudged the music entirely and were losing market share to the indies, who were busy scouring the South to find the next Elvis. Sam Phillips for one was well positioned, with a roster of explosive new talent that he was ready to unleash. Thousands of "cats" from all over the country (and in the United Kingdom) were getting into the act as well, forming bands and recording demos. *Billboard* and *Cashbox* magazines sensed an epochal moment. A March 1956 *Cashbox* editorial entitled "Rock and Roll May Be the Great UNIFYING FORCE" stated that "The overwhelming sensation in the record business this week is the fact that two records which started essentially in the country field" (Presley's "Heartbreak Hotel" and Carl Perkins' "Blue Suede Shoes"), "have become hits also in the pop and rhythm and blues area." This demonstrated that the "possibilities exist . . . of bridging all three markets with one record." On February 16, 1957, *Billboard* announced a new format category— rock and roll. A revolution was underway.

Meanwhile, many in the industry were still uneasy with the growth of rock and roll. It was too sexual, vulgar, and obscene; its singers and songs carried a defiant attitude toward authority; and, especially in the South, it sounded "too black." Nonetheless, many black R&B artists had been enjoying significant commercial success throughout the 1950s. Some adopted a strategy of singing more sentimental or sing-along type songs that would appeal to whites, the downside of which was to cut them off from much of their black audience. Others sang in a more intuitive style with great crossover success to both black and white audiences.

In the early days of rock and roll, regional differences were an important part of the story. Just as Sun Records had defined the sound of Memphis, studios in New Orleans and Chicago helped define the sound of those cities, where Fats Domino, Little Richard, Bo Diddley, and Chuck Berry, the first rock and roll crossover artists, made their most important records.

The New Orleans Sound

ANTOINE "FATS" DOMINO

Except for Elvis Presley, Fats Domino (1929–) sold more records than any other rock pioneer from the 1950s—65 million of them! Born in New Orleans, he was playing the piano in juke joints and honky tonks in the city by the time he was ten years old. Domino's easy-going charm and demeanor made him likeable and non-threatening to his mainstream audience, as did his distinctive Creole patois and his boogie woogie piano playing. In the mid 1940s, Domino joined the band of trumpet player **Dave Bartholomew,** who helped him secure a contract with Lew Chudd and his newly formed Imperial Records in 1949. The first session produced the hit song "Fat Man" (number 6), which ended up selling a million copies.

Domino's native New Orleans had long been one of the most important music cities in America, with a rich mix of styles and influences from all over the world. The distinctive New Orleans R&B from the fifties had loose shuffle rhythms (from jazz), tight bands (from gospel) and a preference toward walking bass lines (from boogie woogie). The piano and tenor sax were the predominant instruments. Dave Bartholomew became a key figure as a songwriter, producer and bandleader for many of the hits that were recorded in the city, most notably those of Domino. Engineer **Cosimo Matassa** also played a seminal role in defining the New Orleans sound at his **J&M Recording Studio** on the corner of Rampart and Dumaine Streets (later at 525 Governor Nicholls Street). Often using **Red Tyler** and **Lee Allen** on sax, **Earl Palmer** on drums, **Huey Smith** on piano, and **Frank Fields** on bass (all from Bartholomew's band), among the recordings made by Matassa were Roy Brown's original version of "Good Rocking Tonight" in 1947, Lloyd Price's "Lawdy Miss Clawdy" in 1952, Little Richard's "Tutti Frutti" in 1955, and many of Domino's hits.

Box 2-4 The New Orleans Sound

Characteristics of the New Orleans Sound
1. Shuffle 'swing-like' rhythm influence from jazz
2. Walking bass lines borrowed from boogie woogie
3. Extremely tight ensembles consisting of piano, bass, drums and horn section

Key New Orleans Recordings
- ❏ "Good Rocking Tonight"—Roy Brown, 1947
- ❏ "Fat Man"—Fats Domino, 1949
- ❏ "Lawdy Miss Clawdy"—Lloyd Price, 1952
- ❏ "Tutti Frutti"—Little Richard, 1955

By the mid-1950s, Domino's records were consistently selling in the hundreds of thousands, but his greatest hits came between 1955 and 1960, including "Ain't That a Shame" (1955, number 10), "I'm in Love Again" (1956, number 3), "Blueberry Hill" (1956–57, number 2) and "Blue Monday" (1957, number 5). Since 1955, Domino has garnered nine gold singles and thirty-seven Top Forty hits. He still lives in New Orleans. Box 2–4 lists the characteristics of the New Orleans sound and some key recordings.

LITTLE RICHARD

See Appendix A, "Tutti Frutti" by Little Richard. Track 7 on enclosed CD.

Little Richard (1932-), born in Macon, Georgia as Richard Wayne Penniman, was in many respects the opposite of Fats Domino—an aggressive, in your face, wild man who didn't sing, but shrieked and hollered, and didn't play the piano, but pounded it into submission. Growing up in a devout Seventh Day Adventist family, Richard learned to sing gospel music and play the piano at a local church. At age 13, he was kicked out of his family's house (reportedly because of his homosexuality); by 1951 he was performing on the radio with a jump band. In 1955 Richard sent a demo to Specialty Records in Los Angeles where it caught the attention of producer **Bumps Blackwell.** Blackwell brought him into New Orleans's J&M studio in September 1955 where Richard recorded his first hit, "Tutti Frutti." With its opening battle cry, "Awop bop a loo mop a lop bam boom! Tutti Frutti! Aw rooty," "Tutti Frutti" went to number 17 in early 1956 and set the mold for many of Richard's hits to come, including "Long Tall Sally" (1956, number 2), "Lucille" (1957, number 1 R&B) and "Good Golly, Miss Molly" (1958, number 10).

Little Richard's gospel-influenced vocals and hard-driving piano playing was augmented by one of the tightest and most dynamic bands in early rock and roll. He often used **stop time** to punctuate vocal parts and honking saxophone solos. His lyrics were among the most sexually suggestive of the era. (The original lyrics to "Tutti Frutti," which included lines such as "Tutti Frutti, good booty/If it don't fit, don't force it/You can grease it, make it easy" had to be cleaned up by local songwriter Dorothy La Bostrie at the session.) On stage he was wild and aggressive, standing

Stop time is the interruption of a regular beat pattern in the rhythm section.

up while he played the piano. He took Presley's sexuality one step further, becoming rock's first androgynous performer by wearing mascara, lipstick and a pompadour hairstyle combed high.

In 1957, at the height of his career, Richard left music to become an ordained minister. Among the reasons he gave were witnessing the Soviet satellite Sputnik fly overhead at an outdoor concert and a dream in which he claimed to have had a vision of the apocalypse. After throwing thousands of dollars worth of jewelry into the ocean, he entered a Seventh Day Adventist college in Alabama "to work for Jehovah and find that peace of mind." In 1962, Richard slowly began his return to music, but his greatest successes were behind him. His influence is undeniable, not only from his songs (which have been covered by the Beatles, Rolling Stones, and many others) but also from his outlandish, over-the-top stage persona.

Chicago R&B

BO DIDDLEY

Meanwhile, up north in Chicago, a different sound was emerging from Chess Records. Ellas McDaniel had moved to the city from Mississippi as a child and became a regular at the South Side clubs, calling himself Bo Diddley (1928–). In 1955 his first recording, "Bo Diddley" (on Checker Records, a Chess subsidiary) went to number 1 on the R&B charts. The song consisted almost entirely of a one-chord vamp set to a repeating rhythm—*chunk-chunk-chunk-a-chunk, chunk a-chunk-chunk*—which has since become known among musicians as the "Bo Diddley rhythm" (and has been co-opted by Buddy Holly ["Not Fade Away"], The Who ["Magic Bus"] and several others). "Bo Diddley" was backed with "I'm a Man," a bump and grind blues number built on the five-note riff from Willie Dixon's song " I'm Your Hoochie Coochie Man."

Bo Diddley has a large, distinctive persona, often wearing cowboy hats and huge horn-rimmed glasses and playing unusual rectangular-shaped guitars. Although he never achieved the fame of other fifties crossover R&B artists, he was an important guitar innovator who is the link between T-Bone Walker and Jimi Hendrix. His use of reverb and tremolo to enhance the sound of his guitar was as pioneering for the fifties as the distortion and feedback that Hendrix used in the sixties. He played his guitar as if it was a percussion instrument, giving his music a hypnotic, rhythmic feel. Diddley often propelled these rhythmic grooves with the unusual use of maracas. His bands frequently included female musicians, which was unusual for the time.

CHESS RECORDS

Bo Diddley was one of several artists who recorded for Chess Records and helped define the Chicago R&B sound. **Phil Chess** and **Leonard Chess** were Polish immigrants who came to Chicago as children in 1928. After dabbling in various business ventures, they eventually went into the nightclub business, owning and operating the Macomba Lounge on the South Side. In 1947 they sold the Macomba and invested in Aristocrat Records, (which they later bought outright and renamed Chess in 1950) to record the artists they had seen performing in their club. Their earliest successes came with transplanted Delta musicians such as Muddy Waters and Howlin' Wolf, but by 1954 they were expanding into the growing crossover market, recording hits by doo woppers—the Moonglows and the Flamingos.

In 1957 they also moved into a larger building at 2120 South Michigan Avenue in which they built an in-house recording facility where all of their artists recorded until 1967 (the building remains today as a museum). Since South Michigan Avenue at the time contained the offices of several independent labels (such as Vee-Jay, Brunswick, and Constellation), distributors, rehearsal spaces, and other studios, it became known as Record Row. Many of the Chess sessions included veteran players Willie Dixon on bass, Fred Below on drums, Otis Spann on piano, and Little Walter on harmonica. Dixon was also influential as a composer, penning the blues standards "Wang Dang Doodle" and "Spoonful." In 1955 Chess signed the man who might easily qualify as the father of rock and roll: Chuck Berry. Box 2-5 lists some characteristics and key recordings of the chess R&B sound.

CHUCK BERRY

Chuck Berry (1926-) was born in St. Louis and grew up listening to gospel, country, blues, R&B and popular crooners such as Nat "King" Cole and Frank Sinatra. After becoming somewhat successful in the local club circuit, Berry went to Chicago in May 1955 with hopes of making a record. There he met Muddy Waters, who referred him to Leonard Chess, who in turn set up a session to record Berry's tune "Ida Red." Although Chess liked the song, he knew of another with the same title, so he suggested renaming "Ida Red." Combining scorching guitar work, a country beat, and a compelling story line, "Maybellene" shot up the

---

Box 2-5 The Chess R&B Sound

Characteristics of the Chess R&B Sound
1. Raunchy, powerful, defining the Chicago blues sound
2. Instrumentation: distorted electric guitar, bass, drums, piano, sometimes harmonica

Key Chess Rock R&B Recordings
❑ "Bo Diddley"—Bo Diddley, 1955
❑ "Maybellene"—Chuck Berry, 1955
❑ "Laura Lee"—Bobby Charles, 1956
❑ "Johnny B. Goode"—Chuck Berry, 1957

charts, hitting number 5 by the end of August. Over the next three years, Berry had four more Top 10 hits—"School Day" and "Rock and Roll Music" (number 3 and number 8 respectively, 1957), and "Johnny B. Goode" and "Sweet Little Sixteen" (number 8 and number 2, 1958).

Chuck Berry was the first great lyricist in rock and roll. His songs were interesting, humorous, and often-ironic tales of teen life that transcended the usual boy-meets-girl story line. For instance, "School Day" told of racing down to the local juke joint as soon as the 3 o'clock bell rang. "Roll Over Beethoven" contained the warning "tell Tschaikowsky the news" to "dig these rhythm and blues," while "Sweet Little Sixteen" told a tale of a girl all dressed up ready to go out and rock, but who still needed mommy and daddy's permission. Berry also occasionally tackled deeper issues, as in the condemnation of racial injustice in "Brown Eyed Handsome Man." Many of these songs not only told great stories, but also contained unforgettable sing-along hooks, such as *"Go! Go! Johnny, Go! Go! Go!"* and *"Hail, Hail, Rock and Roll,"* which made them among the earliest rock and roll anthems. Berry combined elements of blues and country in his songs, and while this was a reflection of his early influences, it was also a calculated effort on his part to capture the widest crossover audience. He also sang very clearly, as did his crooner idols.

Berry was also the archetypal rock guitarist, creating double note lead lines that are among the most copied in rock. It is not inconceivable to believe that every rock guitar player since 1960 has learned to play the introductions to both "Roll Over Beethoven" and "Johnny B. Goode." Berry used imaginative call and response interplay between vocal and guitar on "School Day," recorded live in an era before overdubbing was common. His signature duck walk also inspired an entire generation of guitarists to put on a better show.

Berry's initial success was due in part to Alan Freed, who recognized the hit potential of "Maybellene" early on and gave the song constant airplay. In return for his help, Leonard Chess credited Freed with 1/3 of the song's authorship, therefore assigning him a third of the royalty payments (the other 1/3 was assigned to Chess' landlord, Russ Fratto)—all without Berry's knowledge. This and other forms of outright **payola** were typical of how the industry operated in the mid-1950s. Within a few years, the practice of paying off DJs to get airplay would erupt into a major scandal that would shake the music business to the bone.

In 1959 Berry ran into trouble. While on tour in the southwest, he met Janice Escalante, a fourteen-year-old Mexican-Indian girl, and brought her back to St. Louis to work at his nightclub, Club Bandstand. After Escalante was picked up on prostitution charges, police launched an investigation into Berry on charges of violating the Mann Act, which prohibits transporting minors across state lines for immoral purposes. After two blatantly racist trials (the first was overturned), Berry was convicted in 1962 and spent two years in federal prison. When the embittered Berry returned to music, the British Invasion was underway, sweeping him and many other R&B artists out of the limelight. However, there is no doubt that the Beatles, Rolling Stones, and other British groups that came to prominence in the 1960s owed much of their success to the influence of Chuck Berry's musical genius.

See Appendix A, "School Day" by Chuck Berry. Track 8 on enclosed CD.

Payola was a term coined by *Variety Magazine* in 1938 to describe the practice of payments made to DJs in the form of gifts, favors, or cash by record labels to entice the playing of a record.

Other Important Rock and Roll Artists

Meanwhile Back in Memphis . . .

After selling Elvis Presley's contract in late 1955, Sam Phillips was able to quickly turn his finances around. He began to turn his attention away from blues and R&B toward country and rock and roll. Whether his motives were racist, as some have claimed, is uncertain. What is known is that a number of talented, young, white Elvis wannabes started showing up at his front door to audition for him. Even though Sun was still an independent label, it now had a high profile and national credibility, and it was up to Sam Phillips to seize the moment. While selling Presley's contract was viewed by some as a lost dream, to Phillips a golden opportunity lay ahead in promoting whatever new artists he was able to discover and nurture as he had done with Presley.

Although he did have success in launching the career of a few country artists such as **Johnny Cash** and **Charlie Rich,** most of Phillips's success in the last half of the 1950s came from his rockabilly artists. The biggest of these, Carl Perkins and Jerry Lee Lewis, quickly exploded to the top of the charts, but could not sustain any commercial success. In hindsight, we are able to see that their greatest records, like those of Elvis Presley, were those that were made early in their careers under Phillips's supervision. **Roy Orbison,** on the other hand, achieved his greatest success *after* leaving Sun, with nine Top Twenty hits between 1960 and 1964 for Monument Records, including "Running Scared" and "Pretty Woman," both going to number 1. In trying to turn the balladeer Orbison into a rockabilly singer, Sam Phillips made one of the few artistic miscalculations in his career.

The Later Years of Sam Phillips and Sun Studios

In spite of the stunning success that Sam Phillips had during the fifties, the glory years for Sun Studios were over by 1960. That was the year that he moved into a brand new, state of the art studio just a few blocks from his original location. Even though the new facility was much larger, the atmosphere was sterile and lacked the creative warmth of the cramped former studio. Phillips grew tired of the recording business and sold Sun in 1969. For a time he owned and operated WHER-AM, an all-female radio station in Memphis; he also was one of the original investors in Holiday Inn. The studio at 706 Union Avenue was eventually reopened as a tourist attraction, but still remains open today as a recording studio. Sam Phillips spent the last thirty-some years of his life as a sort of living rock and roll legend. He died at age 80 on July 30, 2003.

THE SUN ROCKABILLY ARTISTS

Carl Perkins

Carl Perkins (1932-1998) was born to poor sharecropping parents in northwest Tennessee. Despite his impoverished youth, he was able to start a band with his brothers Jay and Clayton, playing the honky tonk circuit in the early 50s. During these years, Perkins was composing his own songs and developing his own rockabilly guitar and singing style. After hearing Presley's "Blue Moon of Kentucky" on the radio in 1954, the Perkins brothers auditioned for Phillips, and released two very country sounding singles in 1955 with modest sales success. Their next release was a monster.

After a concert in Amory, Mississippi in which they both appeared in the fall of 1955, singer Johnny Cash suggested that Perkins write a song based on a saying he had often heard while in the service, "Don't step on my blue suede shoes." Amazingly, a few nights later, Perkins heard the same comment on the dance floor in a Tennessee bar. At three o'clock the next morning, Perkins awoke with the song in his head, and wrote the lyrics down on an empty potato bag. Recorded and released in December 1955, "Blue Suede Shoes" shot up the charts, successfully fighting off numerous cover versions to end up at number 2 (Presley's "Heartbreak Hotel" kept it from going to number 1). By March 1956, the song was near the top of the country and R&B charts as well, becoming Sun's first million seller. Unfortunately, tragedy struck on March 21. Perkins and his brothers were on their way to make their network TV debut on the *Perry Como Show* in New York when their car slammed into a poultry truck in Delaware. Carl suffered a broken shoulder and cracked skull, was laid up for six months in the hospital and never made it to New York.

Carl Perkins was never able to come up with another hit, and his career floundered. Although he continued his career after recovering from the auto accident, his sound (and even his look) was just a little too country for the emerging rock and roll audience. However, on a tour of England in 1964, he was received as a conquering hero, and met some of his most adoring fans, a certain moptop musical quartet. "I sat on the couch with the Beatles sitting around me on the floor," he later recalled. "At their request, I sang every song I had ever recorded. They knew each one. I was deeply flattered." The Beatles further showed their respect by covering both "Everybody's Tryin' to Be My Baby" and "Honey Don't" on their fourth album *Beatles for Sale*.

Jerry Lee Lewis

Jerry Lee Lewis (1935-) was the first bad boy of rock and roll. Born in Ferriday, Louisiana, Lewis's childhood, like Presley's and Perkins's, was spent in poverty. The cousin of tele-evangelist Jimmy Swaggart, Lewis was thrown out of bible college his first night after tearing into a boogie woogie version of "My God Is Real." By the time he auditioned for Sam Phillips in 1956 at age twenty-one, he had been married twice, in jail, and turned down by the Louisiana Hayride and every label he had auditioned for in Nashville. But Phillips took a chance on Lewis. In February 1957, after one lackluster release, Jerry Lee recorded "Whole Lotta Shakin' Going On," which quickly shot up the charts to number 3, earning him a spot on the *Steve Allen Show* in July. He quickly followed up "Shakin'" with 'Great Balls of Fire," which went to number 2 in December, and "Breathless," which hit number 7 in March 1958. After the Carl Perkins disappointment, Sam Phillips finally had a star that he could bank on.

But, again, disaster struck. In May 1958, Lewis arrived in England for a promotional tour. With him was his newlywed third wife, Myra Gale. She was 13 years old—and *his cousin!* To make matters worse, Lewis married her before he was even divorced from his second wife. As the British press honed in on the scandal, Lewis was taken off the tour. Assuming that the Brits were just being their usual haughty selves, Lewis and his entourage retreated back to the safety of the states. Unfortunately, the American music industry reacted in much the same way as the British, and he was blacklisted from the Top Forty and cancelled from bookings on Dick Clark's *American Bandstand.* Even though Sam Phillips tried to make a quick buck off of the situation by releasing the novelty song "The Return of Jerry Lee" (which included lines from Lewis records such as: "What did Queen Elizabeth say about you?/Goodness, gracious, great balls of fire!"), Lewis's career went into a tailspin less than a year after it started.

Despite his short stay at the top, Jerry Lee Lewis carved a niche for himself as one of rock and roll's originals. His story is of the very essence of rock and roll: a rebellious spirit, a natural-born performer, with an outrageous personality. Driven by one of the biggest egos in history, and an ongoing conflict with his lifestyle and his religious upbringing, he nicknamed himself "The Killer" (ironically, there is suspicion that he in fact killed his fifth wife, who was mysteriously murdered in their New Orleans home). He literally attacked his instrument, or as rock journalist Andy Wickham noted, "Elvis shook his hips; Lewis *raped* his piano." Jerry Lee Lewis drank too much, abused drugs, and avoided paying taxes and the IRS. And he is still alive to tell about it.

See Appendix A, "Great Balls of Fire" by Jerry Lee Lewis. Track 9 on enclosed CD.

OTHER ROCKABILLY ARTISTS

Two rockabilly artists that are often linked are **Eddie Cochran** (1938-1960) and **Gene Vincent** (1935-1971). Both emerged with hits in the late 50s, Vincent with "Be-Bop-A-Lula" in 1956, Cochran with "Summertime Blues" in 1958. Both bore a resemblance to Elvis—a definite plus—and both seemed to be potential stars. Unfortunately, while on tour together in England in 1960, the car in which they were riding crashed, killing Cochran and seriously wounding Vincent. Although he lived, Vincent never recovered from his friend's death and his career fizzled until his own early death at age 36.

Buddy Holly

Unlike many of the early rock and roll pioneers, Buddy Holly (1936-1959) grew up in a stable, middle-class home in Lubbock, Texas. His was a musical family, and young Buddy learned how to play several instruments, and his singing won a talent contest at age five. Much of his early influences came from listening to country music on the numerous barn dance radio programs, and unlike most west Texas kids, Holly was fond of listening to R&B on black radio stations. As a teenager, he played in a country band, Buddy and Bob (with friend Bob Montgomery), that in 1955 opened for both Elvis Presley and Bill Haley. Meeting Presley made a profound impact on Buddy, who began to cultivate rockabilly influences into his music. With his reputation growing as a singer, guitarist, and songwriter, Holly signed with Decca Records and in early 1956 took off for Nashville, sure of becoming the next Elvis.

By this time, Holly had turned into a prolific songwriter, and his sessions with Decca yielded five single releases. At one of the sessions, drummer Jerry Allison persuaded Holly to rename one of his songs to honor his fiancée; thus "Cindy Lou" became "Peggy Sue." Another song, "That'll Be the Day" was recorded, but Decca refused to release it. By the end of the year, with all of the records selling poorly, Holly and Decca mutually parted, and Holly returned to Lubbock.

In February 1957, Buddy and his newly formed band, the Crickets, began recording at the **Nor Va Jak Studio** in Clovis, New Mexico, which was owned and operated by musician **Norman Petty.** Petty gave the Crickets unlimited access to the studio, and Holly took the opportunity to learn and experiment with the technical side of music production, including **multi-tracking.** In return, Petty was granted partial writing credits on Holly's songs. One of the first songs recorded in Clovis was a revamped, faster version of "That'll Be the Day," which shot up the charts, hitting number 1 by August. Following in quick succession were "Peggy Sue" (number 3, November) and "Oh, Boy" (number 10, December). By late 1957, the Crickets were booked into tours of the U.S., England and Australia (the U.S. tour included a stop at Harlem's Apollo Theatre, where the audience was surprised to find out the group was white). By 1958, Buddy Holly and the Crickets were living in Greenwich Village in New York.

By this time, important changes were beginning to take place in Holly's life. In August, he married Maria Elena Santiago after proposing to her on their first date. He recorded "True Love Ways," a song written by singer Paul Anka that was orchestrated with syrupy strings. The Crickets, tiring of New York and sensing the loss of camaraderie with the newlywed Holly, parted ways with their leader and returned to Lubbock. Holly also took steps to sever the informal contractual arrangements he had with Norman Petty, and the ensuing legal battle tied up his finances for what seemed to be the foreseeable future. To raise needed cash, he reluctantly agreed to join the

See Appendix A, "Peggy Sue" by Buddy Holly and the Crickets. Track 10 on enclosed CD.

Multi-tracking is recording technology that allows separate recording on individual tracks, with the ability to combine tracks recorded at separate times into a finished product.

Unlike many of the early rock and roll pioneers, Buddy Holly grew up in a stable, middle-class home.
AP/WIDE WORLD PHOTOS

Winter Dance Party tour in early 1959 that was to include several mid-western stops.

On the tour, Holly was featured with **Ritchie Valens** (Richard Valenzuela) and Beaumont, Texas DJ the **Big Bopper** (Jiles Perry Richardson), both up and comers with hits on the charts ("Oh, Donna" and "Chantilly Lace"). After the second show at the Surf Ballroom in Clear Lake, Iowa, the three stars chartered a plane to take them to the next show in Moorhead, Minnesota. They were supposed to take a bus, but wanted to arrive early to get their laundry done and get some extra rest. Flying into a quickly forming winter storm with a pilot that was not certified to fly with navigational instruments, the plane crashed eight miles north of Clear Lake in the early morning hours of February 3, 1959, killing everyone on board.

Buddy Holly left an immense legacy, especially considering the brevity of his two-year career. He pioneered the four-piece combo of two guitars, bass, and drums that would be widely copied throughout the sixties. Influences of his well-crafted, innocent love songs can be heard in the early works of the Beatles, the Hollies (who named themselves in his honor), and other groups. When the Beatles (who in fact renamed themselves from the Quarry Men to something that they thought would sound more like Holly's Crickets) made their first record in a small studio in Liverpool, the song they recorded was "That'll Be the Day." As an artist, Holly was the complete package: guitarist, singer, songwriter, and producer. He was the first of many rock guitarists to use the new Fender Stratocaster guitar. Holly was also one of the first rock musicians to push the limits of studio technology to enhance his recordings.

The Everly Brothers

Don Everly (1937–) and **Phil Everly** (1939–) were born in Kentucky in the late 1930s to the country western stars Ike and Margaret Everly. The family toured together while the brothers were children, and the boys learned to sing in a traditional (and thought by some to be outdated) Appalachian style. In 1957, Don and Phil signed with the small independent Cadence Records, where the husband/wife songwriting team Felice and Boudleaux Bryant was assigned to write songs for them. The Bryants supplied most of their early hits, including "Bye Bye Love" and "Wake Up, Little Susie" (number 2 and number 1 respectively in 1957), and "All I Have to Do Is Dream" and "Bird Dog" (both number 1, 1958). In 1960 the Everlys moved to Warner where they recorded "Cathy's Clown" (number 1, written by Don) and "When Will I Be Loved" (number 8, written by Phil). Recording in Nashville, the Everly's slick studio production was achieved in part by using veteran session musicians such as Chet Atkins and Floyd Cramer.

The Everly's distinctive sound of acoustic guitars and high vocal harmonies was influential to the Four Seasons and Beach Boys, as well as later sixties folk rock groups such as the Byrds. Although they disappeared from the charts after 1962, the Everlys continued to tour extensively. After struggling with amphetamine addiction for several years, the brothers broke up in 1973 after a bitter, on-stage argument, but reunited in 1983 at the Royal Albert Hall in London.

The End of an Era

Even though rock and roll created a musical and cultural revolution, the initial shock wave did not last long. A variety of forces came into play in the late 1950s and early sixties that brought sweeping changes to the music—changes that were not all good. The transitional second phase of the history of rock music is the subject of the next chapter.

Chapter 2
Study Questions

1. Describe some of the changes that were taking place in American society in the years leading up to the birth of rock and roll.

_____

_____

_____

2. Describe some of the changes that were taking place in the music business in the years 1946-54?

_____

_____

_____

3. What were some differences between the major and independent labels, both in how they operated and in what kind of music they specialized in?

_____

_____

_____

4. What role did radio play in the explosion of rock and roll, and who were the important personalities?

_____

_____

_____

5. Why was Bill Haley important to the rock and roll explosion?

_____

_____

_____

6. Why was Sam Phillips important to the rock and roll explosion?

_____

_____

_____

7. Why are Elvis Presley's Sun recordings considered to be more important than his RCA recordings?

_____

_____

_____

_____

8. Describe the differences between the R&B that emerged from New Orleans and the R&B that emerged from Chicago in the fifties.

_____

_____

_____

_____

9. What are some of the important contributions that Chuck Berry made to rock and roll?

_____

_____

_____

_____

10. What are some of the important contributions that Buddy Holly made to rock and roll?

_____

_____

_____

_____

The Transition to Mainstream Pop

The Changing Landscape

THE END OF THE CLASSIC ROCK AND ROLL ERA

As the 1950s came to an end, the winds of change were once more blowing across the American landscape. After eight years of the conservative and staid administration of President Dwight D. Eisenhower, the young charismatic John F. Kennedy was elected president. With his now famous call to action from his inaugural address, "Ask not what your country can do for you, ask what you can do for your country," Kennedy's youthful vigor and idealism made the nation's young people feel that they could make a difference in making the world a better place. His social programs included the Alliance for Progress, the Peace Corps, and new legislation to promote civil rights and fight poverty. With his pretty wife, Jacqueline, and two small children, the Kennedys represented a changing of the guard—old was out, young was in.

Rock and roll was changing as well. A series of unrelated events that can only be chalked up to bad luck and bad timing caused the rebels of the first or 'classic' rock era to disappear from the scene:

❑ Elvis went into the army in early 1958, and would never regain the energy and excitement of his early career.

❑ Carl Perkins's career went unfulfilled after the car accident that almost killed him in 1956.

❑ Little Richard retired to the ministry in 1957.

❑ Jerry Lee Lewis was shunned after news of his scandalous marriage broke in 1958.

❑ Chuck Berry was arrested in 1959 for violating the Mann Act.

❑ Tragic accidents claimed the lives of Buddy Holly in 1959 and Eddie Cochran in 1960.

These events were remarkably well timed for the major labels, which by 1960 were busy packaging a more refined and less vulgar product to a maturing audience. By this time, many of the teens that had originally embraced rock and roll were becoming adults and entering the world of mortgages, jobs, marriage, and children. They weren't so rebellious any more, and their music tastes were changing. Suddenly they were buying more LPs than singles (like their parents had done in the fifties), and were 'turning down the volume' so to speak, listening to music that wasn't quite as wild as five years ago. With a maturing audience, an increasingly watered-down product, and the exiting of an entire generation of rock stars, many were inclined to believe that rock and roll was dead.

While this chapter focuses on how the pop music industry reclaimed its audience, two other important strains of pop were also emerging at the same time that will be covered in subsequent chapters. Chapter 4 will cover folk music, which was finally breaking through to the mainstream after languishing for years in the backwoods of rural

America. Chapter 5 will cover soul music, which emerged from the fusion of gospel and R&B in the fifties to become one of pop music's most popular forms in the sixties.

THE BACKLASH

At the same time as the first generation of rock and rollers were fading from view, a number of battles associated with the music were being waged on a variety of fronts. The first of these was a conservative back-lash from religious, government, and parental groups, who from the beginning had warned that rock and roll was causing a breakdown of morals among youth. Some even believed it was a subversive Communist plot and that the government should step in and do something. "I Hate Elvis" clubs sprang up throughout the country, as did boycotts of the TV shows that he performed on. Many blamed the DJs who played the music as the real culprits for poisoning the impressionable young minds of their listeners, and accused them of no less than brainwashing. This complex battle also crossed over into issues of class and race, as rock and roll was viewed by many as the music of lower-class blacks and southern whites, and that it encouraged miscegenation. To an extent, this battle continues to this day.

The Teen Idols

THE BOY NEXT DOOR

The second battlefront was the ongoing one between the major labels and the independents. By the dawning of the sixties, the major labels were fighting back and began to regain control of the teen and young adult market by cultivating a new crop of singers that were clean-cut, wholesome, non-offensive—and white. The teen idols, as they became known, were groomed for stardom not on the basis of their talent, but instead on their 'boy-next-door' good looks. Many of them were of Italian ancestry who Anglicized their names to present a more All-American image—accordingly, Francis Avalone became **Frankie Avalon,** Walden Robert Cassotto became **Bobby Darin,** Concetta Franconero became **Connie Francis.** Unlike most of the classic rock and rollers, the teen idols did not write their own songs, but instead recorded songs written by professional songwriters who consciously smoothed out the rough edges of earlier rock and roll. The typical teen idol song contained little or no beat, lavish orchestration, and non-sexual, safe romantic themes of idealistic teen love. Among the most popular teen idols were Avalon, who had thirteen Top Forty hits between 1958 and 1962; **Paul Anka,** with twenty-two during the same period; and Francis, with twenty-eight. Other popular teen idols included **Fabian** (Fabiano Forte), **Bobby Rydell** (Robert Ridarelli) and **Freddy Cannon** (Frederick Picariello).

One teen idol whose career extended beyond the early sixties was **Ricky Nelson.** Nelson had actually grown up in front of the nation as a

Teen Idols were the clean cut, wholesome singers that the major labels promoted in the late fifties and early sixties to counter the success of independent label R&B and rock and roll.

Key Teen Idol Recordings

- ❏ "Who's Sorry Now?"—Connie Francis, 1958
- ❏ "Venus"—Frankie Avalon, 1959
- ❏ "Puppy Love"—Paul Anka, 1960

cast member of the popular family TV program *The Adventures of Ozzie and Harriet,* named for his parents, the stars of the show. Although Nelson's popularity was strongest before the British Invasion swept all the teen idols aside, he remained popular until his death in an airplane accident in 1985. Between 1957 and 1964 he had thirty-three Top Forty hits, two of which went to number 1 ("Poor Little Fool" in 1958 and "Travelin' Man," 1961").

PHILADELPHIA, DICK CLARK, AND AMERICAN BANDSTAND

One reason for the huge success of the teen idols was their constant exposure on a television program that began broadcasting on Philadelphia's WFIL-TV in 1952. Originally called *Bandstand* and hosted by Bob Horn, the show was taken over by station staff announcer **Dick Clark** in 1956 after Horn was arrested for drunk driving (ironically right in the middle of a 'Don't Drink and Drive' promotion the station was running). In 1957 the show was picked up by the national ABC-TV network and renamed *American Bandstand.* Within two years, it was being broadcast on over 100 stations to an audience of twenty million. It aired until 1987.

The format of *American Bandstand* was simple: pack a TV studio with 150 clean-cut teenagers who dance to the latest hit singles, with weekly appearances by pop singers who lip-sync along with their records. Clark, who looked like a teenager himself, wielded enormous power by picking which songs were played and how often, and his choices mostly favored the pop-oriented teen idols and other non-threatening singers, including local Philadelphia boys Fabian, Avalon, and Rydell. Dick Clark also began building a music empire by investing in local record companies, publishing firms, a management company, and a pressing plant. Powered by the success of *American Bandstand,* Philadelphia played an important role in the pop music industry in the early sixties.

DANCE CRAZES AND NOVELTY TUNES

The most important record labels in Philadelphia at this time were **Cameo/Parkway, Chancellor,** and **Swan** (which was half owned by Clark). For a few years in the late fifties and early sixties, these companies were among the industry leaders in creating a pop music product, sometimes (in the case of the teen idols) literally creating stars out of less than stellar talents. Said Chancellor owner Bob Marcucci of meeting Fabian: "Somehow I sensed that here was a kid who could go. He looks a little bit like Presley. . . . I figured he was a natural. It's true that he couldn't sing. He knew it, and I knew it." Cameo/Parkway hit upon a tremendously successful strategy by producing a series of novelty dance tunes, starting with the 1960 number 1 hit "The Twist" by **Chubby Checker.** Checker was local unknown singer Ernest Evans; his new name was conceived by Dick Clark's wife, Bobbie, as a play on the name Fats Domino. The label followed up "The Twist" with other dance tunes, including "The

Box 3-1 Dance Crazes from the Early 1960s

Twist	Pony	Fly
Dog	Madison	Popeye
Watusi	Loco-Motion	Hitch-Hike
Harlem Shuffle	Limbo	Swim
Wiggle Wobble	Bristol Stomp	Boston Monkee
Hully Gully	Cool Jerk	Duck
Mashed Potato	Monkee	Funky Chicken

Hucklebuck," "Pony Time," "The Fly," and "Limbo Rock" by Checker, and "The Fish," "The Wah Watusi," the "Mashed Potato," and several more by other artists. The dance craze scheme worked so well that "The Twist" returned to the number 1 spot again in 1962, the only single since charting began in 1955 to top the charts twice. Usually, instructions for the dance were found somewhere in the lyrics, and with exposure on *American Bandstand,* they quickly spread throughout the teenage nation. Box 3-1 lists dance crazes from the early 1960s.

Novelty tunes appeared from time to time as well, including:

❑ Sheb Wolley's "The Purple People Eater" (number 1, 1958)

❑ Brian Hyland's "Itsy Bitsy Teenie Weenie Yellow Polka Dot Bikini" (number 1, 1960)

❑ Bobby "Boris" Pickett's "Monster Mash" (number 1, 1962).

Dave Seville came up with the best pop gimmick of all time when he created the Chipmunks by recording overdubs of his own voice at half speed and playing them back at full speed (making them sound an octave higher). He had two number 1 hits in 1958 alone: "Witch Doctor" and "The Chipmunk Song."

Along with *American Bandstand,* other national TV programs began presenting rock 'n roll as well, albeit in small doses. At the time, variety shows were popular that presented comedians, acrobats, and jugglers, as well as musical groups. Although they attracted some criticism from conservatives, the variety shows of Arthur Godfrey, Jackie Gleason, Steve Allen, Milton Berle, and Ed Sullivan all made a point of putting rock on their shows once they realized it increased ratings. *The Ed Sullivan Show,* on the air from 1948 to 1971 and one of the most watched programs on TV, was particularly important for rock artists to gain national visibility. Appearances on the Sullivan show were milestones in the early careers of Elvis Presley, the Beatles, and the Rolling Stones.

Payola

THE PAY FOR PLAY SCANDAL

The third battle being waged at the time was a particularly ugly one. Although **payola,** the practice of DJs accepting cash, favors, and other

payola is the practice of DJs accepting cash, favors, and other gifts from record companies to play their songs was not specifically illegal at the time (unless one considered it bribery), it was certainly unethical.

gifts from record companies to play their songs was not specifically illegal at the time (unless one considered it bribery), it was certainly unethical. It was also so widely accepted as standard business practice that the entire industry shuddered when congress decided to investigate the issue in 1959. The timing of the probe was convenient for politicians who wanted to score points among their constituents who hated rock and roll: 1960 was an election year. When the Special Subcommittee on Legislative Oversight, chaired by Arkansas Democratic Representative Oren Harris, found that 335 DJs had been paid "consulting" fees totaling $263,245, a witch hunt commenced to find out who the guilty ones were. Although a few DJs were fired and some stations produced affidavits showing they were monitoring their jocks, the focus of the committee quickly turned to the two most highly visible rock entrepreneurs, Dick Clark and Alan Freed.

There were a number of issues suggesting that Clark had improper deals going on, including his ownership of publishing companies, 162 song copyrights (145 which had been given to him as gifts) and co-ownership of Swan Records. Since Clark often played songs on *American Bandstand* that benefited these business arrangements, it appeared that he was manipulating the system for his own profit. But because he did not actually accept cash for playing songs and profited legally from the performance royalties once the songs were played, Dick Clark successfully defended himself as merely taking advantage of business opportunities. He also divested himself from most of his various interests (except *Bandstand*) by the time he was called to testify before the committee in April 1960. After two days of questioning that at times seemed to implicate that there was a case to be made against him, the clean cut and youthful looking Clark was released without further investigation.

Alan Freed was not as fortunate. His problems actually began in 1958 when he was arrested for inciting a riot at a concert he promoted in Boston. He was promptly fired by his employer, WINS. By 1959, Freed was working at WABC radio in New York and facing new problems in light of the impending payola investigation. Although he never admitted to taking money from record labels to play records (although he later acknowledged being paid by distributors for "consultation work"), he would not sign an ABC Network affidavit saying as much and was fired by WABC in November. Always more controversial and outspoken than the boyish, likeable Clark, Freed quickly became the scapegoat of the entire scandal. Even *Cashbox Magazine* noted as much, with an editorial stating that Freed "suffered the most and was perhaps singled out for alleged wrongs that had become a business way-of-life for many others."

Unable to find a job with a major radio station, Alan Freed drifted from one small station to another and was hounded by investigators until finally forced to plead guilty to accepting commercial bribes in 1962 (by this time payola was illegal). A federal Grand Jury then indicted him for $38,000 of income tax evasion from the unreported payola. At this point, unable to get a job in radio and with a growing drinking problem, Alan Freed's career and life quickly went down the drain. He died penniless and broken from the emotional and financial toll of the scandal in 1965 at age 43.

Top 40

The payola scandal was the final blow to the dominant era of the DJ, as radio stations began hiring music directors to help determine which records would be played. The power and authority of DJs had already begun to erode with the increasing popularity of the programming format known as Top 40, the brainchild of **Todd Storz,** owner of KOWH in Omaha. While at a tavern located across the street from the station one night in 1955 (although some say the year was 1953), Storz and his companions noticed that patrons were plugging the jukebox to play the same songs over and over, and when the bar closed, the waitresses took their tip money and played those songs again. Storz and his program director wrote down the names of the top songs and began playing them throughout the day on KOWH, eliminating the classical, country, and other programs the station had been playing. Within two years, KOWH went from last to first in the Omaha market, and Storz was able to buy other stations in New Orleans, Kansas City, Minneapolis, and Miami, which he formatted in the same way. Top 40 was popular with listeners because they knew that they were never more than a few minutes away from hearing their favorite song played, and it quickly spread throughout the industry. Ultimately, the Top 40 format had a homogenizing effect on radio, limiting playlists all over America to mainstream pop singles. It also further diminished the power of the DJ, who in the end was shut out from selecting the songs that he played on his show.

Brill Building Pop

Aldon Music

In New York, where the Tin Pan Alley composers had ruled pop music since the 1880s, a new breed of songwriters was beginning to emerge in the late fifties. Rock and roll had presented a paradigm shift in the pop music business, and show tunes written in the Tin Pan Alley mold would not work anymore. New songs had to be written with a rock beat with story lines that related to teenagers but were not offensive to adults. Many of the older, established songwriters were simply not up to the task, leaving the door open for a new crop of younger writers. By the early sixties, this new pop songwriting scene was clustered in and around the **Brill Building** at 1619 Broadway, where over 150 music businesses were located. These songwriting shops became so influential to the industry that the pop music of the late fifties and early sixties became known as "Brill Building Pop." One of the most important, **Aldon Music,** at 1650 Broadway just across the street from the Brill Building, was founded in 1958 by songwriters **Al Nevins** and **Don Kirshner.** Nevins and Kirshner, who preferred their writers to work in pairs, assembled a stable of pop songwriting superstars that included the teams of **Neil Sedaka** and **Howard Greenfield, Barry Mann** and **Cynthia Weil** (who would marry soon after teaming up), and **Carole**

King and **Gerry Goffin,** two nineteen-year-olds who were already married. (Interestingly, there was yet another highly successful Brill Building husband and wife team, **Ellie Greenwich** and **Jeff Barry,** although they didn't work for Aldon.)

Working at Aldon Music was typical of the Brill Building scene: each day writers worked out song ideas in cubicles with upright pianos, often soliciting suggestions and criticisms from other company writers at the end of the day. The songs were then pitched to record companies, whose A&R men, arrangers, and producers cranked out product. It had all the glamour of an assembly line, but with impressive results. By 1962 Aldon had eighteen writers on staff who had placed hundreds of hits on the radio, led by the top three writing teams of Sedaka/Greenfield, Mann/Weil, and King/Goffin. They were not only good, they were young—none were over the age of twenty-six. Box 3–2 lists some Aldon hits that helped define Brill Building Pop.

"Will You Love Me Tomorrow," while extremely popular, was also revolutionary for its time. While most songs of the era were stories of idealistic teenage love, this song was more direct. Being pressured by her boyfriend to submit to his desires, the girl wants assurance that he will still love her in the morning—after all, her reputation was at stake. "The Loco-Motion" was inspired by King and Goffin's babysitter, seventeen-year-old Eva Narcissus Boyd, who was dancing while the two were working on some new material. Goffin asked what the name of the dance was—to him it looked like a locomotive train. After finishing the song, Goffin and King let Eva—who became "Little Eva"—sing it, and it became the first of her four Top Forty hits.

Box 3-2 Aldon Hits That Helped Define Brill Building Pop

Neil Sedaka/Howard Greenfield:
"Stupid Cupid"—recorded by Connie Francis, number 14, 1958
"Breaking Up Is Hard to Do"—Neil Sedaka, number 1, 1960
"Calendar Girl"—Neil Sedaka, number 4, 1960

Barry Mann/Cynthia Weil:
"On Broadway" (with Jerry Leiber and Mike Stoller)—The Drifters, number 9, 1963
"You've Lost That Lovin' Feelin'" (with Phil Spector)—The Righteous Brothers, number 1, 1964
"We Gotta Get Out of This Place"—The Animals, number 13, 1965

Carole King/Gerry Goffin:
"Will You Love Me Tomorrow"—the Shirelles, number 1, 1961
"The Loco-Motion"—by Little Eva, number 1, 1962
"Go Away Little Girl"—Steve Lawrence, number 1, 1963

LEIBER AND STOLLER

As important as the Aldon Music writers were to the era, the real architects of early pop/rock were **Jerry Leiber** and **Mike Stoller.** The two came from remarkably similar backgrounds—both were Jewish East Coasters who moved to Los Angeles with their families in 1949. Both were also ardent fans of R&B music. They met in 1950 when they were both seventeen, and soon began writing songs together. Their first taste of success came in 1953 with Big Mama Thornton's number 1 R&B hit "Hound Dog." After forming their own Spark record label in 1954, Leiber and Stoller began to write songs for the R&B vocal quartet the **Robins,** including the classics "Smokey Joe's Café" and "Riot in Cell Block 9." Their first number 1 pop hits came in 1956 when Elvis Presley recorded his own version of "Hound Dog" along with "Love Me Tender." Presley's version of "Hound Dog" stayed at number 1 for eleven weeks, a record for longevity that stood until 1992. Presley had another number 1 Leiber and Stoller hit with "Jailhouse Rock" in 1957. In all, he recorded twenty-four of their songs.

In 1957 Leiber and Stoller moved to New York and the Brill Building area and began an unusual (for the time) association with Atlantic Records as independent producers. By this time they had hit upon a formula of telling mini-stories with humorous lyrics, which they referred to as "playlets." They were also paying meticulous attention to every detail in the recording process, spending hours in the studio recording as many as fifty takes of a song if necessary. Claiming that "We don't write songs, we write records," Leiber and Stoller pushed the art of record production into new, uncharted territory with the use of string orchestration, Spanish guitars, marimbas, and other exotic percussion instruments and Latin rhythms.

Their formula was well served in the string of nine Top Forty hits between 1957 and 1959 for the **Coasters** (the name given the newly reorganized Robins). These included the classics "Searchin'" and its flip-side "Youngblood," "Yakety Yak" (number 1, 1958), "Charlie Brown," "Along Came Jones," and "Poison Ivy." In addition to their success with another vocal group, the **Drifters** ("There Goes My Baby," "On Broadway," both Top Ten hits), they had two more Top Ten's with Ben E. King—"Spanish Harlem" (written by Leiber with Phil Spector) and "Stand By Me." In 1964 they founded another label, Red Bird, which produced many of the hits of the so-called "girl groups." Although their songwriting productivity fell in the mid sixties, many artists continued to record their songs, including the Beatles ("Kansas City"), Peggy Lee ("Is That All There Is?") and Luther Vandros ("I [Who Have Nothing]").

Leiber and Stoller helped make the independent producer an important part of the production process. Their songs are still among the most enduring in rock history, using clean, witty lyrics teenagers could relate to, set to R&B chord progressions, rhythms, and melodies. They were also tremendously influential to the next generation of producers and songwriters, such as Phil Spector, Barry Gordy of Motown, and Brian Wilson of the Beach Boys.

See Appendix A, "On Broadway" by the Drifters. Track 11 on enclosed CD.

The Girl Groups

PHIL SPECTOR

Phil Spector (1940–) was an understudy of Leiber and Stoller who created his own legacy as one of the era's most important pop producers. Born in the Bronx, he moved to California as a teen and started his own group, the Teddy Bears, which consisted of one female and three male singers (himself included). He wrote and produced their first recording in 1958, "To Know Him Is to Love Him"—the title coming from his father's tombstone (who had recently committed suicide)—which sold over a million copies and went to number 1. With the help of Lester Sill, a West Coast producer who had helped launch the careers of Leiber and Stoller, Spector moved back to New York to work with the two songwriters. Over the next few years, he co-wrote "Spanish Harlem," played guitar on some of the Drifters sessions, and produced a few hits for Gene Pitney and other artists. He quickly developed a reputation as not only a genius in the studio, but as an overbearing control freak and an eccentric loner.

In 1961, Spector moved back to Los Angeles and formed Philles Records with Sill. Sensing that an all-female vocal group might succeed after years of male doo wop groups dominating the charts, Spector began producing records for the **Crystals,** which consisted of five schoolgirl singers. Their first two records, songs of innocent love and devotion to ones boyfriend, charted in the Top Twenty. Their third release, "He Hit Me (And It Felt Like a Kiss)," written by King and Goffin, was banned due to the controversial subject matter. The next two records were smashes: "He's a Rebel" went to number 1 in 1962 and "Da Doo Ron Ron" (written with Ellie Greenwich and Jeff Barry) went to number 3 in 1963.

The success of the Crystals was mirrored by other so called "girl groups" who quickly materialized. The themes were simple and predictable: the glory of boyfriends and how worthless the girl's lives were without them. The **Ronettes,** led by Veronica Bennett (who was later married to Spector from 1968–74) had a number 2 hit in 1963 with "Be My Baby," written by Spector and Greenwich/Barry. The **Chiffons** hits

See Appendix A, "He's So Fine" by the Chiffons. Track 12 on enclosed CD.

Phil Spector—He's a Rebel

The story of "He's a Rebel" is an interesting commentary on Spector's role as visionary, and the record industry as well. Convinced the brand new song (written by Gene Pitney) was going to be a number 1 hit for the Crystals, Spector quickly booked time at LA's Gold Star Studio, even though the Crystals themselves were unavailable. Spector brought in another group, the Blossoms (led by **Darlene Love**) to sing the song but released it as the Crystals anyway, since they already had name recognition. No one seemed to notice. In essence, the song and the production had become more important than the singers themselves.

include "He's So Fine" (number 1, 1963) and the King/Goffin "One Fine Day" (number 5, 1963). The **Dixie Cups'** "Chapel of Love" (another Spector/Greenwich/Barry tune) went to number 1 in 1964, as did "Leader of the Pack" by the **Shangri-Las.** "Leader" was another of the many Greenwich/Barry collaborations, this time with producer **George 'Shadow' Morton.**

THE WALL OF SOUND

While Spector was becoming a force in the success of the girl groups, he was also developing his famous 'Wall of Sound' production technique. To achieve his goal of getting the biggest sound possible on record, Spector combined large instrumental groups with multi-track overdubbing and liberal doses of reverberation from a giant echo chamber. "I want my records to sound like God hit the world and the world hit back," he once said. Spector was fond of using as many as twelve musicians in the rhythm section: three to five rhythm guitars (all playing the same part), two or three pianos (ditto), two bass guitars, a drummer, and several percussionists. To this he added large string and horn sections. From the first Wall of Sound production, "Da Doo Ron Ron," to the many which followed, records produced using this technique exerted tremendous influence on the industry for their innovative use of studio technology. Interestingly, Spector mixed everything to one monophonic track instead of the emerging industry standard two-track stereo, which he was suspicious of.

Like the teen idols, the British Invasion killed off the girl groups, so Spector turned his attention to the blue-eyed soul group the **Righteous Brothers.** Working his magic once again, he produced "You've Lost That Lovin' Feeling" (number 1, 1964), (co-written by Spector with Barry Mann and Cynthia Weil), and the King/Goffin "Just Once in My Life" (number 9, 1965). However, his luck and career turned abruptly when his final and perhaps biggest wall of sound production, **Ike and Tina Turner's** "River Deep, Mountain High" flopped in 1965 without charting. Taken as a sign

The Girl Groups is the name given to the young female vocal groups that emerged in the early sixties, primarily through the promotion of Phil Spector. Story lines for girl group songs usually included references to boyfriends and the worthlessness of the girl's lives without them.

Key Girl Group Recordings

❑ "Da Doo Ron Ron"— the Crystals, 1963
❑ "Be My Baby"—the Ronettes, 1963
❑ "He's So Fine"—the Chiffons, 1963
❑ "Leader of the Pack"— the Shangri-Las, 1964

Blue-Eyed Soul

Soulful hits by white rock groups have been a constant presence on the charts since the sixties. In addition to the Righteous Brothers, one of the most popular of the decade was the **Young Rascals** (later simply the Rascals). Led by the expressive lead vocals of organist Felix Cavaliere, the group had thirteen Top Forty hits and three number 1s between 1966 and 1969 ("Good Lovin'," "Groovin'" and "People Got to Be Free"). Other blue-eyed soul groups and artists from the sixties include the **Box Tops** ("The Letter," 1967), the **Soul Survivors** ("Expressway to Your Heart," 1967), **Joe Cocker** (see Chapter 7) and **Van Morrison** (see Chapter 8). The genre continued into the seventies and eighties with artists such as Hall and Oates, Michael McDonald, and Michael Bolton.

that the pop world was moving in a new direction without him, Spector sank into reclusiveness and paranoia. He resurfaced in 1969 as producer of the Beatles *Let It Be,* and the Ramones *End of the Century* in 1980. After years of reclusiveness, Spector made headlines in early 2003 after his arrest for the murder of a woman in the foyer of his L.A. mansion. At the time of this book's publication, the case had not yet gone to trial.

Surf and Instrumental Rock

THE SURF CULTURE

Meanwhile, another pop music scene was developing on the West Coast. Surf music was not the brainchild of the record industry; rather, it was the offshoot of a lifestyle that was unique to its time and place. During the early sixties, the sport of surfing spawned an entire subculture in Southern California that included carefree laid-back lives, hot rods, wood-paneled station wagons (called "woodies"), Hawaiian shirts and sandals, its own vernacular and its own music. Surfing was brought to California from Hawaii around the turn of the 20th century, where it was enjoyed by a relatively few hardy souls until Hollywood brought it to the rest of the country with a series of bikini beach party movies made between 1959 and 1963. The first, *Gidget,* was followed by others such as *Beach Blanket Bingo, Bikini Beach,* and *Beach Party,* starring Annette Funicello and Frankie Avalon. These movies tended to portray surfers and their girls as clean cut, wholesome, and good looking, leading affluent lives free of adult supervision. Unfortunately, the surf music in these movies was generally watered down, once again to offend as few viewers as possible. Box 3–3 lists some characteristics and recordings of surf style music.

The real music of the surf culture was driving, high energy, and primarily instrumental, dominated by the electric guitar. It had a raw, garage-band edge to it and was not overly produced. The first important surf

---

Box 3-3 Surf and Instrumental Rock

Characteristics of Surf
1. Instrumental music (except the Beach Boys and other later groups), with combo consisting of guitar, bass, and drums, with an occasional organ or horn player. Guitar usually plays the melody.
2. 'Garage band' what-you-hear-is-what-you-get sound
3. High energy

Key Surf/Instrumental Rock Recordings
❏ "Rebel Rouser"—Duane Eddy, 1958
❏ "Miserlou"—Dick Dale and the Del-tones, 1962
❏ "Pipeline"—the Chantays, 1963
❏ "I Get Around"—the Beach Boys, 1964
❏ "Good Vibrations"—the Beach Boys, 1966

band was **Dick Dale and the Del-tones,** who had what is considered to be the first surf hit in 1961 with "Let's Go Trippin'." Of Lebanese descent, Dale often employed downward glissandos in his guitar playing to imitate the sound of waves, and tremolos that were reminiscent of the bouzouki music of his native culture. These tricks are evident in the 1962 hit "Miserlou," which is based on a Middle Eastern folk song. Dale worked closely with **Leo Fender,** the creator of the first solid body electric guitar, to develop the Dual Showman amplifier, which had two 15" speakers that made it possible to play loud, use distortion, and add reverberation. Because the Del-tones were extremely popular in Southern California, they were reluctant to tour and, therefore, never achieved any substantial recognition in other parts of the country. It was up to other Southern California groups to take surf music to national prominence. Among the first to do so were the **Marketts,** whose "Surfer's Stomp" went to number 31 in 1962, the **Chantays** with "Pipeline" (number 4, 1963), and the **Surfaris** with "Wipe Out" (number 2, 1963). Although Dick Dale was dubbed the "King of Surf Guitar," he became disillusioned with music after his initial success and retired in 1965.

See Appendix A, "Miserlou" by Dick Dale and the Del-tones. Track 13 on enclosed CD.

INSTRUMENTAL ROCK

Before surf music became popular, there were other instrumental rock hits by non-California bands in the late fifties and early sixties that had a similar sound but no connection to surfing. These included the **Bill Doggett** hit "Honkey Tonk" (number 2, 1956), the **Champs'** "Tequila" (number 1, 1958) and **Link Wray's** "Rumble" (number 16, 1958). The two most important instrumental groups of this era were **Duane Eddy and the Rebels** and the **Ventures.** Eddy's "twangy" guitar effect, created by turning up the reverb and the tremolo on his amp, was the signature sound of his 1958 hit "Rebel Rouser" (number 6). Eddy was featured on *American Bandstand* often and had fifteen Top Forty hits by 1963. Another Seattle band, the Ventures, burst on the scene in 1960 with "Walk, Don't Run" (number 2) and "Ghost Riders in the Sky," and eventually recorded sixteen albums that made the Top Forty. Their fame was further cemented when they recorded the theme song to the TV program *Hawaii Five-O,* which went to number 4 in 1969.

Louie, Louie

Closely related in spirit to the instrumental rock groups of the era, the Seattle-based **Kingsmen** might have gone unnoticed to the rest of the world if not for their 1963 recording of the obscure calypso tune "Louie, Louie." After hitting number 2 in November, its poorly-sung lyrics began to receive notoriety as being obscene, making the song's popularity endure for years among college students and eventually prompting an FBI investigation (which concluded that the lyrics were unintelligible). Today "Louie, Louie" is a cult classic.

THE BEACH BOYS

Although surf first appeared as instrumental music, ironically the most famous of the surf groups was known for its beautiful vocal harmonies. Hailing from Huntington Beach, California, the Beach Boys consisted of three brothers—**Brian Wilson** (1942-), **Dennis Wilson** (1944-1983), and **Carl Wilson** (1946-1998)—their cousin **Mike Love** and family friend **Al Jardine.** The Wilsons' father, Murry, was a frustrated part-time songwriter who was physically and emotionally abusive to his sons, often punishing them with beatings or humiliation. (Brian's deafness in one ear reportedly came from one such childhood beating. This may have been a factor in his preference for monaural mixes, although he was also a devotee of Phil Spector, who also preferred monaural over stereo.)

The one salve in the Wilson household was music. Murry built a music room in the garage, and with his encouragement the boys all learned to sing and play instruments at an early age. It soon became clear that the most talented son was Brian. For his sixteenth birthday, Murry gave Brian a Wollensak tape recorder, which he used to record himself singing vocal arrangements that were inspired by the popular fifties vocal group the Four Freshmen. With their parents out of town for the Labor Day weekend in 1961, the Wilson Boys, Jardine, and Love (who were by now informally a band, calling themselves the Pendletones) wrote and recorded "Surfin'" to try to cash in on the burgeoning surf craze. The song became a regional hit and helped secure a contract with Capitol Records. They also changed their name around this time at the suggestion of a local record distributor. In the beginning, Murry served as their manager.

The Beach Boys in a 1966 publicity photo. Clockwise from bottom center: Dennis Wilson, Al Jardine, Mike Love, Brian Wilson, Carl Wilson.

AP/WIDE WORLD PHOTOS

The Beach Boys formula was simple: combine the driving rock and guitar licks of Chuck Berry with the lush vocal harmonies of the Four Freshmen. Over the next four years, they released seven albums with an impressive string of seventeen Top Forty singles, including their first hit, "Surfin' Safari" (number 14, 1962), and two number 1s, "I Get Around" (1964) and "Help Me Rhonda" (1965). The subjects were girls, cars, hanging out with schoolmates, and, of course, surfing. The primary songwriter was Brian, who also arranged the intricate vocal harmonies and produced the records. During these years, Capitol put intense pressure on Brian to write as many songs as possible before the surf craze passed, and his output was astonishing. Eventually, however, the emotional stress of writing hit songs, producing, arranging, singing, and touring became overwhelming, and in December 1964 Brian made the decision to stop touring with the band. By this time, he had begun to use marijuana and other hallucinogens heavily, and in the next few years would become reclusive and increasingly unstable mentally. Despite his deteriorating state of mind, in late 1965 he began working on the monumental achievement of his career, the album *Pet Sounds.*

PET SOUNDS

Pet Sounds was inspired upon hearing the newest Beatles release, *Rubber Soul.* Intrigued that they could record an album that contained only good songs and no "fillers," Brian set out to make "the greatest rock and roll album ever." The LP is a tour de force of Brian's writing, arranging, and producing skills (although his friend, **Tony Asher,** wrote the lyrics, they were inspired by Brian). By this time, he had become a studio perfectionist, and spent many hours meticulously crafting the album, which cost an unheard of $70,000. Session musicians were brought in—the other Beach Boys were on tour—including future country star Glen Campbell and jazz legend Barney Kessel on guitars. An array of unconventional (for rock) instruments and sounds were used, including tympani, Japanese percussion, harpsichord, glockenspiel, bass harmonica, and even barking dogs. The songs are generally all short in length with intricate and difficult vocal melodies and arrangements; most have a quiet, reflective, or otherworldly nature to them. The lyrics are about a young man's difficult coming of age; at the time, Brian Wilson was 24 years old.

Pet Sounds sold over a half million copies, and two of its songs hit the charts, "Sloop John B" (number 3), and "Wouldn't It Be Nice" (number 8). Still, by Beach Boys standards, those figures were a disappointment. Although critics hailed it as a masterpiece, the public by now expected a certain type of song from the group, and did not find them on the album. This was definitely *not* surf music. The innovations Brian Wilson brought to *Pet Sounds* were powerful motivation to the Beatles, however, who realized Wilson had thrown the creative gauntlet back at them. Giving Brian Wilson credit for inspiring them, the next year the Beatles responded with their own masterpiece, *Sgt. Pepper's Lonely Hearts Club Band.*

A Teenage Symphony to God

Immediately after finishing *Pet Sounds,* Brian started working on another masterpiece, the seminal "Good Vibrations." The 'mini-symphony' as he called it, took six months to finish, using ninety hours of tape at an astounding cost of $50,000 (the cost of an expensive *album* at the time). It is as unlikely a pop tune as there ever was, utilizing exotic instruments such as the **Theremin,** a complex form with constant key changes, and state of the art studio effects. Nonetheless, "Good Vibrations" was as catchy as it was innovative and went to the top of the charts in December 1966. Before "Good Vibrations" was even completed, however, Brian was already starting on what he determined was going to be his greatest achievement yet. Amid sky-high expectations, the next album, at first named *Dumb Angel* but eventually renamed *Smile,* was to be "a teenage symphony to God," and establish new standards of recording excellence. Ultimately, the enormity of the task, coupled with his excessive drug abuse, bogged the project down, and it was never completed (although the unfinished tracks were released in 1997). There would be more hits to come, but Brian Wilson's moment at the vanguard of the pop music world was more or less over.

The Beach Boys could never quite escape their clean cut, wholesome image, and their popularity began to wane in the midst of the psychedelic era. They unwisely backed out of an appearance at the 1967 Monterey Pop Festival, which may have reinvigorated their image as that of a hipper band. In the seventies and eighties, the Wilson brothers eventually succumbed to the hedonistic Southern California lifestyle of too many drugs, too much partying, and too much self-indulgence. Drummer Dennis Wilson became friends with aspiring songwriter Charles Manson for several months in early 1968 but broke off the friendship just weeks before Manson and his family brutally murdered Sharon Tate and six others on August 9, 1969. Dennis drowned in a boating accident in 1983; Carl Wilson died of cancer in 1998. After years of mental and physical problems in the seventies and eighties, Brian Wilson has returned to recording and touring, while Al Jardine and Mike Love have established their own solo careers.

The **Theremin** is an electronic musical instrument that produces a tone whose pitch is determined by the distance between the player's hands and the instruments two antennae.

Other Sixties Pop

Jan and Dean

See Appendix A, "The Little Old Lady (from Pasadena)" by Jan and Dean. Track 14 on enclosed CD.

Jan and Dean were **Jan Berry** and **Dean Torrence,** two high school buddies in Los Angeles who put a band together and recorded their first hit "Jennie Lee" (number 8, 1958) in Berry's garage. Over the next eight years, they had fourteen more Top Forty hits, including the number 1 "Surf City" in 1963, which was co-written by Brian Wilson, and "The Little Old Lady (from Pasadena)" in 1964. Jan and Dean were friends with the Beach Boys, and the two groups often sang on each other's records. The hits stopped in 1966, when Berry was critically injured in a car accident and suffered partial paralysis and brain damage. He later recovered enough for the two to make occasional concert appearances.

BURT BACHARACH AND HAL DAVID

Perhaps the most prolific pop composer of the last half of the 20th century has been Burt Bacharach (1928–). His first hit came in 1957 when "The Story of My Life," recorded by country artist Marty Robbins, went to number 15. It was also Bacharach's first collaboration with lyricist Hal David (1921–), with whom he would write most of his hits in the sixties. After writing a few hits for Perry Como, the Drifters, and others, the two began to focus their attention on writing songs for **Dionne Warwick,** who was, at the time, a session singer aspiring to be a star. Between 1962 and 1972, Warwick recorded more than sixty of their songs, twenty-three of which hit the Top Forty. Box 3–4 lists some Bacharach/David hits recorded by Dionne Warwick.

Other artists found success with Bacharach/David tunes as well, including:

- ❏ Jackie DeShannon with "What the World Needs Now Is Love" (number 7, 1965);

- ❏ Tom Jones with "What's New Pussycat?" (number 3, 1965);

- ❏ Sergio Mendes & Brasil '66 with "The Look of Love" (number 4, 1968);

- ❏ Herb Alpert with "This Guy's in Love with You" (number 1, 1968);

- ❏ Aretha Franklin with "I Say a Little Prayer" (number 10, 1968);

- ❏ B.J. Thomas with "Raindrops Keep Fallin' on My Head" (number 1, 1969);

- ❏ The Carpenters with "(They Long to Be) Close to You" (number 1, 1970).

The final tally for the duo was sixty-six Top Forty hits, twenty-eight Top Ten, with six going to number 1.

Box 3-4 A Partial List of Bacharach/David Hits Recorded by Dionne Warwick	
❏ "Walk on By"	number 6, 1964
❏ "Alfie"	number 15, 1967
❏ "I Say a Little Prayer"	number 4, 1967
❏ "Do You Know the Way to San Jose"	number 10, 1968
❏ "This Girl's in Love with You"	number 7, 1969
❏ "I'll Never Fall in Love Again"	number 6, 1969

While Bacharach and David never wrote about social or political change, their songs provided the soundtrack for much of the pop music world in the sixties and seventies. David's lyrics usually contained adult storylines that were straightforward and clever, while Bacharach's music often included interesting key changes and odd meters; his arrangements were usually pop savvy yet idiosyncratic. Although they split up in 1973, they reunited in 1993 for a project with Warwick. In the late nineties, Bacharach began collaborating with **Elvis Costello.**

DOC POMUS AND MORT SHUMAN

Doc Pomus (1925–1991) began his career as a white blues singer in the forties before turning his attention to songwriting. In 1958, he teamed up with writer Mort Shuman (1936–1991), with whom he set up shop in the Brill Building. Over the next few years Pomus and Shuman wrote for:

❏ Dion and the Belmonts ("Teenager in Love," number 5, 1959),

❏ the Drifters ("This Magic Moment," number 16, and "Save the Last Dance for Me," number 1, both 1960)

❏ Andy Williams ("Can't Get Used to Losing You," number 2, 1963),

❏ Elvis Presley recorded more than 20 of their songs, including "Surrender" (number 1, 1961), "Little Sister" (number 5, 1961), "(Marie's the Name) His Latest Flame" (number 4 1961), and "Viva Las Vegas" (number 29, 1964).

Although Pomus was eleven years older than Shuman, the two died within months of each other in 1991: Pomus from cancer, Shuman from complications after liver surgery.

THE MONKEES

The ultimate manifestation of industry-manufactured pop came in 1965, when an ad was placed in *Daily Variety* magazine, announcing a casting call for "Folk and rock musicians-singers for acting roles in a new TV series; Running parts for four insane boys, age 17–24." The idea of the program was to capture the fun of the Beatles *Hard Days Night* with four American mop tops. After narrowing down the 400 applicants (including Stephen Stills, who was turned down because he wasn't good looking enough) to four—**Michael Nesmith, Davy Jones, Micky Dolenz,** and **Peter Tork**—the Monkees were born. During the two-year lifespan of the TV show (1966–68), the Monkees hit the Top Forty eleven times, with two number 3, one number 2, and three number 1 hits. Screen Gems, (run by the former head of Aldon Music, Don Kirshner) who conceived of the Monkees, hired L.A. veterans Tommy Boyce and Bobby Hart to write songs such as "Last Train to Clarksville" in the mold

Bubblegum

The Monkees unleashed a short-lived strand of insipid pop that became known as bubblegum. Aimed at pre-teens, bubblegum was generally produced in the studio by session players working from carefully crafted sing-along songs. Among the "classics" of the genre are the unforgettable hits "Yummy, Yummy, Yummy" by the Ohio Express, "Simon Says" by the 1910 Fruitgum Co., and "Sugar, Sugar" by the Archies. Other bubblegum groups besides the Monkees that had their own TV shows were the Archies (an animated cartoon), the Partridge Family, and the Osmonds.

of the Fab Four. The group also performed songs by Neil Diamond, Carole King, and others. They broke up after the TV show was cancelled and band members complained that they were not allowed to play their own instruments on recordings.

Chapter 3
Study Questions

1. What were some of the factors that made some observers believe that rock and roll was dead by the early sixties?

   _____

   _____

   _____

2. Describe the influence that Dick Clark and *American Bandstand* had on the music business.

   _____

   _____

   _____

3. What is payola and how did it affect the music and radio industries?

   _____

   _____

   _____

4. Describe the Brill Building scene and the major figures involved with it.

   _____

   _____

   _____

   _____

5. Why are Leiber and Stoller important?

   _____

   _____

   _____

6. What are some of the contributions that **Phil Spector** made to rock and roll?

_____

_____

_____

_____

7. Describe the surf culture, how it came into **being** and its music.

_____

_____

_____

_____

8. Describe the formula used by Brian Wilson **to achieve** the Beach Boys sound.

_____

_____

_____

_____

_____

9. Why is *Pet Sounds* so important?

_____

_____

_____

_____

10. Describe the formula that Burt Bacharach **and Hal** David used to achieve such remarkable success in the sixties.

_____

_____

_____

_____

The Folk Influence

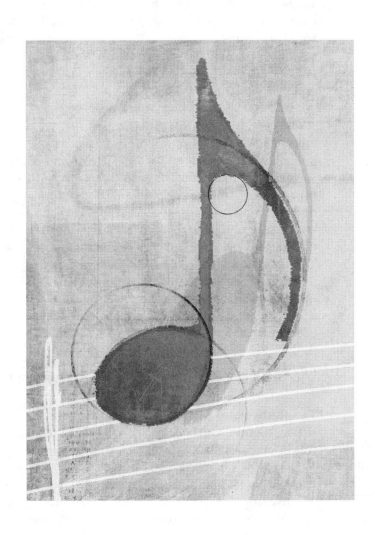

71

The Folk Tradition

THE LEFT WING FOLK SONG CONSPIRACY

Just after the turn of the 20th century, there was an upswing in interest in traditional American folk music. Part of this interest came from preservationists who feared that the music would disappear due to the increasing urbanization of the country. However, folk music was also becoming popular as a tool for political organizations and labor unions to rally support and foster solidarity among their members. One union in particular, the International Workers of the World (IWW, or popularly known as the "Wobblies"), used folk songs to build morale, recruit new members, and stir up publicity for their cause. In 1911, the Wobblies published the first of thirty editions of their songbook entitled *IWW Songs: Songs of the Workers to Fan the Flames of Discontent,* which unofficially became known as *The Little Red Songbook.* Because many folk songs were protest songs against big business and government policies (such as America's involvement in World War I) and were often used by socialist groups and the fledgling Communist Party, by the 1920s conservatives began to speak of a "left wing folk song conspiracy." This association between folk music and social activism and liberal politics endured well into the 1960s.

By the 1930s, another folk music revival was underway. Folk radio shows began appearing, such as *The Wayfaring Stranger* hosted by folksinger **Burl Ives** on the CBS network. Folk songs also began to get published in newspapers. In 1933, **John and Alan Lomax,** a father and son team of musicologists from the Library of Congress began taking trips through the backwoods of the South with a portable recording device to find and preserve folk songs. On their first trip, they discovered an inmate at the Angola State Prison in Louisiana named **Leadbelly** (Huddie Ledbetter) who was a gifted singer, songwriter, and guitarist. Through the Lomaxes persistence, Leadbelly was released in 1934 and went on to become an important influence to folk and blues performers until his death in 1949. Leadbelly also wrote countless numbers of folk songs, including his two most famous, "Goodnight Irene" and "Midnight Special."

WOODY GUTHRIE AND PETE SEEGER

See Appendix A, "Pretty Boy Floyd" by Woody Guthrie. Track 15 on enclosed CD.

The thirties also saw the emergence of the most important early folk singer, **Woody Guthrie** (1912-67). Guthrie's impoverished childhood was spent in Oklahoma and Texas, where he witnessed first hand the tough life of the lower class during the depression. He saw how easily banks were willing to evict farm families whose crops had been ruined by dust storms and other calamities. Guthrie himself was the victim of several tragedies in his youth, including his sister's death in an explosion and his mother's commitment to an insane asylum. He was on his own and living on the streets by age thirteen, singing and playing the harmonica to earn a living. At the age of twenty-five, Guthrie began a lifelong crusade to help band the common folk together to fight for their rights through unions and other organizations. He traveled the country, often hobo style on trains, talking to people, and singing the songs he wrote. Guthrie's songs included dust bowl ballads, pro-union songs, anti-Hitler songs, and songs about the plight of migrant workers and common people. In all, it is estimated that he wrote well over 1,000 songs during his lifetime, including "The Great Dust Storm," "Pastures of Plenty," "Roll on Columbia," and his most famous, "This Land Is Your Land." Guthrie also developed a unique talking blues style of half singing and half speaking the lyrics to his songs while accompanying himself on guitar. With his songs, his idealism, and his working class blue jeans and uncombed hair, Guthrie became a hero and a legend in the folk community.

HOOTENANNIES AND WITCH HUNTS

In 1940, Guthrie met twenty-one year old singer/guitarist **Pete Seeger** (1919–) at a benefit concert for migrant workers. Seeger's father, Charles, was a university professor who had registered as a conscientious objector during World War I, and had exposed his son to folk music at an early age. Throughout the forties, Guthrie and Seeger traveled the country as part of the **Almanac Singers,** singing original and traditional folk songs at **hootenannies** and rallies. In 1949 Seeger went on to form the **Weavers,** one of the first folk groups to break into mainstream visibility when their recording of Leadbelly's "Goodnight Irene" became a number 1 hit in 1950. But both men fell on harder times in the fifties, as did the folk community in general. Guthrie fell ill to Huntington's chorea, a central nervous system disorder that leads to distorted speech and progressive degeneration of the brain that kept him in and out of hospitals until it finally killed him in 1967. Seeger ran into problems of a political nature.

Hootenanny is a folk jam session where traditional folk songs are sung.

The conservative and Cold War climate of the fifties did not bode well for the folk community. Like many other folk singers, Seeger's liberal politics began to catch the attention of the FBI, and he was blacklisted in the 1950 publication *Red Channels: The Report of Communist Influence in Radio and Television.* Among other charges, the book exposed that he had joined the Young Communist League while a student at Harvard in the thirties. In light of the revelations, Decca Records dropped the Weavers, as the group was suddenly too controversial. Seeger left the Weavers in 1953 to tour college campuses across the country as a soloist, singing political songs and inviting audience participation. But by 1955 Congress was on his trail: he was asked to testify before the **House Un-American Activities Committee,** which by now was on their own Communist witch-hunt. Seeger appeared, but refused to cooperate. He was indicted, tried, and convicted on ten counts of contempt of Congress, although he was cleared in 1962 after a lengthy court battle. Seeger continued to be a political activist and went on to write some of the most important songs of the folk movement, including "If I Had a Hammer," "Where Have All the Flowers Gone," "Turn, Turn, Turn," and reworking an old spiritual into the civil rights anthem "We Shall Overcome."

The Fifties Folk Revival

THE CALYPSO FAD

The anti-Communist furor that engulfed the nation's attention for much of the 1950s forced many folk musicians to go underground. However, by the late fifties, there was another popular folk revival. Many people who were turned off by the vulgarities of R&B and rock and roll were drawn to the socially conscious nature of folk music. College students, in particular, saw folk as music that addressed the need for positive change in society, and much of its groundswell of support was fostered at coffeehouses and study halls on campus. One of the first signs that folk was about to have a revival came when actor and singer **Harry Belafonte** scored a series of calypso hits in 1956 and 57. **Calypso,** the folk music of Jamaica, has a different rhythmic quality than traditional American folk, but the narrative verse structures and storylines are similar. Belafonte's commercial success, which included the 1957 number 5 hit "Banana Boat (Day-O)" started a short-lived calypso fad that was instrumental in renewing interest in folk.

The real start to the fifties folk revival came in 1958 when the record "Tom Dooley" by the **Kingston Trio** became a number 1 hit. The song was a traditional folk song about a convicted murderer named Tom Dula who was sentenced to death by hanging in 1866. The group was obviously influenced by the calypso fad (naming themselves after the Jamaican capital city), but played folk music that was pop oriented and without much trace of political protest. To help foster a squeaky-clean image, they wore crew cuts and matching clothes. By 1963 the group had racked up ten Top Forty hits.

THE QUEEN OF FOLK

See Appendix A, "House of the Rising Sun" by Joan Baez. Track 16 on enclosed CD.

In the summer of 1959, the first **Newport Folk Festival** was held in Newport, Rhode Island. One of the artists that performed was angel-voiced **Joan Baez** (1941–), who had been a favorite at Cambridge's Club 47 while a student at Boston University. Baez was beautiful, wore plain peasant clothes, sang traditional folk songs, and was committed to political and social issues. By embracing the values of the common person, Baez became the darling of the traditional folk crowd, who began calling her the "Queen of Folk." She also quickly developed a large mainstream audience as well—her second album *Joan Baez 2* went gold in 1961. Around this time, she met Bob Dylan, with whom she fell in love and brought on her concert tour in the summer of 1963, introducing him to her loyal fans. Because Baez stuck to traditional folk songs and resisted commercial pressures, she did not have any chart success until 1971 when her cover of The Band's "The Night They Drove Old Dixie Down" went to number 3.

In 1961, **Peter, Paul and Mary** made their debut performance at New York's Bitter End. **Peter Yarrow, Noel Paul Stookey,** and **Mary**

Travers, came from different backgrounds—only Yarrow was a folksinger; Travers was an off-Broadway singer, Stookey a comedian. They ended up becoming the most popular folk group of the sixties with twelve Top Forty hits, including two—"Lemon Tree" (number 35) and Pete Seeger's "If I Had a Hammer" (number 10)—from their eponymous first album. Like Baez, Peter, Paul and Mary were involved with the social issues of their songs. Although Seeger wrote "Hammer" as a pro-union song, it became a civil rights anthem in the sixties partly because of Peter, Paul and Mary's recording. The group appeared at numerous protests, rallies, and marches, including the 1963 March on Washington where Dr. Martin Luther King gave his famous 'I Have a Dream' speech. Also like Baez, Peter, Paul and Mary gave a boost to the early career of Bob Dylan, recording two of his songs in 1963 that outsold Dylan's own versions: "Blowin' in the Wind" (number 2) and "Don't Think Twice, It's All Right" (number 9).

THE GREENWICH VILLAGE SCENE

In the wake of the commercial success of performers like the Kingston Trio, Joan Baez, and Peter, Paul and Mary came other popular folk groups such as the Highwaymen ("Michael Row the Boat Ashore," number 1, 1961), the New Christy Minstrels ("Green Green," number 14, 1963) and the Rooftop Singers ("Walk Right In," number 1, 1963). Coffeehouses, cafés and small clubs all over the country began to hire folk performers, and important folk scenes sprang up in New York, the Boston/Cambridge area, Ann Arbor, Michigan, Berkeley, California, and other cities. The most important of these was in New York's Greenwich Village.

The Village had long been a magnet for artists, musicians, writers, and bohemians, and by 1960 young aspiring folk musicians seemed to be everywhere. Among the struggling folk performers in the Village at this time were **Dave Van Ronk, Tom Paxton,** and **Phil Ochs,** who often took part in impromptu hootenannies on Sunday afternoons in Washington Square Park. These gatherings routinely drew so many listeners that police had to stop traffic. Folk music could also be heard in the many clubs and coffeehouses in the area, most of which had open-mic policies on Tuesday nights where singers, both unknown and famous, could get up and perform a set. The most important were:

- ❏ **The Gaslight,** a basement coffeehouse on MacDougal Street;
- ❏ **Café Wha?,** across the street from the Gaslight where Bob Dylan made his first New York appearance;
- ❏ **Gerde's Folk City** on West 4th Street (an Italian restaurant during the day);
- ❏ **Bitter End** on Bleecker Street.

Folk music was so popular that for a while even the **Village Vanguard,** New York's premier jazz club, was featuring it on off nights.

BROADSIDE

In February 1962, Pete Seeger and three other folk musicians began publishing a mimeographed biweekly newsletter called *Broadside.* Designed to showcase new folk and protest songs and provide articles about protests, festivals, and recent record releases, *Broadside* provided a forum for the new generation of folk musicians to get their original songs noticed. However, somewhat of a controversy was already brewing in the folk community, and *Broadside* only fanned the flames. Folk purists had always dedicated themselves to preserving traditional folk songs and furthering the folk agenda of political activism. Even though the pop-oriented folk groups like the Kingston Trio and Peter, Paul and Mary had widened the definition of folk and brought renewed interest in the music, folk purists viewed them with suspicion. Nonetheless, having an outlet like *Broadside* was powerful motivation for a struggling, young songwriter like Bob Dylan to write topical songs inspired by current events. One of Dylan's first songs, "Talkin' John Birch Paranoid Blues," a satirical piece about searching for Communists, was printed in the inaugural issue of the magazine. The next few years would be some of the most prolific in the long career of one of the most important figures in the history of American music.

Bob Dylan

BOY FROM THE NORTH COUNTRY

Bob Dylan was born Robert Zimmerman in Duluth, Minnesota on May 24, 1941 to Abe and Beatty Zimmerman. Bob received a good

Bob Dylan is one of the most important and innovative musicians in American history. AP/WIDE WORLD PHOTOS

Jewish upbringing, although his father made sure he was well versed in the Bible as well. The family moved north to Hibbing in 1947, where Bob stayed until he finished high school. He became interested in music, playing the piano and guitar and forming a rock and roll combo called the Golden Chords. His musical idols included Hank Williams, Little Richard, and Elvis Presley. It was in high school that he began to call himself Bob Dylan in honor of an idol, Welsh poet Dylan Thomas. Dylan enrolled at the University of Minnesota in the fall of 1959 and quickly became a fixture of the hip section next to campus known as Dinkytown. Because the Dinkytown coffeehouse scene was heavily tilted toward folk, Bob's interest in rock and roll began to wane. He learned the traditional folk

Beat Writers

Writers such as Jack Kerouac, William S. Burroughs and Allen Ginsberg who gained notoriety in the fifties and espoused a philosophy of existentialism and a rejection of materialism. Kerouac himself coined the phrase Beat Generation, and defined it for the Random House Dictionary: "Members of the generation that came of age after World War II, who, supposedly as a result of disillusionment stemming from the Cold War, espouse mystical detachment and relaxation of social and sexual tensions."

songs and performed them in his own idiosyncratic and sometimes humorous style, unlike the solemn way in which most Dinkytown folkies presented themselves. During this time, Dylan read and was inspired by the works of the **beat writers,** but his biggest influence was Woody Guthrie's memoir *Bound for Glory.* In the book, Guthrie created fictional characters that used unusual speech patterns such as clipped words, double negatives, and non-sequiturs. Dylan began to adopt these in his own speech, along with a fascination for Guthrie and his music. Deciding he had to meet the folk hero, Dylan left for New York in late 1960.

Dylan arrived in Greenwich Village in late January 1961 and performed an open-mic set at the Café Wha? his first night in town. Within a week, he succeeded in meeting Guthrie, who by this time was bedridden and delusional from his battle with Huntington's chorea. After the meeting, Dylan wrote his first important song, "Song to Woody" and began to write other songs in Guthrie's talking blues style. Performing open-mic night sets and hanging out in the Village, Bob started to establish himself and make friends with locals such as Dave Van Ronk, Ramblin' Jack Elliot, Paul Stookey, and Joan Baez. He played harmonica on a Harry Belafonte album, which helped him get noticed by Columbia Records executive John Hammond. His big break came when *New York Times* writer Robert Shelton gave him a glowing review of a performance at Gerde's Folk City on September 29, 1961. Entitled "Bob Dylan: A Distinctive Song Stylist," the column convinced Hammond to sign Dylan to a five-year contract. Box 4–1 lists some famous Dylan recordings.

Box 4-1 Key Dylan Recordings

- ❑ *The Freewheelin' Bob Dylan,* 1963
- ❑ *The Times They Are a Changin',* 1964
- ❑ *Bringing It All Back Home,* 1965
- ❑ "Like a Rolling Stone," 1965
- ❑ *John Wesley Harding,* 1968

HAMMOND'S FOLLY

Dylan's first album was a vocal, guitar, and harmonica recording done in two days called simply *Bob Dylan*. It contained two originals, including "Song to Woody" and an assortment of blues and traditional folk songs. The album sold poorly; around the Columbia offices it became known as 'Hammond's Folly.' In spite of the setback, Dylan began to compose new songs with a fervor. They came through him with ease, as if he was channeling them from some unknown source. As Tom Paxton said, "He felt he wasn't writing songs, he was [just] writing them down. They were there to be captured." He wrote everywhere, all the time; songs of topical interest, social commentaries, protest songs, love songs. "The Death of Emmett Till" was about the murder of a fourteen-year-old black boy in Mississippi. "Let Me Die in My Footsteps" was a commentary on America's preoccupation with fallout shelters and air raid drills. Two were strong anti-war songs, "Masters of War" and "A Hard Rain's A-Gonna Fall." Two more were about failing relationships, "Don't Think Twice, It's All Right" and "Tomorrow Is a Long Time."

Dylan's second album, *The Freewheelin' Bob Dylan*, consisted almost entirely of his new original material, including his first great anthem "Blowin' in the Wind." "Blowin' in the Wind" was composed in a café across the street from the Gaslight Club in just a few minutes, and within weeks it was being played throughout the Village by other folk singers. The song struck a chord with many in the community who pondered the meaning of its questioning lyrics. Peter, Paul and Mary's 1963 cover of "Blowin' in the Wind" went to number 2 on the charts, putting Bob Dylan on the national map for the first time. When they performed the song at the Newport Folk Festival in July, Peter, Paul and Mary brought Dylan onstage, introducing him as "the most important folk artist in America today" to a thunderous ovation. Bob had also endeared himself to the folk community in May when he refused to appear on the *Ed Sullivan Show* when the producers, fearing a lawsuit, requested that he not perform his intended selection "Talkin' John Birch Paranoid Blues." Later in the summer, he sang at the March on Washington with Joan Baez and Peter, Paul and Mary. Around this time, his on-and-off love affair with Baez began as she took him on tour with her; he was an appropriate folk "King" for the "Queen."

See Appendix A, "A Hard Rain's A-Gonna Fall" by Bob Dylan. Track 17 on enclosed CD.

THE TIMES THEY ARE A CHANGIN'

Released in early 1964, Dylan's third album, *The Times They Are a Changin'* solidified his leadership of the folk community. The title track was a rallying call to action that struck a chord with many of the nation's youth. Also on the album were protest songs such as "With God on Our Side," "Only a Pawn in Their Game," and "The Lonesome Death of Hattie Carroll." However, just as his audience was warming up to their new prophet, Dylan suddenly changed directions with his next LP, *Another Side of Bob Dylan*, which turned away from political activism toward a more introspective stance. The album contained no protest songs—the dominant themes were about relationships—which was noted with consternation by critics. Even the album's title **seemed** to signal that Dylan was abandoning his role as leader of the **folk** movement. When he appeared at the 1964 Newport Festival in **July, D**ylan's crowd response was lukewarm—a noticeable change from **the** enthusiastic reception from the previous year.

Still, Bob was now a major celebrity, **and when** in the summer of 1964 the Beatles came to New York, a **meeting wa**s set up at the Hotel Delmonico. It was at this famous meeting **that D**ylan reportedly turned the Fab Four on to marijuana, although **there is ev**idence to suggest that they were already experimenting with it **and othe**r hallucinogens on their own. At the end of December, Dylan **record**ed his fifth and possibly most important album, *Bringing It All Back Home*. It was clear by now that he was not interested in staying **within** the narrow parameters of acoustic folk music, and wanted to inc**orporate** the energy of electric rock. In the process, the songs on side one, **record**ed with a rock rhythm section, did nothing less than redefine **popular** music. By combining original, thought provoking and poetic **lyrics with** an electric rhythm and blues sensibility, Dylan changed rock **forever.** From this moment on, rock artists such as the Beatles began to **write lyrics** that went beyond girls and cars and tackle issues of social **significanc**e. In addition, Dylan paved the way for the creation of folk rock, **a style** that would be further defined by the Byrds, Crosby, Stills, Nash **and Young**, and others (in June 1965, the Byrds took their pop-oriented **version of** "Mr. Tambourine Man" to number 1). Although side two of *Bringing It All Back Home* was made up of all acoustic material, (including **the** original version of "Mr. Tambourine Man"), the die had been **cast. Pre**dictably, folk purists reacted angrily, but the album peaked at **number** 6, higher than any of Dylan's previous LPs.

Newport 1965

Dylan's most controversial moment came **at the** Newport Folk Festival on July 25, 1965. Appearing before an **audience of** primarily traditional purists, he performed his new electric **mate**rial with the **Paul Butterfield Blues Band.** The audience **was** stunned and angry. To many, like folk singer Oscar Brand, "The **electric gu**itar represented capitalism . . . the people who were selling out." **In** attendance was Pete Seeger, who was so angered by the music **that he** tried to cut the power to the band. After performing three songs, **the band** left the stage to lusty boos from the crowd. Dylan did return **in a few** minutes to play "Mr. Tambourine Man" by himself, with acoustic **guitar** and harmonica. This time he was cheered.

Later in 1965, *Highway 61 Revisited* **was re**leased, an album that continued to explore the sound of *Bringing It All Back Home* and contained one of Dylan's most powerful rock **songs,** "Like a Rolling Stone." Rising to number 2, it was to become the **highest** charting single of his career. In September, Dylan toured with the **Hawks,** a band from Canada who would later be known simply as the **Band.** Each concert consisted of Bob doing a solo acoustic set, followed **by an** electric set with the Hawks. As expected, each night the acoustic **set w**as warmly applauded, the electric set was booed. During breaks in the tour, Dylan went to Nashville and recorded *Blonde on Blonde,* using members of the Hawks and Nashville session players. The album contains a variety of songs, some of which can be considered the hardest rocking of his career. *Blonde on Blonde* also includes the absurd and jovial "Rainy Day Women number 12 & 35" and the poignant "Sad Eyed Lady of the Lowlands," written for his wife Sara Lownds, whom he had married the previous November.

THE BASEMENT TAPES

In the summer of 1966, Dylan was involved in a motorcycle accident that to this day is shrouded in mystery. Bob, Sara, and their children had purchased a mansion outside of the artistic community of Woodstock, New York in July 1965, which they named Hi Lo Ha. On the morning of July 29, Bob apparently fell off his bike somewhere along the winding, wooded roads surrounding their home. The extent of his injuries has been the subject of considerable debate ever since—some say he was only bruised, some say his neck was broken, rumors even flew for a while that he had died. Dylan was in fact injured to some extent, but the accident may have actually been a blessing, allowing him to get away from the intense pressure of his celebrity. While recuperating, Dylan centered his attention on his family life in the peaceful settings of upstate New York, out of the public eye for the first time in nearly three years. He also started to record new songs with the Band, who had moved into a nearby house they called Big Pink (so named because of its exterior paint color). These recordings were originally distributed by Dylan's publishing company to artists looking to record his songs, but over time they fell into the hands of bootleggers who sold them illegally. They became known as the Basement Tapes. Because of the mystery surrounding Dylan's accident and his reclusiveness during this time, the Basement Tapes were widely copied; they were officially released in 1975.

John Wesley Harding, released in January 1968 and Dylan's first album in almost two years, was recorded in Nashville and signaled yet another paradigm shift in his career. Released at a time when big productions like *Sgt. Peppers* and *Pet Sounds* were in vogue, the album is quiet and reflective with simple instrumentation. Its influences lie in the music of Hank Williams and the Bible—Dylan called *JWH* "the first biblical rock album." It includes one of his classics, "All Along the Watchtower," a modern morality parable, as well as other songs that flirt with country influences. His next album, *Nashville Skyline,* continued the country trend to an even greater degree. Dylan's voice seemed to have changed into a smoother sort of croon, most noticeable on the album's only hit, "Lay Lady Lay." Once again, the critics complained, this time because country music was not currently 'in' with the rock establishment. However, the album proved to be immensely influential in creating the country rock genre. Dylan continued to confuse fans with the release of *Self Portrait,* an album comprised entirely of cover tunes. Once again, the critics were less than enthusiastic.

DYLAN'S LATER CAREER

Throughout the seventies, Bob Dylan's career continued to evolve. In 1971 a book of his poetry and prose entitled *Tarantula* was published. In 1972 he acted in and scored Sam Peckinpah's movie *Pat Garrett and Billy the Kid,* which included his song "Knockin' on Heaven's Door." In 1974 he resumed touring for the first time since 1966, once again backed by the Band. In 1975 Dylan toured with the **Rolling Thunder Revue,** a loose collection of friends that included Joan Baez, Ramblin' Jack Elliot, Alan Ginsberg, and other assorted musicians. In 1976, his album *Desire* was released and went to number 1 for five weeks, a testament to his continuing and loyal fan base.

Sometime in early 1979, Dylan converted to Christianity. Throughout his career his songs had contained references to religion, and although he was raised a Jew, he had always had a strong connection to Christian teachings. Three albums followed that reflected his new faith: *Slow Train Coming, Saved,* and *Shot of Love.* The albums, together with Dylan's new habit of opening concerts with sermons, had a negative effect on his career, and record sales and concert audiences dwindled. In 1988, at a particularly low point in his career, Dylan recorded an album with his friends George Harrison, Tom Petty, Jeff Lynne, and Roy Orbison who called themselves the **Traveling Wilburys.** It was a major commercial success. He has continued to record and tour into the 21st century, recently winning a Grammy in the Contemporary Folk Album category in 2001 for *Love and Theft,* which ranks among the best LPs of his career.

THE DYLAN LEGACY

Bob Dylan is one of the most important and innovative musicians in American history. He brought to rock and roll the idea that lyrics can be poetry, a call to action, a political commentary, or a personal statement. He was a major influence on the music of the most popular group of the sixties, the Beatles. Emerging at a time when pop music was increasingly a manufactured product, Dylan was raw, a warts-and-all performer who was not a particularly good singer or guitar player, inspiring an 'anybody can be a rock star' ethic that continues to be an important part of what rock and roll is all about. He brought the worlds of folk, country, R&B and rock and roll together as no one else had previously done. He was influential to the late sixties singer/songwriters (of which he was the first), and in the creation of folk rock and country rock, two genres that continue to flourish to this day.

Chapter 4
Study Questions

1. Why did folk get a reputation as the music of left wing radicals?

   _____

   _____

   _____

2. Why were Woody Guthrie and Pete Seeger so important, and what were some of their contributions to folk music?

   _____

   _____

   _____

3. Who were some of the important players in the fifties folk revival and what roles did they play?

   _____

   _____

   _____

4. How did Jamaican music influence the folk scene in the fifties?

   _____

   _____

   _____

5. Why was the Greenwich Village scene so important?

   _____

   _____

   _____

6. In what ways did Woody Guthrie influence Bob Dylan?

_____

_____

_____

_____

_____

7. Describe some of the difficulties Bob Dylan encountered with critics' and his audience's expectations of him in the mid 1960s.

_____

_____

_____

_____

_____

8. What are some of the later rock styles that Bob Dylan was influential to?

_____

_____

_____

_____

_____

9. What were the Basement Tapes?

_____

_____

_____

_____

10. How did his motorcycle accident affect Dylan's career?

_____

_____

_____

_____

_____

Soul Music

The Origins of Soul

THE FIRST SOUL RECORD

Soul Music is a more pop-oriented version of R&B containing heavy influences from gospel that is associated with the 1960s. Characteristics of soul include a powerful rhythmic drive from the bass and drums, melismatic singing, and, in some cases, heavy orchestrations.

Soul music comes from the merging of rhythm and blues and gospel music. It seems entirely natural that these two styles would find common ground—they are the secular and the sacred counterparts of the black musical experience of the mid 20th century. However, the music of the church and the music of the nightclub traditionally served different purposes for different people, and until the mid fifties the idea of marrying the two was strictly taboo. Although there were a few R&B recordings from the early fifties that contained hints of gospel influence, the first real fusion of the two styles came in 1954 with Ray Charles's landmark record "I Got a Woman."

Charles' formula was simple—and shocking. He transformed the traditional hymn "I Got a Savior, Way over Jordan" into "I Got a Woman" by secularizing the lyrics ("Savior" became "woman," "Jordan" became "across town") and adding a rhythm and blues beat. The result: "I Got a Woman" created the blueprint for soul music, and inspired other R&B singers, doo wop groups, and crossover artists to incorporate their own gospel roots into their records. Although black clergy vilified him, Ray Charles became nothing short of a hero to the rest of the black community.

SOUL AND THE CIVIL RIGHTS MOVEMENT

Key Soul Recordings

- ❏ "I Got a Woman"—Ray Charles, 1954
- ❏ "You Send Me"—Sam Cooke, 1957
- ❏ "Papa's Got a Brand New Bag"—James Brown, 1965
- ❏ "Respect"—Aretha Franklin, 1967

1954 was also the year that the U.S. Supreme Court handed down the *Brown vs. Board of Education of Topeka, Kansas* ruling that effectively made legal segregation unconstitutional and jumpstarted the civil rights movement. Throughout the late fifties and sixties, black political coalitions, often spearheaded by clergymen such as the Rev. Martin Luther King, Jr., became active throughout the South, demanding social changes and racial equality. King's strategy of using non-violent demonstrations resulted in dramatic gains for the cause, even though there often were confrontations that did turn violent. During these years, black Americans experienced a general sense of optimism and expectation that their dreams of freedom from racism and discrimination could finally be achieved. The zenith of the civil rights movement came between the years 1964 and 1968, when the two major Civil Rights Acts and the Voting Rights Act were passed. However, King's assassination on April 4, 1968 was one of several events that caused a re-examination of expectations; many blacks became pessimistic and disillusioned by decade's end, and the dream of integration and equality seemed to fade.

Not coincidentally, the ascent and decline of soul music mirrors that of the civil rights movement. While record sales rose impressively through the early sixties, soul's popularity was greatest in the last half of the decade. Motown Records alone had fourteen number 1 singles on the pop charts and twenty number 1 hits on the R&B charts between 1964 and 1967. Likewise, the best selling soul artist at Stax Records was

Otis Redding, whose greatest chart successes came in the two years before he died in a plane crash in 1967. Although Stax artist Isaac Hayes had impressive sales in the late sixties and early seventies with his albums *Hot Buttered Soul* and *Shaft,* by this time soul was evolving into the style that would become known as funk. Both Motown and Stax went into decline by the mid seventies.

What Is Soul?

As soul became popular in the sixties, the word came to have a number of cultural associations outside of its musical context. First and foremost, to have soul described a sense of pride in being black, of cultural solidarity, and aligning oneself with black consciousness and culture, as opposed to white middle-class culture. It was hip to "have soul," or to be a "soul brother." The soul experience extended as well to hairstyles (the "Afro"), handshakes, "soul food" (ribs, chitlins, collard greens, etc.), clothing, and slang vernacular, all of which became ways of identifying with a sense of racial pride. These associations were often adopted by whites as well, especially Southern white musicians who played soul music.

The music itself took on great diversity, much of it on the account of regional origins. In the South, where the music was born, soul had a raw, gritty, and powerful sound. In the Northern cities, such as Detroit, Chicago, and Philadelphia, soul took on a smoother, more pop-oriented sound. Regardless of these differences, the essence of all soul music is the emotional expression of the black experience in the sixties—pride, struggle, love, ecstasy, hope, pain, and sorrow. Even though very little soul music from the sixties actually addressed the issues of the civil rights movement directly, the songs were often adopted by the black community and used as rallying cries to identify with the ongoing struggle.

Soul vocalists, using the melismatic delivery of gospel as well as a variety of moans, shrieks, and cries, sing in an uninhibited way that often gives the listener the impression that they are about to lose control at any moment. In doing so, they create a sense of anticipation and hope, as if they have just one more ounce of emotion left to give. As author Peter Guralnick has stated, soul is music that "keeps hinting at a conclusion, keeps straining at the boundaries of melody and convention that it has imposed upon itself." Add to this percolating, syncopated bass lines and the heavy drum backbeat of rhythm and blues, and you've got soul music.

The story of soul begins in the 1950s in the rural South. The main characters in the early years were Ray Charles, James Brown and Sam Cooke.

The First Important Soul Artists

Ray Charles

Ray Charles Robinson (1930–) was born in Albany, Georgia and grew up in Greenville, Florida. After losing his sight at age six from glaucoma, his parents enrolled Ray at the St. Augustine School for the Deaf and the

Ray Charles was the pivotal figure in the creation of soul music.
Courtesy Lincoln Journal Star Library

Blind where he learned how to play a variety of instruments while specializing in piano. During his youth he was exposed to jazz, R&B, gospel, and country music from listening to the radio and other sources. By the time he was seventeen, he was on his own and had moved to Seattle where he established himself in the city's nightclub scene, leading a piano trio patterned after crooner Nat King Cole's and mentoring the young fifteen-year-old Quincy Jones. In 1948 he made his first record, "Confession Blues" and changed his name to Ray Charles to avoid confusion with the middleweight boxing champ Sugar Ray Robinson.

The Archetype

By 1954, Charles signed with Atlantic Records after Ahmet Ertegun and Jerry Wexler heard him play "I Got a Woman" at a nightclub in New Orleans. To Ertegun and Wexler, the song was the "archetype" of a new music that, as of yet, had no name. For Charles, the song was nothing special. "I'd been singing spirituals since I was three, and I'd been hearing the blues for just as long. So what could be more natural than to combine them? It didn't take any thinking, it didn't take any calculating." Using the same hymn-to-pop formula, he also recorded "This Little Girl of Mine" (based on "This Little Heart of Mine") and several other songs that became minor R&B hits before his first big breakthrough came in 1959 with "What'd I Say (Part 1)." The song captures the essence of Ray Charles's ability to galvanize different musical elements:

❏ Gospel (pleading call and response vocals),

❏ The blues (the 12 bar form),

❏ R&B (the underlying riff played by the electric piano),

❏ jazz (the horn section).

It became his first Top Ten hit, peaking at number 6.

Soon after the success of "What'd I Say (Part 1)," Charles left Atlantic to sign with ABC. Two number 1 hits followed, "Georgia on My Mind" in 1960 and "Hit the Road Jack" in 1961. In 1962 to the shock of many, Charles turned his attention to country music, but he was a convincing enough country stylist to earn another number 1 hit, "I Can't Stop Loving You." From the early sixties on, his career has focused more on pop and easy listening, resulting in twenty-two more Top Forty hits. Although he has been the target of some criticism over the years for his pop leanings,

Charles always gives every song his own highly personal rendition with a singing style that is one of the most influential and widely copied in all of pop and rock. The pivotal figure in the creation of soul music and an American icon, Ray Charles continues to tour and record to this day.

James Brown

Alternately known as "Soul Brother Number 1," "The Godfather of Soul," and "The Hardest Working Man in Show Business," James Brown (1933–) unquestionably fits all three descriptions. He not only was one of the most consistent contributors to the soul catalogue of the 1960s, but played an important role in the music's evolution into seventies funk, as well as being inspirational and influential to the birth of hip hop. His stage shows are legendary displays of athleticism and showmanship, and his many dance moves have been widely copied throughout the era of music videos.

James Brown was born in Barnwell, South Carolina in 1933 and raised in Augusta, Georgia by his father. Small of stature and dirt poor, Brown was picked on by other kids in his rough neighborhood and was often forced to defend himself. He came to school barefoot, and regularly resorted to searching through garbage cans for food and clothing. Early on, his self-determination and ambition became apparent: classmates recall that he had to be the best at everything he did, which included singing the national anthem at school every morning. At sixteen he ran afoul of the law and was sentenced to 8–16 years of hard labor on an armed robbery conviction. In prison Brown began to focus his attention solely on becoming an entertainer (he was a standout boxer and base-ball player as well), and joined a gospel vocal group that incorporated dancing and choreography into their stage shows. After his release in 1952, Brown kept the group together, named it the Flames, and began tailoring the act to include more R&B material. In 1956, the Flames caught the attention of Cincinnati's King Records, who signed the group to their subsidiary Federal label. Their first recording, "Please, Please, Please," was a showcase for Brown's sobbing, gospel-influenced vocals and the Flames doo wop styled background vocals. It became a regional hit in the South, eventually selling a million copies.

See Appendix A, "Papa's Got a Brand New Bag, Pt. 1" by James Brown. Track 18 on enclosed CD.

Mr. Dynamite

By this point, the band, now called James Brown and the Famous Flames, was touring extensively, playing some three hundred shows a year on the chitlin' circuit. The stage show gradually incorporated a backup band called the JB's, an emcee, and precisely executed chore-ography. One of the highlights of the show was Brown's being carried off stage after apparently succumbing to heart failure, only to dramati-cally return with a sweep of his cape. The band was so well rehearsed and tight by this time that they were equipped to record a new song at any time in any city, which they often did, usually in one take. Although his recordings for the next two years generally sold poorly, Brown's exciting live performances, which included at least ten costume changes and a cast of two dozen, were approaching legendary status, earning him yet another nickname, "Mr. Dynamite." In 1958 he had his first number 1 R&B hit with "Try Me," which, with a decidedly rougher R&B style, was a portent of future recordings. Over the next six years, six more Top Forty hits followed.

In 1962 Brown reached a turning point in his career with the release of *Live at the Apollo,* recorded at the legendary Apollo Theatre in Harlem. With King unwilling to take a risk on releasing an entire album rather than just singles, the self-determined Brown financed the project himself. It is a tour de force of grit and sweat, power and raw energy that in one fell swoop made Ray Charles' style of soul seem old and stodgy. Once *Live at the Apollo* hit the charts, it stayed there for fourteen months, peaking at number 2, a testament to his status as a hero in the black community and a new crossover appeal to whites. In 1965 Brown had his biggest chart successes with two Top Ten singles, "Papa's Got a Brand New Bag Part 1" (number 8) and "I Got You (I Feel Good)" (number 3). By now the James Brown sound had been stripped of all unnecessary elements and distilled to its essence: rhythm. While Brown shrieked, screamed, grunted, and wailed (often shouting his characteristic "Good God!"), the melodic and harmonic instruments in the band—guitar, bass, organ, horns—were played in short, staccato, non-melodic ways that essentially turned them into rhythm instruments. The entire band became a patchwork quilt of polyrhythms—only occasionally were chords played. Brown even went so far as to disperse with the traditional verse/chorus format, often utilizing the **minimalist** concept of simple one or two-bar repeating phrases to create a trance-like effect.

Minimalism is the use of short repeating musical phrases to create a hypnotic effect.

The Spokesman

Throughout the later sixties and seventies, James Brown further pursued this avant-garde, rhythm-oriented approach, which became the bedrock of the emerging seventies styles funk and rap. Although his music became too rooted to Africa for white audiences, his success made him a symbol of pride and cultural identity for many blacks—a black man who triumphed over the white-run record industry on the strength of his own convictions and self-determination. Brown did not take his role as spokesman lightly, with such records as 1968's "Say It Loud, I'm Black and I'm Proud" and 1971's "Get Up, Get Into It, Get Involved" becoming true civil rights anthems. His bands became veritable schools of funk, showcasing players such as **Maceo Parker** on tenor sax, **Clyde Stubblefield** on drums, **Fred Wesley** on trombone and **Bootsy Collins** on bass. As an inspiration to many current R&B and hip hop artists, in many ways James Brown's music is even more influential today than it was during his peak years.

SAM COOKE

Unlike Ray Charles or James Brown, Sam Cooke (1931–1964) was an established star in the gospel world when he made his first pop recordings, and stirred up even more shock and controversy as a result. His 1957 number 1 hit "You Send Me" was easily the biggest crossover hit of the 1950s, selling nearly two million copies. His good looks, suave and debonair image, and sophisticated musical settings allowed him to quickly grab hold of a huge audience of both blacks and whites that could have served him well for a long and enduring career. Unfortunately, he was murdered at age thirty-three in a bizarre incident that is largely unexplained to this day.

Perfection

Cooke was born in Clarksdale, Mississippi (as Sam *Cook*), but grew up in Chicago, one of eight sons of a Baptist minister. As a teenager, he became a member of the Highway QCs, a gospel vocal group whose inspiration was the Soul Stirrers, one of gospels most popular groups. Cooke's charisma and looks drew positive reviews from gospel insiders, and when the lead vocalist of the Soul Stirrers, Robert Harris, suddenly quit in 1950, Cooke was chosen to replace him. Almost immediately, Cooke's warm, velvety croon won over the older, established Soul Stirrers audience, and gained legions of new, younger gospel fans. But by 1956, Cooke was setting his sights on the pop world, and recorded his first pop tune "Lovable" under the name Dale Cook, hoping not to offend his loyal gospel fan base. The thinly veiled ploy did not work; shock and outrage followed. Cooke's next record was "You Send Me." It cemented him firmly in the pop world for the rest of his career.

Part of the appeal of "You Send Me" was the sweet, soulful, and restrained delivery that became Cooke's trademark. Jerry Wexler of Atlantic Records called him "the best singer who ever lived, no contest . . . everything about him was perfection." Cooke managed to appeal to young and old, black and white, transcending any and all barriers. In the wake of "You Send Me" came twenty-eight more Top Forty hits—mostly crooning, romantic ballads—including "Wonderful World" (number 12, 1960) and "Twistin' the Night Away" (number 9, 1962). As his popularity grew, he moved from the chitlin' circuit to performing in Las Vegas and the upper tier of white nightclubs such as the Copacobana in New York.

Tragedy

Cooke's ambitions did not limit him to singing: with his partner J. W. Alexander, he created Kags Music publishing company, the SAR record label, and a production/management company that were beginning to establish him as a visionary black music entrepreneur. With such a bright future before him, the sordid events that led to Sam Cooke's death on December 11, 1964 are puzzling. Picking up a young model at a restaurant in Los Angeles, Cooke drove her to the $3-a-night Hacienda Motel where he reportedly began to sexually assault her. After she escaped with his pants and disappeared, Cooke became enraged and went to the office of night manager Bertha Lee Franklin. A violent altercation ensued, in which Franklin shot Cooke once with a pistol in self-defense. He died at the scene. As grief and disbelief overtook the pop world, 200,000 fans viewed Sam Cooke's body as it lay in state in both Chicago and Los Angeles. His most fitting epitaph was the posthumous release of "A Change Is Gonna Come," a spiritually fused comment on the state of race relations in America, and a response to Bob Dylan's "Blowin' in the Wind."

Motown

HITSVILLE, U.S.A.

At the pinnacle of black popular music in the 1960s was Motown Records, founded in 1959 by songwriter, producer, and erstwhile professional boxer **Berry Gordy.** Borrowing $800 from his family, Gordy bought an eight-room house at 2648 West Grand Boulevard, and put up a sign over the front door that read "Hitsville, USA." He then proceeded to create the largest black-owned business in the United States in the 1960s. Gordy's business strategy was simple: to bring young, black talent in off the streets of Detroit (where they seemed to be in unlimited supply), groom and cultivate them, back them up with highly polished production, and sell them to the largest possible crossover audience. He accomplished his version of the American dream with huge ambitions, autocratic control, hard work, and the production techniques he learned while working on the assembly line at the local Lincoln Mercury plant in 1955.

Motown's beginnings go back to 1957, when Gordy, then an independent producer, met **William 'Smokey' Robinson,** aspiring songwriter and lead vocalist of local group the Miracles. Gordy talked his way into producing the group's next single, "I Got a Job," the answer to the Silhouette's "Get a Job." The song went nowhere, but established an important working relationship between Gordy and Robinson, who would become Motown's first important songwriter and producer. Gordy at first used United Artists or Chess Records to distribute his records, but Robinson convinced him to start his own label and distribute them himself. In early 1959, Gordy formed Tamla Records and Jobete Music, a music publishing firm, both of which eventually fell under the Motown umbrella, and began signing local talent. Gordy formed another important business relationship in 1959 when he produced the number 23 pop hit "Money" by singer **Barrett Strong,** who in time became another one of Motown's top songwriter/producers. ("Money" was later covered by the Beatles, who turned the song into a rock and roll classic.) The upstart label's first blockbuster hits came in 1960 with the Miracles "Shop Around" (number 2, 1960—Motown's first million seller) and the Marvelettes' "Please Mr. Postman" (1961—Motown's first number 1 hit).

THE ASSEMBLY LINE

Motown was a tightly controlled business run by Berry Gordy, but his family played important roles as well. His father helped renovate the offices; two sisters worked as fiscal officers; brother-in-law Harvey Fuqua worked in production. Family outsiders were also drawn into the fold, some of whom eventually became stars: both Martha Reeves and Diana Ross started at the company as secretaries; Marvin Gaye originally was a session drummer who later married Gordy's sister Anna. Another important aspect of Motown was the attention to quality control. Gordy and other company executives held meetings each Friday to vote on whether to release each of that week's recordings. A no vote meant the song either died or had to be redone. Although there were producers and songwriters on staff that were in competition with each other (much like Aldon Music and the Brill Building scene), Gordy closely supervised every major decision that was made. This tight control of power later contributed to dissension within the company.

Because Motown was actively involved in the artistic development of each of its stars, careers were often patiently nurtured over a period of years. For instance, both the Temptations and the Supremes were signed in 1961, a good three years before either group had a hit single. The Motown process of transforming street singer into pop star was a model of assembly line efficiency that gave their artists a consistent look and sound that was innovative in the music business at the time. The process is outlined in Box 5–1.

The results were stunning: during its peak years, from 1964 to 1967, Motown had fourteen number 1 pop singles, twenty number 1 R&B singles, forty-six more Top Fifteen pop singles, and seventy-five more Top Fifteen R&B singles. In 1966 alone, its best year, seventy-five percent of Motown's releases made one or more of the charts, far above the industry average of charting less than fifteen percent of releases.

THE SOUND OF YOUNG AMERICA

Above all else, Motown's greatest achievement was the music it produced. Gordy looked to the success of Phil Spector and the 'wall of sound' to produce music that was thick in horns, strings, and background vocals, backed by a rhythm section with a hard driving back beat. Gordy called it "The Sound of Young America." Motown's recording studio, located in the basement of 2648 West Grand was a tiny room

---

Box 5-1 The Motown Process

Step 1: Finishing School. Modeling expert **Maxine Powell** taught the proper way to walk, talk, and dress as successful young debutantes and debonair gentleman.

Step 2: Dance Lessons. Choreographer **Cholly Atkins,** a well-known dancer from the heydays of the Swing Era in 1930s and 1940s Harlem, taught dance steps and graceful body moves coordinated to the music.

Step 3: Stage Presence. **Maurice King,** executive musical director, taught stage patter, presence, and projecting a friendly, non-confrontational persona.

Step 4: Music Production: In-house songwriters, arrangers, producers, session musicians, and engineers produce the music to fit the individual sound of each artist.

Step 5: Record Distribution. Records are pressed and distributed throughout the country by the various Motown labels.

Step 6: Talent Agency. Artist contracts, management, and touring schedules are overseen by the in-house talent agency.

Overdubbing is a feature of multi-track tape recorders that allows the recording of additional parts independently of each other while listening to previously recorded tracks with headphones.

affectionately called the **'Snakepit'.** Although at first all the musicians and singers were recorded together using two and three track recorders, in 1964 the Snakepit installed an eight-track recorder that allowed Motown producers to record more elaborate productions in stages, **overdubbing** strings, horns, and percussion on top of the rhythm section and vocals. Characteristics of and key Motown recordings are listed in Box 5-2.

From the very beginning, the core of the Motown sound was the in-house rhythm section, known as the **Funk Brothers.** Although the personnel changed somewhat over the years, the core of the Funk Brothers was **James Jamerson** on electric bass, leader **Earl Van Dyke** on piano, drummer **Benny Benjamin,** and guitarist **Robert White.** Jamerson in particular was important in creating a syncopated bass style that helped define soul music and has been widely copied over the years by nearly all that have played the instrument. Gordy kept tight control over the Funk Brothers, not allowing them to go on tour or play sessions at other studios (although he did pay them well—reportedly $50,000 each per year).

HOLLAND DOZIER HOLLAND

Although Gordy used a variety of writers and producers, including **Smokey Robinson, Barrett Strong, Norman Whitfield,** and Nicholas Ashford and Valerie Simpson **(Ashford and Simpson),** the most successful was the team of Lamont Dozier and brothers Brian and Eddie Holland, known as **Holland/Dozier/Holland** (or simply HDH). From their first hit, 1963's "Mickey's Monkey" (recorded by the Miracles) to the end of 1967 when they left the company, HDH racked up an astonishing forty-six Top Forty hits, including twelve that went to number 1. Although HDH's credits include hits for Martha and the Vandellas ("Heat Wave," number 4, 1963) and Marvin Gaye ("How Sweet It Is [To

---

Box 5-2 The Motown Sound

Characteristics of the Motown Sound
1. Pop oriented, smoothing over most of the rough edges of other soul music
2. Rock solid groove, anchored by Benny Benjamin's drums and James Jamerson's innovative syncopated electric bass
3. Heavy use of string and horn orchestration and reverberation, ala Phil Spector's Wall of Sound
4. Use of added percussion to emphasize the backbeat
5. Vocal harmonies used extensively

Key Motown Recordings
❏ "My Girl"—the Temptations, 1965
❏ "You Keep Me Hangin' On"—the Supremes, 1966
❏ "Reach Out I'll Be There"—the Four Tops, 1966
❏ "I Heard It through the Grapevine"—Marvin Gaye, 1968

Box 5-3

Holland/Dozier/Holland Number 1 Hits Recorded by the Supremes

1964:	"Where Did Our Love Go"
	"Baby Love"
	"Come See about Me"
1965:	"Stop! In the Name of Love"
	"Back in My Arms Again"
	"I Hear a Symphony"
1966:	"You Can't Hurry Love"
	"You Keep Me Hangin' On"
1967:	"Love Is Here and Now You're Gone"
	"The Happening"

Be Loved by You])," (number 6, 1964), their best material was written for the Four Tops and the Supremes. Their hits for the Four Tops included "I Can't Help Myself" (number 1, 1965), "Reach Out I'll Be There" (number 1, 1966), "Standing in the Shadows of Love" (number 6, 1966), and "Bernadette" (number 4, 1967). When Gordy assigned HDH to the Supremes in 1964, they pulled off an amazing string of ten number 1 hits over the next three years. HDH not only wrote the songs (melodies primarily by Dozier, lyrics primarily by Eddie Holland) but produced the sessions as well, with Brian Holland engineering at the mixing console. These hits are listed in Box 5-3.

THE DECLINE OF MOTOWN

By the late sixties and early seventies, many of Motown's artists began to leave the company. Many were angered over Berry Gordy's stingy contracts and royalty agreements that insured that those at the top—Gordy and family members—received the lion's share of the profits, while the artists themselves got little. Other artists got fed up with Gordy's overbearing control. When the Holland/Dozier/Holland team left in 1967, it was a harbinger of things to come. Although Stevie Wonder and Marvin Gaye stayed with Motown, it was because they had enough clout to sign new contracts that gave them near complete artistic control—and more money. Mary Wells, the Temptations, Four Tops, Jackson 5, Ashford and Simpson, Martha and the Vandellas, and others were all gone by the early seventies.

In 1971, Gordy shut down the Detroit operations of Motown after a two-year gradual exodus to Los Angeles to be closer to the film and entertainment industry. By the early eighties, Gordy began to realize that the company's best years were over. In 1982 he signed a distribution agreement with MCA, and later sold the business outright to the media giant for $61 million in 1988. Despite selling his Motown labels, Berry Gordy retained ownership of Jobete Music, the hugely profitable publishing firm that holds the copyrights for virtually all the hits from the Motown catalogue.

Important Motown Artists

SMOKEY ROBINSON AND THE MIRACLES

William 'Smokey' Robinson (1940–) has been called "America's greatest living poet" by no less than Bob Dylan. His work as lead singer and primary writer/producer for the Miracles produced twenty-seven Top Forty singles, six of which hit the Top Ten. Robinson also made significant contributions to the Motown catalogue as a songwriter for other artists, including the Temptations ("My Girl," "The Way You Do the Things You Do" and "Get Ready"); Mary Wells ("My Guy"); and the Marvelettes ("Don't Mess with Bill"). Robinson was able to write love songs that spoke directly to such subjects as passion, loneliness, and forgiveness, as well as using clever rhyming schemes and metaphor. His **falsetto** singing was among the most soulful of all the Motown artists.

Robinson formed the Miracles (originally called the Matadors) in 1955 when all four singers were attending Detroit's Northern High School. It was when they auditioned for Jackie Wilson's manager, Nat Tarnopol, in 1957 that they met Berry Gordy, which led to their signing with Motown and eventually their first Top Ten hit, "Shop Around" in 1960. Among the other Miracles Top Ten hits to follow were "You Really Got a Hold on Me" (number 8, 1963), "I Second That Emotion" (number 4, 1967), and "The Tears of a Clown" (number 1, 1970). Robinson left the group in 1972 to pursue a solo career that produced nine more Top Forty hits. He was inducted into the Rock and Roll Hall of Fame in 1987.

THE MARVELETTES

The Marvelettes were formed in 1960 by five schoolgirls attending Inkster High in suburban Detroit. After signing with Motown in 1961, they had their biggest hit with their first release, "Mr. Postman," which also became the company's first number 1 pop hit. Over the next seven years, nine more Top Forty hits followed. The Marvelettes were in some ways a link to the past as the most purely 'girl group' of any of the Motown vocal groups, and were ultimately swept aside by the more contemporary sound of such groups as the Temptations and the Supremes. Interestingly, the group refused to record Holland/Dozier/Holland's "Baby Love" when it was presented to them in 1964; the song was given to the Supremes, who turned it into a number 1 hit.

STEVIE WONDER

The blind and multitalented Steveland Morris (1950–) was rechristened "Little Stevie Wonder" by Berry Gordy soon after he signed with Motown at age ten in 1960. In less than three years Wonder had his first number 1 hit with "Fingertips—Pt 2." The record is a live recording that features Wonder's harmonica playing and singing—which along with playing

Falsetto is a technique where male singers sing in a very high 'head' voice that is beyond their natural vocal range.

drums, piano, and organ were often part of his live performances. Presented initially in the Ray Charles mold (partly because both were blind), Wonder eventually forged his own unique and soulful singing style. He had twenty more Top Forty hits over the next eight years, including eleven Top Tens. Then, when turning twenty-one in 1971, he renegotiated his contract, giving him complete artistic control of his recordings, as well as more money (he had only earned $1 million up to that point, while Motown had kept over $30 million of his profits for themselves). By this time, Wonder was playing nearly all of the instruments himself on his records, as well as producing, singing, arranging, and writing the songs.

With his new contract, Wonder's career after 1972 blossomed well into the eighties as he explored the possibilities of synthesizer layering and fusing funk, jazz, reggae, R&B, soul, pop, and African rhythms. Beginning with the number 1 singles "Superstition" and "You Are the Sunshine of My Life," he had twenty-four more Top Forty hits, nine of which went to number 1, and placed nine albums in the Top Ten. He also won an amazing fifteen Grammy Awards.

MARVIN GAYE

The son of a Washington, D.C. minister, Marvin Gaye (1939–1984) grew up singing and playing organ in his father's church. As a member of the Moonglows (led by Berry Gordy's brother-in-law, Harvey Fuqua), Gaye was discovered and signed by Gordy in 1961; soon afterward, he married Gordy's sister, Anna. Working at first as a session drummer on Miracles recordings, Gaye began his solo career in 1962, which yielded a remarkable forty Top Forty hits, including three that went to number 1:

❏ "I Heard It through the Grapevine" (1968)

❏ "Let's Get It On" (1973),

❏ "Got to Give It Up (Pt. I)," (1977).

From 1967 until 1970, he often teamed with **Tammi Terrell,** with whom he had seven Top Forty hits. Terrell died in 1970 from a brain tumor, three years after collapsing in Gaye's arms onstage during a concert in Virginia.

Like Stevie Wonder, Marvin Gaye was able to renegotiate his contract in 1971, bringing him more artistic control. That same year, he released the album *What's Going On,* which contained three Top Ten singles that were politically charged statements on Vietnam ("What's Going On"), the environment ("Mercy Mercy Me [The Ecology]"), and civil rights ("Inner City Blues [Make Me Wanna Holler]"). His bitter divorce from Anna was the inspiration for the dark and very personal album *Here, My Dear* in 1978 (so personal in fact that Anna considered suing him for invasion of privacy). Gaye's conflicts with his hedonistic, cocaine abusing lifestyle and his religious upbringing brought much self-inflicted anguish to his later life. In 1983, he moved in with his father, with whom he quarreled constantly. After one such heated argument on April 1, 1984, his father shot him to death from point blank range.

THE FOUR TOPS

The Four Tops

❏ Levi Stubbs
❏ Lawrence Payton
❏ Renaldo Benson
❏ Abdul Fakir

After meeting at a birthday party in 1954 while all four were high school students in Detroit, **Levi Stubbs, Lawrence Payton, Renaldo Benson,** and **Abdul Fakir** began singing together and soon secured a contract from Chess Records. After several years of record flops and countless appearances in Detroit area supper clubs, the group signed with Motown in 1963. Berry Gordy originally had the group record a jazz-oriented album, which was never released; he then switched their style back to R&B and hooked them up with producers Holland/ Dozier/Holland in 1964. The results were immediate: their first release, "Baby I Need Your Loving" went to number 11; the next year they hit the Top Forty four times, including the number 1 "I Can't Help Myself." By the end of 1971, they had thirteen more Top Forty hits, including another number 1, "Reach Out I'll Be There" in 1966.

With their distinct sound of the gritty lead vocal of Stubbs pleading and wailing over the creamy backup vocals, the Four Tops have remained together for nearly fifty years without a single change in personnel. Although they stagnated for a while when HDH left the label in 1967 (they resorted to recording cover tunes for a few years, such as "If I Were a Carpenter"), they continued on with a variety of other Motown producers before leaving the label in 1971.

THE TEMPTATIONS

Formed in 1960 by three Southerners, a Los Angeles transplant, and one Detroit native, the Temptations were the most commercially successful male vocal group of the sixties. The group came together when two existing groups, the Primes and the Distants, combined, initially calling themselves the Elgins. By 1961 they had changed their name to the Temptations and signed with Motown. After languishing with poor record sales for several years, the group's luck changed in late 1963 when lead vocalist **David Ruffin** was added and Berry Gordy assigned them to producer Smokey Robinson. Their next release, "The Way You Do the Things You Do" hit number 11, the first of thirty-eight Top Forty hits, fifteen of which went Top Ten and four to number 1. The group's primary attractions were their precise choreography, the best of any of the Motown groups, and the alternating lead vocals of **Eddie Kendrick's** high falsetto and David Ruffin's low husk.

Things began to change for the Tempts in 1966, when Norman Whitfield began producing with an eye toward a rougher hewn soul style, evidenced by the number 13 hit "Ain't Too Proud to Beg." In 1968, David Ruffin quit the group to pursue a solo career, and the group recorded the socially conscious song "Cloud Nine" (number 6). Although "Cloud Nine" contained drug allusions, it became Motown's first Grammy Award winner. More socially aware songs followed, including "Message from a Black Man," "War," and "Papa Was a Rolling Stone," which went to number 1 in 1972. Like many of the other original Motown groups, the Temptations left the label in the mid-seventies.

THE SUPREMES

Unquestionably the most commercially successful of all the Motown groups, the Supremes hit the American radio waves in 1964 with unprecedented fury: ten of their first fourteen releases, all produced by Holland/Dozier/Holland, went to number 1, including a run of five in a row in 1964–65. By the time Diana Ross left the group in 1970, their Top Forty total had reached twenty-five, with two more number 1 hits, "Love Child" in 1968 and Ross' 1969 farewell, "Someday We'll Be Together."

Originally known as the Primettes, the sister group to the Primes (later the Temptations), **Diana Ross** (1944–), **Mary Wilson,** and **Florence Ballard** grew up in Detroit's Brewster

The Supremes were unquestionably the most commerically successful of all Motown groups. Ten of the their first fourteen releases went to number 1.
© Bettmann/CORBIS

housing project. Rejected at their first audition with Berry Gordy because they were still in high school, the girls hung around Hitsville and sang in backup roles on recording sessions before Gordy finally signed them in 1961. After nine unsuccessful singles over the next three years, Gordy assigned the HDH team to produce the group in 1964. By focusing on Ross' sultry and dramatic vocal style, HDH hit on a winning formula for the group, which Gordy skillfully parlayed into weekly TV appearances and nightclub shows in Las Vegas and at the Copacabana in New York. As the attention increasingly centered on Ross (in 1967 they became known as "Diana Ross and the Supremes"), Ballard became disenchanted and left, replaced by **Cindy Birdsong.** Following her departure from the group, Ross went on to a successful film career (managed by Gordy), which included starring roles in 1972's *Lady Sings the Blues* (for which she received an Oscar nomination), *Mahogany,* and *The Wiz.*

The Supremes

❏ Diana Ross
❏ Mary Wilson
❏ Florence Ballard

See Appendix A, "You Keep Me Hanging On" by the Supremes. Track 19 on enclosed CD.

MARTHA AND THE VANDELLAS

Martha Reeves (1941–) and her friends **Annette Beard** and **Rosalind Ashford** began singing together in high school in Detroit as the Del-Phis and had one single under their belt, when in 1961 Reeves began working as a secretary at Motown. One day on short notice they were called in as background singers on a session for Marvin Gaye, which eventually led to their signing with the label as Martha and the Vandellas. With twelve Top Forty hits (including 1963's number 4 "Heatwave" and 1964's number 2 "Dancing in the Street"), the Vandellas were not one of the most commercially successful Motown groups, but were one of the earthiest and most soulful.

THE JACKSON 5

Originally from Gary, Indiana, the five Jackson brothers (**Tito, Jermaine, Jackie, Marlon,** and **Michael)** were the progeny of Joe Jackson, a professional, albeit part-time, musician. By the mid, sixties under their father's management, the brothers were performing together locally and throughout the region. In 1969 they were signed by Motown, and immediately hit paydirt, as their first four singles "I Want You Back," "ABC," "The Love You Save," and "I'll Be There" all went to number 1. It was the first time in history such a feat had been accomplished, and came at a fortuitous time for Motown, whose fortunes were beginning to fade. Early on, it became obvious that the focus of the group was the young and talented Michael, who was only 11 years old when the first single hit. Berry Gordy decided to pattern Michael's style after Frankie Lymon, lead singer of the fifties doo wop group, the Teenagers. Although he officially stayed with the group until the early eighties, Michael began his solo career in 1971 with his release of his first single "Got to Be There" (number 4). The Jacksons left Motown in 1975, like many others, in a dispute over artistic and financial control.

The Jackson 5

- ❏ Tito
- ❏ Jermaine
- ❏ Jackie
- ❏ Marlon
- ❏ Michael

Stax Records

BACK TO MEMPHIS

At the same time that Motown was establishing itself in Detroit, a small record company was emerging in Memphis that would one day become its most formidable soul challenger. Unlike Motown, there was no advance business plan laid out for Stax Records—the company just sort of evolved with large doses of luck, being at the right place at the right time and of course, hard work. Stax also benefited from the unique "transracial" (as historian Peter Guralnick has called it) environment in Memphis at the time. Although the city was as segregated as any Southern city in the early 1960s, there existed a harmonious relationship between blacks and whites that allowed them to mingle socially at many of the nightclubs around town. Especially among musicians, there were no prejudices based on the color of one's skin; the only thing that mattered was whether or not you could play.

The Stax story begins in 1957 when **Jim Stewart,** a country fiddler who worked at Memphis' First National Bank during the day, began a small record label out of a friend's garage at night. He named the company Satellite—"satellites were big at the time," he later recalled in reference to the Soviet Union's Sputnik. By 1958 he had piqued the interest of his sister **Estelle Axton,** ten years his senior, to the point where she invested in the company by buying a monaural Ampex 350 tape machine with which better recordings could be made. The fledgling business quickly became a passion for the two, who spent all of their off hours (she worked at Union Planters Bank) working with local talent producing records, none of which made any significant sales.

STAX IS BORN

In the summer of 1960, the operation moved to the abandoned Capitol Theatre at 926 East McLemore Avenue, where a recording studio was set up in the theatre and a recording booth on the stage. Because money was tight, the sloped floor of the theatre was not leveled out. There was also no heating or air conditioning, which meant that summer sessions were stifling hot while winter sessions were so chilly that musicians often wore their coats. A record store, the Satellite Record Shop, was set up in the popcorn concession area to bring in extra money. Around this time, local legend and DJ Rufus "Bear Cat" Thomas (see chapter 2) brought his daughter Carla to the studio and recorded a duet called "Cause I Love You," which sold around thirty thousand records. The record caught the attention of Jerry Wexler of Atlantic Records, who for $1000 leased the master and took out a five-year option on all other duets by Rufus and Carla (or at least that's how Jim and Estelle interpreted it—more on that later). Wexler was impressed with the raw energy that came from the studio, something that was lacking from the professional arrangers and session musicians he was used to working with in New York. The association between the two companies that started with "Cause I Love You" would last until 1967, by which time the small mom and pop studio was firmly established as a major music production center.

Meanwhile, two recordings established the foundation for what would become the Stax sound. In the summer of 1961, a band of high school students calling themselves the Royal Spades (which included Estelle Axton's son Packy) released a single called "Last Night," which to everyone's surprise, went all the way to number 3 on the national pop charts. With national exposure, the Royal Spades decided to change their name to the **Mar-Keys;** simultaneously, Jim and Estelle changed the name of the studio to Stax (derived from their last names: **St**ewart and **Ax**ton) to avoid a lawsuit with a label in California also named Satellite. The second important recording came in the summer of 1962 when two members of the Mar-Keys, guitarist **Steve Cropper** and bassist **Donald 'Duck' Dunn,** joined two other local musicians, **Booker T. Jones** on Hammond organ and **Al Jackson** on drums, and recorded a simple blues jam which they called "Green Onions." Again, surprisingly, "Green Onions" rose to number 3 on the national charts. The quartet began calling themselves **Booker T. and the MG's** (MG stood for 'Memphis Group' or the English sports car, depending on who is telling the story), and became established as the houseband for most of the recordings that came out of Stax over the next several years. Unusual for the times, but mirroring the unique workplace environment that emerged at Stax, the MG's were an integrated band: both Cropper and Dunn were white, Jones and Jackson were black.

SOULSVILLE, U.S.A.

Stax grew quickly. Realizing that their destiny was in soul music, the company put up the words "Soulsville, U.S.A." on the theatre marquee outside the studio. Over the next fifteen years, more than 800 singles and

Box 5-4 The Stax Sound

Characteristics of the Stax Sound
1. Raw, gritty, powerful, emotional
2. Bare bones instrumentation of bass, drums, guitar, piano or organ, horn section
3. Very tight yet uncluttered groove in rhythm section
4. Horns scored in punchy unison lines and chords
5. Generally no vocal harmonies or backup vocals; vocalists have more 'elbow room' with bare bones arrangements

Key Stax Recordings
❑ "Green Onions"—Booker T. and the MG's, 1962
❑ "In the Midnight Hour"—Wilson Pickett, 1965
❑ "Soul Man"—Sam and Dave, 1967
❑ "(Sittin' on) The Dock of the Bay"—Otis Redding, 1967

300 albums were released that comprise one of the most enduring catalogues of American music. More than 160 singles made the Top 100 pop chart, while nearly 250 of them made the Top 100 R&B chart. By the start of the seventies, the label (which included the subsidiary Volt Records) had over 100 artists signed and more than 200 employees. Like Motown, a variety of in house songwriters were used to crank out hits, the most important of which were **Isaac Hayes** and **David Porter,** who wrote more than twenty for Sam and Dave, including "Hold On, I'm Comin'" (number 21, 1966), "Soul Man" (number 2, 1967), "I Thank You" (number 9, 1968), and "When Something Is Wrong with My Baby." Steve Cropper of Booker T. and the MG's was also an important contributor, co-writing such soul classics as "634-5789" (number 13, 1966) and "Knock on Wood" (number 28, 1966) with Eddie Floyd, "In the Midnight Hour" (number 21, 1965) with Wilson Pickett, and "(Sittin' on) The Dock of the Bay" (number 1, 1968) with Otis Redding. Some characteristics of the Stax sound and some key Stax recordings are listed in Box 5-4.

Sessions at Stax were conducted very differently than they were at Motown. Everything was done in a live and spontaneous environment, rather than the assembly line production using composers, arrangers, and overdubbing. Songs were often composed on the spot, as was the case with "Green Onions," "In the Midnight Hour," and others. As Jerry Wexler said, "Memphis was a real departure, because Memphis was a return to head arrangements, to the set rhythm section, away from the arranger. It was a reversion to the symbiosis between the producer and the rhythm section, and it was really something new." Compared to Motown, the Stax sound is punchier, more direct and emotional, and not as overly produced, and, in effect, more authentic.

THE DEMISE OF STAX

Unfortunately for Stax, buried in the fine print of their original contract with Atlantic was a clause that gave Atlantic ownership of all the Stax/Atlantic master tapes, a small (!) matter that Jim Stewart and Estelle Axton did not realize until early 1968. They promptly ended their associa-

The Rebirth of Stax

After Stax closed, federal marshals seized the theatre at 926 East McLemore Avenue, and Union Planters Bank (ironically where Estelle Axton used to work) sold the building to a church for $10 in 1980. Eight years later, it was torn down. However, like a phoenix rising up from a deserted vacant lot, the Stax Foundation, spearheaded by former employee Deanie Parker, has built an exact replica of the theatre (including the famous marquee) at its former location as a museum and civic landmark. It is called the Stax Museum of American Soul Music.

tion with Wexler, and sold the company to Gulf and Western for just under $3 million. The assassination of Dr. Martin Luther King, Jr. on April 4, 1968 just a few blocks away from Stax at the Lorraine Motel also contributed to the company's downfall. With the heightened racial sensitivity that engulfed Memphis in the months that followed the assassination, tensions between white and black employees increased, and the casual atmosphere of racial harmony sadly came to an end. While Stax continued growing for the next few years, it became mired down in questionable accounting practices that resulted in an IRS investigation in 1973. By 1975, with the company in a downward spiral, Stax was unable to make payroll to its employees, and the doors were shut for good in January 1976.

Important Stax Artists

BOOKER T. AND THE MG'S

As previously mentioned, the MG's were the Memphis version of Motown's Funk Brothers, serving as the house rhythm section for many of the Stax classic soul recordings. They also had their own chart successes, with six more singles beside "Green Onions" hitting the Top Forty, including "Hang 'Em High" (number 9, 1968) and "Time Is Tight" (number 3, 1969).

OTIS REDDING

Otis Redding (1941–67) was born in Dawson, Georgia, 100 miles south of Macon. As a youth, he sang gospel music at church and played the drums in a school band. As he grew older, he became a Little Richard-inspired lead singer with the group the Pinetoppers, and it was with them that Redding first recorded at Stax in October 1962. Although the song, "These Arms of Mine" only cracked the R&B chart at number 20, Redding began to make a name for himself over the next several years as one of the hottest performers on the chitlin' circuit, performing with the Memphis based backup band the Bar-Kays.

Redding's career was flourishing through the mid sixties, especially after his electrifying performance at the July 1967 Monterey Pop

Important Stax Artists

❑ Booker T. and the MG's
❑ Otis Redding
❑ Wilson Pickett
❑ Sam and Dave

Festival, which introduced him to a much larger white fan base. By this time he had chalked up seven Top Forty hits, including his classic "Respect" (number 35, 1965). Just as his career was beginning to take off, on December 9, 1967 his private plane crashed on the way to a concert in Madison, Wisconsin, killing Redding and most of the members of the Bar-Kays. Three days before his death, Redding made his last recording, the melancholy "(Sittin' on) The Dock of the Bay." Released posthumously, the song became his only number 1 hit.

WILSON PICKETT

Although Wilson Pickett (1941–) signed with Atlantic in 1964, his records were not selling until Jerry Wexler brought him to Stax in May 1965. That session resulted in the soul classic "In the Midnight Hour," the first of sixteen Top Forty hits over the next seven years. After his second hit, "634-5789" in late 1965, Pickett recorded at Fame Studio in Muscle Shoals, Alabama as the Stax/Atlantic association began to dissolve. Pickett is known as the "Wicked Pickett" for his roughly hewn, aggressive style and husky voice.

SAM AND DAVE

See Appendix A, "Soul Man" by Sam and Dave. Track 20 on enclosed CD.

Sam Moore (1935–) and **Dave Prater** (1937–88) were a hot Miami-based nightclub act when Wexler signed them to Atlantic and brought them to Stax in early 1965. There they were assigned to the Hayes/Porter writing team, who wrote more than twenty hits for the duo over the next two years, including the classic soul anthem "Soul Man." Despite the fact that their live shows were among the most exciting in the industry, the two became estranged after Prater shot his wife in a domestic dispute and did not talk to each other offstage for several years. They broke up in 1970. Both experienced drug problems over the next several years; Prater died in an automobile accident in 1988.

Muscle Shoals and Aretha Franklin

FAME STUDIOS

Nestled in the northwest corner of Alabama, 150 miles east of Memphis, lies the sleepy metropolitan area known as Muscle Shoals. Actually made up of four small towns—Florence, Sheffield, Tuscumbia, and the township of Muscle Shoals (where Sam Phillips was born in 1923)—the area started on its way to becoming an unlikely music center in 1959 when local guitarist and entrepreneur **Rick Hall** opened a small recording studio and named it Fame Music (Fame being an acronym for Florence Alabama Music Enterprises). After a number of regional hits allowed him to move into a larger custom-built studio, Hall began to attract clients from Atlanta and Nashville, and eventually Jerry Wexler from Atlantic

Records in New York. Like Motown and Stax, one of the chief attractions to the recording environment at Fame was its houseband, which through the sixties became well known simply as the **Muscle Shoals Rhythm Section.** Important members of the MSRS were drummer **Roger Hawkins,** guitarist **Jimmy Johnson,** bassists **Junior Lowe** and **David Hood,** and pianists **Spooner Oldham** and **Barry Beckett.**

Muscle Shoals first came to the pop world's attention in the spring of 1966 with the release of "When a Man Loves a Woman" by local R&B singer **Percy Sledge.** With the help of local DJ Quinn Ivy, the song was brought to the attention of Jerry Wexler, who bought the distribution rights as it shot to number 1 on the pop chart. Once Wexler realized the benefits of recording at Fame (at a time when Stax was getting too busy with their own artists), he began bringing his Atlantic artists to Muscle Shoals. The most notable of these were Wilson Pickett, and in the spring of 1967, Aretha Franklin.

ARETHA FRANKLIN

Although Aretha Franklin (1942–) was born in Memphis and grew up in Detroit, her first recording contract came from neither Motown nor Stax, but Columbia Records. Her father, the Reverend L. C. Franklin, was the nationally known pastor of the 4,500 member New Bethel Baptist Church in Detroit, where Aretha began singing at age eight. By the age of fourteen, she released her first album, comprised entirely of gospel music recorded live at her father's church. At age eighteen she was signed by the legendary John Hammond of Columbia, who tried to make her into the jazz/pop mold of his earlier discovery, jazz great Billie Holiday. After six years and ten albums that resulted in only one hit (the unremarkable "Rock-a-bye Your Baby with a Dixie Melody"), Aretha left Columbia and signed with Atlantic. Jerry Wexler immediately scheduled a session in Muscle Shoals in January 1967.

Although the session was the only one Aretha ever did in Muscle Shoals, it produced the landmark "I Never Loved a Man (the Way I Love You)," a number 9 hit. Under Wexler's direction, for the first time Franklin was allowed the freedom to do what she did best, and her career took off. Following the Muscle Shoals session, Aretha moved to Atlantic's New York studios (taking the Muscle Shoals Rhythm Section with her) and recorded Otis Redding's "Respect," her first number 1 hit. Over the next three years she sold millions of records, hitting the Top Ten constantly with "Baby I Love You" (number 4), "(You Make Me Feel Like) a Natural Woman" (number 9) and "Chain of Fools" (number 2), all from 1967 alone. Franklin has the ability to take a remarkably wide variety of songs and give them definitive soul renditions, as in Carole King's "Natural Woman," the Beatles' "Eleanor Rigby," or Simon and Garfunkel's "Bridge over Troubled Water." She is also a fine pianist and composer in her own right, having penned "Think," "Since You've Been Gone," and many others. Like Ray Charles's voice, her ecstatic, gospel-filled voice is an American institution, and one of the most recognizable and influential in the history of pop music. She also did a credible acting job in her role in the 1980 movie *The Blues Brothers,* singing both "Respect" and "Think."

Chapter 5
Study Questions

1. Describe how Ray Charles created the first soul recording.

_____

_____

_____

_____

2. Describe the close connection between the civil rights movement and soul music of the sixties.

_____

_____

_____

_____

3. How did James Brown influence soul and later black music styles?

_____

_____

_____

_____

4. Describe the key elements to the way business was run at Motown.

_____

_____

_____

5. What were some of the right and wrong things that Berry Gordy did in running Motown?

_____

_____

_____

6. Describe the differences between the way sessions were run at Motown and Stax.

_____

_____

_____

_____

_____

7. What were some of the differences in the Motown sound and Stax sound?

_____

_____

_____

_____

_____

8. How did the "transracial" atmosphere in Memphis affect the operation of Stax?

_____

_____

_____

_____

_____

9. What important role did Jerry Wexler of Atlantic Records play in the soul music of the 1960s?

_____

_____

_____

_____

_____

10. Briefly describe why Atlantic was successful in making a star out of Aretha Franklin but Columbia wasn't.

_____

_____

_____

_____

_____

The British Invasion

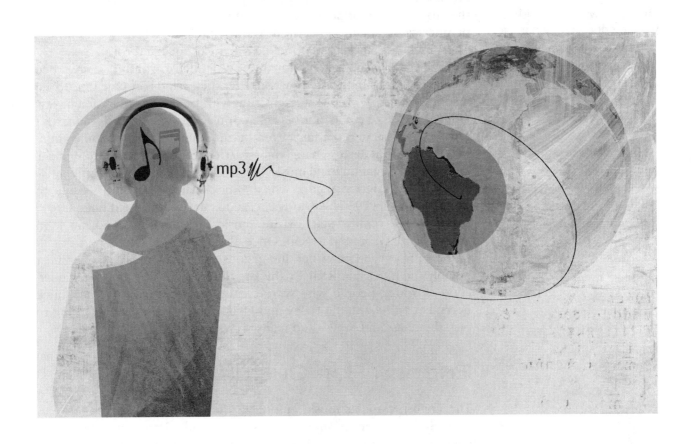

The British Pop Scene in the 1950s

POSTWAR ENGLAND

In early 1964, the Beatles came to America for the first time. Their arrival had been highly anticipated for weeks: bumper stickers reading "The Beatles Are Coming" were everywhere; grown men suddenly started wearing moptop wigs; the press was reporting the group's every move. When they finally touched down at New York's Kennedy Airport on February 7, there was somewhere between 4,000 and 10,000 screaming fans waiting (mostly teenage girls) who would have literally torn the group apart if not for the police officers on duty. By the last week in March, they held the *top five* positions on the *Billboard* pop chart, with seven more records in the Top 100, while their first two LPs were positioned at number 1 and number 2 on the album chart. But the Beatles were just the beginning. Like a dam bursting open, a flood of other English groups soon followed, sweeping American rock stars aside as they took control of radio playlists and record sales. The British Invasion of America had begun in earnest. And the music the Brits were playing? Their own unique style of good old American rock and roll.

Trad jazz was the English term to describe traditional New Orleans jazz, sometimes called Dixieland.

Skiffle was a do-it-yourself music played by small groups using guitars, washboards, empty jugs, etc.

Throughout the years following WWII, English youth had absorbed whatever American music they could get their hands on. One of the first manifestations of this was a fascination with **trad jazz**—traditional New Orleans jazz. Trad jazz bands became popular throughout the country for a while, and a few recordings even became hits in the U.S. Somewhere in the mid fifties, tastes changed to **skiffle,** an English adaptation of traditional American jug band music. The most popular English skiffle musician was **Lonnie Donegan,** whose "Rock Island Line" also became an American hit in 1956. Skiffle was easy to play, and the fad encouraged many British youth to start playing music, including Liverpudlians John Lennon and George Harrison. Once the skiffle fad wore out, British music fans turned to other indigenous American music styles, most notably the blues and R&B. By the late fifties, there was an entire generation of young people who were turning on to Muddy Waters, Chuck Berry, Little Richard, Bill Haley, and Elvis Presley. Many were learning to play the blues and R&B—and many were forming their own bands.

ENGLISH POP CULTURE

The English popular music culture in the fifties and early sixties was very different than in America. There were only three radio stations to choose from, all of which were run by the government sponsored British Broadcasting Corporation (BBC). The closest any of these came to programming pop was the BBC Light, which played light opera, musical comedy, and light orchestral music for dancing—hardly the kind of station where one might hear American R&B. There were only four major record labels, the largest of which were **EMI** and **Decca.** There were few independent labels willing to take risks on wannabe pop stars like there

Box 6-1

Top Ten Hits in America by British Artists, 1962–69

1962: 2	1966: 30
1963: 1	1967: 22
1964: 32	1968: 16
1965: 36	1969: 11

Pirate Radio Stations in England

Early sixties British rock and roll fans could still get a fix of their music even though the BBC wouldn't program it. Many turned to **Radio Luxembourg,** the "Fabulous 208" (for its frequency at 208 on the British dial), which had been catering to a youth audience since the late fifties. The 208 featured American style DJs and even had Alan Freed—on tape. In the early sixties, illegal stations began broadcasting from ships offshore the British coast—the so-called pirate radio stations—that were largely funded by American record companies. These stations—which included Radio Caroline (named for John F. Kennedy's daughter), Radio London, Radio Veronica and Radio Nord—enjoyed tremendous ratings until 1967, when the British government outlawed them. The BBC finally relented to the demands of the youth market when their own pop station, Radio One went on the air on September 30, 1967.

were in America, and American records heavily dominated the English pop charts. With few opportunities to break into the national music scene, up until the early sixties, most rock and roll bands in the UK were pale imitations of their American counterparts. This balance of power shifted dramatically in 1964, however, as the Beatles and other British bands began to assert dramatic influence on the American charts. Box 6-1 illustrates this.

Of course, the British Invasion started with the Beatles, and our story begins with them.

The Beatles

It has now been forty years since much of the world was introduced to the Beatles, and they are still very much with us. In many ways, they changed almost everything—not just in rock and roll, but *everything*. Sure, they had an enormous impact on pop culture—hair, clothes and fashion—but they also changed us on a much broader social level. Although they wrote music that became very popular, it was also meaningful. It spoke of making the world a better place; it challenged us to become better people; it made social commentary but provided hope; it was about the essence of what it is to be human.

The Beatles

- John Lennon
- Paul McCartney
- George Harrison
- Ringo Starr

Key Beatles Recordings

- *A Hard Day's Night,* 1964
- *Revolver,* 1966
- "Strawberry Fields Forever"/"Penny Lane," 1967
- *Sgt. Pepper's Lonely Hearts Club Band,* 1967
- *The White Album,* 1968
- *Abbey Road,* 1969

The Beatles—**John Lennon** (1940-80), **Paul McCartney** (1942-), **George Harrison** (1943-2001), and **Ringo Starr** (1940-)—were *the* cultural phenomenon of the 1960s. They were smart, funny, irreverent, idealistic, and eclectic, and the baby boom generation ate them up. In many ways, everything about the sixties can be looked at from a Beatles perspective. At the start of the decade as they emerged with their infectious pop tunes, there was optimism, a feeling of hope of how we were going to make the world a better place. In the middle sixties, life became more complicated: there were drugs and a sexual revolution, there was a counterculture and an older, conservative generation locked in ideological warfare. The Beatles' music, in turn, became more complicated, asking questions that made us search for the answers. When the sixties came to a crashing halt, the Beatles broke up. With the country in turmoil in the wake of political assassinations, an unpopular war and troubling civil rights issues, we had to face the future without them.

But today, it is the music that matters most. One of the most astounding things about the Beatles was their constant appetite for growth and change. Their music literally matured in front of our eyes. By the time they broke up in 1969, they were writing innovative art that still sounds fresh today. Looking at record sales alone, the numbers are impressive, with fourteen number 1 albums and twenty number 1 singles, but they do not begin to measure the true impact of the Beatles. Box 6-2 lists some ways the Beatles impacted rock.

In short, they had a greater impact on rock and roll than any other artist or group of the era. Then there are the members themselves. Ways the members impacted rock are listed in Box 6-3.

Producer George Martin also played a huge role. It was he who guided the band in the early years, and turned them on to the possibilities of orchestration, new instruments, and studio technology. He was also smart enough to never say, "You can't do that" to the curious questions and imaginative ideas that emerged from the group in the studio.

At the heart of the Beatles magic is the coming together of two powerful yet very different musical forces that in friendly competition brought out the best in each other. John Lennon and Paul McCartney

Box 6-2 The Beatles' Impact on Rock

1. They made rock and roll the dominant pop music format; previously, it was strictly for teenagers.
2. They changed the way music was recorded and presented; they constantly pushed the envelope with their use of studio technology; they provided the basic format for today's music videos; they were innovative in their packaging as well.
3. They transcend generation; although they are a symbol of the sixties, neither they nor their music sounds out of date today. It is still fresh and meaningful, and still appeals to all ages.
4. They combined exceptional songwriting and performing both live and in the studio as no other artist(s) in the 20th century.
5. They forced the recognition of pop music as art, and were the forerunners of art rock.

Box 6-3 The Contributions of John, Paul, George and Ringo

1. All four were great musicians; even Ringo, albeit not the greatest drummer of the era, made impressive contributions to the band.

2. The variety of instruments they played was staggering: Paul, the bassist, also played piano, acoustic and electric guitar, and drums; John played guitar, piano, harmonica, and banjo; George played guitar, sitar, tamboura, bass, violin, synthesizer, and organ; and Ringo played drums and all sorts of percussion instruments.

3. They were great singers. John and Paul were simply two of rock's greatest. The combination of John, Paul, and George singing harmony was powerful and exciting on rockers, gorgeous on ballads.

4. Their compositions cover a diversity of styles that was unprecedented: from hard rockers ("I Saw Her Standing There"); to tender ballads ("She's Leaving Home"); world music ("Within You, Without You"); the avant-garde ("Revolution 9"); children's songs ("Yellow Submarine"); folk ("You've Got to Hide Your Love Away"); to Tin Pan Alley-like ("When I'm Sixty-Four"). Although Lennon and McCartney often wrote together to one degree or another, each had unique styles. John tended to write songs that were more complicated rhythmically, simpler melodically and often more avant-garde. Paul was a superior pop craftsman in the Brill Building mold, writing some of the most endearing pop tunes of the last 50 years ("Yesterday" has been covered by more artists than any song in history), while also bringing a classical music influence.

5. The lyrics, among the most meaningful of their generation (along with those of Bob Dylan), reflect the different styles of the two main writers (one way to tell the authorship of a Beatles song is by identifying the lead singer). John tended to write songs about himself, asking questions and seeking answers that were both personal, yet could be viewed in the larger communal sense as well. Paul tended to write songs about other people, pointing out the peculiarities of their lives or situations they were in. Of course, there were exceptions to this rule—John's "Good Morning, Good Morning" is written in the fashion of Paul; Paul's very direct and personal "Let It Be" is more typical of John.

6. Often the important contributions of George and Ringo are overlooked. George was simply one of the best guitarists in the 60s: he was a master in the studio with a large palette of sounds and effects. He played some of the most melodic and lyrical solos on record. In addition, he turned into a great songwriter as well. His "Something" is the second most covered Beatles tune, and he turned in several other masterpieces as well ("Here Comes the Sun," "Taxman"). His fascination with Indian music and culture inspired the conception of the world music movement. Ringo was the perfect compliment for the other three, never competing for attention, often playing understated but perfect parts. And, he contributed some of the most memorable lead vocals as well ("Yellow Submarine").

could never have achieved the greatness they did on their own. They clicked immediately—they were inseparable in the early days, writing songs together, harmonizing together, or letting the other finish a song when they got stuck. But the competitive nature of their friendship was also hard work, and in the end, when it finally burned itself out, the group broke up.

THE EARLY YEARS

The story of the Beatles begins in Liverpool in the early 1940s as Britain was engaged in World War II. As an important seaport on Britain's northwest shore, the city was a target for German bombers and had suffered mightily during the Battle of Britain in the fall of 1940. The very night John Lennon was born, October 9, 1940, bombs were falling outside the maternity home where he lay with his mother Julia. Sunken ships littered the Mersey River. But the city survived.

Liverpool in the 1950s was an interesting town: despite its working class ethic and depressed economy, it was a sponge for pop culture from America, especially the rock and roll records brought over by sailors. As the rock and roll culture of American youth flourished, the English counterpart of the 'cat' was born: the **teddy boy.** Teddy boys greased their hair up and wore leather jackets, boots, and sneers. Although young John Lennon was not yet a teddy boy in 1956, he was so completely taken with Elvis Presley that he put together his own group called the Quarry Men—named after the Quarry Bank Grammar School he attended. Sometime after Paul McCartney first heard the group play on July 6, 1957, he ended up auditioning for them—and got the job. Lennon and McCartney had one thing in common besides their love for music: both of their mothers had recently died, and their pain clearly had a bonding effect on them. Both would later write love songs to their mums— Lennon's "Julia," and McCartney's "Let It Be." McCartney soon brought along his schoolmate, George Harrison, to play lead guitar. Even though he was only fourteen years old at the time, George could play solos, while John and Paul could only strum chords. The drummer was Lennon's friend **Pete Best,** who stayed with the group until 1962.

THE AUDITION

By 1960, the group had changed its name to the Beatles, and added **Stu Sutcliff** on bass (Sutcliff quit the next year to pursue a career in art). Beginning in August, they played the first of a string of engagements over a two-year period in the raunchy clubs in the **Reeperbahn** section of Hamburg, Germany. It was here that the Beatles honed their group sound, as they were often required to play for up to eight hours a night. In early 1961, they first appeared at Liverpool's **Cavern Club,** a dank, underground pub where they performed nearly 300 times over the next two and a half years. By the time they played their last Cavern Club show, they were drawing long lines to see their polished, high-energy shows. The Beatles were becoming a phenomenon, both locally and regionally.

In late 1961, **Brian Epstein,** the manager of the nearby NEMS record store, became the Beatles' manager and quickly went to work. Over the next few months, the group's teddy boy image changed to more upscale, matching mohair suits with white shirts, thin ties and mop top haircuts. Although Epstein searched for a record contract for the group, his initial efforts were in vain: the only label that even showed enough interest to let them audition was industry giant Decca Records (who turned them down). Finally, as Epstein was exhausting his options, he managed to get his foot in the door at EMI's small **Parlophone** subsidiary. His contact was **George Martin,** a classically trained composer and staff producer at EMI, who was willing to give the group a chance at an audition. On June 6, 1962, the Beatles went into the London office building on Abbey Road where the EMI studio was located and recorded four songs. Martin decided to sign them, although he was admittedly not so much impressed with their music as he was with their personal charm. "It was love at first sight . . . we hit it off straight away . . . the most impressive thing was their engaging personalities."

BEATLEMANIA!

After the Beatles signed with Parlophone, things began to happen very quickly. The band went to work on their first album amid a hectic touring schedule. After the audition, Martin told them they had to replace Best, which they did with their friend Richard Starkey, who went by the name Ringo Starr. Four songs were recorded on various off days, and the other ten were recorded in one ten-hour marathon on February 11, 1963. The resulting album was called *Please Please Me.* Eight of the songs on the LP were originals, highly unusual at the time for a debut album. At this point, many of the songs were written by John and Paul 'eyeball to eyeball'; however, even in the early days, the two were also writing apart from each other, often only getting help from the other for a hook or extra phrase. The Beatles first single, "Love Me Do," (written by Paul) and their first number 1 (UK), "Please Please Me," (written by John), came from these sessions. Ringo did not play on two of the songs—producer Martin felt that his playing wasn't up to par, so session drummer Andy White was used instead.

The band continued their hectic touring schedule as their popularity soared throughout England. By July 1963, they went back into the studio to start on the second album entitled *With the Beatles.* It was released on November 22, 1963, (the day that John F. Kennedy was assassinated) and immediately went to number 1 (UK) where it stayed for twenty-one weeks. The album is a mix of originals (including "All My Loving" and "I Wanna Be Your Man") and covers (such as "Roll over Beethoven" and "You Really Got a Hold on Me"). By this time, the group was constantly being mobbed by fans all over England whenever they appeared in public. After a performance at London's Palladium in October, the *Daily Mirror* coined the term 'Beatlemania!' in a headline, and it stuck.

COMING TO AMERICA

Beatlemania went largely unnoticed in America until the beginning of 1964, but it hit with sudden and tremendous impact. The group's first appearances on the *Ed Sullivan Show* on February 9th, 16th, and 23rd were viewed by approximately seventy-three million people each, the largest audiences in the twenty-three year history of the program. EMI's American subsidiary, Capitol Records, had been slow to release any Beatles singles, but when the first, "I Want to Hold Your Hand," was finally released in January 1964, it shot straight to number 1 where it stayed for seven weeks. By the end of March, the Beatles held the top five records in America: number 1: "Can't Buy Me Love," number 2: "Twist and Shout," number 3: "She Loves You," number 4: "I Want to Hold Your Hand," and number 5: "Please, Please Me."

July of 1964 saw the release of the third album, *A Hard Day's Night.* It went to number 1 and stayed there for twenty-one weeks (in the UK, only to be knocked off by the group's next album). *A Hard Day's Night* is significant on several accounts: it is the first Beatles album in which a 4-track tape machine was used, which allowed them to overdub parts and begin using the studio in more innovative ways. It is also their only album consisting entirely of Lennon and McCartney songs. *A Hard Day's Night* was a tie-in to the pioneering feature film of the same name, whose jocular plot evolves around whether the Fab Four would make it through

The Beatles perform on the *Ed Sullivan Show* in New York on February 9, 1964. Left to right: Paul McCartney, Bass; George Harrison, Guitar; John Lennon, guitar; in back: Ringo Starr, drums.
AP/WIDE WORLD PHOTOS

another madcap day of being chased by fans. Directed by Richard Lester, the film is a blueprint for many of the first music videos made in the 1980s. The album itself is a tour de force for Lennon, who wrote most of the songs, including the title track (inspired by one of Ringo's favorite catch phrases), the lovely "If I Fell" and "I Should Have Known Better." McCartney's contributions, while fewer in number, were still noteworthy, including "Can't Buy Me Love" (a beautifully disguised 12-bar blues) and the tender "And I Love Her."

The fourth album, *Beatles for Sale,* released in December 4, 1964, was the first Beatles LP to receive luke-warm critical acclaim. In many ways, it is a reflection of the rigors of Beatlemania—constant touring, constant screaming mobs, no privacy—which made writing difficult. As George Martin put it, the band was "war weary." However, there were still some gems: "Eight Days a Week," a collaborative effort from John and Paul actually fades *in,* on of the first examples of the group trying out new ideas in the studio. John's "I'm a Loser" philosophically questions the high price of fame. The album was filled out with several covers, including Chuck Berry's "Rock and Roll Music," Leiber and Stoller's "Kansas City," and two Carl Perkins tunes, "Everybody's Tryin' to Be My Baby" and "Honey Don't."

MEETING DYLAN

The first album to signal the experimental future of the Beatles recordings was *Help!,* released on August 6, 1965. Part of the evolution was the result of the famous meeting with Bob Dylan in the summer of 1964 at New York's Hotel Delmonico. Dylan and the Beatles reportedly spent several hours chatting, laughing, and smoking marijuana. The meeting was an epochal moment in the history of the Beatles, as Dylan's influence was immense and immediate, revitalizing the group at the very moment that they were ready to evolve both musically and lyrically. From this point on, the lyrics of McCartney and particularly Lennon and Harrison began to take on increasing social, political, and cultural significance. The group also began to expand into more musically diverse styles, evidenced on *Help!* by the use of outside session musicians for the first time (a flautist at the end of "You've Got to Hide Your Love Away" and strings on "Yesterday"). Lyrically and musically, from this moment on the Beatles would begin to change rock and roll into an art form.

Help! was the first album in history to have an advance order of over one million copies. It was also a tie in to the group's second movie, once again directed by Richard Lester. The title song, composed by John, was written as an expression of his self-loathing 'Fat Elvis' period: tiring of the trappings of wealth and fame, he was drinking and eating too much, bored with his marriage and with living in the suburbs. Dylan's influence is overpowering on Lennon's "You've Got to Hide Your Love Away." Tucked away near the end of Side B is McCartney's masterpiece "Yesterday," uniquely set to only acoustic guitar and string quartet accompaniment (arranged by Martin). It became the most performed pop song in the world for the next several years.

Coming of Age

Rubber Soul is often considered the Beatles 'coming of age' album. Released on December 3, 1965, it is comprised of fourteen original songs written over a four-week period. With a number of songs tackling social issues, *Rubber Soul* shows more lyrical depth and intelligence than any previous release. Musically and instrumentally the album is a harbinger of things to come, as the Beatles introduce a variety of new instruments, including sitar on Lennon's "Norwegian Wood" and fuzz bass on Harrison's "Think for Yourself." There is also a baroque piano solo played by George Martin on John's autobiographical "In My Life" recorded at half speed to make it sound like a harpsichord when played back at normal speed.

On August 5, 1966, the Beatles released *Revolver,* an album that many call their finest work. It is also considered to be the first album of the psychedelic era because of its use of exotic instruments, studio effects, and several drug allusions. Where *Rubber Soul* headed, *Revolver* continued on to the next level. There are no 'fillers' on the album, as every song has merit, most are brilliant. George Harrison contributed three strong tracks: "Taxman," a social commentary about the high taxes in Britain for the wealthy; "Love You To," written specifically for sitar and tablas (recorded using only himself and Indian musicians), possibly the first piece of the coming 'world music' movement; and "I Want to Tell You." Lennon contributed six, including three with drug references ("She Said She Said," "Dr. Robert," and "Tomorrow Never Knows"). "Tomorrow Never Knows" was inspired by Timothy Leary's *The Psychodelic Experemce,* a guide to spiritual enlightenment through the use of LSD based on the *Tibetan Book of the Dead.* McCartney's contributions were more of his usual well-crafted pop gems, including the haunting "Eleanor Rigby," the tender "Here, There, and Everywhere" inspired by Brian Wilson's "God Only Knows," and the sing-along children's song "Yellow Submarine."

Sgt. Pepper's

After the release of *Revolver,* the Beatles announced their decision to discontinue touring. Although they had toured worldwide since 1963 with spectacular success, live concerts were plagued by poor sound reinforcement and screaming mobs; now their music was getting too dependent on studio technology to be reproduced adequately in a live setting. Their last concert was at Candlestick Park in San Francisco on August 30, 1966. The announcement fueled rumors that the Beatles were about to break up, which the lack of their expected year-end album release only intensified. To silence critics, on February 17, 1967 the band released "Penny Lane" and "Strawberry Fields Forever" as two A sides on one single. Both songs are remembrances of real places in Liverpool from McCartney and Lennon's childhoods.

"Penny Lane" and "Strawberry Fields Forever" were originally supposed to be included on the group's next album, the highly anticipated

Sgt. Pepper's Lonely Hearts Club Band, released on June 1, 1967. Restless fans and critics were overjoyed: *Sgt. Pepper's* is arguably the most important album in rock history. For several months in the summer of 1967, it literally captivated the world of popular culture. The album took five months and 700 hours to record and cost an unheard of $100,000. Stemming from Paul's idea to fabricate an alter ego band where each Beatle could assume the role of another musician, the album was originally intended to give the experience of having attended a royal performance, with each song segueing into the next. In the end, only the first two songs were done this way, but with an overture to open Side A, a reprise of the overture and an encore to close out Side B, the effect is nearly the same. *Sgt. Pepper's* is often called rock's first concept album, although some give that distinction to the Beach Boys *Pet Sounds. Sgt. Pepper's* also contains what is arguably the most famous music album cover in history, showing celebrities and famous people gathered around the Beatles in costume. The album is the first ever to print the song lyrics on the inside of the cover. *Sgt. Pepper's* is also noteworthy for the stunning use of studio technology, used with great skill and effect throughout. The album's encore, the Lennon/McCartney collaboration "A Day in the Life" is a chilling commentary on bureaucracy, materialism, and the specter of nuclear annihilation, and is perhaps their finest work.

ALL YOU NEED IS LOVE

After the release of *Sgt. Pepper's,* the Beatles took part in the first world-wide satellite TV broadcast on the program *Our World,* performing Lennon's "All You Need Is Love" live to 350 million viewers. Then, in August, the band suffered a major setback when manager Brian Epstein died from an accidental drug overdose. From this point on, the Beatles would try to manage themselves, one of the first of many bad business decisions that ultimately contributed to the group's downfall. In February 1968, the band, along with actress Mia Farrow and her sister Prudence, the singer Donovan, Mick Jagger, the Beach Boys' Mike Love, and assorted girlfriends all went to the ashram of guru **Maharishi Yogi** in Rishikesh, India to learn about Transcendental Meditation. Within just a few weeks the group ascertained that the Maharishi was a charlatan, and one by one returned home to England. Lennon later wrote the vindictive "Sexy Sadie" about the experience, which appeared on the upcoming *White Album.*

Magical Mystery Tour, a six-song double EP (an 'extended play' 45-rpm) was released on December 8, 1967, accompanying the film of the same name. The movie and artwork of the EP was inspired by the cross-country journey of Ken Kesey and his Merry Pranksters in their psychedelic bus Further. Although the EP was panned by the critics as too self-indulgent, sloppy, and not very good, it did contain John's brilliantly bizarre and surrealistic "I Am the Walrus," whose two note melody was inspired by the sound of an English police siren. In the months following the release of *Magical Mystery Tour,* the Beatles released two singles written by Paul, "Lady Madonna" and "Hey Jude," which ultimately became their best selling single with sales of nearly ten million copies.

Impending Doom

By the time *The Beatles* (aka *The White Album*) was released on November 22, 1968, the inner tensions that would eventually break the band apart were surfacing. Lennon and McCartney were losing control of their song publishing rights, and their new music company Apple was losing money due to mismanagement. John's new lover Yoko Ono was a constant presence, and an often-unwelcome one at that (she would often submit criticisms at recording sessions, and at one point when she was ill, John even rolled a bed into the studio for her). Other signs of impending dissolution were becoming apparent: George began recording a solo album, Ringo quit for a few days when he discovered that Paul was re-recording the drum parts himself after Ringo left the studio. Nonetheless, *The White Album* is a remarkable double album with thirty songs that cover a wide range of styles. Many of the songs were recorded without the full group in attendance, giving the effect of John, Paul, and George essentially taking turns doing solo pieces with backing musicians. Still, some of the groups best material can be found on *The White Album,* including John's "Happiness Is a Warm Gun," "Julia," and the avant-garde "Revolution 9"; Paul's "Blackbird," "I Will," and "Ob-la-di, Ob-la-da"; and George's "While My Guitar Gently Weeps" (featuring his friend Eric Clapton on guitar) and "Piggies."

1969 saw the release of *Yellow Submarine,* which is often called the worst Beatles album, a manifestation of the ever-worsening band morale. Only six songs are on the album, two of which had already been released. Side B of the album contains orchestral scorings by George Martin from the accompanying movie.

The End

The next album recorded was not immediately released. *Let It Be* was originally planned as a no overdubs, back-to-live concept to be called *Get Back.* To get a truly live recording, the Beatles staged a surprise noontime concert on the rooftop of Apple's Savile Row offices on January 30, 1969 and performed five songs (including Paul's "Get Back") before the police shut them off because of neighbor's complaints. The concert was filmed, as were most of the sessions, and were included in the accompanying documentary of the same name. However, with tempers flaring over Paul's overbearing control and the worsening management situation, the task of finishing the project was just too much for the band. George Martin quit; George Harrison walked out for a few days. By the time the recording was done, no one wanted to stick around to mix it, so the job was left to a session engineer. The resulting mixes were too sloppy with too many mistakes, so Phil Spector was brought in to re-produce the entire album. Spector added lush string orchestration to some of the songs, including Paul's "The Long and Winding Road," which angered McCartney. *Let It Be* was not released until May 8, 1970, after the Beatles had broken up.

The last album recorded by the Beatles was *Abbey Road,* (released September 26, 1969), and it is perhaps their finest work. George Martin was persuaded to return as producer, and by this time the studio had installed a new eight-track recorder for the band to use for the first time. Synthesizers were also used for the first time on several of the songs. Once again, George Harrison contributed two very fine songs, "Something" and "Here Comes the Sun." Lennon's contributions include "Come Together," based loosely on Chuck Berry's "You Can't Catch Me" and "Because," inspired by hearing Yoko play Beethoven's "Moonlight Sonata" backwards. The centerpiece and masterstroke of *Abbey Road* is the sixteen-minute, eight-song medley that closes Side B. The songs, written mostly by Paul, seamlessly segue together and cover a variety of styles, from the serenely beautiful "Sun King," the polka-like "Mean Mr. Mustard," the tongue-in-cheek "Polythene Pam," and ending up with the rocking "The End." The last song features a jam session where Lennon, McCartney, and Harrison trade two-bar guitar solos before closing with the words, "And in the end, the love you take/Is equal to the love you make." A fitting finale to leave their millions of fans.

The Beatles breakup was messy. Although Paul had lobbied the others on the idea of a return to performing live at small clubs without public announcement, John had had enough. In September he announced to the rest of the band that he "wanted a divorce," but was persuaded by McCartney to remain silent to keep from jeopardizing pending business dealings. In the ensuing months, McCartney went to work on his solo album debut, and ultimately came to the conclusion that he too wanted out. When *McCartney* was released on April 10, 1970, it included a faux self-interview in which Paul implied that the Beatles were done. Lennon, who had kept his desire to quit a secret out of respect for Paul, felt betrayed. Business entanglements, lawsuits, and Lennon's anger would continue on for years, but one thing was clear: the Beatles would never record or perform together again.

THE AFTERMATH

After the breakup of the band, solo albums were forthcoming from Lennon and McCartney. Now that they were no longer chained together, each was free to pursue separate music careers. McCartney continued to write well crafted pop tunes, but without Lennon's gravity they became lightweight and sugary sweet. In 1972 he formed **Wings** with wife **Linda Eastman,** whom he married in 1969. Nine number 1 hits followed, including duets with Stevie Wonder and Michael Jackson. In 1971, George Harrison organized the first ever All-star concert to raise money for a cause, the **Concert for Bangladesh,** which raised over $10 million for the people of that country. In 1988 he formed the Traveling Wilburys with friends Bob Dylan, Tom Petty, Jeff Lynne, and Roy Orbison. He died of cancer on November 29, 2001. Ringo, after having two number 1 hits in 1973 went on to a career in TV and movie acting.

John Lennon had a turbulent and brief post-Beatles life. In the early seventies, his festering anger over what he perceived was McCartney's double-crossing sent him into primal scream therapy, which was reflected in his dark and disturbing 1970 album *Plastic Ono Band.* In 1971 he released *Imagine,* which contained the poignant title track as well as "How Do You Sleep," a scathing attack on McCartney. As he and Yoko settled down at their Dakota apartment in New York to raise their family, Lennon was gradually becoming more at peace with the world by the late seventies. Just as hopes of a long awaited Beatles reunion were rising, Lennon was murdered outside the Dakota by crazed fan Mark David Chapman on December 8, 1980.

The Rolling Stones

IMAGE

In the 1960s, the Rolling Stones began calling themselves "The World's Greatest Rock and Roll Band," and by many standards they were. But because their rise to fame so closely followed that of the Beatles, to many they were the world's *second* greatest band. The Stones were forced early on to portray themselves as dangerous and surly, creating a sort of 'anti-Beatles' image as a way to find a niche for themselves in the midst of Beatlemania. The ploy worked. There are two ironies to the public images of the Stones and the Beatles: the first is that despite the public's perception of the Beatles as middle class and lovable versus the low class and dangerous Stones, the Stones came from a generally higher class upbringing than the Beatles did. The second is that the Stones have been much more influential and widely imitated in this regard than the Beatles. The marketing of rock musicians as rebellious hoodlums has become an accepted part of the rock and roll canon.

The Rolling Stones were the quintessential "kick ass" rock and roll band throughout much of the sixties and seventies. Unlike most British bands of the era that cut their teeth playing American-influenced blues and R&B and then moved on to their own brand of pop, the Stones only occasionally strayed far from their roots, and always returned (their worst digression was a brief flirtation with disco in the late seventies). Their on-stage image, in the persona of Mick Jagger, was the most boldly sexual and threatening of their time. Off stage, the scandals and bad behavior of their personal lives only served to intensify their scoundrel images. During their most creative period from 1965 to 1972, the Rolling Stones created some of rock and rolls most memorable anthems and produced four albums that are nothing short of masterpieces.

THE EARLY YEARS

Mick Jagger (1943–) and **Keith Richards** (1943–) both grew up in London and briefly went to the Dartford Maypole County Primary School together. Around 1950, Richards moved to a housing project on the other side of town and the two did not see each other again until a chance meeting on a commuter train in 1960. The two fledgling guitarists began jamming together after discovering their common love for American rhythm and blues. **Brian Jones** (1942–69), also an aspiring blues guitarist, had grown up in the exclusive resort city of Cheltenham

Key Rolling Stones recordings

- ❏ "(I Can't Get No) Satisfaction," 1965
- ❏ *Beggars Banquet,* 1968
- ❏ *Let It Bleed,* 1969
- ❏ *Sticky Fingers,* 1971
- ❏ *Exile on Main Street,* 1972

before joining Alex Korner's influential Blues Incorporated. Jones became acquainted with Jagger and Richards through London's blues bar scene, and by mid 1962 the three musicians, along with Dick Taylor on bass and Mick Avory on drums, played their first gig as the Rolling Stones at the Marquee Club (taking their name from a Muddy Waters tune). By January 1963, Taylor and Avory had been replaced by **Bill Wyman** (1936–) on bass and **Charlie Watts** (1941–) on drums, and the Stones personnel for the next six years was set.

Sometime in the spring of 1963, public relations man **Andrew Loog Oldham,** a former employee of Brian Epstein, heard the Stones at the Crawdaddy Club, where they had established a residency. After taking on the group as clients, Oldham realized that "In just a few months the country would need an opposite of what the Beatles were doing," and went about packaging the group as such. On the advice of George Harrison (by this time the two bands had become acquainted), Decca Records signed the group, and in May 1963 they released their first single, a cover of Chuck Berry's "Come On," which went to number 21 in the UK. Their second single, the Lennon and McCartney tune "I Wanna Be Your Man" was released in October and hit the British Top Fifteen. Other early recordings included covers from their American role models: Willie Dixon's "I Just Want to Make Love to You," "Little Red Rooster," and "I Want to Be Loved," Holland/ Dozier /Holland's "Can I Get a Witness" and Buddy Holly's "Not Fade Away," which went to #3.

BREAKING THROUGH

Starting in late 1963, the Stones embarked on an arduous three-year touring schedule. On their first tour, they warmed up for the Everly Brothers, Bo Diddley, and Little Richard; in early 1964, they headlined their own tour of the UK. Crowds at their concerts were decidedly more aggressive than Beatles audiences, and often times the band could only perform four or five songs before violence erupted. At a concert in Dublin, fans rushed on stage and tackled Jagger while Wyman was crushed against a piano. One report said "three boys were throwing punches at Brian while two others were trying to kiss him." When the Stones went on their first American tour in June 1964, they had moderate success in the larger cities while being virtually ignored in the Midwest. The tour ended on a high note when Oldham booked a recording session at Chicago's Chess Studio that was attended by idols Muddy Waters, Willie Dixon, and Chuck Berry. From that session came their first number 1 hit in the UK, a cover of Bobby Womack's "It's All Over Now." Of their Chicago concert, *Vogue Magazine* wrote: "The Stones have a perverse, unsettling sex appeal with Jagger out front of his team-mates . . . To women, he's fascinating, to men a scare."

By the end of 1964, the Stones were finally beginning to break through in the United States. They released their first LP, *England's Newest Hit Makers/The Rolling Stones,* and by the end of 1965 they had four hits break into the Top Ten. Jagger and Richards by this time were composing their own material (initially under the pseudonym Nanker Phelge), with Richards typically writing the music and Jagger the lyrics.

The Rolling Stones March 26, 1971 farewell performance at London's Marquee Club, where they played their first show in 1962. Left to right: Mick Jagger, unidentified, Mick Taylor, Keith Richards, Charlie Watts.
AP/WIDE WORLD PHOTOS

After two Top Ten hits in late 1964 and early 1965 ("Time is on My Side" and "The Last Time"), in June the Stones finally hit number 1 in the States with "(I Can't Get No) Satisfaction," which stayed at the top for four weeks. Richards reportedly conceived the song's memorable guitar riff in the middle of the night in a motel room in Florida. Within a year, the Stones had two more U.S. number 1 hits, "Get Off My Cloud" and "Paint It Black," and two more Top Ten hits. Five more Top Tens in 1966, including the number 1 "Paint It Black" in which Brian Jones played sitar (an obvious Beatles influence), signaled that the Stones had finally conquered America.

Rock and Roll Bad Boys

Meanwhile, the Stones were living up to their bad boy image. In January 1967 they appeared on *The Ed Sullivan Show* with the intention of performing their risqué (for the time) "Let's Spend the Night Together." While CBS censors protested, the group played the song anyway, with Jagger either mumbling the words "the night" or changing them to "some time," depending the viewer's perception. Then, on February 12 both Richards and Jagger were arrested after police raided a party at Richards' home—Richards for allowing drugs on his property, Jagger for possession of amphetamines. The same day that the two appeared at the court hearing, Brian Jones was arrested at his London flat for possession of cocaine, Methedrine, and marijuana. Although Jagger and Richards were convicted and sentenced to serve jail time, their convictions were overturned. Jones, however, continued to be harassed by police, and was later arrested again. Because of his eventual conviction, touring abroad became impossible, as most countries refuse to grant visas to convicted drug felons.

From their earliest years, Brian Jones had been the most flamboyant member and the de facto leader of the group. However, Jagger's athletic and sexually suggestive onstage antics and Richards' high-energy guitar playing had shifted the public focus of the group to them away from him. Jagger and Richards were also taking artistic control of the Stones with their songwriting, further relegating Jones to the sidelines. As Brian Jones sensed he was being reduced to the role of a second-class citizen within the band, his paranoia increased, as did his drug use. With the band unable to tour for nearly three years due to his drug conviction, Jones finally left the group in June 1969 to clean himself up and turn his life around. Less than one month later on July 3, he was found dead in his swimming pool. The official coroner report cited the cause as "death by misadventure." Two days later the Stones performed at Hyde Park in London before 250,000 fans who heard Jagger open the show by reading from Percy Shelley's *Adonais:* "Peace, peace! He is not dead, he doth not sleep." Brian Jones was replaced by guitarist **Mick Taylor.**

CREATIVE TRIUMPH, TRAGEDY

Despite the inner turmoil, the Rolling Stones in 1968 were entering their most creative period. Following the critically panned release of the psychedelic *Their Satanic Majesties Request* (which the group patterned after the Beatles *Sgt. Peppers*), the Stones hired producer **Jimmy Miller,** who went about giving the band a rougher sound by making Richards's guitar more prominent and highlighting percussion instruments. The first Miller production, released in May 1968 was the classic "Jumpin' Jack Flash," which went to number 3. Next up was *Beggars Banquet,* released in December, which contained two of the Stones most memorable anthems, "Sympathy for the Devil" and "Street Fighting Man." Both songs made powerful musical and lyrical statements: "Sympathy" was a commentary on the dark side of contemporary society, while "Street" became a rallying cry for students to take political action. In May 1969, the Stones released yet another rock classic, "Honky Tonk Women," which became their fifth number 1 single. The November 1969 release of *Let It Bleed,* which contained two more masterpieces, "Gimme Shelter" and "You Can't Always Get What You Want," was warmly greeted by critics and fans alike. Some viewed *Let It Bleed* as a satirical take on the Beatles' soon to be released *Let It Be,* and "You Can't Always Get What You Want" as a response to "Hey Jude." Whether they were or not is arguable, but it was more proof that the Stones seemed destined to live in the shadow of the Beatles.

As the Stones wound up their first American tour in five years at the end of 1969, plans were made to stage a free "thank you America" concert in the San Francisco Bay Area. After several possible locations were turned down, the site was set at the last minute for the Altamont Raceway, just south of San Francisco. Hastily prepared, the event was mismanaged from the start. Hell's Angels were hired to provide security (and paid in *beer*); the stage was inadequate, as were the restroom facilities. Throughout the early performances by Santana, Jefferson Airplane, Crosby Stills Nash and Young and others, the Angels' applied brute force to keep order among the overflow crowd. By the time the Stones took the stage, chaos and violence were erupting in the crowd. Then, with cameras rolling (for the documentary film *Gimme Shelter*) and the band playing "Under My Thumb," the Hell's Angels violently stabbed to death audience member Meredith Hunter directly in front of the stage. With order breaking down and fearful for their lives, the Stones fled the scene in a helicopter.

Although Altamont dealt the Stones another serious public relations setback, it had surprisingly little effect on the intensely creative streak they were undergoing. In April 1971, they released *Sticky Fingers,* recorded in part in Muscle Shoals, Alabama. Critics hailed it as one of their best albums. The album contained the number 1 hit "Brown Sugar," which became the latest of the Stones songs to draw criticism as being misogynistic (others included "Under My Thumb," "Stupid Girl," and "Honky Tonk Women"). What drew perhaps the most attention to the album however was the cover, conceptualized by **Andy Warhol,** which contained a real zipper within a photo of a man's jeans. The album also introduced for the first time the famous Ruby Mazur designed tongue and lips logo on the inner sleeve. In May 1972, the fourth Jimmy Miller produced album, *Exile on Main Street,* was released to mixed reviews. *Exile* is swampy, bluesy, and captures the essence of the Mississippi Delta, with elements of rock and roll, soul and country thrown in as well. Over time, many have come to view the double album as the Stones' best ever.

THE LATER YEARS

Since the early seventies, the Stones have continued to tour and record. Since *Exile on Main Street,* they have hit the Top Forty eighteen more times, eight of which went to the Top Ten. Six of their post-*Exile* albums have hit number 1, although none since 1981. Their personnel has stayed remarkably consistent over the years, with the exceptions of Mick Taylor leaving in 1975, replaced by **Ron Wood** (formerly of the Faces), and mainstay Bill Wyman leaving in 1994 after more than thirty years, replaced by bassist **Darryl Jones.** In the last few years, they have stayed naughty, although no longer dangerous, and have become more venerable institution than creative force.

The Who

THE EARLY YEARS

Although never as commercially successful as the Beatles or the Rolling Stones, the Who were unquestionably one of the most influential bands in rock history. Not only were they the prototype of the 'power trio' format, they were inspirational to several later rock genres, including punk, heavy metal, and art rock. They were among the first rock and roll bands to incorporate synthesizers into the compositional process rather than just as an effect. They brought stage violence and theatrics to rock like no other band before them. They also produced a catalogue of highly unique and powerful original music that had social relevance and relied heavily on the exceptional musicianship of the four group members. And, in 1969 they produced the first rock opera *Tommy*, which was universally hailed as a masterpiece and was later made into not only a feature film but also a Broadway musical. The Who did all this despite (or perhaps because of) the friction caused by the constantly clashing personalities within the band.

Roger Daltrey (1944-), **Pete Townshend** (1945-), and **John Entwistle** (1944-2002) grew up in the west London suburb of Shepherd's Bush and went to school together. All three were drawn to music: Townshend and Entwistle played in a trad jazz band for a while before Entwistle left in 1962 to join the Detours, a rock band which included Daltrey on lead guitar. In 1963, Daltrey switched to lead vocals and Townshend joined as lead guitarist. When Detours drummer Doug Sandom quit that same year, **Keith Moon** (1947-78), who had been in a surf group called the Beachcombers, replaced him. With a repertoire that consisted primarily of American R&B covers, the Detours developed a popular fan base and often performed on the same bill with the Rolling Stones and the Hollies. In early 1964, after discovering that another band already was named the Detours, they changed their name to the Who.

THE MOD SCENE

Around this time, public relations man **Pete Meaden** took over management of the Who and repackaged them with the look of **London's mod scene.** The mods were easily identified: snappy dressers with short hair, owning scooters decorated with lots of chrome mirrors and lamps and consuming large quantities of amphetamines that allowed them to "dance like a madman" as Townshend said. Meaden also inflicted yet another name change on the band, this time to the High Numbers, another mod reference. After one unsuccessful single release, the band split with Meaden, teamed up with new manager Kit Lambert, and changed their name back to the Who. Under Lambert's management, the band toured in the summer of 1964 with the Beatles, the Kinks, and pub singer Tom Jones.

One night in late 1964 while playing at London's Railway tavern, Townshend broke the neck of his guitar when it accidentally hit the club's low ceiling. In a fit of anger, he proceeded to smash the rest of the instrument to bits all over the stage and throw pieces to the audience. The notoriety that followed the incident helped secure a contract with Decca Records and the January 1965 release of "I Can't Explain," which featured session guitarist Jimmy Page on rhythm guitar. The record was selling poorly until the Who appeared live on the British TV show *Ready, Steady, Go*, and Townshend and Moon destroyed their equipment. As a result of the publicity over the incident, the group's popularity soared and "I Can't Explain" went on to sell over 100,000 copies, reaching number 8 on the British charts. In late 1965, the group's first album *(The Who Sings) My Generation* was released, featuring a mix of R&B covers and

Key Recordings by the Who

❏ "My Generation," 1965
❏ *Tommy*, 1969
❏ *Live at Leeds*, 1970
❏ *Who's Next*, 1971

Townshend originals, including the title track, which hit number 2 in the UK. "My Generation" was a rebellious attack on the establishment, older people and anyone else who wasn't young ("Hope I die before I get old"), and established Townshend as a spokesman for the teenage nation. The record ends in a flurry of feedback and drum cacophony, predating the violence and anger of punk.

MONTEREY

In early 1967, the second album *A Quick One* was released (titled *Happy Jack* in the U.S.) which featured a ten-minute mini-opera and the single "Happy Jack," which hit number 24 in the U.S. With little success in the U.S. market up to that point, the Who embarked on a tour of America in the summer of 1967 that included a stunning performance at the Monterey Pop Festival in June that concluded with Townshend and Moon again destroying their equipment. The band capitalized on the media stir that followed with the hit "I Can See for Miles," which at number 9 became their best ever U.S. chart appearance. With Townshend's deafening power chords and Moon's bombastic drumming, "I Can See for Miles" is a predecessor to heavy metal. The song was part of the late 1967 album release *The Who Sell Out,* which contained another mini-opera, faux advertising songs, and radio jingles recorded from the offshore pirate radio station Radio London.

By this time, the Who's stage act was a flurry of perpetual motion: Townshend attacked his guitar with a windmill right hand as he leapt across the stage; Moon was a wild man on his huge drum set which included two bass drums; when not screaming into the microphone, Daltrey would swing it by the cord as if he was roping cattle. In the midst of all this, bassist Entwistle stood statue-like, seemingly oblivious to everything. Much of the fury on stage was fueled by the constant amphetamine and alcohol usage by the band members, which also intensified the frequent personality clashes between Daltrey and Townshend, who battled over control of the band. (At one point, Daltrey was even kicked out of the band for a while and was not let back in until he promised to become less combative.)

TOMMY

In 1968, Pete Townshend became a follower of the spiritual guru **Meher Baba,** and began to reduce his drug consumption and reflect upon ways to define his own moral responsibilities through music. He came up with the idea of telling a story of spiritual enlightenment through song lyrics rather than the conventional spoken narrative accompaniment. It would be, in effect, a rock opera, the first of its kind. Released in 1969 and named after its main character, *Tommy* is the story of a boy who traumatically loses all sensory skills—becoming deaf, dumb, and blind—and becomes famous for his superior skills at playing pinball. After he is miraculously cured, he is manipulated into selling his secrets and exposed as a fraud. The story line was one that could be interpreted on several levels by a wide range of people; but most of all, the music in the 90-minute *Tommy* is exceptional, from "Underture," "Pinball Wizard," "See Me, Feel Me," "We're Not Gonna Take It," and others. *Tommy* became a critically acclaimed hit and put the Who at the front of the creative vanguard in rock. It was turned into a controversial film in 1975 and a Broadway musical in 1993.

In August 1969, the band appeared at Woodstock, and their set is one of the highlights of the documentary film. In 1970 *Live at Leeds* was released, one of the most dynamic live recordings in rock history. Not taking time to bask in the glory of *Tommy*, Townshend began work on his next project, which was to be a science fiction film entitled *Lifehouse*. Because the enormous scope of the project proved to be too much for Townshend, *Lifehouse* was never fully realized. However, four of the songs were included in the 1971 LP *Who's Next*, which like *Tommy* and *Live at Leeds* went to number 4 on the album charts. Included on *Who's Next* are two stunning and innovative pieces, "Baba O'Reilly" (named for Meher Baba and minimalist composer **Terry O'Reilly**) and "Won't Get Fooled Again," in which Townshend programmed an ARP 2600 synthesizer to provide a sequenced foundation for the songs to be built upon. Both songs became staples of FM radio playlists.

FINAL TRIUMPH, TRAGEDY

In 1973 Townshend completed his second rock opera, the double album *Quadrophenia*, which charted at number 2. The hero, Jimmy, is a member of the mid sixties London mod scene with a four way split personality, which reflected the personalities of each of the Who's band members. The story is a "study in spiritual desperation" which leads Jimmy to the realization that "the only important thing is to open [his] heart." Like *Tommy*, *Quadrophenia* was critically hailed and turned into a film in 1979. In 1978, the aptly named *Who Are You* was released as Townshend began to experience somewhat of an identity crisis as he agonized over becoming an elder statesman in the wake of the punk scene. Almost simultaneously, on September 7, 1978, Keith Moon died of an overdose of a sedative he had been taking to treat alcoholic seizures. Although the group continued on for another three years with **Kenney Jones** on drums (formerly of the Small Faces), the group was never the same again.

Throughout the seventies, the members of the Who involved themselves in solo album projects and regrouped periodically to tour. In October 2001 they played the Concert for NYC, a benefit concert for families of the victims of the September 11 attack on the World Trade Center. Pete Townshend still performs as a solo act, although he is afflicted with tinitus, a constant ringing in his ears. However, since the June 2002 death of John Entwhistle, Townshend and Daltrey have officially drawn the final curtain on the Who.

Other British Invasion Bands

THE MERSEY BEAT GROUPS

In the wake of the Beatles success, many of the first wave of British Invasion bands sounded predictably very much like the Fab Four. Because there was a reported 350 bands in Liverpool alone in the early sixties, it was inevitable that a few would make it to the charts. The style of these bands—upbeat and joyous, with a relentless drive—became known as **Mersey Beat** (from the Mersey River), or simply beat. One of the first Liverpool groups was **Gerry and the Pacemakers,** who like the Beatles, were signed by Brian Epstein, played Hamburg and the Cavern Club, and produced by George Martin. Formed in 1959 as a skiffle band, the Pacemakers had three U.K. number 1 hits in 1963 and hit in the States with "Don't Let the Sun Catch You Crying" (number 4) in 1964 and "Ferry Across the Mersey" (number 6) in 1965. Also from Liverpool were the **Searchers,** whose sound could best be described as a precursor to the Byrds—tight, four-part harmony and chiming guitars. Their biggest hit came in 1964 with "Love Potion Number Nine" (number 3 U.S.). **Billy J. Kramer and the Dakotas** were another Epstein/Martin group from Liverpool, although Kramer was more of a fifties-type pub crooner than a rock singer.

By 1964, groups from other English cities had emerged. Manchester was home base to **Herman's Hermits,** the **Hollies,** and **Freddie and the Dreamers.** Freddie Garrity, with Buddy Holly-nerdish looks, started out playing skiffle; with the Dreamers his biggest hit was "I'm Telling You Now" (number 1 U.S., 1965). The Hermits, led by Peter Noone, were as cute and cuddly as the Beatles, with whom they actually went toe to toe with in record sales for a while. Between 1964 and 1967, they had eleven Top Ten hits, six of which were in 1965, when they practically dominated the charts. They hit with two number 1s that year: "Mrs. Brown You've Got a Lovely Daughter" and "I'm Henry the Eighth, I Am." When the Hermits were unable to musically evolve out of lightweight pop, they quickly fell from grace. The Hollies, led by **Graham Nash,** formed in 1962 and became best known for their Everly Brothers-influenced harmonies and jangly guitars. They began making inroads into the American market in 1966 with Top Ten hits "Bus Stop," "Stop Stop Stop," and "On a Carousel," but by 1968 Nash had become unhappy with the group's direction and left for the U.S. (and helped start Crosby, Stills and Nash). From Tottenham came the **Dave Clark Five,** whose peak years also were from 1964 to 1967. Their first hit, 1964's "Glad All Over" (number 6 U.S.) was the first of seventeen; they also were the second British group (after the Beatles) to appear on Ed Sullivan, and ultimately did so a total of eighteen times.

THE BLUES-ORIENTED GROUPS

Also starting around 1964, groups with a rougher, blues orientation started emerging from Britain. These groups tended to be sinister and menacing looking, with rude and defiant attitudes—definitely more Rolling Stones than Beatles. The two most prominent and influential were the **Animals** and the **Kinks.**

Led by singer **Eric Burdon,** the Animals were formed in Newcastle in 1962. In addition to Burdon, the group included **Alan Price** (keyboards), **Bryan "Chas" Chandler** (bass), **Hilton Valentine** (guitar), and **John Steel** (drums). The group's first album, *The Animals,* was recorded in one day in 1964 at EMI's Abbey Road studio and included their only number 1 hit (U.K. and U.S.), "House of the Rising Sun." The song is one of two traditional folksongs from the album that were also on Bob Dylan's first album—an indication of one of the group's main influences. However, it was the reciprocal influence that ultimately had the biggest impact on rock history: upon hearing the Animals play "House of the Rising Sun" while touring England in 1964, Dylan is reported to have said, "My God, ya oughta hear what's going down over there. Eric Burdon, the Animals, ya know? Well, he's doing "House of the Rising Sun" in rock. Rock! It's fucking wild! Blew my mind." The group disbanded in 1966; Burdon reformed it as Eric Burdon and the Animals later that same year. Chandler went on to a management career, and played an important role in the discovery of Jimi Hendrix.

Brothers **Ray Davies** and **Dave Davies** (vocals and guitars), **Mick Avory** (the original Rolling Stones drummer), and **Peter Quaife** (bass) formed the Kinks in London in 1963. Their first hit single came the following year, "You Really Got Me" (number 1 U.K., number 7 U.S.), which was followed in 1965 with "All Day and All of the Night" (number 7 U.S.) and "Tired of Waiting for You" (number 6 U.S.). The Kinks' sound was heavily based on blues-based distorted power chords—making them an important predecessor to hard rock and heavy metal. Even though the group continued to record and perform after their early hits, for the next ten years or so they went largely unnoticed until punk and metal bands rediscovered their power chord-filled catalogue of songs (Van Halen recorded "You Really Got Me" in 1978). That catalogue also includes one of rocks all time sing along anthems, 1970's "Lola."

Chapter 6
Study Questions

1. What were some of the differences between the British and American pop scenes in the fifties and early sixties?

_____

_____

_____

_____

2. Describe how John Lennon and Paul McCartney wrote songs in the early years.

_____

_____

_____

_____

3. In what ways did songs written by Lennon differ from those written by McCartney?

_____

_____

_____

4. Name three significant things about the album *Revolver.*

_____

_____

_____

5. What were some of the factors that led to the breakup of the Beatles?

_____

_____

_____

_____

6. What were some of the ways in which the early years of the Rolling Stones were different than those of the Beatles, including their public relations, records and audience reaction?

_____

_____

_____

_____

_____

7. What were the most important Rolling Stones albums?

_____

_____

_____

_____

8. What later music styles did the Who influence, and how?

_____

_____

_____

_____

9. What were some of the difficulties encountered by the Beatles, Rolling Stones and the Who in live performances?

_____

_____

_____

_____

10. Describe the differences between the Mersey Beat groups and the blues oriented groups that emerged from the British pop scene in the 1960s.

_____

_____

_____

_____

1960s Blues and Psychedelia

The Sixties Counterculture

SEEDS OF DISCONTENT

By the mid 1960s, another generation of American youth was becoming dissatisfied with their lives and began to question the middle class values of their parents. These values—the traditional ones—included being achievement oriented, acquiring material goods, becoming wealthy, and "keeping up with the Jones's." Although discontent was nothing new to the realities of being a teenager, the world was a much different place in 1965 than it was in 1955, or even 1960 for that matter. New social pressures were emerging that had a strong impact on youth, giving them even more reason to reject the establishment. Foremost among these were the civil rights movement, the Vietnam War, and the increased use of hallucinogenic drugs. During the last half of the sixties, a youthful counterculture developed in San Francisco and other cities that wrapped itself in rock music as it dropped out of society.

Although the civil rights movement began in earnest in 1954 with the U.S. Supreme Court's *Brown vs. Board of Education of Topeka, Kansas* ruling, the struggle to end racism and discrimination was by no means over by the mid sixties. Many white youth identified with and supported the cause of the oppressed black population with the same sense of idealism that turned them away from their parents. On the other hand, many older middle class Americans resisted any and all social change and saw support of this issue by the young as merely an opportunistic reason to rebel. The murders of civil rights activists Medgar Evers in 1963, Malcolm X in 1965, and Dr. Martin Luther King, Jr. in 1968 were violent indicators that helped define exactly how much work was yet to be done in the area of race relations in our country.

By the mid sixties, however, the issue that most clearly divided the nation was the war in Vietnam. For young men, getting drafted and sent to Vietnam represented a very real personal threat and became an ideological battleground that extended beyond whether you were for the war or against it. The older generation, who had come together for the common good of the nation during the Depression and World War II, could not understand why young people would question the government's authority and its reasons for committing troops to a war thousands of miles away against the spread of Communism. Many youth saw the war as pointless and imperialistic, and as the war escalated, protesting increased and sometimes became violent. The first large-scale anti-war rally was staged by the radical Students for a Democratic Society in Washington, D.C. in April 1965; by 1967 protests and rallies were common on college campuses all over the country. The year 1968 saw bloody confrontations between police and protesters in Chicago during the Democratic National Convention. When the draft lottery was installed in late 1969, many of draft age defiantly burned their draft cards or became 'draft-dodgers' by fleeing to Canada. On May 4, 1970, four students were killed by National Guard troops during a demonstration on the campus of Kent State University, resulting in angry nationwide protests and the closing of hundreds of college campuses for several days.

DRUGS

Another issue that became a weather vane of the sixties was the increasing recreational use of psychoactive drugs such as LSD, marijuana, hashish, and mescaline. Many young people preferred these drugs to alcohol and 'uppers' such as amphetamines (speed) because they tended to induce a general state of increased creativity and enlightenment rather than aggressive behavior. Rock musicians such as Bob Dylan, the Beatles, and others were quick to experiment with these drugs and explore their mind-expanding possibilities. In June 1967, Paul McCartney announced that he had taken LSD four times in the past year, and that it made him "a better, more honest, more tolerant member of society, brought closer to God." The Beatles album *Revolver,* released in August 1966 and often called the first album of the psychedelic era, contains several allusions to drugs, most notably in the song "Tomorrow Never Knows." Other sixties rock songs of the era that reportedly had drug connotations include Jimi Hendrix's "Purple Haze" (a type of LSD), the Byrds' "Eight Miles High," Jefferson Airplane's "White Rabbit," and the Amboy Dukes' "Journey to the Center of the Mind."

Unlike marijuana, which had been used illegally for years by jazz musicians and others, LSD (lysergic acid diethylamide, or simply acid) was relatively new, and in fact was legal in the U.S. until October 1966. Discovered in 1938 by a Swiss chemist, acid became widely known in part through highly publicized experiments by Harvard psychologist **Dr. Timothy Leary** (whose book *The Psychedelic Experience* John Lennon used as the inspiration for "Tomorrow Never Knows") and author **Ken Kesey** (*One Flew Over the Cuckoo's Nest,* 1962). Kesey first encountered the drug at the Stanford Research Institute just outside San Francisco, and began sharing it with his friends (who became known as the **Merry Pranksters**) at parties called 'acid tests.' Acid tests featured live music by Bay area bands like the Warlocks (who later changed their name to the Grateful Dead), light shows, and acid-spiked Kool-Aid. Previous to the acid tests, Kesey and the Merry Pranksters had journeyed to New York in the summer of 1964 in their day-glow painted school bus named Further, dropping acid and playing crude homemade music to astonished onlookers along the way. Author Tom Wolfe chronicled the Merry Pranksters in their heyday in his book *The Electric Kool-Aid Acid Test.*

San Francisco and Acid Rock

THE HIPPIE CULTURE

The focal point of the new underground culture was San Francisco, a well-established haven for creative intellectuals, bohemians, radical political activists, and eccentrics. The San Francisco Bay area was the West Coast base for beat poets Allen Ginsberg and Jack Kerouac, the birthplace of the free speech movement (at the Berkley campus of the University of California), and with cheap rents and safe neighborhoods, a magnet for free-spirited young people who came by the thousands. By the mid sixties, there was an air of spontaneity about the city that fostered an anything goes, 'lets try something and see what happens' attitude. When the liberal use of psychoactive drugs was thrown into the mix, there was an explosion of long hair, incense, peace signs, tie-dyed shirts and bell-bottom pants, beads, and free sex—and the hippie culture was born. The name was apparently a derivative of the fifties word hipster—these kids were only *slightly* hip—that had been coined by a local newspaper reporter in September 1965.

Hippies eschewed the trappings of the rat race, often living communally in large houses where they shared chores, listened to music, consumed drugs, and pursued peaceful and artistic activities. The largest concentration of hippies was in the **Haight-Ashbury** neighborhood (named for the intersection of Haight and Ashbury Streets), where stores and boutiques such as the Psychedelic Shop, the Blushing Pony, and the I/Thou coffee shop served their various spiritual and other needs. But the counter culture was also apparent all over the city, with the emergence of radical theater groups such as the San Francisco Mime Troupe, run by promoter Bill Graham, nightclubs like the Matrix, operated by Marty Balin of the Jefferson Airplane, and bookstores like **City Lights Books,** owned by **Lawrence Ferlinghetti.** A loose collective that called itself the **Family Dog** formed in 1965 with the sole purpose of promoting dances where there was no booze but where hallucinogens were available. Their first event, called **A Tribute to Dr. Strange,** was held at Longshoreman's Hall on October 16, 1965 and featured bands such as the Charlatans, Jefferson Airplane, and the Great Society (which included singer Grace Slick). The event was so successful that others like it soon followed, and were often staged at one of the many older ballrooms in the city such as the **Avalon,** the **Fillmore,** and the **Carousel.**

THE SUMMER OF LOVE

By January 1966, the San Francisco scene was in full bloom. Ten thousand people showed up at Longshoreman's Hall for the three-day **Trips Festival** (January 21–23) organized by Kesey and his Merry Pranksters that featured music by the Grateful Dead and Big Brother and the Holding Company, among others. The event also included Native American tepees, strobe lights, slide shows, poetry readings and free acid samples dispensed by local chemist/acid activist **Owsley** (Augustus Owsley Stanley, III). It was publicized with colorful and stylized **psychedelic posters** that became in themselves part of the flair of the local scene. Another creation that emerged from the San Francisco scene was the **psychedelic light show,** which used the crude technology of the time: colored liquids that pulsated over classroom overhead projectors onto bare walls and dancers. By early 1966 the Fillmore and Avalon Ballrooms were having concerts nearly every weekend. Legendary promoter **Bill Graham** used the Fillmore to stage his shows, while **Chet Helms,** manager of Big Brother and the Holding Company worked the Avalon. Free concerts in city parks were not unusual either—as Mickey Hart of the Grateful Dead recalled: "I loved playing for free. It felt good to give the music away and let people who couldn't afford the music hear it."

On January 14, 1967, the **Human Be-In Festival** drew 20,000 to the Polo Grounds in Golden Gate Park to hear Allen Ginsberg, Lawrence Ferlinghetti, Dr. Timothy Leary, and radical activist Jerry Rubin speak and listen to the Jefferson Airplane, Quicksilver Messenger Service, and Big Brother and the Holding Company. Newspaper writer Ralph J. Gleason described the audience as "a wild polyglot mixture of Mod, Paladin, Ringling Brothers, Cochise, and Hell's Angels' formal." The event was among the first in the year that culminated in the so-called 'Summer of Love.' By the summer, Haight-Ashbury was a tourist attraction, the focus of national media attention and overflowing with hippies and other eccentrics. There was even a song, "San Francisco (Be Sure to Wear Flowers in Your Hair)," written by John Phillips of the Mamas and the Papas and sung by Scott McKenzie that celebrated (and capitalized on) the moment. The highpoint of the summer occurred on the weekend of June 16–18, when the **Monterey International Pop Festival** was held at the Monterey County Fairgrounds, just south of San Francisco. This landmark event was the first major outdoor rock festival, and was a blueprint for the many that followed in the next few years, including Woodstock. Monterey was instrumental in launching the careers of Jimi Hendrix, Janis Joplin, and other Bay area bands that were 'discovered' by the major record executives who were in attendance.

The Summer of Love spawned what has become the standard-bearer of rock journalism, *Rolling Stone Magazine.* The first issue appeared on November 9, 1967 with a photo of John Lennon wearing a WWI doughboy helmet on the set of the film *How I Won the War* on the cover. The brainchild of local journalists Jann Wenner and Ralph J. Gleason, *Rolling Stone* has distinguished itself through the years as more than just a fanzine by reporting on the *culture* of rock music, as well as covering political and social issues. Part of the magazine's success has been due to the quality of its writers, which have included Cameron Crowe (now a Hollywood film producer), Ben Fong-Torres, Joe Eszterhas, and Hunter S. Thompson, among others. To be on the cover of Rolling Stone is considered such an achievement that it inspired the 1973 song "The Cover of Rolling Stone" by Dr. Hook and the Medicine Show (which earned the group a cover photo on the March 29th issue).

PROGRESSIVE ROCK RADIO

The San Francisco scene also was important in the emergence of **underground** or **progressive rock radio.** In spite of the burgeoning psychedelic music culture, the city's AM radio stations were still programming Top 40, which effectively excluded any local bands from getting airplay. Although the FM band broadcast in stereo and was of superior quality to AM, in the mid sixties it was still routinely programmed with classical music and jazz. Then in 1967, music entrepreneur and former DJ **Tom Donahue** was sitting around with his wife and friends one evening listening to Doors and Judy Collins records when he asked "Why isn't anyone playing this kind of music on the radio?" After calling a number of stations to offer his services, Donahue found San Francisco ratings cellar-dweller KMPX-FM was willing to give him a shot (the station was in such dire straights that their phone had been disconnected). On April 7, 1967 the charismatic Donahue took over the evening slot at the station and began playing an eclectic mix of blues, R&B, the Beatles, comedy, and local artists, interspersed with his unconventional low, spaced-out conversation that he backed with Indian ragas. The program proved to be such a hit that, by November, Donahue was featured in a *Rolling Stone* article and eventually became known throughout the industry as the 'Father of Free Form.' As the new format became popular across the country, it allowed many rock artists to get airplay for music that was too long, too non-commercial, or too experimental for Top 40. Although radio programmers began to replace it with tighter formatting in the early seventies, progressive rock was the format that turned FM radio into the most popular band for listening to music.

ACID ROCK

The lively music scene that developed in San Francisco in the sixties was a mirror image of the anything goes ethos of the city. Because of the association with the drug culture (especially LSD), the music became known as **acid rock** or psychedelic rock. Unlike earlier rock styles, the term acid rock really describes the music that emerged from San Francisco more than it denotes a specific set of style characteristics. Acid rock bands played a wide variety of music styles, although that is not to say that some common elements did not emerge. For one, there was an almost jazz-like approach to spontaneous improvisation that most often presented itself as extended, free form, distorted guitar solos. The lyrics were not about romantic love and relationships, but instead were more socially relevant, often critical of the establishment or extolling the virtues of altered states of consciousness or free love. Bands promoted an egalitarian image of themselves, downplaying the notion of a leader or a star within the group. Generally speaking, acid rock had a decidedly non-commercial bent that did not easily mesh with AM radio formatting. There was a noticeable lack of 45-rpm single success among the acid rock bands, although many received substantial FM airplay: for instance, the Jefferson Airplane had only two Top Forty singles in the sixties, the Grateful Dead none. The most notable exception to the lack of commercial success in AM radio among Bay area bands of the time was Creedence Clearwater Revival, whose country/pop leanings placed them somewhat outside the acid rock mold. Characteristics of acid rock and some key acid rock recordings are listed in Box 7–1.

Important San Francisco Acid Rock Performers

JEFFERSON AIRPLANE

In the spring of 1965, folksinger **Marty Balin** went about putting together a house band for the Fillmore Street folk club he managed

Box 7-1 San Francisco Acid Rock

Characteristics of San Francisco Acid Rock
1. Umbrella term encompassing a wide variety of stylistic approaches
2. Typical instrumentation: distorted electric guitar, acoustic guitar, bass, drums, piano or organ; backup singers frequently used
3. Long, free-form guitar improvisations common (hard rock influence)
4. Socially-relevant lyrics (folk influence) rather than pop-oriented songs of romance; references to drugs and their usage common
5. Communal lifestyles—bands often lived together and promoted an egalitarian image
6. Lack of commercial awareness

Key San Francisco Acid Rock Recordings
- ❏ *Surrealistic Pillow*—Jefferson Airplane, 1967
- ❏ *Cheap Thrills*—Big Brother and the Holding Company, 1968
- ❏ *American Beauty*—Grateful Dead, 1970

San Francisco Acid Rock Performers

- ❏ Jefferson Airplane
- ❏ Grateful Dead
- ❏ Big Brother and the Holding Company/Janis Joplin
- ❏ Charlatans
- ❏ Quicksilver Messenger Service
- ❏ Country Joe and the Fish
- ❏ Santana

called the Matrix. He enlisted folk musician **Paul Kantner,** blues guitarist **Jorma Kaukonen,** bassist **Jack Casady,** drummer **Skip Spence** (who was actually a guitar player), and vocalist **Signe Anderson.** Named after a friend's dog, Blind Thomas Jefferson Airplane, the group made their debut in August 1965. By the end of the year, their repertoire was evolving from folk to electric psychedelic, which helped secure a contract with RCA (making them the first Bay area acid rock band to sign with a major label). Just as their first RCA album, *Jefferson Airplane Takes Off* was about to be released in the summer of 1966, Anderson quit and moved home to Oregon to care for her newborn baby; Spence departed soon after to form the group Moby Grape. Anderson's replacement was **Grace Slick** (1939–), who had previously sung with another local group, the Great Society.

Slick brought with her a more powerful voice than Anderson, and two songs from the Great Society's repertoire, "Somebody to Love" and "White Rabbit." Both songs were included on the Airplane's second album *Surrealistic Pillow* (released in February 1967), and both hit the Top Ten that year (number 5 and number 8, respectively). In many ways these two songs capture the essence of San Francisco psychedelia: "Somebody to Love" extols the virtues of free love, while "White Rabbit," inspired by Lewis Carroll's *Adventures of Alice in Wonderland* criticizes the misguided older generation and suggests that the listener "feed your head," commonly interpreted as an invitation to take drugs. After two less successful album releases, the Airplane in 1969 released the anti-establishment manifesto *Volunteers,* which included the lyric "Up against the wall, motherfucker" in the song "We Should Be Together." By this time, the group was at its creative peak, and performed at the Monterey, Woodstock and Altamont festivals.

The seventies brought shifting personnel and several name changes. In 1970, drummer **Spencer Dryden** (who had replaced Spence) left to form New Riders of the Purple Sage, Kaukonen and Casady left to form Hot Tuna, while Slick and Kantner had a baby together. Founder Marty

Balin left in 1971. After taking some time off, in 1974 the group reformed as the Jefferson Starship, and released *Red Octopus* in 1975, which became the group's (Airplane or Starship) only number 1 album. When Kantner departed in 1984, he took the legal rights to the word, "Jefferson," so the group continued on as simply "Starship" until 1989 when Jefferson Airplane regrouped once more with nearly all the original members. In all, the various renditions of the band placed twenty-one albums in the Top Forty charts.

GRATEFUL DEAD

Although the Grateful Dead were the heart and soul of the San Francisco scene during the sixties, their legacy extended well into the nineties as one of the most consistent live performing groups in rock history. The roots of the Dead go back to 1964, when banjo player **Jerry Garcia (1942–95)**, guitarist **Bob Weir**, keyboardist **Ron "Pigpen" McKernan**, and two others formed the bluegrass band Mother McCree's Uptown Jug Champions. In 1965 they electrified, added drummer **Bill Kreutzman** and bassist **Phil Lesh**, and changed their name to the Warlocks. Before long they became the house band for Ken Kesey's acid tests, playing for the tripping participants at the all night multimedia affairs. Sometime around 1966 they again changed their name, borrowing a phrase from an Egyptian prayer that Garcia had seen in a dictionary, and moved into a house at 710 Ashbury to become the quintessential communal hippie band. The Dead's music was an eclectic mix of folk, country, bluegrass, blues, and rock—a reflection of the diverse musical backgrounds of the members. Garcia originally played bluegrass, Kreutzman and Weir were rock and rollers, Pigpen was a blues musician, while Lesh previously played classical trumpet with the Oakland Symphony. In 1967 drummer/percussionist **Mickey Hart** joined the band, bringing his interest in Native American and world music.

In 1967 the Grateful Dead signed with Warner Brothers and released three albums over the next three years. The lengthy non-commercial compositions resulted in poor record sales, however, and by 1970 the band was $100,000 in debt to the label. Despite their inability to sell records, the Dead was earning a reputation as one of the top live attractions in rock, and appeared at both the Monterey and Woodstock festivals. Their shows often lasted three hours or more, and featured long improvisational jams that regularly took them into uncharted musical waters. Initially bankrolled by the acid chemist Owsley, the group accumulated a huge twenty-three ton sound system that included over 600 speaker cabinets on stage, making them legendary for the extreme volume they produced. The band also built up the one of the most devoted following of hard core fans in rock history, known as **Deadheads**, who followed them from city to city wearing tie-dyed shirts and other hippie garb and ingesting hallucinogens, recreating the spirit of Haight-Ashbury well into the nineties.

Because of their focus on live concerts rather than record sales, the Grateful Dead had only modest success with album sales and but one hit single—1987's "Touch of Grey" (number 9). In 1970 they released two albums that are often considered to be among their best, *Working Man's Dead* and *American Beauty.* Songs from these albums, such as "Casey Jones," "Truckin'," and "Ripple" received considerable FM airplay, and became staples of their live shows. In 1989 they toured with Bob Dylan, and released the live album *Dylan and the Dead.* However, their hedonistic lifestyle was beginning to catch up with them: Pigpen, a heavy drinker, died in 1973 from liver disease; his replacement, Brent Mydland died from a drug overdose in 1990. Garcia developed diabetes, a condition that was complicated by his involvement with heroin and other drugs. He died on August 9, 1995 at California's Serenity Knolls drug treatment facility of a heart attack, effectively bringing an end to the Grateful Dead.

BIG BROTHER AND THE HOLDING COMPANY/JANIS JOPLIN

Another Bay area band that went from modest beginnings to stardom was Big Brother and the Holding Company. The band (which included **Sam Andrews** and **Jim Gurley** on guitars, **Peter Albin** on bass, and **Dave Getz** on drums) emerged from the 1965 Wednesday night jam sessions that Family Dog member Chet Helms was running out of the basement of a condemned mansion on Page Street in Haight-Ashbury. Under Helms's management, Big Brother quickly became a fixture on the local scene, performing at the Trips Festival and as the house band at the Helms produced Avalon Ballroom shows. By early 1966 however, the band felt the need for a strong lead vocalist, and Helms recommended Texas blues singer **Janis Joplin** (1943–70), whom he had met a few years earlier when she visited San Francisco. In June 1966, Joplin returned to join Big Brother.

Joplin was born in Port Arthur, Texas. She was a self-conscious loner who gravitated to music, poetry, and painting as a teen. At seventeen she ran away from home and moved to Austin where she sang in coffeehouses and became a part-time student at the University of Texas. Music emboldened her, allowing her to develop a tough as nails nonconformist persona to hide her vulnerabilities. Her singing style, inspired by blues singers Bessie Smith and Big Mama Thornton, was rough edged, gritty, and raw. With her dynamic ability to move from a barely audible whisper one moment to full tilt screaming the next, she transfixed audiences. When Big Brother performed at the Monterey Festival, they stole the show with their powerful performances. (The crew filming the festival, not knowing who they were, passed over their Saturday afternoon performance; the band agreed to perform again on Sunday evening so they could be filmed and included in the resulting documentary.) On the strength of their appearances at Monterey, the group signed with Columbia Records and released *Cheap Thrills* in the summer of 1968; the album went to number 1 where it stayed for eight weeks. The single "Piece of My Heart" from the album also charted at number 12.

Shortly thereafter, Joplin left Big Brother over her concerns about their musicianship (or lack thereof), and formed a new band, the **Kozmic Blues Band.** Although they appeared with her at Woodstock, they disbanded in January 1970 after one album release. By this time, she seemed to be getting her life in order after years of living life in the fast lane (with well-known appetites for booze, sex, and heroin). In April, Joplin assembled a new band, the **Full Tilt Boogie Band,** began work on her next album, *Pearl* (her nickname), and became engaged. However, she lapsed back into heroin addiction and on October 4, 1970 she was found dead with fresh needle marks in her arm at Hollywood's Landmark Hotel. Coming less than two weeks after the death of Jimi Hendrix, Joplin's drug overdose death was an omen to many that perhaps the self-indulgent hippie era was coming to an end.

Pearl was released posthumously and went to number 1 in early 1971. The single "Me and Bobby McGee" (written by Kris Kristofferson) also hit number 1. Two other songs from *Pearl* left chilling legacies: "Buried Alive in the Blues" is missing the vocal overdub that Joplin did not live to record, and the a cappella "Mercedes Benz," recorded three days before her death is ironically full of pain and whimsy at the same time—and is perhaps her greatest recording.

OTHER BAY AREA ACID ROCK BANDS

Even though the **Charlatans** were more or less an amateur group, they are acknowledged by many to be the first acid rock band in the Bay area. Led by visual artist **George Hunter,** the band got its start playing at the Red Dog Inn in Virginia City, Nevada in the summer of 1965, wearing cowboy outfits and long hair and performing to a sound sensitive light box. **Quicksilver Messenger Service,** formed in 1965, was on par with the Grateful Dead as a quintessential acid rock jam band. Led by guitarist **John Cipollina,** QMS was a fixture in the San Francisco ballroom scene throughout the late sixties, and recorded four albums that charted in the Top Forty between 1969 and 1971. The group is perhaps best known for the song "Fresh Air" (1970), which became an FM radio staple despite never hitting the charts. **Country Joe and the Fish,** also formed in 1965 by **Joe McDonald** and **Barry Melton,** was the most political of the Bay area bands. Originally a loose knit skiffle-type band, in 1966 the band electrified and released what was to become their most famous recording, the Vietnam protest song "Feel Like I'm Fixin' to Die Rag." The Fish appeared at Monterey and Woodstock, and their performance of "Fixin' to Die" preceded by the 'Fish Cheer' ("Give me an *F,* give me a *U,* give me a *C,* give me a *K* . . . ") is one of the highlights of the Woodstock documentary film.

One group from the San Francisco Bay area that lent a slightly different slant to the local music scene was **Santana,** led by Mexican guitar virtuoso **Carlos Santana** (1947–). Santana put together his band in 1967 from musicians that he jammed with regularly in San Francisco's Latin district. Their public debut at the Fillmore in 1968 electrified the audience and won them a spot at Woodstock, where their performance of "Soul Sacrifice" had a similar effect. In the ensuing years, the group had ten Top Forty hits, including 1970's "Evil Ways" and "Black Magic Woman" (number 9 and number 4, respectively). The Santana sound is steeped in Afro-Latin instruments and rhythms, the Hammond B-3 organ and Carlos

Santana's unique guitar styling. It is one of the few bands to reach pop superstar status without a clearly defined lead vocal identity—their popularity stems from their infectious dance rhythms and the guitar wizardry of their leader. Santana has remained one of rock's most venerable bands, and scored a dramatic comeback in 1999 with their multi-Grammy Award winning album *Supernatural.*

WOODSTOCK AND THE ERA OF THE ROCK MUSIC FESTIVAL

The psychedelic era also marked the beginning of an era when large outdoor music festivals became popular. The first of these was the Monterey Pop Festival in June 1967, which drew an audience of approximately 30,000 and was both an artistic and a financial success (with a profit of nearly $250,000). In addition, the resulting documentary film *Monterey Pop* showed the rest of the rock world just how much fun a three-day marathon of music, psychedelia, peace, and love could be. In Monterey's wake, other festivals in Palm Springs, Toronto, Los Angeles, Atlanta, and other cities were held, some of which drew upwards of 150,000 fans. Although there were occasional problems—bad drug trips, not enough restroom facilities or first aid, trouble with local authorities over the influx of longhaired youth—in large part most went off without major disruptions.

The landmark event of the festival era was the **Woodstock Music and Arts Fair,** held from August 15–18, 1969. Originally scheduled for the small artist's community in upstate New York, problems with local townsfolk forced a last minute move to Max Yasgur's farm in nearby Bethel, fifty miles away from Woodstock. Despite assurances by festival organizers that no more than 50,000 would attend, an estimated 450,000 showed up, creating a mini-nation of counter-culture youth who, for the most part, enjoyed the music and behaved themselves (and closed down the New York State Thruway with one of the worst traffic jams in history). More than thirty artists were signed, including some of the top names in the business: Jimi Hendrix, the Who, the new supergroup Crosby, Stills, Nash & Young, the Grateful Dead, Janis Joplin, and Jefferson Airplane. New groups that made stunning debuts included Sly and the Family Stone, Santana, and English blue-eyed soul singer Joe Cocker. The festival in time became an indelible icon of the hedonistic sixties peace-love generation, and a cultural bookmark of the times. The documentary film and accompanying soundtrack double album were also released to great fanfare, capturing many of the remarkable musical moments of the festival.

Although Woodstock left many with a renewed hope in the goodwill of the human spirit, much of the innocence of the entire sixties era was shattered with the disaster of the Altamont Festival outside San Francisco just four months later (discussed in chapter 6). Even if Altamont wasn't the only event that sent counter culture spirits crashing, it hit much closer to home for many in the rock audience. Woodstock performers are listed in Box 7-2.

Box 7-2 Woodstock Performers

Joan Baez	Iron Butterfuly (did not appear)
Blood, Sweat and Tears	It's a Beautiful Day (dismissed)
The Jeff Beck Group (cancelled)	Janis Joplin
The Paul Butterfield Blues Band	The Jefferson Airplane
The Band	The Joshua Light Show
Creedence Clearwater Revival	Melanie
Canned Heat	Mountain
Country Joe McDonald & The Fish	Quill
	John Sebastian
Crosby, Stills, Nash & Young	Ravi Shankar
Joe Cocker	Sly and the Family Stone
Arlo Guthrie	Bert Sommer
Grateful Dead	Santana
Tim Hardin	Sweetwater
Jimi Hendrix	Ten Years After
Richie Havens	Johnny Winter
Keep Hartley	The Who
The Incredible String Band	

The Sixties Los Angeles Psychedelic Scene

THE STRIP

Meanwhile, Los Angeles was developing its own music scene in the mid sixties. For many young people in the city, there was the same independent spirit of infinite possibilities that characterized the era. "The universe was changing," observed Ray Manzarek of the Doors, one of the many groups that emerged during this time. At the center of L.A.'s live music scene were the clubs clustered along **Sunset Strip** that increasingly turned to rock and roll to attract young affluent customers. These included the **Whisky-A-Go-Go**, the **Galaxy**, the **London Fog**, the **Unicorn**, the **Troubador, Three Experience**, the **Trip** and **Sneaky Pete's.** Amid the neon and bright lights, the Strip was almost a 24-hour party. The party atmosphere began to come apart in the summer of 1967 (the "Summer of Love" up north in San Francisco), when police began to hassle longhaired kids who gathered in the area late at night. As tensions mounted, several incidents occurred that approached riot proportions, inspiring both the film "Riot on Sunset Strip" and the song "For What It's Worth" by Buffalo Springfield ("Stop children, what's that sound/Everybody look what's going down"). By the end of the decade, things turned ugly when the zeitgeist of the Strip became more about drugs than music. Characteristics of the L.A. Psychedelic Scene and some key recordings are listed in Box 7-3.

Box 7-3 L.A. Psychedelia

The L.A. Psychedelic Scene
1. More theatrically oriented than San Francisco bands
2. Instrumentation included electric guitar, keyboards, drums, bass
3. Darker lyrics, eschewing the peace and love ethos of San Francisco bands
4. Wide variety of styles and influences

Key L.A. Psychedelic Recordings
- ❏ *Freak Out!*—Frank Zappa and the Mothers of Invention, 1966
- ❏ *The Doors*—the Doors, 1967

L.A.'s music scene was more musically diverse than San Francisco's. As an important center of the record industry, L.A. was home to a well-established pop scene that was dominated in the early sixties by Phil Spector and the Beach Boys, among others (as previously discussed in chapter 3). Whereas the San Francisco scene eschewed commercialism as part of its ethic, Los Angeles drew many musicians who specifically wanted to be part of the mainstream pop scene. Starting in 1965, Los Angeles-produced singles began to take control of the pop charts away from New York and London. That same year, the folk rock movement (discussed in chapter 8) was finding its legs with the emergence of groups like the Byrds ("Mr. Tambourine Man," number 1) and the Mamas and the Papas ("California Dreamin'," number 4).

In spite of L.A.'s proclivity to be a pop center, the city's cinematic and dramatic bent inspired a lively psychedelic scene that produced two of the most theatrical and lyrically provocative groups of the sixties, the Doors and the Mothers of Invention. Both groups eschewed the peace and love ethos of the San Francisco scene, and explored darker messages in their lyrics. Both groups also explored a wide variety of musical approaches and influences as well.

THE DOORS

The Doors were formed in 1965 after **Jim Morrison** (1943–71) recited one of his poems to fellow UCLA film student and classically trained pianist **Ray Manzarek,** who suggested the two collaborate on writing songs. Within a few months, they had a guitarist, **Robby Krieger,** a drummer, **John Densmore,** and a name, taken from Aldous Huxley's book about the hallucinogenic drug mescaline, *The Doors of Perception.* By the summer of 1966, the Doors were performing their original material at the London Fog and later at the Whisky-A-Go-Go, where they became the house band. One of their songs, "The End," contained a dramatic recitation with explicit Oedipal allusions that got the band fired from the Whisky; however, by this time, they had signed with Elektra Records. Their first album, *The Doors,* went to number 2 in the summer of 1967, powered in part by the number 1 hit single "Light My Fire." Over

The Doors

❏ Jim Morrison
❏ Ray Manzarek
❏ Robby Krieger
❏ John Densmore

Ostinato is a short, repeated musical phrase, either melodic or rhythmic.

the next four years, the group released eight albums, seven of which ended up in the Top Ten, and one more number 1 hit, 1968's "Hello, I Love You."

The handsome and sexually suggestive Morrison quickly established himself as the focal point of the Doors. As a former film student, he understood the power of the theatrical presentation of rock music. Morrison was also greatly influenced by the theatre of the absurd, a confrontational genre of theater that was emerging at the time, and adopted the Lizard King persona, a concept taken from **Julian Beck's Living Theatre.** His lyrics were poetically brilliant, yet were full of dark references to death and excess. The music of the Doors was unlike any other of the era, and perhaps in rock history. Manzarek's Vox combo organ sounds distinctively different than the Hammond organ employed by most sixties groups; Krieger's jazz-influenced guitar playing is clean, unlike the distorted sound most psychedelic guitarists preferred. One of the most unique aspects to the sound of the Doors was the trance-like **ostinato** keyboard bass parts played by Manzarek with his left hand to compensate for the lack of a bass player.

As the Doors became popular, Morrison became obsessed with inciting audiences to do whatever his whims dictated, and over time his behavior became increasingly unpredictable. He was arrested in December 1967 in New Haven, Connecticut for public obscenity, and again in 1968 for disorderly conduct aboard a plane. The low point came in March 1969 when he was arrested for lewd and lascivious behavior for "exposing his private parts and by simulating masturbation and oral copulation" during a concert in Miami. Although authorities could produce no photographs or actual witnesses of the incident, it tied Morrison and the band up in court proceedings for nearly a year and made concert promoters skittish about hiring them, lest similar incidents occur. Morrison was also becoming increasingly argumentative and aggressive from heavy drinking and taking large amounts of LSD and other drugs.

The Doors, in an undated publicity photo. Left to right: John Densmore, Robbie Krieger, Ray Manzarek, Jim Morrison.
AP/WIDE WORLD PHOTOS

Soon after the group's seventh album, *L.A. Woman* was completed in early 1971, Morrison took an extended break from the group and moved to Paris with his girlfriend Pamela Courson. On the evening of June 3, 1971, after having dinner with friends, Morrison returned to his apartment alone; Pamela later found his dead body. It was quickly sealed in a coffin and buried at the Pere-Lachaise cemetery in Paris. Because there was no autopsy and the police and doctor who arrived at the scene could not be traced, rumors have persisted that he is still alive. The mysterious circumstances surrounding his death have only served to enhance the legendary status of one of rocks most charismatic and mysterious figures.

FRANK ZAPPA/THE MOTHERS OF INVENTION

Frank Zappa (1940–93) was one of rock's most controversial musicians—and most brilliant. He was a musical anarchist who tore down musical convention and accepted norms in creating some of rocks most sophisticated and intellectual music. Unlike Jim Morrison's, Zappa's lyrics were often humorous, biting and satirical, vulgar, and sometimes downright gross. As an admirer of the absurdist traditions of avant-garde 20th century composers and artists such as Salvador Dali, his musical stylings ranged from doo wop parodies to garage band jams to jazz to avant-garde electronic. He was one of the most skilled guitarists to emerge in the sixties, yet with more than sixty albums to his credit, his virtuosity as a performer is often overshadowed by his talent as a bandleader, composer, arranger, and studio innovator.

Zappa was born in Baltimore. His father was a guitar-playing government research scientist who worked a variety of jobs that forced the family to move frequently during Frank's childhood. Eventually the Zappas scttlcd down in Lancaster, California in 1954. By this time, Frank had developed in interest in 20th century classical music after listening to records of Edgard Varese's *Ionisation* and Igor Stravinsky's *The Rite of Spring*. As he grew older, he started listening to doo wop, R&B and blues, began playing the guitar, and throughout high school played in a variety of garage bands. After high school he composed music for two low budget films and briefly flirted with college. In 1964, Zappa joined a band called the Soul Giants, which he ultimately took control of and renamed the Mothers (appropriately on Mother's Day, 1965 while playing a gig at a go-go bar in Pomona).

As they worked their way into the L.A. club circuit (including the Whisky-A-Go-Go) and began playing Zappa's original compositions, the Mothers attracted the attention of producer Tom Wilson of MGM, which led to their first record contract. The double album *Freak Out!* was released in 1966, but only after MGM insisted that the words "of Invention" be added to their name (apparently to somehow make it less offensive). *Freak Out!* is a manifesto of individual freedom and non-conformity, with lyrics that are openly critical of American society. The music ranges from electronic sci-fi to doo wop parody to an eight-minute collage of sound called "Help, I'm a Rock." The album was unlike anything that came before it, and a harbinger of things to come from Zappa. It received critical acclaim but attracted little attention from buyers.

Over the next five years, Zappa and the Mothers of Invention recorded an astounding thirteen albums. In this phase of his career, Zappa continued his sharp-tongued attacks on subjects that he viewed as contemptible: hippies, drug use, mindless conformity, pop culture, and government control. His 1967 album, *Absolutely Free,* included the song "Plastic People"; 1968's *We're Only in It for the Money* was a parody of *Sgt. Pepper's Lonely Hearts Club Band* (which sold surprisingly well, hitting number 30). He also experimented with mixing taped noise and sound effects into his music (an influence from Varese), which he used along with a 50-piece orchestra and chorus on the 1968 album *Lumpy Gravy.* By 1969 Zappa was starting to experiment with jazz/rock fusion, evident for the first time on *Uncle Meat* and coming to full fruition with the critically acclaimed *Hot Rats,* 1972's *Grand Wazoo,* in which he used a jazz big band, and the Miles Davis influenced *Waka/Jawaka.* The diversity of other music styles that Zappa was exploring was mind-boggling: 1967's *Cruising with Ruben & The Jets* consisted of doo wop parodies; *Burnt Weeny Sandwich* was mostly complex instrumentals, while *Weasels Ripped My Flesh* paid homage to free jazz musician Eric Dolphy while also including the pre-punk anthem "My Guitar Wants to Kill Your Mama."

Zappa worked on several film projects during his life, most notably 1971's *200 Motels,* a self-parody about a band playing a series of one nighters that starred Ringo Starr and Keith Moon. In addition to working on other theatrical projects, including the ill-fated science fiction stage musical *Hunchentoot,* Zappa wrote orchestral music which he performed with symphony orchestras around the world, toured extensively and released rock albums at an exhausting rate (at least twenty-one during the seventies alone). In December 1972 at a concert in London, a fan pushed Zappa into the orchestra pit, damaging his spine, fracturing his skull and crushing his larynx, which lowered his singing voice by a third of an octave. After recovering, his new baritone voice was featured in 1973's *Overnight Sensation,* which included the cult hit "Don't Eat the Yellow Snow." In 1975 the Mothers of Invention disbanded, and all future Zappa recordings were released under his name. In the eighties, Zappa started working with the **Synclavier,** a state of the art digital synthesizer that allowed him to compose and orchestrate music in the studio. Albums such as *The Perfect Stranger* (1984) and *Jazz from Hell* (1985) are innovative ventures into computer-based music. He also had one Top Forty hit, 1982's "Valley Girl," a satirical look at privileged teen airheads sung by his daughter Moon Unit. In the late eighties, Zappa attempted to thwart the many bootleggers of his live concerts by releasing a series of six two-CD sets of his live work entitled *You Can't Do That on Stage Anymore.*

In the years preceding his death, Zappa became a politically active voice against the censorship of rock lyrics. In 1985 he appeared as a dissenting voice before a Senate subcommittee inspired by the **Parents Music Resource Center** (PMRC), a group led by Tipper Gore (wife of future Vice President Al Gore) that advocated warning labels on CDs whose lyrics were determined to be offensive (see chapter 12). For a short while he also became a trade representative for the Czech Republic, named to the post by Czech President Vaclav Havel, a longtime fan. In 1991, Frank Zappa was diagnosed with the inoperable prostrate cancer from which he died in 1993.

British Blues and the Emergence of Hard Rock

MEANWHILE, ACROSS THE POND . . .

The British rock scene in the mid to late sixties was gearing up for a second assault on American shores with a sound that was harder, louder, and more blues oriented than the first invasion. Leading the pack were two guitar players that would become rock legends by the end of the decade, Eric Clapton and Jimi Hendrix. Clapton, a native son who had inspired London graffiti proclaiming, "Clapton Is God" while still barely twenty years old, grabbed the world's attention when he formed the power trio Cream in 1966. Hendrix, a transplanted American who would do nothing less than redefine guitar playing before his untimely death in 1970, was a well-kept secret in the U.S. until his appearance at the 1967 Monterey Pop Festival. Before we examine the lives of these two guitar heroes, a little background on the thriving London blues scene in the mid sixties is in order.

As mentioned in chapter 6, the British had a long-standing fascination with American music, as evidenced by the trad jazz, skiffle, and R&B fads in the forties and fifties. By the early sixties, a burgeoning blues scene was also developing in London, led by guitarist **Alex Korner** and guitar/harmonica player **Cyril Davies,** who in 1962 formed the band **Blues Incorporated.** Their 1962 LP *R&B from the Marquee,* recorded live at the famed London club, was the first ever full-length British blues album. Over the next few years, Blues Incorporated's changing lineup would include bassist Jack Bruce (later of Cream) and most of the members that would become the Rolling Stones. The band also inspired a young **John Mayall** to start his own blues group, the **Bluesbreakers** in January 1963. Like Blues Incorporated, the Bluesbreakers' lineup was constantly changing, and at one time or another included Jack Bruce, John McVie and Mick Fleetwood (later of Fleetwood Mac), Mick Taylor (later of the Stones) and Eric Clapton. During Clapton's brief tenure with the band (1965–1966), Mayall released the landmark album *Blues Breakers—John Mayall with Eric Clapton* that put the guitarist on the map and hit the Top Ten in Britain.

HARD ROCK—THE FORERUNNER TO HEAVY METAL

Blues Incorporated and the Bluesbreakers, along with British Invasion bands the Who, the Animals, and the Kinks, were influential to the emerg-

Box 7-4 Hard Rock

Characteristics of Hard Rock

1. Instrumentation: electric guitar, bass, drums; occasionally Hammond organ
2. Songs often based on blues riffs, often using power chords
3. More intense, louder, bombastic than previous rock styles
4. Guitar player emerges as the focal point of the group

Key Hard Rock Recordings

❏ *Are You Experienced?*—the Jimi Hendrix Experience, 1967
❏ *Disraeli Gears*—Cream, 1968
❏ *Electric Ladyland*—the Jimi Hendrix Experience, 1968

ing style that became known as **hard rock** or blues rock. English bands such as the Yardbirds, Cream, Deep Purple, and the Jimi Hendrix Experience, as well as American bands such as **Steppenwolf, Iron Butterfly, Grand Funk Railroad,** and **Vanilla Fudge** were among the earliest to play in this style. Hard rock songs were often based on blues riffs and power chords; the guitar is usually distorted, and all the instruments (bass, drums, guitar, and sometimes Hammond organ) are played with more intensity—louder, in other words—than previous styles. These bands also tended to include blues-based guitar solos, which were often of extended length. Because of these characteristics, hard rock is considered to be the forerunner to heavy metal of the seventies. Some characteristics of hard rock and some key recordings are listed in Box 7-4.

ERIC CLAPTON/CREAM

Throughout his forty-year career, Eric Clapton (1945–) has established himself as one of rock's premier guitarists while performing in a variety of different groups and musical settings. Although he has become a pop icon as the leader of several commercially successful bands and has written a number of pop hits, he has never strayed far from his true calling— playing the blues. Clapton had a rocky childhood, having been raised by his grandparents after his mother abandoned him in his infancy. As a teen, he attended art school for a brief time, but turned his attention to music and the guitar after being expelled for poor grades. From the beginning, Clapton was drawn to American blues and R&B while immersing himself in the records of Robert Johnson, B. B. King, Muddy Waters, and Chuck Berry. In October 1963 he joined the Yardbirds, an up and coming R&B cover band with a growing following. Soon after Clapton joined, the Yardbirds' replaced the Rolling Stones as the house band at the Crawdaddy Club. As the Yardbirds audience began to expand, there was growing sentiment from within the band to pursue a more pop-oriented direction as many other British R&B bands had successfully done. As they moved away from the blues and R&B toward psychedelic pop, Clapton grew increasingly dissatisfied, and eventually quit in March 1965. Just as the Yardbirds finally made a breakthrough on to the pop charts with "For Your Love" (number 6 U.K.), Eric Clapton was laboring as a construction worker.

His construction career did not last long, however—in late spring, John Mayall asked Clapton to join the Bluesbreakers. Although he only stayed with the band for slightly over a year, during his tenure, Clapton established himself as Britain's premier blues guitarist and developed a devoted cult following. In July 1966 he left Mayall and formed the seminal hard rock power trio Cream with bassist **Jack Bruce** and drummer **Ginger Baker.** Clapton had played with Bruce and Baker at informal jam sessions, and although the two did not personally get along, they agreed to put their differences aside for the sake of the group. After their debut at the 1966 Windsor Jazz and Blues Festival, Cream concerts became renowned for their high volume extended blues jams. Audiences in the U.S. seemed to especially like this aspect of their shows: "When we saw that in America they actually wanted us to play a number for a whole hour—one number—we just stretched it," Clapton later said.

Cream became immensely popular in both the U.K. and America, eventually selling fifteen million records. After their first album *Fresh Cream* failed to chart, their second, *Disraeli Gears* went to number 4, propelled by the hit single "Sunshine of You Love" (number 5, 1968). The song is a 24 bar blues based on one of the most memorable blues riffs in all of rock. Clapton's guitar solo is a masterpiece of lyricism and understatement. The groups next LP, *Wheels of Fire,* was a live/studio double album partially recorded at the Fillmore Ballroom, which contained the hit "White Room" (number 6, 1968) and an inspired electric cover of Robert Johnson's "Cross Road Blues" entitled "Crossroads." However, by mid 1968 the fragile Bruce/Baker truce was beginning to unravel, and Clapton was becoming increasingly tormented by the pressures of being a guitar idol. At the height of their popularity, Cream disbanded after giving a farewell concert at the Royal Albert Hall on November 26, 1968. The final album *Goodbye Cream,* which included the Clapton/George Harrison effort "Badge," was released early the next year, and went to number 2 in the U.S.

Clapton's life and career was on a roller coaster of change over the next several years. His first musical endeavor was the so-called 'supergroup,' **Blind Faith,** which included Baker again on drums, **Rick Gretch** on bass and violin, and blue-eyed soul singer/keyboard player **Stevie Winwood,** who had become popular with the Spencer Davis Group and Traffic. Despite a successful concert tour and a self-titled number 1 album, Clapton quit after six months. In 1970, he released two solo albums, *Eric Clapton* and *Layla and Other Assorted Love Songs. Layla* was released under the pseudonym Derek and the Dominoes, a short-lived group made up of studio musicians Jim Gordon, Carl Radle, Bobby Whitlock and **Duane Allman** of the Allman Brothers Band on guitar. The title song, written about Clapton's unrequited love for George Harrison's wife Patti (who would later leave Harrison and marry Clapton), is one of rock's greatest anthems, with soaring guitar work by Clapton and Allman and a beautiful extended coda written by drummer Gordon. Despite an amazing string of popular successes and a standing in the rock world that was approaching legend-in-his-own-time status,

Clapton sunk into several years of heroin addiction and alcohol abuse. By the time he released the number 1 selling *461 Ocean Boulevard* in 1974, he was on the road to recovery, and for the first time was comfortable with his status as a pop star. Although his recent years have had rocky moments, most notably the tragic death of his son Conor in 1991, Clapton has emerged remarkably healthy from his troubles, with two more number 1 albums in the nineties and thirteen Top Forty hits since 1974's number 1 single "I Shot the Sheriff."

JIMI HENDRIX

Although Jimi Hendrix (1942–1970) was only an international superstar for less than four years, in that time he expanded the sonic possibilities of the electric guitar as well as redefined the relationship between music and noise with his startling use of feedback and other guitar effects. In addition to establishing himself as perhaps the most innovative guitarist in history, he became the premier showman and studio technician of his generation. Although his musical universe included electric psychedelia, jazz, hard rock, R&B and folk, his music was always deeply rooted in the blues. When he died in 1970 at age twenty-seven, Jimi Hendrix left a profound legacy that is still highly influential to musicians of all stripes.

He was born in Seattle as John Allen Hendrix. John's childhood was unsettled—his father was away at war in his early years, his mother abandoned the family when he was ten. He taught himself to play the guitar from listening to his father's jazz and blues records, and by fifteen he was playing in cover bands in Seattle area clubs. In 1959 Hendrix joined the army and served in the 101st Airborne as a paratrooper at Fort Bragg, North Carolina. After a medical discharge in 1962 from an ankle broken during a jump, John moved to Nashville and started to get work in the city's club scene as a rhythm guitarist. Working under the name Jimmy James, he became a sought after sideman, working in the bands of Little Richard, Sam Cooke, B. B. King, Wilson Pickett, and the Isley Brothers. In 1964, he moved to New York City, where his show-stopping performances with his band Jimmy James and the Blue Flames began to attract the attention of the city's rock elite. It was while playing at Greenwich Village's Café Wha? in early 1966 that Hendrix was heard by Chas Chandler of the Animals, who advised him that he would become a star if he moved to England and let Chandler be his manager. In September, Hendrix left New York for London.

ARE YOU EXPERIENCED?

In England, Hendrix quickly made the rounds and was introduced to the Beatles, Eric Clapton, Pete Townshend, and others in the London rock scene. Seeking a power trio format as a working band, he and Chandler put together the **Jimi Hendrix Experience** with **Mitch Mitchell** on drums and **Noel Redding** on bass. After playing their debut gig at Paris's Olympia Theatre in October, the trio recorded their first single, "Hey Joe," which hit number 6 on the U.K. charts in January 1967. Two more singles followed in quick succession, "Purple Haze" (number 3) and "The Wind Cries Mary" (number 6), which combined with appearances on national TV, made sensations out of Hendrix and the group. In May 1967, these singles and fourteen other Hendrix originals were released on astonishing debut album *Are You Experienced?* The LP is perhaps the definitive artistic statement of the psychedelic era, and a stunning showcase for Hendrix the guitarist, composer, and studio experimentalist. The musical styles cover jazz jams ("Third Stone from the Sun," "Manic Depression"), Dylan-influenced electric folk ("The Wind Cries Mary"), hard rock ("Purple Haze," "Fire"), the blues ("Red House") and

Although Jimi Hendrix was only an international superstar for less than four years, in that time he expanded the sonic possibilities of the electric guitar as well as redefined the relationship between music and noise with his use of feedback and guitar effects.
AP/WIDE WORLD PHOTOS

Beatles-influenced psychedelia ("Are You Experienced"). Hendrix also makes innovative use of spoken poetry, backward tapes, occasional Dylanesque 'talking blues' style vocals, and an array of guitar-produced sound effects, along with his distinctive use of feedback and noise. Redding and particularly Mitchell also make substantial contributions with powerful supporting roles. Mitchell's frenetic drumming reflects an influence from jazz drummer Elvin Jones as well as carrying on the tradition of powerhouse English drummers such as Keith Moon and Ginger Baker. The album was a hit in the U.K., going to number 2.

As a live performer, Hendrix is perhaps unparalleled to this day. A left-handed guitarist, he played the Fender Stratocaster upside down, strung in reverse order. He played it behind his back, over his head, and with his teeth, techniques that had not been used since T-Bone Walker in the forties. His startling feedback effects were created with an array of processing pedals, including a Vox wah-wah, a Fuzz Face (for distortion) and a Univox Univibe (for a phasing effect). He also played with incredible volume produced by stacking English made Marshall amplifiers on top of each other—the 'Marshall stack.'

COMING TO AMERICA

Even though he was becoming a star in England, Hendrix was still pretty much of a stranger in his native America until his June 1967 performance at the Monterey Pop Festival. Performing on the last night of the festival before final act the Mamas and the Papas, the Experience played an electrifying show of six songs that concluded with a slow, hard rock version of the Troggs' "Wild Thing." Watching "Wild Thing" (it is included in the documentary film of the festival), one gets to see the complete Hendrix package: coaxing feedback out of his guitar, playing it behind his back, using it as a phallic symbol, and ultimately setting it on fire and smashing it. Even though the performance got mixed reviews from critics, it put Jimi Hendrix on the map in America. *Are You Experienced?* went to number 5 on the U.S. charts, and the Experience began their first tour of the U.S. as the unlikely warm up band for the Monkees (they were quickly dropped, however, as the band was too psychedelic for the Monkees audience).

The year 1968 saw Hendrix busy releasing two new albums, touring extensively, and beginning construction on his dream studio in New York City, **Electric Ladyland.** The albums *Axis: Bold as Love,* released in February, and *Electric Ladyland,* released in November were commercial successes, hitting number 3 and number 1, respectively. The critics, who were divided on the merits of *Are You Experienced?* were coming around as well: *Rolling Stone* reviewer Jon Landau called for Hendrix to win the magazine's Performer of the Year Award for *Electric Ladyland. Axis: Bold As Love* contained a cover of Bob Dylan's "All Along the Watchtower" that has become *the* definitive version (Dylan himself adopted this version for his live shows).

In 1969, Redding and Mitchell tired of the road and returned to England, and in May Jimi was arrested in Toronto for possession of heroin, a charge that was later dismissed. The highlight of the year came at Woodstock where, with a loosely organized band called the Electric Sky Church, Hendrix performed his now legendary version of "The Star Spangled Banner" as the festival's headline act. (Because the Sunday night program, which Hendrix was supposed to close, ran long, his performance took place on Monday morning in front of just a few thousand fans.) On New Year's Eve, he played New York's Fillmore East Ballroom with a new trio, the Band of Gypsys, consisting of **Billy Cox,** an old army buddy on bass and **Buddy Miles** on drums, a band mate from the Wilson Pickett days. The concert was recorded and released on the May 1970 album *Band of Gypsys.*

In 1970, Hendrix saw his studio finally completed, Mitchell's return on drums, and his last self-authorized album recorded, *Cry of Love.* He also made plans to record with jazz/rock fusion pioneer Miles Davis. Unfortunately, he was using increasingly large quantities of alcohol and drugs, and while in England on the morning of September 18, he died "as a result of an inhalation of vomit due to barbiturate poisoning"—an overdose of sleeping pills. He was brought back to the U.S. and buried in Seattle. Hendrix' last concert was in August at the Isle of Wight Festival in England.

Chapter 7
Study Questions

1. What were some of the social issues that led to the formation of a youth counterculture in the sixties?

   _____

   _____

   _____

   _____

2. How and why did San Francisco give birth to the hippie movement?

   _____

   _____

   _____

   _____

3. What were some of the events and cultural trappings that resulted from the San Francisco scene and the Summer of Love?

   _____

   _____

   _____

4. What were some of the musical and non-musical influences on acid rock?

   _____

   _____

   _____

5. Name some similarities and differences between the early careers of the Jefferson Airplane and the Grateful Dead.

   _____

   _____

   _____

6. What were some of the differences between the psychedelic scenes in San Francisco and Los Angeles?

_____

_____

_____

_____

_____

7. Describe some of the reasons that the Doors sound was unique.

_____

_____

_____

_____

8. Describe some of the different music styles that Frank Zappa experimented with and the albums that they are found on.

_____

_____

_____

_____

9. What were some of the hallmarks of Cream's sound, and why did they break up after such a short existence?

_____

_____

_____

_____

10. Name three reasons why *Are You Experienced?* is considered to be a landmark album.

_____

_____

_____

_____

Changing Directions

The Seventies

THE CHANGING LANDSCAPE

As the nation entered the seventies, the cultural landscape seemed once again to be changing. Turmoil had seemingly reigned for the last several years, casting a dark cloud over the optimism and hope of the early sixties. The assassinations of Dr. Martin Luther King and Senator Robert Kennedy in 1968 had certainly thrown their share of cold water on any momentum that had been gained by the anti-war and civil rights movements. In November 1968, Republican candidate Richard M. Nixon, who campaigned on a promise of bringing an end to the Vietnam War, was elected President. However, many young people viewed Nixon with suspicion, and their fears seemed to be justified when he ordered the invasion of Cambodia by U.S. troops in 1970—an obvious expansion of the war. In response, protests broke out on college campuses all over the country. Nixon would continue to be a provocateur throughout his presidency, polarizing the young and old, liberals and conservatives, political agitators and the so-called 'silent majority.'

Rock was going through a similar rite of passage. Chief among the events that defined a new sense of reality (or was it pessimism?) were the deaths of Jimi Hendrix, Janis Joplin, and Jim Morrison from drug overdoses within a span of nine months; the tragedy at Altamont in December 1969 which seemed to kill the momentum of Monterey and Woodstock; and the breakup of the Beatles in late 1969. Haight-Ashbury and L.A.'s Sunset Strip turned ugly and violent, sure signs that there was a definite downside to the drug culture. The cumulative effect of all this mayhem was to numb much of the rock audience into retreat and reevaluation, at least for the time being.

FRAGMENTATION

For a variety of reasons, rock was also beginning to fragment into a number of different styles and musical paths by the seventies. Rock had matured significantly during the sixties, and the pursuit of different paths of expression is a natural part of the growing process of any art form, which rock had indeed become. Through the leadership of Beatles and others at the creative vanguard, musicians had witnessed the expansion of rocks musical boundaries, and many were ready to begin pursuing their own musical paths. The breakup of the Beatles actually encouraged the fragmentation of rock, as there was no longer a clear-cut leader for musicians to line up behind and follow. The rock audience had also expanded tremendously during the sixties, and by 1970 rock was no longer the music of the counterculture, but the music of the mainstream culture. This larger audience, which now cut across two generations, was itself much more diverse and fragmented, and also willing to accept a number of different forms of expression within the rock context.

The radio and record industries also contributed to the fragmentation. Late sixties progressive rock radio, with its free form, anything goes programming, was by 1970 deemed too haphazard and inefficient; radio executives began to tightly format their stations to target specific segments of the audience. These new formats included soft rock (target group: women), urban contemporary (blacks), oldies (mature adults), and AOR, or album-oriented rock (young white males). The expanded rock audience was also buying more records: in the early seventies the record industry was growing at an astounding twenty-five percent a year. A million seller was no longer a benchmark—the biggest selling records were now expected to go platinum or even multi-platinum. Like the radio industry, record companies also bought into the strategy of marketing rock as a *product,* and assigned user friendly labels to the newly emerging music styles: folk rock, singer/songwriters, country rock, soft rock, art rock, and so on.

This chapter will examine the new mainstream pop styles and artists that began emerging in the late sixties and early seventies that changed the face of the rock world. Other styles that emerged in the seventies will be covered in later chapters: heavy metal and art rock in chapter 9; funk, jazz/rock fusion and disco in chapter 10; and punk in chapter 11.

Folk Rock

The Dylan Influence

Folk rock actually had its beginnings well before the onset of the seventies, and, in reality, many of the genres pioneering groups had already disbanded by that time. As discussed in chapter 4, Bob Dylan's first experiments into combining the folk philosophy with rock occurred as early as 1964 with his *Bringing It All Back Home* LP. From there the movement took off: in June 1965 the Byrds had the first folk rock number 1 hit with Dylan's "Mr. Tambourine Man"; a month later Dylan made his infamous appearance at the Newport Folk Festival with the Paul Butterfield Blues Band. Later that year, Dylan released *Highway 61 Revisited,* which included the number 2 single "Like a Rolling Stone," and in December Simon and Garfunkel's "The Sounds of Silence," a folk song with an overdubbed rhythm section went to number 1. Although the folk community vilified Dylan for abandoning traditional folk and "selling out," folk rock caught on. The late sixties and early seventies saw the emergence of a number of other popular folk rock groups that helped further define the style, including Buffalo Springfield, the Nitty Gritty Dirt Band, the Mamas and the Papas, the Lovin' Spoonful, and Crosby, Stills, Nash & Young. Some characteristics of Folk Rock and some key folk rock recordings are listed in Box 8-1.

Folk rock combines the essential elements of folk music—socially relevant lyrics, strumming guitars and a softer manner—with the electric instruments of rock. The style can also be identified by its emphasis on beautiful choral singing, which often includes three and four-part harmonies. Many of the important groups emerged from the burgeoning music scene in Los Angeles, including the band that, perhaps more than any, pioneered the new style, the Byrds.

Box 8-1   Folk Rock

Characteristics of Folk Rock
1. Commercial pop oriented, combining elements of rock and folk
2. Instrumentation built around strumming acoustic guitar with rock rhythm section
3. Generally softer dynamics
4. Emphasis on rich choral vocal harmonies, often three and four part
5. Emphasis on lyric story lines, which could include romantic love, social or political themes, traditional folk songs, etc.

Key Folk Rock Recordings
- ❏ *Bringing It All Back Home*—Bob Dylan, 1964
- ❏ *Mr. Tambourine Man*—the Byrds, 1965
- ❏ "For What It's Worth"—Buffalo Springfield, 1967
- ❏ *Bridge over Troubled Water*—Simon and Garfunkel, 1970
- ❏ *Déjà Vu*—Crosby, Stills, Nash and Young, 1970

THE BYRDS

The Byrds

- ❏ Roger McGuinn
- ❏ Gene Clark
- ❏ David Crosby
- ❏ Chris Hillman
- ❏ Michael Clark

The Byrds were led by **Roger McGuinn,** a singer/guitarist from Chicago who had worked with Limeliters, the Chad Mitchell Trio, and Judy Collins before embarking on a solo career in early 1964. That summer he met New Christy Minstrel singer/guitarist **Gene Clark** in Los Angeles, and the two decided to start a group. They soon added to the roster singer/guitarist **David Crosby,** bass player **Chris Hillman,** and drummer **Michael Clark.** After rehearsing for a few months as the Jet Set and then as the Beefeaters, in November they signed with Columbia Records and changed their name to the Byrds (misspelled purposely as homage to the Beatles). In January 1965, they were introduced to Bob Dylan, and with his endorsement, the band recorded "Mr. Tambourine Man." By smoothing out the rough edges of Dylan's original version with beautiful vocal harmonies and adding a rock rhythm section (mostly L.A. studio musicians), the group further defined the folk rock style. "Mr. Tambourine Man" went to number 1 in June. Interestingly, it was McGuinn's prominently featured Rickenbacker electric 12-string guitar and not the group's vocals that was their most distinctive feature.

In November 1965 the Byrds scored their second and last number 1 hit, "Turn! Turn! Turn! (To Everything There Is a Season)," a song whose lyrics were adapted from Ecclesiastics with a melody written by Pete Seeger. Their last Top Twenty hit came in early 1966 with "Eight Miles High" (number 14), a song which probably would have charted even higher if not for being blacklisted by many radio stations for supposedly having drug references (even though the group insisted the title referred to writing the song while flying over the Atlantic Ocean). The song and the LP *Fifth Dimension* from which it came represented something of a style change for the group, moving away from folk rock and toward avant-garde psychedelia. Unfortunately, *Fifth Dimension* was not well received by the general public; meanwhile the group began to fall apart.

Gene Clark left in 1966, followed in 1967 by David Crosby, who had argued frequently with McGuinn. By 1968, the remaining Byrds underwent another style change with *Sweethearts of the Rodeo,* a pioneering country rock album recorded in Nashville. However, it and subsequent albums did not sell well, and the group sputtered along without much success until finally disbanding in 1973.

SIMON AND GARFUNKEL

Paul Simon (1941-) and **Art Garfunkel** (1941-) first got to know each other as classmates in the sixth grade in Forest Hills, New York. Singing together as the folk duo Tom and Jerry throughout their schooldays, they recorded a single called "Hey, Schoolgirl" in 1957 which went to number 49 and earned them an appearance on *American Bandstand.* After their next records flopped, both went off to college, Garfunkel to study architecture and Simon to study English literature. In 1962 they reunited and began working the Greenwich Village folk club scene. Around this time Simon took one of his originals to Columbia Records producer Tom Wilson (Bob Dylan's producer at the time), who bought the song and signed the duo. The resulting album, *Wednesday Morning, Three A.M.,* a combination of traditional folk songs, Simon originals, and Dylan covers, went nowhere. Once again, the two went their separate ways, with Simon moving to England to try to get his career back on track.

Meanwhile, sensing a trend was afoot with the successes of "Mr. Tambourine Man" and "Like a Rolling Stone," Columbia's Wilson took one of the songs from *Wednesday Morning, Three A.M.,* "The Sound of Silence," and added a rock rhythm section and electric guitar without Simon or Garfunkel's knowledge. The results were stunning: within six months it was the number 1 song in the country (December 1965). Simon immediately returned from England and reunited with Garfunkel to go on a college campus tour and record a new album in the folk rock vein. In 1966 the duo placed five singles and three albums in the Top Thirty, including the Top Five hits "Homeward Bound" (number 5) and "I Am a Rock" (number 3). Although their two voices blended perfectly, the real magic in the group came from Simon's songwriting, which mixed pop-oriented melodies with intelligent and relevant lyrics that appealed to a wide audience base. However, after their initial success, Simon's output slowed and the duo did not have another major hit until 1968 when the soundtrack album from the film *The Graduate* and its single release "Mrs. Robinson" both went to number 1. *The Graduate* was followed by *Bookends,* which also went to number 1 (the two albums occupied the top spot on the charts for a combined sixteen weeks). In 1970, after another two-year drought, Simon and Garfunkel released *Bridge over Troubled Water,* which also went to number 1 (for ten weeks), contained the hit singles "The Boxer" (number 7) and "Bridge over Troubled Waters" (number 1) and won the 1970 Grammy for Album of the Year.

Bridge over Troubled Water would be Simon and Garfunkel's last album. Garfunkel began an acting career that included roles in *Catch 22* and *Carnal Knowledge,* while Simon released his eponymous first solo album in 1972. Simon's solo career was in many ways more adventurous

Crosby, Stills, and Nash. From left to right: Stephen Stills, David Crosby and Graham Nash.
Courtesy Lincoln Journal Star Library

and successful than his work with Garfunkel, with nine Top Forty album releases, including 1975's *Still Crazy After All These Years* and 1986's *Graceland,* both of which won Grammy Awards. 1986's *Graceland* was recorded using the South African vocal group Ladysmith Black Mambazo, the Everly Brothers, and Los Lobos, and was important in launching a new awareness of world music.

CROSBY, STILLS, NASH AND YOUNG

Supergroup Crosby, Stills, Nash and Young, perhaps the most influential folk rock band, was formed by four of the movement's most talented and decorated singers and songwriters. Their intricately crafted high four part harmonies are among the most distinctive of the genre. In May 1968, former Byrd **David Crosby** (1941–) began jamming with **Stephen Stills** (1945–) of the recently disbanded Buffalo Springfield; they were soon joined by **Graham Nash** (1942–), a former member of the English group the Hollies. Their first LP, *Crosby, Stills & Nash,* recorded in early 1969, went to number 6 and contained two minor hits, "Marrakesh Express" and "Suite: Judy Blue Eyes" (which Stills wrote for singer Judy Collins). Canadian singer/songwriter **Neil Young** (1945–), also formerly of Buffalo Springfield, joined the band in time for their summer tour, which included a performance at Woodstock. In early 1970, CSN&Y released what is perhaps their finest recording, *Déjà Vu,* which went to number 1 on advance orders of two million copies. The album also contained two hit singles, "Woodstock" (written by Joni Mitchell, number 11) and "Teach Your Children" (number 16). *Déjà Vu* features songs written by each of the members that encompass a wide assortment of musical influences, including acoustic folk, hard rock, country, and pop.

Soon after the release of *Déjà Vu,* the Kent State massacre inspired Young to write "Ohio" ("Tin soldiers and Nixon's comin'/We're finally on our own/Last summer I heard the drumming/Four dead in Ohio"), a number 14 single release. Young later reflected on the song: "It's still hard to believe I had to write this song. It's ironic that I capitalized on the death of these American students. Probably the biggest lesson ever learned at an American place of learning. My best CSN&Y effort. Recorded totally live in Los Angeles. David Crosby cried after this take." The group toured again in the summer of 1970, but afterward broke up due to internal conflicts (Stills and Young had a history of feuding going back to their days in Buffalo Springfield). A live album from the tour, *Four Way Street* was released in 1971, and like *Déjà Vu,* went to number 1. A brief reunion tour in 1974 resulted in their third straight number 1 LP, a greatest hits compilation entitled *So Far.* Since 1977, the group has reunited from time to time without Young and has released three Top Twenty albums as well as three Top Twenty singles.

OTHER FOLK ROCK ARTISTS

One of the earliest and shortest lived folk rock groups was **Buffalo Springfield,** which proved to be a springboard to later success for many of the groups members. Formed in Los Angeles in 1966, the group included singer/guitarists Stephen Stills and Neil Young (later of CSN&Y), **Richie Furay** (later of Poco), drummer **Dewey Martin,** and bassist **Bruce Palmer.** Martin, Palmer, and Young were all native Canadians. Later, bassists **Jim Fielder** (later of Blood Sweat and Tears) and **Jim Messina** (later of Poco and Loggins and Messina) joined the band. The group signed a contract with Atlantic late in 1966 after serving as the house band at the Whiskey-a-Go-Go and touring with the Byrds. Their eponymous first LP, released in 1967, contained Buffalo Springfield's only hit single, "For What It's Worth," written by Stills about the Sunset Strip 'riots' of 1967 (see chapter 7). In spite of the obvious talent and success of the group, they disbanded in May 1968 after four albums due to inner tensions.

Two important folk rock groups emerged from the Greenwich Village folk scene in 1965. **The Lovin' Spoonful** was led by singer/guitarist **John Sebastian,** who along with guitarist Zal Yanovsky had previously been with the Mugwumps (with future Mamas and Papas members Mama Cass Elliot and Denny Doherty). In their short three-year existence, the group released ten Top Forty singles, including 1966's "Daydream," "Did You Ever Have to Make Up Your Mind" (both number 2), and "Summer in the City" (number 1), and supplied the soundtracks to Francis Ford Coppola's *You're a Big Boy Now* and Woody Allen's *What's Up, Tiger Lily?* After the group broke up in 1968, the quintessential hippie Sebastian appeared at Woodstock as a solo act and later wrote the theme to the TV show *Welcome Back, Kotter.* **The Mamas and the Papas** were made up of **Denny Doherty, 'Mama' Cass Elliot,** and husband and wife **John Phillips** and **Michelle Phillips,** all regulars in the New York folk scene. Originally known as the New Journeymen, the group moved to the Virgin Islands to rehearse new material before relocating in Southern California. After serving as backup vocalists in recording sessions, the group signed with Dunhill in 1966 and changed their name to the Mamas and the Papas. Between 1966 and 1968, the group released five albums and ten Top Twenty singles, including 1966's number 1 "Monday, Monday" and 1967's number 2 "Dedicated to the One I Love." The group was known for their strong four part multi-tracked vocals and their good time hippie look. However, by 1968 the Phillips' were having marital problems, which ultimately contributed to the group disbanding. Elliot died of a heart condition in 1974. John Phillips wrote a number of hit songs (including most of the M&P's) before his death in 2001, including Scott McKenzie's 1967 number 4 hit "San Francisco (Be Sure to Wear Flowers in Your Hair)" and the Beach Boys 1988 number 1 hit "Kokomo." The Phillips' had three daughters, including actress McKenzie (TV's *One Day at a Time*) and singer Chynna of the group Wilson Phillips.

Singer/Songwriters

THE DYLAN INFLUENCE (AGAIN!)

By the end of the sixties, a new breed of performers was beginning to emerge who collectively became known as the **singer/songwriters.** Performers that wrote and sang their own songs were not new to rock: Chuck Berry, Buddy Holly, John Lennon, Paul McCartney, Paul Simon, and John Phillips all fit that description. But these men were all identified with the groups that played their songs; the new breed of songpoets were soloists who did not work in the context of an established band. The only rock artist who had established himself as a solo singer/songwriter in rock up to this time was Bob Dylan, which was of course due to his folk background. In fact, the singer/songwriters of the late sixties and early seventies might have been called folkies ten years earlier, but this was a new era where labeling products was essential to the industry. In any event, Dylan's influence manifests itself once again.

Although the sixties were a time of communal thought, sharing, and a spirit of working together to change society, by the seventies many people were ready for a moment of introspection and reflection, with a focus on bettering themselves. This attitude was widespread enough that many observers began calling the seventies the 'me first' decade. The singer/songwriters reflected this mood, and tended to write about themselves rather than socially conscious issues, as the earlier folkies would have done. The personal and confessional themes of these songs—along with a soft, slow, and soothing musical context—connected with the maturing rock audience. Pianos and acoustic guitars became essential instruments. And, for the first time in rock, women performers and their perspectives became important voices, no doubt due at least in part by the concurrent rise of the feminist movement. Some characteristics of the Singer/Songwriters and some key recordings are listed in Box 8–2.

Box 8-2 Singer/Songwriters

Characteristics of the Singer/Songwriters
1. Solo artists who recorded and performed with backup bands
2. Personal, confessional, reflective, narcissistic lyrics
3. Soft, soothing music, with acoustic pianos and acoustic guitars prominent
4. Willingness to experiment with influences from a variety of styles, including jazz, R&B, folk, etc.
5. Important outlet for women performers and their viewpoints

Key Singer/Songwriter Recordings
❑ *Astral Weeks*—Van Morrison, 1968
❑ *Sweet Baby James*—James Taylor, 1970
❑ *Blue*—Joni Mitchell, 1971
❑ *Tapestry*—Carole King, 1971

Beyond those general guidelines, the singer/songwriter designation is a broadly based catchall term, as these performers were also willing to experiment with a wide range of musical influences, including jazz, folk and R&B. Even though many critics hated the singer/songwriters and what they represented (one critic even slashed a poster of James Taylor into bits and wrote about it), in many ways they perfectly reflected the mood of the industry and the country at the end of the sixties, one of the most turbulent decades in our history.

VAN MORRISON

The career of George Ivan Morrison (1945–) has been chameleon-like, ranging from writing enigmatic song stories to poignant love songs to enduring Top Ten classics. His soulful, quirky vocal style and intelligent lyricism have been widely copied, while he in turn has been influenced by a wide range of styles including folk, jazz, soul, and the blues. Morrison was born and raised in a working class family in Belfast, Northern Ireland. At sixteen he quit school to tour Europe for a year with an R&B band; when he returned he formed the group **Them,** which secured a steady gig as the house band at Belfast's Maritime Hotel. Cut in the mold of the Rolling Stones and the Animals, Them became extremely popular in Ireland playing rough R&B influenced rock. In 1964 the group moved to London where they released two albums, the number 2 U.K. single "Here Comes the Night" and Morrison's classic "Gloria" before breaking up in 1966. In 1967 Morrison returned to Belfast before moving to New York, where he signed with Bang Records, who against his wishes released his first solo LP, the bleak and confusing *Blowin' Your Mind.* Despite the fact that the album contained the number 10 hit single "Brown Eyed Girl," it sold poorly and Morrison retreated back to Belfast.

He rebounded quickly. In 1968 Morrison returned to New York and signed with the newly formed Warner Brothers label and in November released one of the most innovative and influential albums of the singer/songwriter genre, *Astral Weeks*. The album is not your typical rock and roll record; in fact, Morrison used a jazz rhythm section (noted session men Richard Davis on bass, Connie Kaye on drums and Jay Berliner on guitar), a vibraphonist, woodwinds, and string quartet to create a jazz/folk/blues/classical hybrid. Recorded in only two days, *Astral Weeks* is an enduring masterpiece that the critics loved; unfortunately, once again sales were poor. Morrison's commercial fortunes began to turn in the early seventies with the release of five albums in four years that cracked the Top Forty *(Moondance, His Band and the Street Choir, Tupelo Honey, Saint Dominic's Preview* and *Hard Nose the Highway)*, and his highest charting single in late 1970 with "Domino" (number 9). Morrison continues to record and tour despite suffering from severe stage fright. Many of his songs have also been covered by other artists, including "Have I Told You Lately That I Love You," a number 5 hit for Rod Stewart in 1993 and "Wild Night," a number 3 hit for John Mellencamp in 1994.

JONI MITCHELL

Perhaps even more than Van Morrison, Joni Mitchell (1943–) has been a restless seeker of musical experimentation throughout her career. Using her beautiful, soprano voice and the Dylanesque technique of using almost too many words in a phrase, Mitchell tells song stories in an intriguing and often subtly humorous manner. She was born Roberta Joan Anderson in Alberta, Canada. After contracting polio at age nine, she

Using her beautiful, soprano voice and the Dylanesque technique of using almost too many words in a phrase, Joni Mitchell tells song stories in an intriguing and often subtly humorous manner. AP/WIDE WORLD PHOTOS

leaned to play guitar and sing while recuperating at a children's hospital. Later, she became a fixture in the local coffeehouse scene and married fellow folksinger Chuck Mitchell in 1965, with whom she moved to Detroit the next year (they divorced soon afterward). Mitchell quickly became a hit in the Motor City, which led to a number of engagements in New York and a contract with Reprise Records in 1967. Her 1968 self-titled debut LP was produced by David Crosby and sold respectfully, while her next, 1969's *Clouds* sold even better, going to number 31. Mitchell's career at this juncture was enhanced by other established artists' recordings of her songs, including Judy

Collins' version of "Both Sides, Now" (number 8, 1968) and Tom Rush's version of "The Circle Game."

In 1970 Mitchell finally broke through to commercial success with the platinum selling *Ladies of the Canyon,* which included "Woodstock," a song that Crosby, Stills, Nash & Young turned into a number 11 hit. The next year she released the masterpiece *Blue,* which firmly established her as one of pop's most gifted artists. Winning praise from both critics and the public (hitting number 15), *Blue* contains painfully confessional lyrics, encompasses an array of musical influences as well as performances by James Taylor and Stephen Stills. Subsequent albums have sold well, despite her shifting musical explorations. Among the most noteworthy were *The Hissing of Summer Lawns,* with its African rhythmic influences and *Mingus,* a collaboration with jazz bassist Charles Mingus, who died before the album's release. Mitchell has also had a sprinkling of Top Forty hits, including 1974's "Help Me" (number 7).

JAMES TAYLOR

Boston born James Taylor's (1948–) life has certainly seen its ups and downs, but he has managed to persevere and become a successful and often imitated star. He is known as the quintessential sensitive soft rock performer, although he has worked in a variety of musical settings that belie that reputation. Taylor began writing songs after being admitted to a mental institution as a teen. Upon his discharge in 1966, he moved to New York and put together the Flying Machine with guitarist Danny Kortchmar. The group split up the next year due to Taylor's heroin addiction, which would plague him until 1969. In 1968 he moved to London and was signed to the Beatles' Apple Records, which produced his little noticed debut LP. After another stay at an institution to clean up his drug habit, he appeared at the 1969 Newport Folk Festival and signed with Warner Brothers. His next album, 1970's *Sweet Baby James* was a monster, hitting number 3 with the help of the autobiographical single "Fire and Rain," which also went to number 3. Taylor went on to record thirteen more Top Forty albums and thirteen more Top Forty singles, including Carole King's "You've Got a Friend," a number 1 hit in 1971. In 1972 he began a ten-year marriage to singer Carly Simon, with whom he had a number 5 hit in 1974, "Mockingbird."

CAROLE KING

Carole King's (1940–) career started as a respected Brill Building songwriter with her husband Jerry Goffin, but in 1971 she reinvented herself as a performing artist with the release of *Tapestry,* which at the time was the largest selling album in history (peaking at number 1, *Tapestry* sold over fifteen million copies and stayed on the charts for six years). In between her two careers, King divorced Goffin and moved to L.A., where she started an ill-fated label, Tomorrow Records. In 1968 she formed a group called the City which never toured due to her intense stage fright, but released one album that contained the songs "Hi-De-Ho" and "You've

Got a Friend," which were successfully covered by Blood, Sweat and Tears and James Taylor, respectively. Taylor encouraged her to embark on a solo career, which led to the Grammy Award winning *Tapestry,* 1971's number 1 Music, 1972's number 2 *Rhymes and Reasons,* 1973's number 6 *Fantasy* and 1974's number 1 *Wrap Around Joy.* She also released thirteen Top Forty singles in the seventies, including the number 1 "It's Too Late," one of two hits from *Tapestry.* In addition to being a pop songwriting genius, King is a fine pianist and possesses a voice that is smoky and soulful.

OTHER SINGER/SONGWRITERS

Other singer/songwriters that emerged in the late sixties and early seventies include **Laura Nyro, Judy Collins, Jackson Browne, Randy Newman, Carly Simon, Cat Stevens, Jim Croce,** and **Gordon Lightfoot.**

Country Rock

DYLAN STRIKES YET AGAIN

As previously discussed in chapter 1, country music was one of the primary influences on the birth of rock and roll, and was an important component of the first rock and roll style, rockabilly. After rockabilly faded in the late fifties, there was minimal country influence on rock for the next several years. However, when Bob Dylan recorded the country influenced *John Wesley Harding* and *Nashville Skyline* in Nashville in 1968 and 1969, respectively, interest in country tinged rock began to resurface. The use of Nashville studio musicians and a guest vocal by Johnny Cash on *Nashville Skyline* made that album a particularly important landmark. However, there were predecessors even to Dylan in the merging of country's ethos with rock. As early as 1963, the Hawks (which later became the Band) were playing music that could be loosely categorized as **country rock;** their association with Dylan in 1965 and 1966 on tours and on the *Basement Tapes* was no doubt mutually influential. Former teen idol Rick Nelson was also on the front end of the movement, recording the country influenced *Bright Lights and Country Fever* as early as 1966. Some characteristics of Country Rock and key recordings are listing in Box 8-3.

The country rock scene was centered in Los Angeles, the home base of such early pioneers as the Nitty Gritty Dirt Band, the Flying Burrito Brothers, Rick Nelson's Stone Canyon Band, and Poco, as well as later country rock artists such as the Eagles, Linda Ronstadt, and Loggins and Messina. One of the most important country rock venues in the city in the mid sixties was the **Troubador,** a watering hole frequented by many local musicians that had been a folk club in the early sixties.

Box 8-3 Country Rock

Characteristics of Country Rock
1. Use of pedal steel guitar and other instruments normally associated with country/western
2. Two-beat country rhythm
3. Occasional use of twangy vocal delivery and vocal harmonies reminiscent of country/western
4. Rock rhythm section

Key Country Rock Recordings
❏ *Music from Big Pink*—the Band, 1968
❏ *Sweethearts of the Rodeo*—the Byrds, 1968
❏ *Bayou Country*—Creedence Clearwater Revival, 1969
❏ *The Eagles*—the Eagles, 1972

THE BAND

Never fully appreciated by the public but loved by rock critics, the Band nonetheless made a unique musical statement in the late sixties and early seventies that, while influential, has never quite been replicated. Their music was an eclectic mix of folk, blues, country, classical, and rock and roll that managed to bring out the unique talents of each individual member. The Band evolved between 1958 and 1963 as the Hawks, the backup band for Arkansas-born rockabilly singer Ronnie Hawkins. One by one, Hawkins assembled the core of the group, adding fellow Arkansan **Levon Helm** in 1958, guitarist **Robbie Robertson** in 1959, and bassist **Rick Danko,** pianist **Richard Manuel,** and organist **Garth Hudson** in 1961. Robertson, Danko, Manuel, and Hudson were all Canadians, picked up as the group played its way through the rough and tumble bars in the mining towns in the middle of the country. The band members' various musical influences meshed well, and the Hawks developed a reputation as one of the hardest rocking bands around. By 1963, the egotistical Hawkins was forced out of his own group, and the group became at various times Levon and the Hawks or the Canadian Squires, with Helm as the de facto leader. In 1964, John Hammond Jr. heard them perform at a Canadian club and arranged a series of recording sessions with him in New York. It was there that they were introduced to Bob Dylan.

The Hawks toured with Dylan in late 1965, and after his motorcycle accident in the summer of 1966, they moved to Woodstock, NY to collaborate with him on the informal recording sessions that would in time be known as the Basement Tapes. Those recordings, many of which were done in the basement of their sprawling pink house, provided the inspiration for the group to begin working on their own material and the eventual release of their first album, *Music from Big Pink* in 1968. The album was a revolutionary surprise; coming at a time when the rest of the rock world was immersed in psychedelia, *Big Pink* is unadorned and earthy, and lacking the flash of albums such as *Sgt. Peppers* or *Are You*

Experienced? Following its release, the group moved to Hollywood where in 1969 they released *The Band,* the album that proved to be their commercial breakthrough, peaking at number 9, and containing their only Top Forty single, "Up on Cripple Creek" (number 25). As the Band's popularity increased, the focus increasingly turned to the charismatic Robertson, the group's primary songwriter, and the egalitarian inner dynamics of the group began to change. Although they released six more LPs, including the Top Tens *Stage Fright* from 1970 and *Rock of Ages* in 1972, their days were numbered. The Band toured for the last time in 1976, concluding with a gala concert on Thanksgiving Day at San Francisco's Winterland Ballroom that included guest appearances by Dylan, Van Morrison, Eric Clapton, Muddy Waters, and many others. The documentary film of that concert, *The Last Waltz,* directed by Martin Scorsese, is one of rock and roll's best.

THE EAGLES

The Eagles were unquestionably the most commercially successful country rock group—their album *Eagles/Their Greatest Hits 1971-1975* was the first ever to be certified platinum by the Recording Industry Association of America, and has sold over 26 million copies worldwide to date. The band came to symbolize all that was good—and bad—about the laid back and glitzy California lifestyle in the seventies, although ironically none of the four original members were from the Golden State. Bassist **Randy Meisner** hailed from Scottsbluff, Nebraska; guitarist **Bernie Leadon** from Minneapolis; drummer **Don Henley** from Texas; and guitarist **Glenn Frey** from Detroit. The group came about as the four worked their way through a variety of influential bands after moving to Los Angeles in the mid sixties. Meisner was a founding member of Poco and worked briefly in Rick Nelson's Stone Canyon Band. Leadon had briefly been a member of the Flying Burrito Brothers, while Frey had worked with Bob Seger and J. D. Souther. Eventually all four found themselves in the studio together in 1971 as session musicians on a Linda Ronstadt album. Later that year David Geffen signed them to his yet to be launched Asylum Records, and, as the Eagles, they released their self-titled debut LP in 1972. Assisted by the hit single "Witchy Woman" (number 9), within a year and a half the album went gold. In early 1973, the group returned to the studio to record their second album, *Desperado,* which also went gold and contained the hit "Tequila Sunrise."

By this time, the Eagles were slowly abandoning the country flavor that characterized their early releases in favor of a harder rock sound. The next two albums, *On the Border* and *One of These Nights* (both 1974) hit the Top Ten, with the latter being the first of their five number 1 LPs. In spite of their success, the shift away from country alienated Leadon, who quit the group in late 1975 and was replaced by **Joe Walsh** of the James Gang (another guitarist, **Don Felder,** had also joined for *On the Border*). After the release of their wildly successful greatest hits compilation in early 1976, the band returned to the studio to record their fifth album, *Hotel California,* which was released in December 1976 and went platinum within one week. Using California as a metaphor, Henley's lyrics paint a dark picture of excesses that yield unsatisfying pleasure. Eventually the album sold over 10 million copies, and contained the number 1 singles "New Kid in Town" and "Hotel California." The album's title track was the group's fourth number 1 and their tenth Top Forty single. Although their next album took nearly three years to complete, *The Long Run* (1979) hit number 1 and contained three more Top Ten singles, including the number 1 "Heartache Tonight." *The Long Run* would be their last album as a group; the creative energies had run dry by 1981, and when Frey began work on a solo album, the Eagles broke up.

The Eagles had many critics during their short-lived but commercially successful existence. For many, the band symbolized the "laid-back, rich, and don't-give-a-shit California lifestyle," as Glenn Frey later complained. They were also viewed as too 'corporate,' the manifestation of manufactured pop product. But in many ways, their soaring harmonies and catchy melodies defined seventies pop music—for better or worse—perhaps more perfectly than any other band of the era.

CREEDENCE CLEARWATER REVIVAL

Formed in 1959 by four junior high school classmates from El Cerrito, California, Clearwater Revival was one of America's most popular bands from 1969 to 1971. Led by brothers **John Fogarty** (guitars/vocals/chief songwriter/producer) and **Tom Fogarty** (guitars/vocals), with **Stu Cook** (bass), and **Doug Clifford** (drums), CCR signed with Fantasy Records in 1964 when they were known as the Blue Velvets. After briefly calling themselves the Golliwogs, the band adopted their permanent name in 1967. CCR scored thirteen Top Forty hits beginning in 1969 with the release of their LP *Bayou Country,* including eleven in the Top Ten and five that went to number 2: 1969's "Proud Mary" (from *Bayou Country*), "Bad Moon Rising," and "Green River," and 1970's "Travelin' Band" and "Lookin' Out My Back Door." The band's sound was easily identifiable with strumming, country influenced rockabilly guitars, and John Fogarty's raspy blues-enriched voice. Although most of their songs have rather down to earth and non-political storylines, 1969's "Fortunate Son" was an attack on the privileged class who could afford to stay out of Vietnam through college draft deferments.

Creedence Clearwater Revival

❏ John Fogarty
❏ Tom Fogarty
❏ Stu Cook
❏ Doug Clifford

OTHER COUNTRY ROCK BANDS

Other bands and artists that played music in the country rock style include **Linda Ronstadt,** the **Flying Burrito Brothers, Poco,** the **Nitty Gritty Dirt Band,** the **Stone Canyon Band, Pure Prairie League,** and **Loggins and Messina.**

Southern Rock

THE RURAL COUSIN

Southern rock is the rural cousin to the citified country rock. Whereas many country rock groups had a close musical connection to folk with strumming guitars and harmonious vocals, Southern rock bands were deeply rooted in country music and the blues. They were grittier, and played louder and harder than their country rock cousins; their lyrics reflected less emphasis on intellectual subjects and more on identifying with 'good old boy' Southern stereotypes and male posturing and swagger. The bands were often bigger as well, sometimes including two lead guitarists (Lynyrd Skynyrd had three), and in the case of the Allman Brothers, two drummers. With its harder edge and blues base, Southern rock is closely related to hard rock of the late sixties, and both styles vied for the predominantly white male audience. The power and drive of Southern rock also made the music popular in concert settings. Some characteristics of Southern Rock and some key recordings are listed in Box 8-4.

LYNYRD SKYNYRD

Formed in 1965 in Jacksonville, Florida, Lynyrd Skynyrd was the prototypical Southern rock band, combining the rebellious attitude of rock and roll with the blues and a country twang. In 1965, while still in high school, classmates **Ronnie Van Zant** (vocals), **Allen Collins** (guitar), **Gary Rossington** (guitar), **Leon Wilkeson** (bass), and **Billy Powell** (keyboards) formed a band they named in mock honor of their gym teacher, Leonard Skinner, who was known to punish students with long hair. After adding drummer **Bob Burns,** the band spent the next several years playing bars throughout the South before they were discovered and signed to MCA Records by producer Al Kooper. After adding third guitarist Ed King, the band recorded their debut album *Pronounced Leh-*

Box 8-4 Southern Rock

Characteristics of Southern Rock
1. Heavier instrumentation, often including two drummers, two or three lead guitar players
2. Harder edge than country rock, similar to hard rock
3. Deep roots in the blues
4. Lyric themes identifying with Southern 'good old boy' image: male swagger, drinking, cheating, fighting, etc.

Key Southern Rock Recordings
❑ *At the Fillmore*—Allman Brothers Band, 1971
❑ "Free Bird"—Lynyrd Skynyrd, 1973
❑ "Ramblin' Man"—The Allman Brothers, 1973
❑ *Second Helping*—Lynyrd Skynyrd, 1974

Nerd Skin-Nerd in 1973, which included the anthemic tribute to Duane Allman, "Free Bird." They also became the warm-up act on the Who's Quadrophenia Tour. By the time their second album *Second Helping* was released in 1974, Lynyrd Skynyrd was acquiring a devoted fan base. The album went multi-platinum, and also contained what was to be their highest charting hit, "Sweet Home Alabama" (number 8), a reply to Neil Young's "Southern Man." Three more albums were forthcoming by late 1976, topped by the triple-platinum double live *On More from the Road.* Then, tragedy struck.

On October 20, 1977, three days after the release of Lynyrd Skynyrd's sixth album *Street Survivors,* the plane carrying the band to a gig in Baton Rouge, Louisiana crashed outside of Gillsburg, Mississippi, killing Van Zant, new guitarist Steve Gaines and Gaines' sister Cassie, a backup singer. The other members were injured but lived to continue on with the band. Ironically, the *Street Survivors* cover showed the band surrounded by flames; after the crash, the flames were removed on a redesigned cover. *Street Survivors* ultimately peaked at number 5, becoming their biggest seller.

The Allman Brothers Band

Although they weren't as commercially successful or typical a Southern rock band as Lynyrd Skynyrd, the Allman Brothers Band was one of America's greatest rock bands, forging a unique combination of blues, boogie, R&B, country, and jazz. Their legendary on-stage jamming outdid even the Grateful Dead, with songs that often lasted 30 minutes or more and featured the tasteful playing of their three main soloists, the brothers themselves, and guitarist Dickey Betts. The band was formed in 1969 in Macon, Georgia, the hometown of guitarist **Duane Allman** (1946-71) and his organist brother **Greg Allman** (1947-). At the time, Duane was a session guitarist at Fame Studios in Muscle Shoals, Alabama, where he had earned a solid reputation by playing on records by Wilson Pickett, Aretha Franklin, and others. At the suggestion of Phil Walden, head of the newly formed Capricorn Records, Allman put together the band by recruiting friends **Dickey Betts** on guitar, **Jai Johanny Johanson** and **Butch Trucks** on drums, **Berry Oakley** on bass and Greg. After some touring to jell their sound, they released their eponymous debut album, which garnered respect from critics and sold modestly, mainly in the South. Two more releases followed in the next two years, 1970's *Idlewild South,* which sold moderately well and peaked at number 38, and the double live *At the Fillmore* from 1971, recorded at the Fillmore East Ballroom. By this time, the Allmans were being praised as "America's best rock and roll group," while Duane was further cementing his reputation as a guitar hero by appearing on Eric Clapton's *Derek and the Dominos* album.

On October 29, 1971, as the band was working on its third album, Duane was killed in a motorcycle accident in Macon. Determined to continue, the rest of the members completed *Eat a Peach,* which climbed to number 4, and added pianist **Chuck Leavell** as a quasi replacement for Allman. But tragedy struck again—before they could finish their next album, bassist Oakley was also killed in a motorcycle accident on November 11, 1972, only three blocks from where Duane had died. Forging ahead once again in the face of misfortune, Dickey Betts assumed the leadership of the band, writing most of the material for 1973's *Brothers and Sisters.* It became their only number 1 album and contained the Allman's highest charting single, "Ramblin' Man" (number 2). The band began to break apart in the mid seventies: Greg married actress Cher (who had a disruptive influence) and later was forced to testify against a band employee in a federal drug trial, alienating him from the other band members.

OTHER SOUTHERN ROCK BANDS

With the success of the Allman Brothers Band and Lynyrd Skynyrd, other Southern rock bands emerged in the seventies that achieved commercial staying power. They include the power trio **ZZ Top** from Texas, with ten Top Forty albums beginning in 1973; South Carolina's the **Marshall Tucker Band,** with eight Top Forty albums starting in 1973; Florida based **.38 Special,** led by Donnie Van Zant (younger brother of the late Ronnie from Lynyrd Skynyrd), five Top Forty LPs; the **Charlie Daniels Band,** led by the former Nashville session guitarist (Daniels' credits include Dylan's *Nashville Skyline*), five Top Forty albums; Georgia's **Atlanta Rhythm Section,** also with five Top Forty LPs; and the L.A. based **Black Oak Arkansas.**

Seventies Country

THE NASHVILLE SOUND

During the sixties, country music was pretty much non-existent to much of the pop world. Although it remained the primary format for many radio stations in the South and West, only a handful of songs by country artists made the pop charts before 1968. Jim Reeves had a crossover hit in 1960 with "He'll Have to Go" (number 2 pop); Patsy Cline's "Crazy" went to number 9 in 1961; and Nashville session pianist Floyd Cramer had three Top Ten hits in 1960–61, including the number 2 "Last Date." There were also a few non-country artists who scored hits during this period, including Ray Charles, Connie Francis, and Brenda Lee. Most of these records were made in Nashville, where record companies had taken steps to update the fifties honky tonk of Hank Williams and Ernest

Box 8-5　The Nashville Sound

1. Pop-oriented presentation of country/western music
2. Heavy orchestrations with strings and backup vocalists
3. Elimination of some of the twangy vocal presentation associated with country/western

Tubb into a smoother, more pop-oriented commercial sound. What became known as the **Nashville Sound** was achieved in part by adding strings and eliminating some of the twangy vocal presentation that characterized earlier country styles.

Then, starting around 1968, country started becoming cool again, no doubt helped by the work of Bob Dylan and others. Leading the pack was former session guitarist **Glen Campbell,** who tallied fourteen Top Forty hits between 1968 and 1977, including 1968's number 1 "Wichita Lineman." Campbell even had his own TV show for a short time. Also in 1968, **Kenny Rogers** started his incredible assault on the pop charts, first with his group the First Edition, then as a solo artist, hitting the Top Forty twenty seven times. Another solo artist, **John Denver** had four number 1 singles and fifteen Top Forty LPs starting in 1971. By the end of the seventies, country music was big business whose audience extended beyond its traditional Southern base. The 1980 film *Urban Cowboy* starring John Travolta made black hats and line dancing all the rage for a few years.

THE OUTLAWS

There was also a bit of a controversy going on in the country music world: a backlash against the citified country sound. Starting in the early seventies, a group of artists collectively known as **"the Outlaws"** began to emerge with songs that bore a closer resemblance to the earlier honky tonk style. These artists included **Willie Nelson, Waylon Jennings, Kris Kristofferson,** and **Jessi Colter.** Nelson had moved to Nashville in 1961 from his native Texas and established himself as a songwriter (including "Crazy," Patsy Cline's 1961 hit). Feeling the need to free himself from the confines of the Nashville scene, Nelson returned to Texas in 1969 and adopted a new image—that of a redneck hippie, with long hair in a pigtail, faded jeans, and earring. This departure from the traditional clean-cut string tie country image made Nelson a rebel. His 1975 concept LP *Red-Headed Stranger* was a hit (number 28) that paved the way for Jennings and others. Jennings had played bass with Buddy Holly during the singer's ill-fated last tour, and had resisted the traditional country mold throughout the sixties. His commercial breakthrough came in 1976 with "Good Hearted Woman," a duet with Nelson. RCA capitalized on the success of Nelson, Jennings, and the rest of the Outlaws with the 1977 compilation LP *The Outlaws,* which became the first country platinum album.

Seventies Pop Stars

MERGERS AND MEGAHITS

By the time the seventies rolled around, rock had become the dominant music format of the mainstream culture, a fact that is reflected in the explosive sales growth of records and tapes. In 1973, music was a $2 billion a year industry; by 1978, sales had grown to $4 billion. As rock was becoming big business, the industry began to consolidate: large corporations started to merge with and acquire record companies and other music related businesses. By the end of the seventies, 80 percent of all record and tape sales were controlled by six of these conglomerates: **Columbia/CBS, RCA Victor, United Artists-MGM, Capitol-EMI, MCA,** and **Warner Communications.** In this new climate of lawyers, accountants, and corporate control, it became imperative to turn a profit, and record labels responded by minimizing their risk whenever possible. Often this meant relying on well-established artists to produce records designed to have the greatest sales potential. These artists became the beneficiaries of massive advertising campaigns and huge contracts as the major labels poured their resources behind them, often with impressive results. Several albums from the seventies are among the best selling of all time, including the Bee Gees' *Saturday Night Fever* (thirty million copies), The Eagles' *Eagles/Their Greatest Hits 1971–1975* (twenty six million), Fleetwood Mac's *Rumours* (twenty five million), and Carole King's *Tapestry* (fifteen million). One of the most bankable stars was Elton John, who held the number 1 album spot for a combined total of 39 weeks with seven of his eighteen Top Forty LPs during the decade.

Unfortunately, there was a price to be paid for the focus the music industry was putting on producing megahits. Many lesser groups relied on stale pop formulas to produce music that was creatively unsatisfying, including Air Supply, Paul McCartney and Wings, Journey, Chicago, Rod Stewart, Three Dog Night, and Foreigner. Each sold a lot of records during the seventies, most of which were less than inspiring. Another side effect of the seventies pop culture was the death of many of the smaller more innovative labels who simply couldn't compete in this new megahit environment. But the independents would not disappear, nor would they stop shaking up the music industry and causing trouble for the majors.

Chapter 8
Study Questions

1. What were some of the reasons that rock began to fragment in the seventies?

    _____

    _____

    _____

2. Why were the Byrds important to the early years of folk rock?

    _____

    _____

    _____

3. Name three important characteristics of Crosby, Stills, Nash and Young.

    _____

    _____

    _____

4. What are some of the common characteristics of the music of the singer/songwriters that emerged in the seventies?

    _____

    _____

    _____

    _____

5. Name two similarities in the careers of Van Morrison and Joni Mitchell.

    _____

    _____

    _____

    _____

6. Name two important artifacts of the sixties and seventies that the Band was involved in.

_____

_____

_____

_____

7. What are some of the differences between country rock and Southern rock?

_____

_____

_____

_____

8. The Allman Brothers were not the prototypical Southern rock band. What made them different?

_____

_____

_____

_____

9. Who were the Outlaws and what did they do that was significant?

_____

_____

_____

_____

10. How did corporate America influence rock in the seventies?

_____

_____

_____

_____

Hard Rock in the Seventies

The Birth of Heavy Metal

THE INDUSTRIAL ROOTS

Heavy metal was born in the dismal, grimy industrial cities of England—places like Birmingham, Aston, and Hertford, where people labored at arduous factory jobs that barely kept food on the table. They were resilient people who had survived the bombings during World War II and went about rebuilding their lives in the years after, persevering and making do as best they could. Nevertheless, it was a dark and troubling world in which their children grew up in the fifties and sixties. The rock that evolved from this time and place was more intense, more powerful, more angrily aggressive and louder than any that had come before it. Said heavy metal protagonist Ozzy Osbourne: "We got sick and tired of all the bullshit, love your brother and flower power forever. We brought things down to reality."

Heavy metal is deeply rooted in the blues, specifically the amplified blues of the British hard rock bands such as the Yardbirds, Cream, and the Jimi Hendrix Experience. The focus of each of these bands was the virtuosity and showmanship of their guitarists—Jeff Beck, Jimmy Page, Eric Clapton, and Hendrix—who essentially redefined how the instrument was going to be used in a rock setting. Heavy metal continued this preoccupation with flashy displays of technical prowess, and produced some of the most skilled guitarists in history. The most prominent features of heavy metal guitar playing are high volume, distortion, and **power chords.** The use of distortion by guitar players was nothing new to rock by the sixties: many of the early recordings from Sun Studios, including the 1951 landmark "Rocket 88" utilized the technique. In 1954, North Carolina guitarist **Link Wray** recorded "Rumble," a tune based around a distorted guitar riff that sold over a million copies in the fifties, and reached number 16 in 1958. But with the end of the classic rock and roll era, further innovation on the guitar moved from America to England.

The most prominent features of heavy metal guitar playing are high volume, distortion, and **power chords.**

One of the first British bands to utilize power chords was the Kinks, whose Top Ten hits "You Really Got Me" from 1964 and "All Day and All of the Night" from 1965 were both based on repeating power chord riffs. The year 1965 also saw the release of several influential British singles that utilized distorted guitar riffs and power chords, most notably the Who's "I Can't Explain," the Rolling Stones' "(I Can't Get No) Satisfaction," and the Yardbirds' "For Your Love." By 1967, when both Cream and the Jimi Hendrix Experience had formed and codified the blues based hard rock style, heavy metal was one evolutionary step away. Unknown to everyone at the time, the name for the music had already been coined by beat writer William Burroughs, who used it in his 1964 novel *Nova Express* (not his *Naked Lunch,* as many have incorrectly reported). However, the phrase had no musical connection until 1968, when songwriter Mars Bonfire used it in the lyrics to his song "Born to Be Wild," which became a hit for Steppenwolf and was used in the biker cult film *Easy Rider.* Bonfire later said he first heard the term in his high school chemistry class. By the time rock critic Lester Bangs began using

---

Box 9-1 Heavy Metal

Characteristics of Heavy Metal
1. Typical instrumentation: electric guitar, bass, drums, vocalist
2. Loud, aggressive, use of feedback, distortion, noise, studio effects
3. Showcase for the technical virtuosity of the lead guitarist
4. Themes of Satanic worship, evil, Goth, witchcraft, death
5. Songs often based on blues riffs and power chords

Key Early Heavy Metal Recordings
❑ *Led Zeppelin*—Led Zeppelin, 1969
❑ "Whole Lotta Love"—Led Zeppelin, 1969
❑ *Paranoid*—Black Sabbath, 1970
❑ *Led Zeppelin IV*—Led Zeppelin, 1971
❑ *Machine Head*—Deep Purple, 1972

---

the phrase in the early seventies, the name—a perfect description of the music—had stuck. Some characteristics of heavy metal and some early recordings are listing in Box 9-1.

Heavy metal became popular primarily because of its power and volume, and its rebellious and aggressive attitude, all of which struck a chord with its core audience—white teenage males who were pissed off at the world. It also represented for many rock fans an extreme rejection of the seventies commercial pop and soft rock styles described in chapter 8. For these and other reasons, it was widely dismissed by rock critics, who considered it amateurish and simple minded. It wasn't until the nineties, when many of the Seattle grunge bands acknowledged its influence that heavy metal began to shake some of the disrespect that had been heaped on it by critics over the years.

The prototypical heavy metal band was a power trio—guitar, bass and drums—with an added vocalist. The songs typically are based on a pounding and thunderous repeated riff, typically played by both bass and guitar in unison. Singers tend to induce distortion into their voices as well, often using screams and yells to create more intensity. Song themes frequently are of death, the occult, mythology, sexual conquest, and drugs. There is also a good deal of macho posturing and swagger in the attitude of the performers, as well as the music itself.

The Earliest Heavy Metal Bands

BLACK SABBATH

There is debate as to who the first heavy metal band was. Many point to the seminal American hard rock bands such as Iron Butterfly and Vanilla Fudge, both of which were formed in 1966, or Britain's Deep Purple. However, the first band to clearly define the conventions of early heavy metal was Black Sabbath, from Birmingham, England. From the beginning, Black Sabbath was fixated in the occult, low sonorities, distortion, and bone-crunching volume. They were one of the first bands to use lower tunings on their guitars, which gave their power chords more depth and intensity. Visually, the band looked menacing, wearing steel crucifixes, black clothes, and long hair, while their live shows often included burning crosses and other images of devil worship. Singer Ozzy Osbourne's plaintive wailing was a departure from rock singing that came before, and was highly influential to later metal bands.

The members of Black Sabbath, guitarist **Tony Iommi,** bassist **Terry "Geezer" Butler,** drummer **Bill Ward,** and **Ozzy Osbourne** (1948–), were schoolmates who all grew up within a mile of each other in the working class city of Aston, just outside of Birmingham, England's second largest city. By the time they began jamming together in 1967, they had encountered their share of tough times: Osbourne had been in jail for six weeks for burglary, while Iommi had lost the tips of two fingers of his right hand while working in a metal press factory. At first they called themselves Polka Tulk, then Earth, but ultimately took Black Sabbath from a novel of the same name by occult writer Dennis Wheatley. After being rejected by fourteen record labels, they signed with the small Vertigo label and released their self-titled debut album in January 1970.

To everyone's surprise, the LP was well received, hitting number 8 in Britain and number 23 in the U.S., and eventually sold over a million copies. In September, their second album, *Paranoid,* was released, and buoyed by the single release of the title track (number 4 U.K.), it went to number 12 in the U.S. and sold four million copies. This was accomplished despite the fact that the band was getting virtually no airplay and bad reviews from critics. With a hectic touring schedule of both England and the U.S., Black Sabbath was able to nurture a strong fan base that enabled all of their first five albums to be certified gold. However, in the wake of the disco and punk movements of the mid seventies, sales began to slow. Osbourne quit in 1979 to pursue a solo career, and although Black Sabbath has stayed together over the years, the band was never the same without him. Osbourne's career bloomed again in 2001 in his family's hit TV series.

LED ZEPPELIN

Although Led Zeppelin would go on to greater fame and influence than Black Sabbath, they were hardly the prototypical heavy metal band. Their music covered a much wider range of styles than any other band in the genre, and as such they almost defy categorization. Transcending their deep blues roots, Zeppelin incorporated many influences: their music was at times bombastically violent and savage, at other times folk-like and lyrical. Nonetheless, they managed to put their own signature sound on everything they did, and sold more than fifty million records while being virtually ignored and disrespected by the rock press.

Led Zeppelin evolved out of the Yardbirds, which **Jimmy Page** (1944–) joined as the bassist in June 1966. Page had carved out a career as a respected studio guitarist in London, having played on hundreds of recordings including the Kinks "You Really Got Me" and "All Day and All of the Night," and the Who's "I Can't Explain." Although he eventually became the Yardbirds lead guitarist and took control of the band after the volatile Jeff Beck was forced out, Page could not stop the internal bickering that eventually broke up the band in mid 1968. Forced to fulfill a series of contractual obligations in Scandinavia, Page went about putting together a replacement group for the tour. He first asked the Who's John Entwistle and Keith Moon, who briefly toyed with the idea before deciding that the new band would sink "like a lead balloon," according to Moon. Undeterred, over the next few months Page brought together **John Paul Jones** (1946–), a producer and bass player who, like Page was a veteran of the London studio scene; **Robert Plant** (1948–), the singer in a band called Hobbstweedle; and **John Bonham** (1948–80), a powerhouse drummer from Birmingham. The electricity of their first rehearsal was palpable. "The room just exploded," Jones later remarked. "And we said, 'Right, we're on, this is it, this is gonna work!'"

After completing the tour of Scandinavia as the New Yardbirds, the band recorded their self-titled debut album in thirty hours without a record contract. Renaming themselves Led Zeppelin (inspired by Moon's comment), they toured America in early 1969 as the opening act for Vanilla Fudge. Meanwhile, manager Peter Grant had secured an unheard of $200,000 advance from Atlantic Records for the album, which shot to number 10 almost immediately after its January release. *Led Zeppelin* contains six originals as well as two songs written by Chicago bluesman Willie Dixon. Promoting themselves with an exhaustive touring schedule, Zeppelin developed a devoted following that took each of the next eight albums to platinum status and either number 1 or number 2 on the charts. In November 1969, *Led Zeppelin II* was released, which stayed at number 1 for seven weeks and included the number 4 hit "Whole Lotta Love." *Led Zeppelin III*, released in October 1970 revealed a more diverse musical direction with the introduction of folk elements, and again hit number 1. Although the unnamed fourth album, released in November 1971 and alternately referred to by fans as *Led Zeppelin IV*

Led Zeppelin in performance. Left to right: Robert Plant, vocals; John Paul Jones, bass; Jimmy Page, guitar; John Bonham, drums.
Led Zeppelin's music covered a much wider range of styles than any other heavy metal band. They almost defy categorization.
© Neal Preston/CORBIS

and *ZoSo* only went as far as number 2, it was the band's biggest selling album, with eventual sales of over twenty-two million copies.

The album is noteworthy for its complete lack of identifying marks on the cover. On the inner sleeve, each band member chose a symbol with which to identify—Page's symbol appeared to read "ZoSo," which many fans began to call the LP. Evidence of the bands preoccupation with the occult was also present on the album cover; Page in particular was fascinated with the writings of renowned Satanist Aleister Crowley, whose former home Boleskine House he had purchased in 1970. *Led Zeppelin IV* also included the bands signature piece, "Stairway to Heaven," a song that become one of the most played songs in radio history despite the fact that it was not released as a single and was over eight minutes long. Starting off quietly on acoustic guitar with overtones of Celtic Renaissance music, "Stairway" is an epic piece that slowly builds a storm of volume and distortion into a tumultuous climax.

Following tours in 1973 and 1975 in which the band broke numerous box office records (many of which had been held by the Beatles), Led Zeppelin was the biggest act in rock and roll. Their album releases from this period, *Houses of the Holy* (1973) and *Physical Graffiti* (1975) both went platinum. By this time the band had redefined the nature of touring by choosing to play only in large cities, forcing many fans to travel hundreds of miles to see them. They also began handling all aspects of promotion and logistics in exchange for a 90% cut of the gate (previously, it was customary for the promoter and band to split the proceeds 50/50). They were also becoming notorious for their off-stage behavior, which included the usual hotel room trashing as well as depraved and sometimes bizarre sexual escapades with the many groupies that were in constant supply. One such incident in Seattle involving a live shark and a naked girl became legendary after it inspired Frank Zappa to write his song "The Mud Shark."

Led Zeppelin by this time had developed an us-against-the-world attitude, largely due to their relationship with the rock press. Rock magazines such as *Rolling Stone, Cream,* and England's *Melody Maker* had all taken hits at the band, as had newspapers on both sides of the Atlantic. Many derided the band for the exhibitionism and pretentiousness of its live shows; others complained that their audience was almost exclusively immature, doped-up white teenage boys, which somehow made the music irrelevant. Throughout the seventies, interviews with the members of Led Zeppelin were hard to come by.

A series of misfortunes hit the band starting in 1975, when Plant and his family were involved in an auto accident that nearly killed his wife Maureen. A year later, his son Karac died from a respiratory virus. Then, on September 25, 1980, as they were preparing for an upcoming U.S. tour, Bonham died at Page's home in Windsor after an all-night drinking binge. He was thirty-two years old. Three months later, Page and Jones released a statement saying that Led Zeppelin was disbanding. All three remaining members continued on with solo careers, including a reuniting of Page and Plant in 1984 with the all-star band the Honeydrippers. In 1995 Led Zeppelin was inducted into the Rock and Roll Hall of Fame.

Other British Heavy Metal Bands

DEEP PURPLE

Formed in 1968 in Hertford, England, Deep Purple was one of the first heavy metal bands to include influences from classical music together with the other staples of the genre: the blues, distortion, and high volume. After a series of early personnel changes, a stable lineup was set with **Ritchie Blackmore** on guitar, **Jon Lord** on Hammond B-3 organ, **Ian Paice** on drums, **Roger Glover** on bass, and singer **Ian Gillan.** The group achieved success almost immediately with covers of Joe South's "Hush" (number 4) and Neil Diamond's "Kentucky Woman" (number 38), both in 1968. In 1969 the group recorded the art rock concept album *Concerto for Group and Orchestra,* a multi-movement orchestral work written by Lord, which generated poor sales. The group then turned their focus to Blackmore's guitar-oriented hard rock material, with which they hit pay dirt. *Machine Head,* released in 1972 (number 7), included the metal classic "Smoke on the Water" (number 4), a song built on one of the simplest yet most memorable riffs in rock history. The lyrics to the song are based on an actual event, the burning of the Montreux Casino in Switzerland during a Frank Zappa concert in 1971. The band had gone to the concert while on break from recording the album in the hallways of the city's abandoned Grand Hotel. Deep Purple released five more albums over the next decade that hit the Top Twenty.

JUDAS PRIEST

Judas Priest was another band that grew up out of the shadows of the steel mills in Birmingham. Formed in 1969, they struggled early on with a revolving lineup, but by 1974 the lineup was set: **K. K. Downing** on guitar, **Ian Hill** on bass, **Glenn Tipton** on guitar, **Rob Halford** on vocals, and **Alan Moore** on drums. Their 1974 debut album *Rocka Rolla* received almost no attention; in fact, it wasn't until the closeted gay Halford started to adopt a leather-and-studs look from underground S&M stores in 1977 that the band began to take off. That year's *Sin After Sin* received positive reviews, while the following year's *Stained Class* put them on the map as a major force in the metal world. The band's 1979 LP *Hell Bent for Leather* is often cited as being influential in the **New Wave of British Heavy Metal** movement of the late seventies and eighties. While on tour to promote the album, Halford would often ride a Harley Davidson on stage, which led to an endorsement deal with the motorcycle company. By 1980 they finally cracked the American Top Forty with *British Steel,* and hit the charts with seven more albums during the decade.

QUEEN

Queen's roots go back to 1967, when guitarist **Brian May** and drummer **Roger Taylor** joined a group called Smile. After several years of struggle, singer **Freddie Mercury** (Frederick Bulsara) and bassist **John Deacon** joined the group, which by now had been renamed Queen. Forsaking live performances for two years while the four were enrolled in college, they released three albums in 1973 and 74: *Queen I, Queen II,* and *Sheer Heart Attack,* the last of which broke through in the American charts at number 12. The band's live act focused on May's astonishing chops and Mercury's Liza Minnelli-influenced flamboyant preening. In the studio, their music was highly produced, using heavy doses of overdubbing on vocals to create a unique and highly identifiable sound. Their breakthrough came in 1975 with *A Night at the Opera* (number 4 U.S., number 1 U.K.), which contained the opera spoof "Bohemian Rhapsody" that reportedly used as many as 180 overdubs of Mercury's voice. The song was such a smash that it stayed at number 1 in England for a record-breaking nine weeks. The band also recorded two stadium rock anthems, 1977's "We Will Rock You," and 1980's "Another One Bites the Dust" (number 1). Although Mercury and the group never publicly revealed the singer's homosexuality, by the late eighties rumors were flying that he was ill with AIDS. Finally, on November 22, 1991 he released a statement confirming his illness; he died two days later. "Bohemian Rhapsody" hit the charts again in 1992 after its inclusion in the film *Wayne's World.*

Queen

- ❏ Brian May
- ❏ Roger Taylor
- ❏ Freddie Mercury
- ❏ John Deacon

American Heavy Metal

ALICE COOPER

America was also getting into the heavy metal scene in the late sixties, as it too had its share of disaffected youth who were sick of the love-your-neighbor generation. One of them was **Vincent Furnier** (1948–), a scrawny and sickly teenager growing up in Phoenix who would become rock's "prince of darkness" as Alice Cooper. Furnier put his first band together, the Earwigs, in 1963 from members of his high school track team. In the early years, the band often practiced in the middle of the desert with a generator hooked up to a telephone pole to power their amps. After a series of personnel and name changes, the band became Alice Cooper in 1968, a name reportedly taken from a seventeenth century witch found on an Ouija board card. Soon afterward, band members **Glen Buxton** (guitar), **Michael Bruce** (keyboards), **Dennis Dunaway** (bass), and **Neal Smith** (drums) persuaded Furnier to actually take on the character of Alice Cooper himself. Armed with a desire to shock their way into the rock world, Furnier and entourage moved to Los Angeles by years end.

Alice Cooper quickly made a reputation for themselves in L.A.; unfortunately, it was for clearing out club patrons faster than a fire alarm. The problem was that the band was just too freaky: in addition, their bizarre

Alice Cooper

- ❏ Vincent Furnier
- ❏ Glen Buxton
- ❏ Michael Bruce
- ❏ Dennis Dunaway
- ❏ Neal Smith

original songs, Cooper and his mates had taken to wearing ghoulish mascara and odd clothes that included among other items, see-through pants. No self-respecting record label was interested until Frank Zappa signed them to his new Straight Records. After two poorly received album releases, the band was $100,000 in debt. Warner Brothers bought Straight from Zappa in 1970, and released the single "Eighteen," which surprisingly became a national hit at number 21. Based on the success of the single, Warner allowed the band to release the LP *Love It to Death,* which Cooper supported with a hectic nonstop touring schedule. The album was a hit, and the band's fortunes changed almost overnight. Subsequent album releases *Killer* (1971), *School's Out* (number 2, 1972) and *Billion Dollar Babies* (number 1, 1973) all went platinum. The single release "School's Out" also went to number 7 in 1972.

In the beginning, Alice Cooper's stage shows included theatrics as a way to distract the audience from their lack of musicianship. As the years went on, the stage antics took on a gruesome and ghastly tone, incorporating sledgehammers, electric chairs, guillotines, and a live boa constrictor that Alice wore around his neck. The shows became legendary—and influential. "David Bowie used to come to our shows in England when he was a folk singer," Cooper recalled. "Elton John was this nice piano player who came to our show at the Hollywood Bowl. The next time I saw him he was in a Donald Duck outfit, wearing huge glasses and doing Dodger Stadium." Furnier eventually tired of being Cooper, and began drinking heavily to cope with the pressures. He left the band in 1975 admitting himself to a psychiatric clinic to treat his alcoholism. He rebounded in the late eighties with the LP *Trash,* which contained the single "Poison" (number 7, 1989). A lifelong baseball fan, he now owns a restaurant in Phoenix appropriately named Cooperstown.

AEROSMITH

One of the most popular heavy metal bands of the seventies, Aerosmith endured attacks from rock critics as a cheap imitation of the Rolling Stones and a lingering drug problem to re-emerge more popular than ever in the eighties. The band formed in 1970 in Sunapee, New Hampshire as a power trio with drummer/vocalist **Steve Tyler,** guitarist **Joe Perry,** and bassist **Tom Hamilton.** By the end of the year, the group added **Brad Whitford** on guitar and **Joey Kramer** on drums (allowing Tyler to front the band as lead vocalist), and moved to Boston, where they signed with Columbia Records in 1972. Although their self-titled debut album sold poorly, its power ballad single "Dream On" was a minor hit that peaked at number 59. The second LP, *Get Your Wings,* did slightly better, benefiting from a hectic tour schedule, but still did not break the Top Forty.

The group's commercial breakthrough came with 1975's *Toys in the Attic,* which, helped by the number 10 single "Walk This Way," went platinum and hit number 11. Meanwhile, "Dream On" was re-released and charted again at number 6. In spite of their phenomenal success, Aerosmith was falling apart from their problems with drugs. Perry quit

Aerosmith

❑ Steve Tyler
❑ Joe Perry
❑ Tom Hamilton
❑ Brad Whitford
❑ Joey Kramer

in 1979, Whitford in 1980, and the group floundered until both returned in 1984 and Perry and Tyler completed drug rehabilitation programs. Aerosmith's long road back to the top was bolstered by their appearance on Run-D.M.C.'s 1986 cover of "Walk This Way" and the prominent airplay the song's video received on MTV. Reintroduced to a new younger audience, Aerosmith had three subsequent Top Ten LPs: *Pump* (number 5, 1989), *Get a Grip* (number 1, 1993) and *Big Ones* (number 6, 1994). Their song about incest, "Janie's Got a Gun," won the 1990 Grammy Award for Best Rock Performance by a Duo or Group.

KISS

Heavily influenced by Alice Cooper, Kiss formed in 1970 when guitarist **Paul Stanley** and bassist **Gene Simmons** found drummer **Peter Criss** and guitarist **Paul "Ace" Frehley** through ads they had taken out in music magazines. Rehearsing in a loft in Manhattan, the band began wearing makeup around their eyes; over time they decided to completely cover their faces with designs that reflected their personalities. In 1973 they were close to a record contract with Warner Brothers, but after the label asked them to abandon their makeup (which they refused to do), the deal fell through and they signed instead with newly formed Casablanca Records. Although critics immediately dismissed the band, they quickly formed a bond with fans—the 'Kiss Army.' In 1975 they scored their first Top Ten LP, *Alive!;* their first Top Ten single "Beth" came the following year. In 1977 Marvel Comics published a Kiss comic book that reportedly contained blood from band members in the red ink. It sold more than 400,000 copies. In 1978 a second comic book was released, and NBC broadcast an animated TV special entitled *Kiss Meets the Phantom of the Park*. At this time, Kiss also began to market their albums on TV and radio, do in-store appearances, and offer promotions through their fan club, all of which were unusual at the time but are common today. After their popularity began to wane in the late seventies, they changed their image in 1983 and appeared without makeup for the first time. To date, the group has sold more than 70 million records.

Kiss

- ❏ Paul Stanley
- ❏ Gene Simmons
- ❏ Peter Criss
- ❏ Paul "Ace" Frehley

VAN HALEN

Van Halen emerged from the Sunset Strip bar scene in the late seventies to become one of the most popular American metal bands in history. Brothers **Eddie Van Halen** (guitar) and **Alex Van Halen** (drums) were born in Nijmegen, Holland, where their father Jan was a part-time clarinet player. Both boys received extensive classical piano training in their youth. In 1963, when Eddie was eight and Alex ten, the family moved to Pasadena, California, where the brothers developed a love for rock and roll. In 1973, while playing in a bar band, they came across the flamboyant singer **David Lee Roth,** who sang in a rival band. Roth and the Van Halens joined forces, added bassist **Michael Anthony,** and began playing at Gazzari's, the Starwood, and other bars along the Strip. In 1977, Gene Simmons from Kiss heard them and financed a demo tape that resulted in a contract from Warner Brothers. Roth's good looks and rock and roll swagger combined with Eddie Van Halen's unbelievable self-taught guitar technique (which includes hammer-ons, pull-offs, and two-hand tapping) were irresistible to casual pop fans and serious musicians alike. Since their self-titled debut album from 1978, the group has produced nine straight Top Ten LPs, including three number 1s in a row (*5150* from 1986, *OU812* from 1988 and *For Unlawful Carnal Knowledge* from 1991), and the number 1 single "Jump" from 1984. In 1985, Roth left to start a successful solo career and was replaced by singer **Sammy Hagar.**

Van Halen

- ❏ Eddie Van Halen
- ❏ Alex Van Halen
- ❏ David Lee Roth
- ❏ Michael Anthony

OTHER METAL BANDS FROM THE 70s

Other important heavy metal bands that emerged in the 1970s included **Blue Oyster Cult, Cheap Trick, Ted Nugent and the Amboy Dukes, Boston, Quiet Riot, Motley Crew,** and **Anthrax.**

Art Rock

THE ORIGINS OF ART ROCK

In the late sixties another rock style fragmented off from the mainstream. Actually, **art rock**—or progressive rock as some called it—was a designation for a diverse and eclectic mix of rock styles that were bound together more by common philosophy than by musical style: to incorporate elements of other forms of music generally described as art or high culture into a rock context. These borrowings usually came from European classical music, although they occasionally included American jazz and the musical avant-garde as well. The first stirrings of art rock came from England, where class distinctions and separation of 'highbrow' and 'lowbrow' art and their audiences are more pronounced than in the U.S. When musicians from the upper classes of English society began developing an interest in rock and roll, they brought a completely different set of social experiences and circumstances to the music than lower and middle class musicians, and their music reflected it. Some characteristics of Art Rock and some key recordings are listed in Box 9–2.

Although the Beatles were not from the upper class themselves, their association with the classically trained producer George Martin gave them the opportunity to experiment with influences from classical music. As early as 1965, the band was using classical instruments and influences, including the chamber string ensemble arrangement on "Yesterday" and the baroque-like piano solo on "In My Life." Both were conceived by Martin, who also played the "In My Life" solo. By the time *Sgt. Pepper's* was released in 1967, the Beatles were making extensive use of classical influences, including the album's quasi-opera setting. A few weeks before the release of *Sgt. Pepper's,* London-based **Procol Harum** released "A Whiter Shade of Pale," whose prominent feature was an organ solo co-opted from baroque composer J. S. Bach's "Aire on a

Box 9-2 Art Rock

Characteristics of Art Rock
1. Umbrella term to describe the philosophy of incorporating elements of European classical music, American jazz and the avant-garde into rock
2. Predominant use of keyboards and synthesizers
3. Use of classical forms such as operas, multi-movement suites; concept albums
4. Use of classical instruments such as string orchestras, flutes, oboes, etc.
5. Virtuoso performers with classical music training

Key Art Rock Recordings
❑ *Days of Future Passed*—the Moody Blues, 1967
❑ "A Whiter Shade of Pale"—Procol Harum, 1967
❑ *Sgt. Pepper's Lonely Hearts Club Band*—the Beatles, 1967
❑ *Tommy*—the Who, 1969
❑ *Close to the Edge*—Yes, 1972
❑ *Dark Side of the Moon*—Pink Floyd, 1973

G String." Also in 1967, Birmingham's **Moody Blues** released the influential *Days of Future Passed*, which utilized a symphony orchestra as well as the **Mellotron,** an early synthesizer capable of reproducing the sound of violins, cellos, and flutes. With the release of the Who's *Tommy* in 1969, the first rock 'opera,' a number of groups and artists on both sides of the Atlantic were incorporating highbrow art music into rock.

In addition to the use of classical instruments and forms, art rock is also typically characterized by the prominent use of keyboards such as the Mellotron and the **Mini-Moog,** one of the first commercially available portable synthesizers developed by electronic music pioneer **Dr. Robert Moog.** Many of the musicians that played the music were virtuoso performers with classical music training, which often contributed to excessive displays of showmanship. Concept albums were common, in which songs were thematically or otherwise related and often connected through the use of segues. In some cases, works of classical literature influenced the lyrics of art rock songs as well.

As in the case of heavy metal, many critics held art rock in contempt. Rock and roll was *supposed* to be simple, lowbrow and rebellious, they said. Art rock was too preoccupied of empty complexity and pretentiousness; it was too clinical. Many young rock musicians felt the same way, and disdain for the music ultimately boiled over in Britain's lower class and disenfranchised youth. The backlash by this faction of society against art rock and other 'corporate' rock from the seventies contributed to the rise of the English punk movement, whose mantra was to return rock and roll to its most rebellious state. Nevertheless, art rock had its fans, and several art rock bands enjoyed high levels of commercial success in the seventies. Yes scored five Top Ten albums between 1972 and 1979; two Moody Blues LPs have reached number 1, most recently in 1981; Pink Floyd's *The Dark Side of the Moon* went to number 1 and stayed on the Top 200 album chart for 741 weeks—more than fourteen years!

Important Art Rock Bands

PINK FLOYD

Perhaps more so than any other band, Pink Floyd was the embodiment of art rock in the seventies. They were at the vanguard of electronic special effects in their recordings; their music and lyrics took on a grand scale normally associated with classical music or opera; their concert performances became spectacles of lasers, lights, and props. And it was Pink Floyd that produced the single most significant artifact of the art rock movement, 1973's *The Dark Side of the Moon.* The Pink Floyd story can be divided into three parts: the Sid Barrett years, from 1965–1968; the Roger Waters years, from 1968–1983; and the later years from 1983 to the present. The band was formed in 1965 in London by guitarist **Syd Barrett,** bassist **Roger Waters,** drummer **Nick Mason,** and keyboardist **Rick Wright.** At first they were a very typical English R&B cover band; in fact, their name was derived from two obscure blues singers from Georgia, Pink Anderson and Floyd Council. However, under the de facto leadership of Barrett, the band soon began to experiment in performance with electronic effects, free-form instrumental breaks, feedback, and psychedelic light shows. By 1967 they had won a devoted following of fans and a record contract from EMI; their first single "Arnold Layne" made the Top Twenty. Their debut album, *The Piper at the Gates of Dawn* was a light-hearted psychedelic epic that some critics put on a par with *Sgt. Peppers.* Unfortunately, Barrett, the group's mastermind, began to exhibit signs of mental instability that ultimately forced his ouster from the group in mid 1968.

Just as Barrett was leaving, guitarist **Dave Gilmour** was brought in, and with the changeover, group leadership shifted to Waters, who reshaped Pink Floyd into a darker, grander, and more experimental unit. Although albums from this period such as *Atom Heart Mother* (number 1, U.K.) were appealing to a growing underground rock audience, Pink Floyd still had not made a dent in the American market. This changed dramatically with *The Dark Side of the Moon,* a state-of-the-art concept album that utilized innovative stereo effects, taped sounds and spoken voices, synthesizers, and dreamy, conceptual pop-oriented songs. Not only did it hit number 1 in the U.S. and yield a number 13 hit ("Money"), but almost overnight it made Pink Floyd international superstars. Subsequent albums *Wish You Were Here* (dedicated to former leader Barrett, 1975) and *Animals* (1977) continued the themes of isolation and insecurity of modern life first expressed on *The Dark Side of the Moon,* and struck a responsive chord with listeners, going to number 1 and number 3 respectively.

In 1979 the group released the concept double album *The Wall,* which contained the single "Another Brick in the Wall," a scathing attack on the British educational system that was made into a music video and ultimately banned by the BBC. Tours during this period included animated films, laser light shows, and elaborate staging—*The Wall* tour featured the building of an actual wall that by shows end had completely obscured the audience's view of the band. In spite of their unparalleled

Pink Floyd

❏ Syd Barrett
❏ Roger Waters
❏ Nick Mason
❏ Rick Wright
❏ Dave Gilmour

successes, the group began to unravel (due in part to Waters's overbearing control), and broke up in 1983 after the release of the LP *The Final Cut.* They reassembled in 1986 without Waters and continued to be nearly as commercially successful as they had in the seventies, including 1994's number 1 LP release, *The Division Bell.*

MOODY BLUES

Formed in the spring of 1964 in Birmingham, the Moody Blues began as a blues-influenced cover band working the city's bar scene. Original members included guitarist **Denny Laine,** keyboardist **Mike Pinder,** vocalist/flautist **Ray Thomas,** bass player **Clint Warwick,** and **Graeme Edge** on drums; by 1966 Laine and Warwick had left and were replaced by **Justin Hayward** on guitar and vocals and **John Lodge** on bass. Although Laine and Pinder were writing original material from the beginning, the group's first hit was a cover of the obscure blues tune "Go Now!" which went to number 1 in the U.K. and number 10 in the U.S. in 1965. In 1967 the group purchased a Mellotron, which facilitated a dramatic change of direction toward orchestrated pop tunes and extended compositions. For their 1968 release *Days of Future Passed,* the Moody Blues also used studio musicians known as the London Festival Orchestra; the album rose to number 3 in the U.S. and spawned two Top Forty singles, "Tuesday Afternoon" and "Knights in White Satin." "Knights" actually hit the charts three times in England between 1967 and 1979, and went to number 2 in the US in 1972. Although in time *Days of Future Passed* has been regarded as the groups most influential LP, their commercial success has continued to this day, with four more albums hitting number 3 or higher in the seventies and eighties. Their most recent tours have included performances with symphony orchestras.

YES

One of the most well respected art rock bands among musicians, Yes has become legendary for its superior musicianship, high three-part vocal harmonies, and intricate and complex compositions. The group has endured a number of personnel changes over the years; the original lineup in 1968 included vocalist **Jon Anderson,** bassist **Chris Squire,** drummer **Bill Bruford,** guitarist **Peter Banks,** and keyboardist **Tony Kaye.** Although they achieved instant acclaim in England, it was not until 1971's *The Yes Album* (number 40) that they broke through in the U.S. By this time Banks had left and was replaced by guitar virtuoso **Steve Howe;** shortly thereafter Kaye left and was replaced by keyboard wiz **Rick Wakeman.** In 1972, Yes released two Top Ten albums, *Fragile* and *Close to the Edge* that included increasingly adventurous pop-oriented songs, including "Roundabout" (number 13). *Close to the Edge* was a paradigm of the progressive rock movement, consisting of three extended pieces, including the four-movement title cut. After its release, Bruford left to join King Crimson, and was replaced by session drummer **Alan White.**

The band's next two albums, the live *Yessongs* and *Tales from Topographic Oceans* were Wakeman's last; he was replaced in 1974 by **Patrick Moraz**. *Tales* was another epic that was loved by some critics and ridiculed by others; it was followed by the jazz/rock fusion undertaking *Relayer.* After a world tour, Wakeman rejoined Yes for the remainder of the decade, but the band broke up in 1980. Subsequently, the band has reformed and continued touring, achieving their only number 1 hit in 1983 with "Owner of a Lonely Heart."

OTHER IMPORTANT ART ROCK BANDS

Other English bands that helped define art rock of the era include **King Crimson,** led by guitar prophet **Robert Fripp; Jethro Tull,** led by vocalist/flautist **Ian Anderson;** the innovative organ trio **Emerson, Lake and Palmer,** led by keyboard virtuoso **Keith Emerson; Genesis** and **Gentle Giant.**

Glam Rock

THE ORIGINS OF GLAM

In the early seventies, a new rock trend emerged that became known as **glam rock** or glitter rock. Glam—a shortening of the word glamorous—was primarily influenced by the pretentious tendencies of art rock and the bluntly audacious qualities of heavy metal. Like art rock, glam encompassed an eclectic mix of stylistic approaches; the glue that held the movement together was the use of flamboyant fashions, alter ego stage personalities and shocking assaults on traditional notions of sexuality, especially male masculinity. Glam rockers learned from Alice Cooper that it was possible to shock and challenge a rock audience by creating a theatrical environment on stage through the use of makeup, staging, and props. Cooper was, after all, an *actor* as much as a musician. By glorifying sexual ambiguity and androgyny, glam was also a backlash of sorts against the sexual revolution of the sixties. The movement was also characterized by the use of makeup, glitter dust, ostentatious and futuristic costumes, and decadence. Most of all, glam rock was outrageous, glitzy, and campy. Some characteristics of glam rock and some key recordings are listed in Box 9–3.

As was the case with several other rock movements, there were parallel scenes in the U.S. and the U.K. The American scene was centered in New York, where at venues like the **Mercer Art Center,** groups such as Eric Emerson's Magic Tramps and the **New York Dolls** performed. The Dolls were performing in drag, lipstick, and makeup as early as 1971, but in spite of using such highly regarded producers as Todd Rundgren and George 'Shadow' Morton ("Leader of the Pack"), they were simply too outrageous to achieve anything other than a cult following. The group included Johnny Thunders (later of the punk rock group the Heartbreakers) and David Johansen, who would later have some pop success as Buster Poindexter.

Box 9-3 Glam Rock

Characteristics of Glam Rock

1. An umbrella term encompassing a side variety of styles held together by the use of flamboyant fashions and assaults on sexual conventions
2. Theatrical presentations: lighting, props, makeup, and costuming
3. Shock value; glitzy, campy, outrageous

Key Glam Rock Recordings

❑ *The Rise and Fall of Ziggy Stardust and the Spiders from Mars*—David Bowie 1972
❑ *Bang a Gong (Get It On)*—T. Rex 1971
❑ *All the Young Dudes*—Matt the Hoople 1972
❑ *Captain Fantastic and the Brown Dirt Cowboy*—Elton John 1975

London was more tolerant of men dressing up in women's clothes than New York was, and the glam scene flourished there. At the forefront was **Marc Bolan,** a product of London's mod scene whose pretty looks and fashion sense as the leader of **T. Rex** set the tone for the burgeoning movement. Bolan disbanded the group in 1975 after eleven British Top Ten hits and one American ("Bang a Gong," number 10, 1972), and then spent the next two years overindulging himself before dying in an automobile accident in 1977. Other bands that followed in the T. Rex mold were **Gary Glitter, Slade,** and **Sweet.** Although Sweet made the biggest impact in America with four Top Ten hits, Glitter had the most enduring song of the era, the sports stadium staple "Rock and Roll Part II" from 1972.

DAVID BOWIE

The most influential glam performer was David Bowie (1947–). Born David Robert Jones (he renamed himself after the Bowie knife to avoid confusion with the Monkees' Davy Jones), during the sixties Bowie released three singles in the mod vein, spent time in a Buddhist monastery, and formed his own mime and experimental art troupes. In 1969 he released the singer/songwriter album *Man of Words, Man of Music* as a way to raise money for his Beckenham Arts Lab. Because the LP and its single release "Space Oddity" (in which he portrayed himself as an extraterrestrial) were hits, Bowie decided to focus his creative energies solely on music. After briefly working with Marc Bolan and producing *Hunky Dory,* a tribute album to pop artist Andy Warhol, Bowie announced in a January 1972 *Melody Maker* interview that he was gay. At the same time, he began to develop his new alter ego, the androgynous, bisexual, alien rock star named **Ziggy Stardust.** Backed by his band the **Spiders from Mars,** Bowie in late 1972 introduced his new persona in *The Rise and Fall of Ziggy Stardust and the Spiders from Mars.* His extravagantly decorated concerts that followed in London and New York in which he dyed his hair orange and wore women's clothing were smash hits. By the end of 1973, Bowie had released two more LPs,

Aladdin Sane and *Pin Ups,* produced albums for Lou Reed, the Stooges, and Mott the Hoople, and then unexpectedly announced his retirement from live performing.

By this time, Bowie had become the only glam rocker who would achieve star status in the U.S. His vocal style—crooning through clenched jaws in the manner of pub singer Anthony Newley—would in time prove to be immensely influential. In his American tour of 1974 (after coming out of retirement) Bowie showed a new obsession with soul music, which he repackaged and named "plastic soul." His 1975 album, *Young Americans,* reflected his new interest, and yielded the number 1 single "Fame," which he co-wrote with John Lennon. Bowie would subsequently have one more number 1, 1983's "Let's Dance." In 1977 he moved to Berlin where he collaborated with synthesizer pioneer Brian Eno on two innovative electronica-pop albums. By this time, he had also launched an acting career, appearing in 1976's *The Man Who Fell to Earth;* later roles included the lead in the Broadway production of *The Elephant Man.*

OTHER IMPORTANT GLAM ROCKERS

If David Bowie was the most influential glam rocker, Reginald Kenneth Dwight was by far the most commercially successful. In 1969 this fledgling singer/songwriter borrowed names from British R&B singer Long John Baldry and saxophonist Elton Dean and became **Elton John** (1947–). Around the same time, he began working with lyricist **Bernie Taupin;** their on and off working relationship over the years have made them the most successful songwriting team since John Lennon and Paul McCartney. Since 1970, John has released twenty-eight Top Forty LPs, fifteen of which went platinum, seven of which went to number 1; and more than fifty Top Forty singles, including eight number 1s. Despite his considerable songwriting abilities and classical training on piano, it took his wild performing antics and outrageous costuming to establish him as a pop star. His turbulent life has included alcohol and cocaine abuse, depression, bulimia, and a marriage in 1984 in spite of his awareness that he was gay.

Another glam rocker, **Rod Stewart,** has released nineteen Top Forty LPs and thirty-three Top Forty singles, including four number 1s. **Roxy Music,** formed in 1971 in London, led by keyboardist **Bryan Ferry** and synthesizer pioneer **Brian Eno,** and **Mott the Hoople,** formed in Hereford, England in 1968 were two other important glam groups that achieved popularity in their native country without making an impact in America.

Chapter 9
Study Questions

1. Describe some of the social and musical influences on the birth of heavy metal.

   _____

   _____

   _____

2. Why is Black Sabbath considered to be the first heavy metal band?

   _____

   _____

   _____

3. Name three things (musical or non-musical) that influenced Led Zeppelin.

   _____

   _____

   _____

4. Why is Led Zeppelin not considered to be the prototypical heavy metal band?

   _____

   _____

   _____

5. Describe the relationship between most heavy metal bands and rock critics in the seventies.

   _____

   _____

   _____

   _____

6. What was Alice Cooper's most important contribution to the rock canon?

_____

_____

_____

_____

7. What were some reasons that art rock originated in England instead of America?

_____

_____

_____

_____

_____

8. What are some common characteristics of art rock?

_____

_____

_____

_____

_____

9. Why did some critics hold art rock in contempt?

_____

_____

_____

_____

10. Name some common practices used by glam rockers to make themselves outrageous.

_____

_____

_____

_____

Black Music in the Seventies

Soft Soul

THE CHANGING SOUL LANDSCAPE

The changes that were taking place in the pop and rock world in the late sixties and early seventies had a detrimental effect on the careers of many established black pop artists. At the same time that the many white-dominated styles were emerging (folk rock, heavy metal, etc.), the popularity of soul music began to wane. The two sixties soul power-houses, Motown and Stax, went into decline, as did the careers of many of the decades most popular soul singers, including James Brown, Aretha Franklin, and Sam and Dave. What happened? For one thing, soul music had been inescapably linked to the civil rights movement, and when that movement began to run out of steam by decade's end, it was only natural that soul would also lose some of its appeal. The most turbulent events of the civil rights movement, including race riots in Newark, Detroit, and the Watts section of Los Angeles, and the assassinations of Malcolm X and Dr. Martin Luther King, Jr. did not sit well with the generally quieter mood of the country in the early seventies.

Radio networks and record companies were co-conspirators in the changes to black pop. Radio programmers were reluctant to play music that was confrontational, or even reminiscent of the conflicts of the sixties, and were only too glad to play newer commercial music by white artists. Record labels also began to shift their attention to white acts that had more commercial appeal. Even Atlantic Records, which had earned a reputation as one of the finest jazz, R&B and soul labels in the fifties and sixties, began to abandon those styles in favor of white rock acts such as Led Zeppelin, Cream, and Crosby, Stills, Nash and Young.

But even as penetrating the pop charts became more difficult for established soul artists, a new generation of black pop stars began to emerge. Many of these stars found success with a newer, more produced and polished sound that became known as **soft soul** or **romantic soul.** Soft soul was a logical extension of the highly produced Motown sound, and because it was not as gritty or raw and contained little if any political content, it was popular with radio programmers and listeners alike. Although soft soul artists were not limited to a particular region or city, the center of its development was Philadelphia, the home base for three of its important producers. Some characteristics of soft soul and some key recordings are listed in Box 10–1.

Soft soul was a highly produced and polished soul from the early seventies that emphasized lush string and horn arrangements and smooth vocal harmonies.

THE SOUND OF PHILADELPHIA

The **Philadelphia Sound** (as some called the soft soul that came from the city in the early seventies) was overly slick, with lush strings and horns and smooth vocal harmonies. Although much of the music was very danceable, torchy, romantic ballads were also popular. Soft soul enjoyed great crossover success and widespread radio play, and became an important influence on not only the disco movement of the mid seventies but also the romantic soul styles of today. The architects of the

Box 10-1 Soft Soul

Characteristics of Soft Soul
1. Highly produced and orchestrated; smooth vocals
2. Medium tempo dance tunes; slow, torchy romantic ballads
3. Influential to disco and current romantic soul styles
4. Center of development: Philadelphia
5. Great commercial and crossover appeal

Key Soft Soul Recordings
❑ "If You Don't Know Me By Now"—Harold Melvin and the Blue Notes 1972
❑ "Then Came You"—Spinners 1974
❑ "For the Love of Money"—the O'Jays 1974

Philadelphia Sound were the songwriting/producing team of **Kenny Gamble** and **Leon Huff,** and independent producer **Thom Bell.** Gamble had apprenticed with Leiber and Stoller in New York before returning to his hometown where he teamed up with Huff. The two began working as independent producers, and scored a number 4 hit in 1967 with their song "Expressway (to Your Heart)" by the white group Soul Survivors. In the wake of that success, they began assembling acts for their own Excel, Gamble, and Neptune labels, before forming **Philadelphia International Records** (PIR) in 1971. Over a five-year period beginning in 1968, Gamble and Huff produced thirty records that went gold. The most important artists at PIR were **Harold Melvin and the Blue Notes** ("If You Don't Know Me By Now," number 3, 1972), the **O'Jays** ("Love Train," number 1, 1973), **MFSB** (an acronym for Mother Father Sister Brother, a band consisting of the studio musicians at Philadelphia's Sigma Sound Studios where Gamble and Huff worked), and the **Three Degrees** ("When Will I See You Again," number 2, 1974).

Bell's rise to fame paralleled Gamble and Huff's, with his first hit coming in 1968 with the Delfonic's "La La Means I Love You," which went to number 4). Among his biggest acts were the **Stylistics** ("Betcha By Golly, Wow," number 3, 1972), the **Spinners** ("Then Came You," number 1, 1974, and six other Top Ten hits between 1972 and 1980). Other soft soul artists that rose to fame in the wake of the success of soft soul included **Al Green** ("Let's Stay Together," number 1, 1971), **Billy Paul** ("Me and Mrs. Jones," number 1, 1972), **Roberta Flack** ("Feel Like Makin' Love," 1974, one of three number 1 hits in the seventies), and **Barry White** ("Can't Get Enough of Your Love, Babe," number 1, 1974).

Funk

FUNK DEFINED

Soul was also evolving in a much different direction beginning around 1970. Even as the Philadelphia Sound was smoothing out the grittiness

Funk was the more primal evolution of R&B and soul that emerged in the early seventies whose most important characteristic is the rhythmic groove.

of soul, a more primal form of R&B was emerging that became known as **funk.** The most important element in funk is not smooth orchestrations: it is the groove, formed by layers of syncopated patterns that form a tightly woven rhythmic fabric. Minimalism is often used: simple one and two-bar repeating phrases that create a trance-like effect. Funk is also loosely structured, with extended jams, long improvisations and stream of consciousness lyrics common. Funk singers employ all kinds of vocal tricks, from shrieks and screams, guttural noises and grunts, sometimes locked in rhythmically to the band, sometimes floating above it out of rhythm. Group vocal chants are also common. Funk was the rawest, earthiest, and most Africanized form of black pop music to date, and as such saw little crossover appeal in the early seventies, as radio stations and much of the mainstream audience retreated from it. However, perspective has shown it to be highly influential to jazz/rock fusion, hip-hop, and rap, as well as many alternative rock bands from the nineties and beyond. Some characteristics of Funk and some key recordings are listed in Box 10–2.

The godfather of funk is James Brown. His work in the mid sixties codified the style, especially 1965's "Papa's Got a Brand New Bag" and 1967's "Cold Sweat." Some scholars view his 1970 recording of "Get Up (I Feel Like Being a) Sex Machine" as the single defining recording of the style. These recordings paved the way for other artists to make innovative contributions to the genre. Besides James Brown (see chapter 5), the two most prominent funk pioneers were George Clinton and Sly Stone.

GEORGE CLINTON

George Clinton (1940–) is one of the most eccentric and colorful musicians of all time. Leading a loose aggregation of musicians known at var-

---

Box 10-2 Funk

Characteristics of Funk
1. Most important element: the rhythmic groove, especially between the bass and drums
2. Typical instrumentation: bass, drums, guitar, electric keyboards, horns
3. Minimalism: simple two and four bar repeating phrases that create a trance-like effect
4. The rawest and earthiest form of black pop to date
5. Vocalists employ shrieks, screams, grunts, etc.; group vocal chants common

Key Funk Recordings
- ❑ "Get Up (I Feel Like Being a) Sex Machine"—James Brown 1970
- ❑ "Thank You (Falettinme Be Mice Elf Agin)"—Sly and the Family Stone 1970
- ❑ *Shaft*—Isaac Hayes, 1971
- ❑ *Innervisions*—Stevie Wonder, 1973
- ❑ "Tear the Roof Off the Sucker (Give Up the Funk)"—Parliament, 1976
- ❑ "Brick House"—the Commodores, 1977

George Clinton is one of the most eccentric and colorful musicians of all time.
AP/WIDE WORLD PHOTOS

ious times as **Parliament, Funkadelic,** the P-Funk All Stars, and the Mothership Connection, Clinton produced some of the most adventurous recordings of the sixties and seventies. Growing up in Plainfield, New Jersey, he founded a vocal group called the Parliaments at age fifteen; twelve years later, Clinton was working as a staff writer at Motown when the group had their first hit with "(I Wanna) Testify" (number 20). Following a legal dispute with Berry Gordy over the name Parliaments, Clinton began recording psychedelic music on the Westbound label as Funkadelic. Although he eventually won the dispute with Berry, Clinton continued to record using both bands, with Parliament (the 's' being dropped) being the more commercial-oriented ensemble, Funkadelic being the more experimental.

Throughout the seventies, Clinton built up a cult following through innovative concept albums and dazzling concert experiences. Performances would often include Clinton, dressed in elaborate costumes (rivaling those of David Bowie), jumping out of a coffin while other band members at various times wore diapers, smoked marijuana, and simulated sex acts. A giant flying saucer named the Mothership descended from a huge denim cap. Musically, Clinton mixed influences from psychedelia, R&B and jazz; lyrically he created cosmic and imaginary worlds with characters such as the Cro-Nasal Sapiens, the Thumpasorus People and Dr. Funkenstein, all of whom engaged in a sort of primeval struggle for existence. One critic described all this as either James Brown on acid or a black Frank Zappa. As you might imagine, Clinton's crossover appeal to white audiences was minimal; his black audience was large enough for him to chart five Top Forty albums in the seventies, three of which went gold, two platinum. Parliament's biggest single hit came with 1976's straight-ahead funk tune "Tear the Roof Off the Sucker (Give Up the Funk)" (number 15) from the album *Mothership Connection.* Clinton's groups over the years have included such heavyweight musicians as former James Brown-ers **Bootsy Collins, Maceo**

Parker, and **Fred Wesley.** One of his musical mottos is "Free your mind and your ass will follow."

SLY AND THE FAMILY STONE

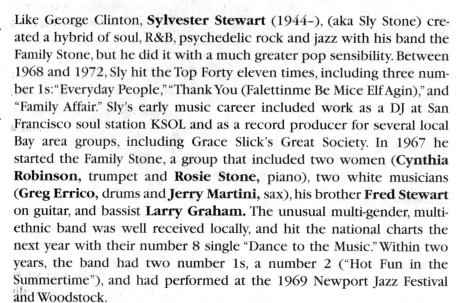

See Appendix A, "Thank You (Falettinme Be Mice Elf Agin)" by Sly and the Family Stone. Track 21 on enclosed CD.

Like George Clinton, **Sylvester Stewart** (1944–), (aka Sly Stone) created a hybrid of soul, R&B, psychedelic rock and jazz with his band the Family Stone, but he did it with a much greater pop sensibility. Between 1968 and 1972, Sly hit the Top Forty eleven times, including three number 1s: "Everyday People," "Thank You (Falettinme Be Mice Elf Agin)," and "Family Affair." Sly's early music career included work as a DJ at San Francisco soul station KSOL and as a record producer for several local Bay area groups, including Grace Slick's Great Society. In 1967 he started the Family Stone, a group that included two women (**Cynthia Robinson,** trumpet and **Rosie Stone,** piano), two white musicians (**Greg Errico,** drums and **Jerry Martini,** sax), his brother **Fred Stewart** on guitar, and bassist **Larry Graham.** The unusual multi-gender, multi-ethnic band was well received locally, and hit the national charts the next year with their number 8 single "Dance to the Music." Within two years, the band had two number 1s, a number 2 ("Hot Fun in the Summertime"), and had performed at the 1969 Newport Jazz Festival and Woodstock.

While Sly's use of irresistible sing-along hooks produced enduring pop staples ("I Want to Take You Higher," "Dance to the Music"), his lyrics sometimes contained harsh social commentary ("Don't Call Me Nigger Whitey," "Sex Machine," "Stand"). The group's most militant statement came with 1971's *There's a Riot Going On,* which was also their only number 1 album. One of the key elements to the sound of the Family Stone was the bass playing of Larry Graham, who developed an innovative 'slap' technique of playing that has become a staple of all subsequent funk and jazz/rock fusion. When Graham left the group in 1972 to start his own band, Graham Central Station, the Family Stone began to flounder. Sly became notorious for no-shows at concerts, and rumors of drug addiction flourished. By the mid seventies, the group had disbanded. Recent years have found many of the Family Stone's most memorable hits being used for high profile national advertising campaigns.

OTHER IMPORTANT FUNK BANDS

By 1974, funk was achieving a surprising degree of crossover success. **Earth, Wind and Fire,** formed in 1969, used Latin rhythms, jazzy horn lines and an interest in Egyptology to achieve fourteen Top Forty hits (including the number 1 "Shining Star" in 1975) and eight platinum albums between 1974 and 1979. **Stevie Wonder** reinvented himself as a singer/songwriter/synthesizer conceptualist with five Top Five albums in the seventies *(Talking Book, Innervisions, Fulfillingness' First Finale, Songs in the Key of Life, Journey through the Secret Life of Plants),* and funk classics such as 1972's "Superstition" and 1976's "I

Wish," which both went to number 1. **Kool and the Gang had twenty-two** Top Forty hits in the seventies and eighties, including "Funky Stuff" and "Jungle Boogie." Other groups that had funk hits included the **Ohio Players** ("Funky Worm," 1973) and the **Commodores ("Brick House,"** number 5, 1977).

Two other artists, **Isaac Hayes** and **Curtis Mayfield,** achieved **pop** success scoring music for what became known as the **blaxploitation films** (movies made by black directors and actors that had **inner city** themes of drug deals and ghetto shootings). Hayes, the **former Stax** writer who broke out onto his own with the landmark LP *Hot Buttered Soul* in 1969, became the first black composer to win an **Academy Award** for Best Score for 1971's *Shaft* soundtrack LP. Mayfield scored **the highly** successful *Superfly* in 1972, emphasizing his high, falsetto **vocals and a** smooth, pop oriented brand of funk.

Jazz/Rock

HORN ROCK BANDS

In the late sixties, rock musicians and jazz musicians began **to experi-**ment with fusing the two styles together. Rock musicians, who **generally** had fewer pretensions about what could or could not be done **stylisti-**cally than jazz musicians, were the first to cross influence **their music.** The first of these bands, the **Electric Flag, Chicago,** and **Blood, Sweat and Tears** were formed in 1967; the following year saw the **creation of Tower of Power, Chase,** and other similar groups. Although **these** bands typically did not incorporate jazz swing rhythms, they **had large** horn sections made up of what were traditionally jazz **instruments** (trumpets, saxophones, and trombones) and incorporated **jazz har-**monies and, in some cases, extended jazz solo improvisations. **Blood,** Sweat and Tears was the first of these bands to break through **to pop suc-**cess, achieving three number 2 hits from their platinum Grammy **Award** winning eponymous LP in 1969. Although the group was **founded by** former Dylan cohort **Al Kooper,** he had been forced out **before the** group hit the charts. The Electric Flag was founded by **former Band of** Gypsies drummer **Buddy Miles** and blues guitarist **Mike Bloomfield** (another former Dylan band mate) in San Francisco, although **they only** stayed together for a year and a half.

The unquestioned pop powerhouse of the horn rock **bands was** Chicago, who shortened their name from CTA (Chicago **Transit** Authority) shortly after the release of their platinum **certified first** album. Under the direction of producer **James William Guercio,** Chicago has sold more than 100 million records since its inception, **with** twenty Top Ten hits and fifteen platinum or multi-platinum **albums.** Tower of Power, while achieving just a modicum of pop success, **was the** funkiest of the horn bands, with a rhythm section powered by **drummer David Garibaldi** and **Chester Thompson** on Hammond **organ, and** the mighty and ultra-precise **Tower of Power Horns,** led by **saxo-**phonist **Emilio Castillo.**

JAZZ/ROCK FUSION

Jazz musicians were much more suspicious of rock than their rock counterparts were of jazz. Since its birth, rock and roll had been steadily eating away at the young jazz audience, a fact that had not gone unnoticed by jazz musicians. Many viewed rock as simple, lowbrow, and mindless; others looked down their noses at the music because of its inherent commercial sensibilities. In addition, most jazz musicians viewed rock musicians as inferior players who were making lots of money playing three-chord drivel. It wasn't until **Miles Davis** (1926–91) began experimenting with rock influences that jazz musicians began to realize that rock could provide a new creative outlet and possibly a much larger audience. Davis, who had been at the forefront of nearly every jazz innovation since the mid forties, first incorporated electric guitar and keyboards in early 1969 with his impressionistic album *In a Silent Way.* It was his next LP, the double album *Bitches Brew,* recorded in New York City at roughly the same time as the Woodstock festival, which effectively created the new genre known as **jazz/rock fusion,** or simply fusion.

Jazz/rock fusion was the jazz style of the early seventies that embraced rock elements such as rhythm, electric instruments, and simpler harmonies.

Fusion incorporates the rhythms, instruments, and simpler harmonies of rock, while maintaining the essential element of jazz—the improvised solo. Fusion was the first jazz style in which horn players or singers were not the main lead instruments; that role was now taken up by synthesizer players and guitarists. Davis himself often used a wah-wah pedal on his trumpet to give it a guitar-like sound. Although *Bitches Brew* and later Miles Davis albums were noted for a very cluttered, improvisational style, with layers of keyboards and guitars over rock grooves, later fusion evolved into a tighter format, some of which was relatively pop oriented. By the late seventies, much of fusion had either become excessively pretentious (the same problem art rock was having) or overtly commercial, and the music lost much of its initial creative impulses. Some characteristics of Jazz/Rock Fusion and key recordings are listed in Box 10-3.

The alumni from Davis' first fusion explorations went on to form the first generation of fusion bands that helped further define the style. Drummer **Tony Williams** and English guitarist **John McLaughlin**

Box 10-3 Jazz/Rock Fusion

Characteristics of Jazz/Rock Fusion
1. Rock rhythms, instruments, performance techniques
2. An emphasis on jazz improvisation
3. Typical instrumentation: drums, percussion, electric bass, electric guitar, saxophone

Key Jazz/Rock Fusion Recordings
❏ *Bitches Brew*—Miles Davis, 1969
❏ *Birds of Fire*—Mahavishnu Orchestra, 1973
❏ *Head Hunters*—Herbie Hancock, 1974
❏ *Heavy Weather*—Weather Report 1977

formed the short-lived **Lifetime** in 1969; McLaughlin later went on to form the **Mahavishnu Orchestra,** one of the most intense and explosive of the fusion groups. One of the most popular and influential with jazz and rock musicians alike was **Weather Report,** formed in 1970 by tenor saxophonist/composer **Wayne Shorter** and keyboardist **Josef Zawinul.** Their 1977 LP, *Heavy Weather,* went platinum, partly on the strength of Zawinul's hit song "Birdland." Keyboardist/composer **Herbie Hancock** hit the pop charts in 1974 with his own platinum LP, the funk-influenced *Head Hunters;* while keyboardist **Chick Corea** formed the art rock-influenced **Return to Forever** in 1970.

Reggae

WHAT IS REGGAE?

Reggae is an indigenous Jamaican music that evolved from the combination of folk music, American R&B, and traditional Afro-Caribbean music. By the late sixties, reggae recordings were starting to filter out of Jamaica and make a presence in the U.S. In 1969 two reggae records by Jamaican artists hit the American pop charts, "Israelites" by **Desmond Dekker and the Aces** (number 9) and "Wonderful World, Beautiful People" by **Jimmy Cliff** (number 25). By the early seventies, American and British rock musicians began co-opting the music: **Johnny Nash** had a number 1 hit in 1972 with the reggae inspired "I Can See Clearly Now" and a number 12 in 1973 with Bob Marley's "Stir It Up." Paul Simon went to the Jamaican capital city of Kingston in 1972 to record his reggae influenced "Mother and Child Reunion," which hit number 4 on the charts. In 1973 the Jamaican film *The Harder They Come* was released, introducing American audiences to the music and its star, Jimmy Cliff. In Boston, a city with a large student population, the film was so popular that one theatre ran it for more than seven years without interruption. In 1974, Eric Clapton's cover of Marley's "I Shot the Sheriff" became the most popular reggae song in American pop history when it went to number 1. Throughout the seventies and eighties, artists and bands such as the Clash, Elvis Costello, the Police, and others were inspired by the infectious rhythms of the music. Reggae in the seventies became the latest form of black music to become trendy in England, following the trad jazz-skiffle-R&B-blues lineage. Two Birmingham groups, the **English Beat** and **UB40,** were among the many that formed in the U.K. in response to the popularity of Jamaican music. In addition, the Jamaican tradition of 'toasting' and creating music through a process known as 'dub' later became important influences on rap music. Some characteristics of reggae and some recordings are listed in Box 10–4.

Each instrument in a reggae band has a clearly defined role to play: while the guitar provides choppy, 'up stroke' strumming on beats two and four, the bass and drums are locked into a syncopated beat that often de-emphasizes the downbeat of each measure. Most reggae is played slowly, allowing the resulting polyrhythms and lyrics to be clearly heard. Because reggae came from the oppressed lower class in the ghettos of

Reggae is the Jamaican music that evolved from the combination of indigenous folk, American R&B, and traditional Afro-Caribbean music.

The primary rhythmic feature of reggae is the **'riddim,'** or the intertwined patterns played by the bass, guitar, and drums.

Box 10-4 Reggae

Characteristics of Reggae
1. Combines influences from Jamaican folk (mento), American R&B, Afro-Caribbean music
2. Intertwined patterns played by the bass, drums and guitar known as 'riddim'
3. Lyrics often refer to social injustices, political dissent, racism
4. Identification with Rastafarian movement

Key Reggae Recordings
❏ "Israelites"—Desmond Dekker and the Aces 1969
❏ *Burnin'*—Bob Marley and the Wailers 1973
❏ "I Shot the Sheriff"—Eric Clapton 1974

the capital city of Kingston, its lyrics often concern political protest, social injustices, racism, and the Rastafarian movement.

RASTAFARI CULTURE

Rastafarianism is a movement whose followers believe they will be repatriated to their African homeland and escape Babylon (a metaphor for their oppressors in the New World). It was inspired by the writings of **Marcus Garvey,** a writer and political activist who wrote of the "crowning of a black king" who will "be the redeemer." In 1916 he moved to Harlem and started a "Back to Africa" movement before eventually moving to the continent himself. When **Haile Selassie** was crowned king of the African nation Ethiopia in 1930, many clergymen in Jamaica saw this as a sign that Garvey's predictions were correct. Rastafarians reinterpreted the Bible to suit their needs, and in time developed their own cultural values that included songs of social and political protest, the smoking of ganja (marijuana) as a sacramental herb, and wearing the hair in **dreadlocks.** As the movement spread throughout Jamaica, Rastafarian songs were mixed with an African drumming style known as **burru** and slowed down. At this point in time, roughly the mid sixties, the Rastafarian culture began to intermingle with the popular music of Jamaica to provide the basis for reggae.

HISTORICAL BACKGROUND TO REGGAE

Reggae's roots go back to the indigenous folk music of Jamaica known as mento, which first appeared in rural areas in the 19th century.

Mento's popularity began to fade in the 1940s, when Swing big bands patterned after those of Benny Goodman and Count Basie rose to popularity in the urban dancehalls of Kingston. To emulate them, local musicians formed road bands that played their version of swing music at public dances. By the late 1950s, Jamaican youth began copying the R&B records of Fats Domino and Louis Jordan they were hearing on radio broadcasts from New Orleans, Miami, and Memphis, and developed their own variation of the music known as **ska.** Ska (an onomatopoeic word originating from the sound of the strong, sharp offbeat accents) is an up tempo music that combines an R&B-influenced walking bass with accents on the offbeats (beats 2 & 4) from mento. Ska was extremely popular on the island in the early sixties, and one ska record even hit the American charts in 1964, **Millie Small's** "My Boy Lollipop" (number 4). The most popular ska band in Jamaica at this time was the **Skatalites,** led by trombonist **Don Drummond.**

In the summer of 1966, temperatures soared on the island, making ska too fast to play or dance to, and a slower, updated version emerged known as **rock steady.** More relaxed and looser rhythmically than its predecessor, rock steady simplified the bass and drum syncopations of ska, but retained the offbeat accents. Rock steady appealed to the Jamaican lower class youth known as the **Rude Boys,** urban hooligans that were generally against the system who sometimes engaged in civil disobedience. Whereas ska lyrics, like those of American R&B, concerned themselves with love and sex, the influence of the Rude Boys and Rastafarian culture into rock steady resulted in songs with themes of social and political protest.

THE DANCEHALL CULTURE

Another factor that had an impact on the evolving music styles in Jamaica during the fifties and sixties was the dancehall culture. The many dancehalls throughout Kingston increasingly became 'safe houses' where the lower class could gather and listen to and dance to music, often provided by portable sound systems that played records. In an attempt to liven up their shows, the DJs that operated these sound systems began to deliver spontaneous commentary on the proceedings, usually in some creative way that involved rhyming, interesting verbal sounds, the use of different dialects and nonsense syllables. This practice became known as **toasting.** In addition, DJs began to mix interesting sections of different songs together—a process known as **dub**—to create even more excitement, and often toasted over the top of the dub. Eventually these styles made their way into recording studios, resulting in hit songs from artists such as King Stitt and U Roy. In the seventies, Caribbean expatriates such as **Kool Herc** and **Grandmaster Flash** took the techniques of dub music and toasting to the Bronx where they played important roles in the creation of rap music.

By 1968 the evolution from rock steady to reggae was complete: the music had slowed down even further, while becoming more intense and hard driving. The word itself comes from the local slang term "raggay," or raggedy. Central to the rise in popularity of reggae worldwide was **Chris Blackwell,** the heir to a British fortune who spent much of his youth living in Jamaica. In 1961, Blackwell founded **Island Records,** the driving force behind Millie Small's "My Boy Lollipop." In 1964, Blackwell met and signed Jamaican singer Jimmy Cliff to Island, launching his career with a series of records that became hits in Europe. Cliff eventually had an American hit ("Wonderful World, Beautiful People") and was the star of the influential film *The Harder They Come.* Blackwell also signed Desmond Dekker in 1964, and released "Honour Thy Father and Mother," a number 1 hit in Jamaica. Dekker later went on to have the 1969 hit "Israelites," which went to number 1 in the U.K. and number 9 in the U.S. In the late sixties, Blackwell turned his attention to rock acts such as Traffic, Jethro Tull, and Emerson, Lake, and Palmer, but in 1972 signed the reggae artist who was destined to be the music's biggest star: Bob Marley.

BOB MARLEY AND THE WAILERS

See Appendix A, "Get Up, Stand Up" by Peter Tosh. Track 22 on enclosed CD.

By the time he died of cancer at the age of thirty-six, Bob Marley (1945–81) had not only become the most famous reggae musician on earth, but a national hero to his fellow Jamaicans. After moving to the shantytown slums of Kingston from rural Jamaica at age fourteen, Marley began playing guitar and writing songs. At seventeen, he recorded several lackluster singles with the help of producer Leslie Kong; the next year he formed the Teenagers, later renamed the Wailing Rudeboys, later simply the Wailers. The original lineup included singers **Peter Tosh** and **Bunny Livingstone.** In spite of occasional singles that were hits on the island, the Wailers endured years of financial hardship—Marley even worked in a factory in Delaware for a period. In 1969, they signed with producer Lee Perry, who beefed up the band with the addition of brothers **Aston and Carlton Barrett** on bass and drums. Over the next three years, the Wailers became enormously popular in Jamaica, and were signed to Island in 1972. Their first Island LP, *Catch a Fire,* received favorable international acclaim; their second, *Burnin'* included two of Marley's most famous compositions, "I Shot the Sheriff" and "Get Up, Stand Up." Both songs illustrate the desperate lives of the Jamaican underclass: "Sheriff" relates a misunderstanding and violent altercation with law enforcement, while "Get Up" exhorts fellow Rastafarians to take action against the system. When Eric Clapton's cover of "I Shot the Sheriff," from his 1974 album *461 Ocean Boulevard* went to number 1 in both England and America, reggae's new prophet was poised for worldwide stardom. Around this time both Tosh and Livingstone quit the group to pursue solo careers, but Marley brought in the **I-Threes** vocal group (which included his wife Rita) for their successful international tour in 1974, their first outside of Jamaica. Leading the wave of reggae's international popularity, the Wailers went on to record six gold albums for Island, including *Rastaman Vibration* in 1976, which went to number 8 on the U.S. charts.

Marley used his growing fame to expound upon his political viewpoints, which included social activism, rebellion against the system, and his belief in Rastafarianism. His reverential stature in his native country climbed to levels normally reserved for popular religious leaders or heads of state. Perhaps as a result, Marley was wounded in an assassination attempt in December 1976 that forced him into exile for more than a year. Then in 1980, after collapsing while jogging in New York's Central Park, he discovered that he had cancer in his brain, liver, and lungs. His final album *Uprising* was released shortly before he died on May 11, 1981. In his short time in the spotlight, Bob Marley defined the music and politics of reggae for the worldwide rock community.

OTHER REGGAE ARTISTS

Other influential Jamaican ska, rock steady and reggae artists to emerge in the sixties and seventies were **Toots Hibbert,** leader of **Toots and the Maytals,** Peter MacIntosh, going by the name **Peter Tosh, Prince Buster, Judge Dread,** and the above-mentioned Desmond Dekker and Jimmy Cliff.

Before he died, Bob Marley had not only become the most famous reggae musician on earth, but a national hero to his fellow Jamaicans. AP/WIDE WORLD PHOTOS

Disco

THE UNDERGROUND REVOLUTION

When **disco** hit the pop music world in the mid seventies, it did it with such sudden, overpowering force that much of the music establishment was caught off guard. In spite of this, disco became the biggest pop music trend in history (in terms of record sales), and for a few short years, from 1976 to 1979, its total control of the American pop scene was comparable only to that of big band jazz during the Swing Era. But by 1980, the disco supernova had burned itself out, due in part to a virulent backlash from the mainstream rock culture. Disco's most important feature was its rhythm and the relentless pounding emphasis on every beat, a streamlined evolution from the late sixties-early seventies funk of James Brown and Sly Stone. Its other musical influences were diverse: the lush string and horn orchestrations from Motown and Philadelphia International Records; percolating percussion from Latin music; vocal chants and honking saxophones from rhythm and blues. It also incorporated new technology, making extensive use of synthesizers and drum machines.

Like Swing, disco was first and foremost music to dance to, and it emerged at a time when much of rock had become too artsy (art rock), too pretentious (heavy metal), or too self absorbed (singer/songwriters) to care about dancers any more. Remember the dance fads of the early sixties, the Twist, the Wah Watusi, the Limbo, and the Swim? Those days, when public dancing was a near ritual, were a distant memory by the early seventies. By then it seemed that the only people to whom dancing was still an important part of community were blacks, Hispanics, and gays—coincidentally the same groups that had been left out by nearly all the new rock trends of the seventies. Disco reconnected rock to dance, and in doing so paved the way for the dance-oriented MTV Generation and its superstars: Michael Jackson, Madonna, and Prince. Disco also was

Disco is dance-oriented pop that incorporates synthesizers, drum machines, and lush orchestrations that emerged in the late seventies.

Box 10-5 Disco

Characteristics of Disco
1. Pop oriented dance music whose most important characteristic is the relentless pounding emphasis on every beat
2. Produced in the studio using synthesizers, drum machines
3. Lush strings orchestrations, predominant use of percussion instruments, vocal chants

Key Disco Recordings
❏ "Love to Love You Baby"—Donna Summer 1975
❏ *Saturday Night Fever* Soundtrack—the Bee Gees and other artists 1977

an important influence on new wave, rap, and hip-hop culture. Some characteristics of Disco and some key recordings are listed in Box 10-5.

Disco's origins were in the European and East Coast dance clubs known as **discotheques** that first became popular during the early sixties. These clubs generally employed DJs to play records rather than hire live bands out of economic necessity. By the early seventies, discos had fallen out of favor with rock's mainstream audience and went underground, catering primarily to the black, Hispanic, and gay subcultures. Around 1973, the popularity of discos started to rebound, a trend that was due in part to the ever-increasing skills of DJs to seamlessly merge one song into the next, using two turntables while keeping the beat constant (disco records often had the beats per minute—bpm—marked on the label). This technique enabled dancers (who were often worked into a frenzy by ingesting cocaine and other uppers) to stay on the dance floor for extended periods of time. Discos initially did not impose dress codes, but it became fashionable for patrons to dress to the nines, enabling them to fantasize, at least for the moment, that they were the featured performers while they did their best dance moves. It was in this environment that disco turned the tables on the established rock culture: the DJs, the producers (who created the music), and the dancers were the stars instead of the rock singers and instrumentalists.

DISCO CONQUERS THE AIRWAVES

Disco records were initially ignored by radio, and did not get extensive airplay until around 1974. It was in that year that the first bona fide disco hits emerged, "Rock the Boat" by the Hues Corporation and George McCrae's "Rock Your Baby." Both entered the Top Forty on June 15th; on July 6th "Rock the Boat" hit number 1 and was replaced the following week by "Rock Your Baby," which stayed there for two weeks. By the following year, disco hits were popping up with regularity, with Van McCoy's "The Hustle," Elton John's "Philadelphia Freedom," and KC and the Sunshine Band's "Get Down Tonight" and "That's the Way (I Like It)" all hitting number 1. Late in 1975, **Donna Summer,** the 'queen of disco' emerged for the first time with the hit "Love to Love You Baby" (number

2). Produced by European producer **Georgio Moroder,** who created a symphony of synthesized sounds over a drum machine beat, "Love to Love You Baby" featured Summer repeating the title over and over in fake orgasmic ecstasy. Summer later went on to hold the number 1 spot for a cumulative thirteen weeks in a one year stretch in 1978 and 1979 with four number 1 hits, including "Bad Girls," which stayed at the top for five weeks in the summer of 1979. Summer later became a born-again Christian and renounced her disco heritage.

By 1976, disco ruled the airwaves, as everybody and everything in pop came under its influence. Among the number 1 hits of the year were Walter Murphy's adaptation of Beethoven's Fifth Symphony, "A Fifth of Beethoven"; Johnny Taylor's "Disco Lady"; and L.A. DJ Rick Dees' "Disco Duck." Even Paul McCartney got into disco mode with "Silly Love Songs" (number 1) with his group, Wings. The year 1976 was also the year that the established-but-floundering English group the **Bee Gees** introduced their new revamped disco sound with "You Should Be Dancing," also a number 1 hit. The song proved to be merely a warm-up for the group, who the following year wrote the soundtrack to the Hollywood smash hit *Saturday Night Fever,* produced by Robert Stigwood and starring John Travolta. The soundtrack album to the film (which also featured the Tramps, MFSB, Kool & the Gang and others) eventually sold thirty million copies worldwide, making it the best selling LP in history at the time. The Bee Gees had three number 1 singles generate from the album—"How Deep Is Your Love," "Stayin' Alive" and "Night Fever"—and had three more number 1s the following year. The movie itself grossed a stunning $130 million. Throughout 1978 and 1979, disco dominated films, TV, radio, and advertising. There were all-disco radio stations; remakes of Beatles, Beach Boys, and classical music set to disco beats were common; even the Rolling Stones couldn't escape disco fever, and profited handsomely with 1978's number 1, "Miss You." For a brief moment at the start of 1979, the most popular band in America was the gay-novelty group the **Village People.**

THE BACKLASH

As early as 1978, the disco backlash was setting in, with "Death to Disco" and "Disco Sucks" T-shirts and buttons becoming popular. On the night of July 12, 1979, Chicago radio station WLUP sponsored a "Disco Demolition Night" between games of a double header at the White Sox' Comiskey Park. Nearly 50,000 people showed up to witness DJ Steve Dahl blow up a crate of disco records. Many of the fans went one step further and stormed onto the field, tearing up turf and causing so much chaos and destruction that the second game had to be cancelled. Surely the anti-disco backlash was caused in part by the music's overwhelming popularity and the inevitable pendulum swing away from it. There was also the natural dislike of the music by those fans who held the musical virtuosity of real performers in high regard, since disco was created largely in the studio using synthesizers and overdubbing technology. But there was an uglier side to the disco backlash as well.

Disco was perceived by many as gay music, and those people with homophobic tendencies found the music to be an irresistible target for their invective. Others with a racist agenda got caught up in the anti-disco craze as a convenient way to openly express their feelings. Anti-gay and anti-black sentiments were common among many angry, young white males who made up the core of rocks mainstream heavy metal audience. Not wanting to alienate this group, many radio stations stopped playing disco records. In fact, many radio stations stopped playing black pop music altogether. By 1980, disco was not only a dirty word, it was dead.

Chapter 10
Study Questions

1. What were some of the reasons for the decline of soul music at the beginning of the seventies?

   _____

   _____

   _____

2. What were some important differences between soft soul and funk?

   _____

   _____

   _____

3. In what ways did James Brown influence funk?

   _____

   _____

   _____

4. Name three differences between the music, bands and careers of George Clinton and Sly Stone.

   _____

   _____

   _____

5. Why were jazz musicians suspicious of and reluctant to incorporate rock influences into their music?

   _____

   _____

   _____

6. In what ways was Miles Davis influential to rock music?

_____

_____

_____

_____

7. How did American music and Jamaican reggae cross influence each other?

_____

_____

_____

_____

_____

8. Why was reggae used for social protest, and describe its relationship to the Rastafarian movement.

_____

_____

_____

_____

_____

9. Where, when and how did disco become popular?

_____

_____

_____

_____

10. Name three reasons why there was a backlash against disco.

_____

_____

_____

_____

Punk and Its Aftermath

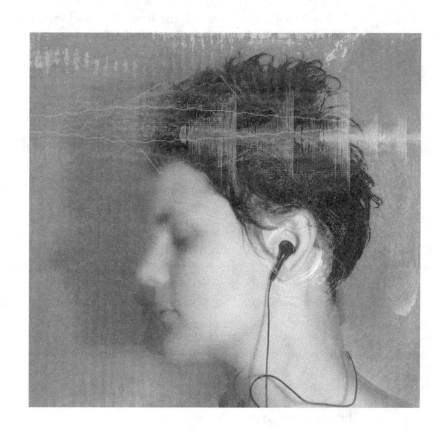

The Origins of Punk

THE ANTI-REVOLUTION

On November 6, 1975, a new band played their first show at London's St. Martin's School of Art. Bands had been performing at schools like St. Martin's for years, and so in the days leading up to the performance, there was no reason to believe that anything out of the ordinary would happen—just some good old rock and roll played by an unknown group looking for a little recognition. However, it soon became apparent that this was indeed going to be a very different type of show. Within minutes, the band members—all scrawny teenagers—began to angrily insult their audience. Their music was raw, noisy, and offensive—that is, if you wanted to call it music. The members of the band made no attempt to hide the fact that they could barely play their instruments. The performance was a combination of noise, anger, invective, chaos, and rebellion. It was also short—after ten minutes the school's social programmer pulled the plug and cut off their power. But in those ten minutes the world got its first glimpse of the Sex Pistols.

The Sex Pistols were not the first punk rock band, but they certainly were the most notorious. **Punk** emerged in the mid seventies as a backlash reaction against nearly everything that rock had brought to the decade:

❏ The conservative and self-indulgent tendencies of folk rock and the singer/songwriters;

❏ The pretentiousness of art rock and heavy metal;

❏ The slick studio production of funk;

❏ The control and manipulation of the marketplace by the rock establishment.

To punks, rock at age twenty was middle aged, soft, and irrelevant. There were too many pampered millionaire rock stars, and too many flashy guitar and keyboard solos that served no purpose other than to let the performers show off. More and more, rock had become the music of the mainstream rather than the music of the outsiders; it had become safe rather than dangerous; and worst of all, it had lost the rebellious attitude that had been its birthright. Punk brought rock back to the streets, back to its primeval days, and in doing so, it dramatically influenced its future evolution.

PUNK CULTURE

Punk was more than just a musical trend, however—it was a culture, defined by its rejection of any and all conventional norms of society. Its mantra was simple: to shock, disrespect, disrupt, offend, and destroy anything in its path, using whatever means possible. But because these nihilistic tendencies were so passionate and universal, punk culture was also full of contradictions. For instance, punk rejected traditional fashion,

---

Box 11-1 Punk

Characteristics of Punk
1. Raw, angry, nihilistic; characterized by a do-it-yourself attitude
2. Typical instrumentation: electric guitars, bass, drums, vocalist
3. Lyrics with themes of nihilism, anger, alienation, desperation, and darkness
4. Counter culture associated with clothing styles, body pins, etc.

Key Punk Recordings
❏ *The Velvet Underground and Nico*—Velvet Underground, 1967
❏ *Raw Power*—Iggy and the Stooges, 1973
❏ *Never Mind the Bullocks, Here's the Sex Pistols*—the Sex Pistols, 1977
❏ *London Calling*—the Clash, 1979

---

but in doing so created its own fashion statement of torn jeans, spiked hair, dog collars, and safety pins worn on the face. Some punks embraced progressive social issues while others adopted racist and fascist stances. And ultimately punk became attractive enough to the rock establishment that major labels began signing groups like the Sex Pistols, in effect making them a part, rather than a rejection, of the status quo. When this happened, the punk movement suddenly lost its credibility. Some characteristics of Punk and some key recordings are listed in Box 11-1.

Even though punk's moment on earth was brief—roughly from 1975 to 1978—it has inspired more journalistic efforts than any other subject in rock (with the possible exception of the Beatles). And rightfully so: the punk movement was one of the most fascinating trends in modern pop culture. Punk's lifetime also roughly paralleled that of disco, and many writers have pointed out the complementing and polar opposite roles of the two movements. Disco's origins were in black music, punks in white (the "whitest music ever" according to historian Jim Curtis). Disco was smooth and sensual—punk jagged and dissonant. Disco was constructed in the studio using sophisticated studio technology—punk was the ultimate anyone-can-do-it music. Disco dancing was coordinated and stylish—in punk, dancing (if you want to call it that) was a pushing, jostling, shoving match called **pogo.** Disco fashion was leisure suits, dresses, and high heels—punk fashion was leather and safety pins. Finally, disco was dismissed by the rock press as escapist, while punk was embraced by many of the same writers as a long awaited return to the rebellious spirit of rock and roll.

The Earliest Punk Bands

GARAGE BANDS

Of course, the rebellious attitude of punk can be traced back to the beginnings of rock and roll. In the broadest definition of the word, many of the early rock and rollers can be described as punks, especially rebel rousers like Jerry Lee Lewis, Little Richard, and Link Wray. By the sixties, punk attitude could be found in "My Generation" by the Who ("Why don't you all f-f-f-fade away") and a growing number of **garage bands** that were populating the suburban American landscape. Garage bands were typically after school endeavors put together by friends for fun and to play for an occasional school dance. Occasionally, a garage band's self-produced single would become a local hit; sometimes these records would even get regional or national attention. Examples of national hits by what were essentially local garage bands include "Louie, Louie" (1963) by Seattle's the Kingsmen; "Psychotic Reaction" (1966) by the **Count Five** from San Jose, California; and "96 Tears" (1966) by the Flint, Michigan based **? and the Mysterians.** The prevailing attitude of the sixties garage band was that anybody could buy a guitar and an amp, learn three chords and start a band. This is also fundamental to the principles of punk.

Two Michigan bands from the sixties were especially influential to punk rock. **The MC5** (short for the Motor City Five) was formed in 1965 in Detroit, a tough industrial city where harsh economic conditions offered little hope for local youth. Their political ranting and sloganeering at concerts earned them a large and devout local following, which led to a contract with Elektra Records in 1968. However, their live debut album *Kick Out the Jams* immediately immersed the band in controversy: the opening track is an evangelical call for revolution ("Brothers and sisters, I wanna wanna see your hands out there . . . "). The title track begins with the proclamation that "Right now it's time to. . . . *kick out the jams, motherfucker!*" After some stores refused to sell the album, the band responded by plastering the windows of one with Elektra stationary that had "Fuck you" scrawled on it. Soon afterward, the label dropped the band.

The Stooges were formed in Ann Arbor, Michigan in 1967 by lead singer (or more appropriately, lead *screamer*) **Iggy Pop** (James Osterberg), a rough and tumble youth who had been raised in a trailer park in nearby Ypsilanti. After seeing a performance by the Doors, Iggy formed the Stooges, who gave their first concert on (appropriately) Halloween night. Stooges concerts were an onslaught of noise and anarchy, as Iggy would often rub raw meat on himself, fling himself into the crowd and even cut himself with broken bottles. The raw power and primal qualities of the Stooges was unprecedented, and their lyrics were a harbinger of future punk. The song "1969," from their self-titled debut album on Elektra took a common punk theme—boredom—and proclaimed "Last year I was twenty-one, I didn't have a lot of fun" and "Another year of nothing to do, It's 1969." After the release of *Raw Power* in 1973, the group broke up. Although they reformed in 1976 and released two albums produced by David Bowie in 1977, sales were poor. Iggy Pop also suffered through periods of heroin addiction and mental institutionalization during this time.

THE VELVET UNDERGROUND

The Velvet Underground was the first important New York band to adopt the lyric themes of despair, drug addiction, and violence that would later be commonly associated with punk. They never sold many records—they were too crude for anything more than a cult following. However, their influence was great, and it has often been said that everyone who bought a Velvets record went out and started a band. The group was formed in 1965 by **Lou Reed** (vocals, guitar) (1942–) and **John Cale** (vocals, electric violin), two classically trained musicians who were involved in New York's avant-garde scene—Reed as a poet, Cale as a composer. Sometime in 1966, they were heard by artist **Andy Warhol,** who invited them to take part in his traveling mixed media show, the Exploding Plastic Inevitable, and perform at his art loft known as the Factory. On Warhol's insistence, European model/singer **Nico** joined the Velvets, and with her they recorded their first album, *The Velvet Underground* and Nico on MGM/Verve. Containing such plaintive Reed compositions as "I'm Waiting for the Man," a song about a white kid trying to get a heroin fix in Harlem, and "Venus in Furs," a song about sado-masochism, sales of the LP were poor. Although they continued to record and tour, by 1970, Reed, Cale and Nico had all left the group to pursue solo careers. Reed's post-Velvet career has been the most commercially successful: in 1973 his single "Walk on the Wild Side" hit number 16 on the U.S. charts.

With their crude sound, lyrics of alienation, desperation and darkness, and their association with the New York arts community, the Velvet Underground was perhaps the most influential of the pre-punk era bands. From them, the torch would soon be passed to a new crop of New York bands who would create the bona fide punk movement.

The New York Scene

CBGB's

The New York punk movement was connected to the city's conceptualist art scene known as the New York School. Conceptualist art, such as that created by abstract expressionist painters such as Jackson Pollock (who laid his canvas on the floor and threw paint at it), eschews technique for an "I-did-it-my-way" approach to creativity. Early pre-punk bands in New York used this tie in with high culture as an excuse for their own lack of musical technique as well as their lack of commercial success (Pollack himself was largely dismissed until after his death in 1956). The Velvet Underground were championed by pop artist Andy Warhol, while the **New York Dolls** first gained notoriety playing at the Mercer Arts Center on the lower East Side. Formed in 1971, the Dolls combined a glam look with an amateurish approach to performing (see chapter 9). For a brief period before they started to fall apart in early 1975, they were managed by **Malcolm McLaren,** a London clothier who was fascinated with the French situationist's strategy of staging media events for the sole purpose of disrupting everyday life. Before returning to England later that year, McLaren had the Dolls perform in red with a Communist flag as a backdrop.

Around this time, a grimy little bar at 315 Bowery in New York's Lower East Side renamed itself **CBGB's** and started to book underground rock bands. Within months, CBGB's (actually named CBGB and OMFUG for Country, Bluegrass and Blues, and Other Music for Urban Gourmets) became the center of the New York punk scene. The only other major club supporting punk at this time was **Max's Kansas City** at 213 Park Avenue South in Greenwich Village. One of the first groups to play at CBGB's was **Television,** a band that included bassist Richard Myers, who went by the name **Richard Hell,** and guitarist Tom Miller, who went by the name **Tom Verlaine** (after the French symbolist poet). Television's influences included avant-garde saxophonists John Coltrane and Albert Ayler, the Rolling Stones and French impressionistic composer Maurice Ravel. Hell was also influential to punk fashion as the first to wear the ripped clothes and just-fell-out-of-bed hairstyle, and as the writer of the first punk anthem, "Blank Generation," whose lyrics seemed to express the hopelessness that many in the rock underground felt. Hell later went on to play with the Heartbreakers and led the seminal band the **Voidoids,** which recorded "Blank Generation."

Another early CBGB artist was **Patti Smith** (1946–), a painter, poet, and rock journalist who began experimenting in 1971 with setting her poems to the musical accompaniment of guitarist **Lenny Kaye** and pianist **Richard Sohl.** In early 1974, the trio recorded "Hey Joe," backed with Smith's "Piss Factory," a song about her experience working at an assembly line job in New Jersey. With the release of the single, Smith's group began a residency at Max's Kansas City alongside Television, after which both bands moved to CBGB's. These successes were instrumental in securing a contract with newly formed Arista Records and the 1975 release of *Horses.* Produced by John Cale, *Horses* is an amalgamation of rock and roll, poetry, and primal experimentation. In spite of this, it was one of the few punk albums of the era that actually charted, going to number 47. Smith also made an alternative punk fashion statement of her own with a white button down shirt and men's tie.

THE RAMONES

The band that is considered by many to be the first true punk band was the Ramones, a group of high school buddies from the Forest Hills section of Queens, New York. The Ramones played rock and roll that was simple (four chords maximum per song), fast (most songs were played at breakneck tempos and were over in less than two and a half minutes), raw, energetic, and fun. Their music was intense and unrelenting (a sort of punk version of Phil Spector's Wall of Sound), while their shows, rarely lasting over twenty minutes, have been called the most powerful in rock history. Taking a surname used by Paul McCartney in his early years, the group was formed in 1974 by **Jeffrey Hyman, John Cummings, Doug Colvin,** and **Tom Erdely,** who became Joey, Johnny, Dee Dee, and Tommy Ramone, respectively. With a uniform of torn jeans and leather jackets, the Ramones played their first show on March 30, 1974 at New York's Performance Studio. By the end of the summer, the band had established a residency at CBGB's, where they played off and on for a year and developed a cult following. Near the end of 1975, they signed a contract with Sire Records and in early 1976 recorded their eponymous debut album for just over $6,000.

In the summer of 1976, the Ramones toured England and created a sensation in the rock underground that helped ignite the British punk movement. Later that year, they recorded their second album, *Ramones Leave Home,* which had limited success in the U.S. (like their first LP) but became somewhat of a hit in England. Capitalizing on their new-found celebrity in the U.K., the Ramones released "Sheena Is a Punk Rocker" in early 1977, which became a Top Forty hit there. Key to the success of the Ramones among punks was their amateurish musical abilities and the fact that they only played their own material. The band wrote their own songs not out of an artistic undertaking but because they couldn't learn other peoples. As Johnny Ramone admitted in an interview, "We put records on, but we couldn't figure out how to play the songs, so we decided to start writing songs that were within our capabilities." Their lyrics, often containing biting sarcasm and mindless humor, also held great appeal to punkers. Songs such as "I Don't Care," "I'm Against It," "I Wanna Be Sedated," and "Teenage Lobotomy" offered welcome relief from the soul-searching confessionals of the singer/song-writers and other types of narcissistic seventies rock.

PUNK GOES POP

Although the Ramones appeared in the Roger Corman 1979 film *Rock N' Roll High School* and Phil Spector produced their 1980 LP *End of the Century,* their audience (at least in America) did not grow much beyond cult status. Two other bands that emerged from the mid seventies New York punk scene that did achieve pop success were **Blondie** and the **Talking Heads.** Blondie, led by bleached blonde singer and former Playboy bunny **Deborah Harry,** achieved remarkable commercial success in the late seventies. After their debut at CBGB's in 1974, the group signed with Chrysalis Records and by 1978 had a number 6 album, *Parallel Lines,* which yielded four British hit singles. At their peak between 1979 and 1981, the group had four number 1 U.S. singles, including the reggae influenced "The Tide Is High." The Talking Heads, also formed in 1974, were the creation of three art students at the Rhode Island School of Design, **David Byrne** (guitar, vocals), **Chris Frantz** (drums), and **Tina Weymouth** (bass). From the beginning, the Talking Heads were different than the other bands on the CBGB scene, where they made their debut in the spring of 1975. First, they were all accomplished musicians; second, they had all attended college. Third and most noticeably different was their music, which revealed a fascination with the rhythms of R&B and the minimalism of contemporary New York composers such as Philip Glass and Terry Riley. The Talking Heads also looked different, wearing slacks and sweaters, and projected an image of nerdy-smart college students. Lead singer Byrne's on-stage moves were described by one rock critic this way: "Imagine an out-of-it kid practicing Buddy Holly moves in front of a mirror." In time, Byrne's self-conscious awkwardness became fashionably cool. In the summer of 1975, the band toured Europe with the Ramones, and later signed with their label, Sire. In 1977 they released their debut album *Talking Heads '77,* which yielded the single "Psycho Killer," inspired by the Norman Bates character from Alfred Hitchcock's film *Psycho.* In the song, Byrne sings in a clipped, almost stuttering sing/speak that in a strange sense fit his stage image. The band continued recording until their breakup in late 1991.

The London Scene

No Future

While New York punk was linked to the city's art scene, the British punk movement was driven primarily by the country's poor economy. In 1975, with unemployment at more than one million and inflation at a record 18%, many British kids had no future to look forward to when they finished school. Many went 'on the dole' (welfare) and there was a general mood of cynicism, despair, and boredom. From these grievances, punk emerged as a legitimate social protest. But dissatisfaction went beyond the economy. There was also a tremendous amount of resentment directed toward the record industry, which was enduring hard times of its own. In 1976, sales of singles leveled off and album sales actually declined in England for the first time in years. To be sure, part of the problem was that kids had less disposable income, but there was also a growing dissatisfaction with the continued promotion of aging British Invasion stars ("boring old farts"), whose best work was years behind them. When sale started to sag, many in the industry, mindful of how the Beatles had revitalized the entire industry back in the early sixties, began looking for the 'next big thing,' the 'new Beatles' that could rev things up again. As industry A&R men and talent scouts started to snoop around, many turned their attention to the small but flourishing pub rock scene.

London's **pub rock** circuit was the seventies version of the sixties R&B scene, where little known and unsigned bands were free to experiment with music that was being ignored by the record industry in an intimate club environment (remember the Beatles and the Cavern Club?). Among the popular pubs in the scene were the **Nashville,** the **Tally Ho,** the **Hope,** and the **Anchor.** By focusing on live performances rather than the more controlled environment of the studio, pub bands were more exciting and energetic than many established recording bands. Although their repertoire often included R&B covers, many pub bands began to put an emphasis on original material, and the scene became a training ground of sorts for new songwriters. The essence of pub rock was from the beginning a back-to-basics, stripped down, guitar-oriented music. Over time, pub bands started to adopt a more aggressive stage attitude, the music got faster and louder, and the beginnings of British punk began to emerge. Among the more popular pub bands were **Brinsley Schwarz** (featuring songwriter **Nick Lowe**), **Dr. Feelgood,**

Bees Make Honey, Eddie and the Hot Rods, City, and the **101ers,** which included guitarist Joe Strummer. Strummer left the 101ers in 1976 to start his own punk band the Clash soon after hearing the Sex Pistols in concert. New wave artist **Elvis Costello** also got his start in the pub scene. There were also a number of small independent record labels that sprang up for pub bands and the burgeoning punk movement, the most important of which were **Stiff** and **Rough Trade.** As is usually the case, the major labels were resistant to taking a risk on the new music.

However, as pub rock evolved into punk, it was only a matter of time before one band would emerge that would be so offensive and so disruptive that the majors could no longer afford to ignore them. That band was the Sex Pistols.

THE SEX PISTOLS

The Sex Pistols were either the perfect antidote for everything that was wrong with rock or a clever act of fraud played on the record industry, the media, and the establishment. The band was crude, amateurish, depraved, offensive, nihilistic . . . we could go on and on. In a period of slightly more than two years, they managed to outrage the British press, offend the Royal Family, confound the radio and record industries, and take punk beyond the limits of anyone's sensibilities. And most importantly, they had a deep impact on the future course of rock music. The Pistols were the brainchild of London clothier Malcolm McLaren, who got his first taste of band management with a short-lived stint with the New York Dolls in early 1975. After the Dolls broke up, McLaren returned to London and his boutique at 430 Kings Road, which at the time sold neo-teddy boy clothing and was named Let It Rock. Anticipating a new trend, McLaren changed the name of the store to **Sex** and began selling leather and metal S&M fashions. Among the frequent store patrons were drummer **Paul Cook,** guitarist **Steve Jones,** and bassist **Glen Matlock** of a band called the Strand. At some point, the three approached McLaren to manage them and to find a suitable (as in, having the right look and attitude) vocalist. In one of McLaren's many strokes of genius, he found the perfect fit in **John Lydon** (1956–), an out of work janitor whose teeth were green from neglect and who had such a nasty attitude that the others began calling him **Johnny Rotten.** It is also worth noting that Lydon had never sung before. At first, McLaren saw the band as a means to advertise his store (hence the name Sex Pistols); but he soon saw the potential in using them as mercenaries in his own nihilistic agenda.

After their first gig in November 1975, the Pistols began playing college campuses in England and writing their own material. One of their first songs, "Anarchy in the U.K." is a three and a half minute diatribe that begins with "I am an antichrist" and ends with "Get pissed, destroy." It was also a rallying cry that effectively put the Sex Pistols at the vanguard of Britain's punk movement. In September 1976, McLaren staged the Punk Rock Festival at London's 100 Club as a showcase for the Pistols and other punk bands, including the Clash, the Buzzcocks, and the Vibrators. The strategy worked: in October the Pistols signed with EMI with a £50,000 advance; in November they released "Anarchy in the U.K." as a single. In December, the group encountered their first scandal when they appeared live on the nationally broadcast *Today* TV program. Host Bill Grundy seemed intent on provoking the band: seconds after Rotten muttered the word "shit" under his breath, Grundy asked Steve Jones to "say something outrageous." This exchange followed:

Jones: You dirty bastard.
Grundy: Go on again.
Jones: You dirty fucker!
Grundy: What a clever boy.
Jones: You fucking rotter!

The uproar that followed caused EMI to drop the Pistols in January 1977, thereby forfeiting their advance to the band. In March the Pistols were signed by A&M, and given another £50,000 advance; one week later they were fired and given £25,000 more as a buyout fee. Around this time, bassist Matlock decided to quit the group; his replacement was **John Ritchie** (1957-79), a friend of Rotten's who went by the name **Sid Vicious.** The band signed with Virgin in May and released their second single "God Save the Queen," a malicious attack on the monarchy that concludes by repeating the line "No future, no future, no future." Although Virgin tried to block it, the release of "God Save the Queen" coincided with the queen's Silver Jubilee in June. In spite of being immediately banned from the radio and the refusal of many stores to sell it, "God Save the Queen" quickly sold 200,000 copies and became the number 1 single in Britain (the official charts listed it with a blank at the number 2 spot). By the end of the year the Pistols released their only LP, *Never Mind the Bollocks, Here's the Sex Pistols* on Warner.

In January 1978, the Sex Pistols undertook a fourteen-day tour of the Southern and Western U.S. After the last concert in San Francisco, Rotten

The Sex Pistols at their last concert at San Francisco's Winterland Park on January 14, 1978. Left to right: Sid Vicious, bass; Johnny Rotten, vocals; Paul Cook, drums; Steve Jones, guitar.
The Sex Pistols were either the perfect antidote for everything that was wrong with rock or a clever act of fraud played on the record industry, the media, and the establishment.
© Roger Ressmeyer/CORBIS

quit (or was fired, depending on who you talk to), and the group broke up. Sid Vicious, a heroin addict, was charged in October with the stabbing death of girlfriend Nancy Spungen in their room at New York's Chelsea Hotel. Although he was released on bail, he died of a heroin overdose in February 1979 before he was brought to trial. After dismissing the Sex Pistols as a farce, John Lydon in 1978 formed the group Public Image, Ltd. Whether or not they were indeed a farce is still being debated; however, there is universal agreement that the Sex Pistols changed rock and roll forever.

THE CLASH

The Clash have always occupied a secondary role to the Sex Pistols in the annals of British punk (and after all, who could top the Pistols?), but in fact they took punk beyond its early narrow focus and outlived the Pistols by nearly ten years. The Clash were also the most political of the English punk bands (working for change rather than just destruction), and incorporated a broad base of musical styles into their recordings. The group formed in 1976 when guitarist/vocalist John Mellor, aka **Joe Strummer,** left his band the 101ers to join forces with guitarist **Mick Jones** and bassist **Paul Simonon** of the London SS. The 101ers were a pub band whose name was taken from the torture room number in George Orwell's novel *1984.* The name for the new band was chosen from a commonly used newspaper term for racial and class conflicts. Also included in the initial lineup was drummer Terry Chimes, aka **Tory Crimes,** and 101ers guitarist Keith Levene, who left shortly after their first show. Managed by Malcolm McLaren associate Bernard Rhodes, the Clash opened for the Sex Pistols in their 1976 summer tour of England, which led to a contract with British CBS in February 1977. After securing a $200,000 advance, the group released its eponymous debut album, after which Chimes left and was replaced by **Topper Headon.**

Although the Clash by this time were becoming popular in Britain, they were virtual unknowns in the U.S. However, in 1979, buoyed by their Pearl Harbor Tour of America and the release of their third album *London Calling* (which went to number 27), they began to make inroads into the American market. That same year, they appeared in the semi-documentary film *Rude Boy,* which featured extensive footage of their live shows. In 1980 the triple album *Sandinista!* was released, an experimental mix of styles that drew mixed reviews (although it was named album of the year by the *Village Voice*). The Clash were not afraid to tackle political and social issues in their music, including racism ("Police and Thieves"), rebellion ("White Riot"), unemployment ("Career Opportunities"), and class consciousness ("What's My Name"). Their music incorporated influences that were beyond the scope of most punk bands, including reggae, gospel, Euro-pop, funk, jazz, R&B, and rap. The fact that they were influenced at all by black American music set them worlds apart from the Sex Pistols and most other punk bands. The Clash also managed to find some commercial success, most notably with 1982's *Combat Rock* (number 7), which included the number 8 single "Rock the Casbah." Another song from *Combat Rock,*

"Should I Stay or Should I Go" was re-released in 1991 after it was featured in a Levi's TV commercial and went to number 1 in the U.K. The band broke up in 1986.

OTHER IMPORTANT PUNK BANDS

The Sex Pistols and the Clash inspired hundreds of other punk bands to form in England in the late seventies. Among the most important were the **Damned,** the **Vibrators,** the **Buzzcocks, Joy Division, Generation X,** and **Siouxsie and the Banshees.** Although punk was not as readily accepted in the U.S., it nonetheless altered the course of American rock forever. There is no doubt that punk's attitude of shock and its radical anyone-can-do-it ethos in one way or another influenced nearly every American rock artist to emerge in its wake, from Michael Jackson and Madonna to Nirvana and the White Stripes. But before we get too far down the road, a discussion is in order of punks two immediate descendants: new wave and hardcore.

The Punk Aftermath

NEW WAVE

After the initial wave of punk bands more or less redefined rock and shook up the record industry, a second or "new wave" of artists appeared that took elements of punk and fused them with a more pop-oriented sensibility. **New wave** bands, on the lead of the Talking Heads and the Clash, began to incorporate other stylistic strains into their music, including American R&B, reggae and even synthesizer based techno-pop. The earliest examples of this could be found in Blondie and the Talking Heads, both of which went as far back as 1974. From Boston, the **Cars** emerged as a major commercial success, with eight Top Forty albums and four Top Ten singles before their breakup in 1988. Akron, Ohio born songwriter/singer/guitarist **Chrissie Hynde** hooked up with three Londoners to form the **Pretenders,** which had five Top Forty LPs in the eighties. Also coming from Akron was **Devo** (short for de-evolution), who combined a futuristic robotic image with techno-pop sensibilities and had a platinum selling LP *Freedom of Choice* in 1980 that yielded the number 14 "Whip It." Another band that relied heavily on image was Athens, Georgia's the **B52's,** whose two female vocalists wore bouffant hairdos. Their biggest hit was 1990's "Love Shack" (number 3). From Detroit, the **Romantics** contributed one of the eighties more memorable anthems, "What I Like About You." Some characteristics of New Wave and some key recordings are listed in Box 11–2.

The English new wave movement was stronger than its American counterpart. In addition to the Pretenders, the most important artists in the British scene were **Elvis Costello** and the **Police.** In 1975, Elvis Costello (DeClan Patrick McManus) (1954–) was married and worked as a computer programmer when he suddenly quit his job to work as a roadie for Brinsley Schwarz. After submitting demos of his own songs, he

Box 11-2 New Wave

Characteristics of New Wave
1. A post punk style with commercial pop sensibilities
2. Utilizes influences from R&B, reggae, techno-pop
3. Synthesizers frequently used

Key New Wave Recordings
❏ *My Aim Is True*—Elvis Costello, 1978
❏ *Synchronicity*—the Police, 1983

secured a contract with Stiff Records in 1976, and eventually released his debut LP *My Aim Is True* in 1978. It was a hit (number 32 in the U.S.) and won critical raves. Since then, Costello's musical focus has been remarkably eclectic, with influences ranging from jazz, R&B, reggae, punk, and lounge music. His intelligent, witty, and sometimes hostile lyrics owe a debt to Dylan. Since his debut, twelve albums and two singles have hit the Top Forty, making him one of the most commercially successful post-punk artists.

The Police were formed in 1977 by bassist Gordon Sumner, aka **Sting,** drummer **Stewart Copeland,** and guitarist **Andy Summers.** The group name seems to have been part of a government agency theme: Copeland's father at one time worked for the CIA; his brother owned a small record label, Illegal Records Syndicate **(I.R.S.)** and a talent agency, Frontier Booking, International (FBI). After forming in 1977, the group lost favor with the punk community by starring in a chewing gum TV commercial, but their first self-produced single sold 70,000 copies in Britain. After signing a lucrative contract with A&M Records, the group toured small clubs in America in a rented van and developed a strong grass roots following. By mixing strong pop melodies, reggae-influenced dance music and blond good looks, over the next ten years the group scored six albums and nine singles in the Top Forty. The high point of their popularity came in the summer of 1983, when "Every Breath You Take," from the LP *Synchronicity* stayed at number 1 for eight weeks. The album also went quadruple platinum and stayed at the number 1 spot for seventeen weeks.

HARDCORE

Based primarily in Los Angeles, hardcore punks developed their own fashion of tattoos, buzz cut haircuts, and Army boots, and their own dance called **slam dancing.** Slam dancing was often accompanied by moshing, in which participants would form pits in front of the stage and smash into each other. Diving into the mosh pit from the stage was also common. Hardcore concerts often erupted in chaos and violence; in fact, bands often seemed intent on inciting audiences into doing just that. Hardcore punk in L.A. emerged as a rejection of the city's laid-back music scene epitomized by bands like the Eagles. One of the most important hardcore bands was **Black Flag,** which included vocalist

Alongside the new **wave** movement came a darker, angrier and even louder evolution of punk that became known as **hardcore.**

Box 11-3 Hardcore

Characteristics of Hardcore
1. A harder edged, darker and angrier evolution of punk
2. Counterculture associations with fashion, slam dancing, mosh pits
3. Scene centered in Los Angeles

Key Hardcore Recordings
❏ *Fresh Fruit for Rotting Vegetables*—the Dead Kennedys, 1980
❏ *Damaged*—Black Flag, 1981

Henry Rollins, who would later become an important rock journalist. Black Flag also included guitarist Greg Ginn, who founded **SST Records** as a way to get the group's music recorded. SST became the most important hardcore independent label in the eighties. Some characteristics of Hardcore and some key recordings are listed in Box 11–3.

Other L.A. hardcore bands included **X,** the **Circle Jerks,** and the **Minutemen.** Outside of L.A., healthy post-punk scenes also developed in Minneapolis, home of **Hüsker Dü,** Washington D.C., home of **Fugazi,** and Austin, Texas. The most political hardcore band, the **Dead Kennedys,** came from San Francisco in 1978. Led by vocalist/activist **Jello Biafra** (Eric Boucher), the band attacked fascism, U.S. imperialism, poverty, California Governor Jerry Brown, and President Ronald Reagan. They also started their own record company, Alternative Tentacles. Biafra ran for mayor of San Francisco in 1979; one of his campaign platforms was that businessmen must wear clown suits to work.

INDUSTRIAL

Like English punk, industrial rock emerged in the mid seventies as a statement against the alienation and hopelessness of modern industrial life. The key musical elements of the movement are the fusing of the punk nihilist attitude, the aggression of metal, and the abrasive usage of synthesizers and avant-garde electronics. The first industrial bands were England's **Cabaret Voltaire,** formed in 1973, and **Throbbing Gristle,** formed in 1975. Throbbing Gristle in particular created music that was so extreme in its use of mechanical noise and assault on obscenity laws that one newspaper labeled them as "wreckers of civilization." The group's live performances often started with a punch clock and ended exactly sixty minutes later when the power cord was pulled. Their first album release from 1976 was entitled *The Best of Throbbing Gristle, Vol. 2.* The more listener accessible Cabaret Voltaire was influenced by the Dadaist art movement and the ambient works of synthesizer guru Brian Eno. Some characteristics of Industrial rock and some key recordings are listed in Box 11–4.

Another early industrial band, Berlin, Germany's **Einstürzende Neubauten** took industrial to the next level by using power tools and

Box 11-4 Industrial

Characteristics of Industrial

1. Abrasive and relentlessly mechanical; pounding jackhammer beat
2. Use of digital samples, avant-garde electronics, taped music and white noise
3. Use of industrial materials (power tools, etc.) in performance
4. Lyrical themes of alienation, despair and dehumanization

Key Industrial Recordings

❑ *Halber Mensch*—Einstürzende Neubauten, 1985
❑ *Mind Is a Terrible Thing to Taste*—Ministry, 1989
❑ *Pretty Hate Machine*—Nine Inch Nails, 1989
❑ *Last Rights*—Skinny Puppy, 1991

large industrial objects (such as giant industrial springs and air conditioning ducts) that they amplified and beat with pipes, hammers, and chains in performance. Formed in 1980, the name is German for "collapsing new buildings." By the early eighties, industrial bands such as Canada's **Skinny Puppy** and Belgium's **Front 242** were evolving the style by adding pounding dance beats, which influenced later American bands such as Chicago's **Ministry** and Cleveland's **Nine Inch Nails.** Led by guitarist/vocalist Al Jourgensen, Ministry's sound combined sampled sounds, angry vocals, and metal guitar riffs into what the leader called "aggro." Nine Inch Nails is the one-man band of writer/arranger/producer/performer **Trent Reznor,** whose 1989 debut LP *Pretty Hate Machine* produced three college radio hits, and earned him a spot on the 1991 Lollapalooza tour. Reznor's later works became more accessible by including more familiar song structures and personalized lyrics. Two albums from the nineties, *Broken* and *The Downward Spiral* (number 2, 1994) achieved platinum status with the help of controversial music videos that included such chilling imagery as a man being sexually tortured and ground up by a machine ("Happiness in Slavery") and genital piercing ("Sin"). Reznor produced *The Downward Spiral* while living in the home where the Manson Family murdered actress Sharon Tate. He also scored Oliver Stone's 1994 film *Natural Born Killers.*

Chapter 11
Study Questions

1. Who were some of the people and bands that were influential to the creation of punk, and what were their contributions?

_____

_____

_____

_____

2. Why was punk so influential to rock, and why did it lose its credibility?

_____

_____

_____

3. What were some important differences between the New York and London punk scenes?

_____

_____

_____

4. Why did New York punk musicians feel it was not necessary to be virtuoso performers on their instruments?

_____

_____

_____

_____

5. How was London's pub rock scene instrumental in the development of the city's punk scene?

_____

_____

_____

6. In what ways did the Sex Pistols manipulate the music industry and how did they contribute to the end of the punk era?

_____

_____

_____

_____

_____

7. In what ways were the Clash unique among punk bands of the era?

_____

_____

_____

_____

_____

8. What were some of the musical influences used by new wave artists such as Elvis Costello and the Police?

_____

_____

_____

_____

_____

9. Describe the differences between hardcore and new wave.

_____

_____

_____

_____

_____

10. What are the defining characteristics of industrial, and how does it differ from punk?

_____

_____

_____

_____

The Eighties

Technology Rules

CHANGING CONSUMER TECHNOLOGIES

As rock entered the eighties, once again the musical landscape was changing. Punk had a sort of wiping-the-slate-clean effect on the music business, clearing the way for a new group of stars and styles to emerge. But at the turn of the decade, the industry faced new challenges: despite the fact that sales of recorded music had doubled in the last half of the seventies to $4.1 billion, they began to fall in 1979, and bottomed out in 1982 at $3.6 billion. Many industry observers blamed the decline on the popularity of prerecorded cassette tapes, which were typically priced lower than albums. First introduced in 1963, the cassette format had steadily gained acceptance with consumers throughout the seventies, and was routinely found in home and car stereos by the early eighties. There was also ample evidence that many consumers were using their cassette decks to record their own copies of their friends LPs, further eroding sales figures. When Sony introduced the pocket-sized portable Walkman in the United States in 1980, it was an immediate hit with young rock fans and spawned a plethora of similar devices on the market. By 1983, sales of prerecorded cassette tapes actually exceeded album sales for the first time ever, providing solid evidence that the format was here to stay.

However, the cassette was *not* here to stay. The year 1983 saw the introduction of the compact disc (CD), a digital format that offered even greater portability and dramatically improved sound quality. CDs were non-linear, meaning that to get from song one to song five, the user simply had to hit a button and wham!, you were there. Cassette tapes were linear, so to get to song five one must fast forward the tape, wait, then hit stop, play, and if you were lucky, you were somewhere near the start of song five. Consumers responded to CDs with enthusiasm, and the demand allowed the record industry to sell them at a higher price than either prerecorded cassettes or LPs, in essence making more money for selling less product. CDs were a rescue line for the music business, and quickly killed off the vinyl LP and eventually cassettes as well.

MIDI AND DIGITAL TAPE RECORDING

Technological advances from the eighties would also dramatically change the way that music was going to be created in the future. When the **MIDI** (musical instrument digital interface) protocol was agreed upon by musical instrument manufacturers in 1983, the way was cleared for the creation of keyboards, **digital samplers,** drum machines, and other digital instruments that could 'talk' to each other and interconnect with computers. When a MIDI controller, such as a keyboard or drum pad, is played, it sends out a digital signal containing such information as what note was played, how hard it was struck, and whether more pressure was applied after the initial strike, and so on. This information can

Digital samplers are synthesizers that digitally record (sample) sounds that can be played back and manipulated from a MIDI instrument.

MIDI

MIDI, an acronym for the Musical Instrument Digital Interface protocol, has transformed the world of music production since its inception in 1984. As commercially produced music synthesizers were becoming increasingly digital in the late seventies and early eighties, the limitation of their interconnectivity was becoming painfully apparent. In the early eighties, engineers from manufacturers Sequential Circuits, Roland and Oberheim began work on a standard that would allow digital instruments to be controlled remotely. The MIDI 1.0 Standard, which was first published in 1983, was an instant success and has become an industry standard that is used by professionals and part-time enthusiasts alike.

be recorded on computer sequencing software, where it can be edited in powerful ways and played back on any other MIDI instrument. In this way, one person can easily play all the synthesized instruments on a recording, and can quickly change a guitar part to a piano part, or change the piece's key to accommodate a singer. Producers and do-it-yourselfers could now use MIDI technology in the same way that tape recorders were used. The eighties saw a dramatic increase in the number of small, home-based studios that could produce music much quicker and less expensively than the large commercial studios, many of which went out of business.

The eighties also saw advancements in digital audio recording technology. Digital multi-track tape recorders, although extremely expensive, allowed never before heard of sonic quality and clarity. Because recorded information stored on digital tape required less space than it did using analog technology, more tracks became available to record on—as many as 48 in some cases. The introduction of Digital Audio Tape (DAT) recording technology in the late seventies allowed for a low cost solution to stereo (two-track) digital recording on tiny tapes that could store up to two hours of material. Throughout the eighties and early nineties, most music recording studios were busy replacing their analog tape recorders with digital ones. By the end of the nineties, digital tape itself began to get phased out in favor of hard disc recording.

MTV

On August 1, 1981, Music Television (MTV) began broadcasting on cable, and almost overnight changed everything about how music was packaged, sold, and consumed. Marketed to the largest record buying demographic—ages twelve to thirty-four—MTV became the fastest growing cable channel in history when its subscription went from 2.5 million to 17 million within two years, despite the fact that only 40% of the country was wired for cable. When it premiered, MTV was essentially a visual version of radio, with non-stop broadcasting of music videos hosted by VJs (video jockeys). At first, music videos from Britain dominated MTV's

The most significant **change in** the music business **in the** eighties came ironically **from** an old technology: te**levision.**

programming because many British bands had already been experimenting with the genre throughout the seventies. In fact, the very first music video shown on the station was by the British group the Buggles. The name of their song was appropriate for the occasion: "Video Killed the Radio Star." The popularity of other British bands such as **Duran Duran** (with five platinum LPs between 1983 and 1986), **Human League, Eurythmics,** and **Flock of Seagulls** in the early eighties can be directly attributed to their exposure on MTV.

The consequence of MTV as a new medium in which to experience music is that the music video essentially became an advertisement for the record, the band, and the record label. Simply stated, a catchy and memorable video that people liked to watch sold records. American labels that had previously looked at music videos as an intangible expense now viewed them as marketing necessities. Although the non-musical attributes of artists—how they looked, what clothes they wore, how well they danced—had always been important in pop music, they suddenly took on even greater significance, and became perhaps even more important than the music itself. MTV rapidly became the most powerful player in the industry, since their programmers decided which videos to play and which not to play. In the first few years, those choices were overwhelmingly white: a mid 1983 survey by *Billboard* found that of the 100 videos in heavy or medium rotation the week of July 16, none were of black artists. MTV, under heavy criticism from just about everyone, feebly tried to defend their programming as the result of extensive market research. But they could not explain how an artist like **Rick James,** whose most recent album *Street Songs,* had sold nearly four million copies couldn't get his videos shown.

It wasn't until the incredible success of Michael Jackson's *Thriller* album and the three videos that accompanied it that the network was forced to change its programming. Although the songs "Beat It," "Billie Jean," and "Thriller" all became Top Ten hits and their videos set new standards for production quality, there were widely circulated rumors at the time suggesting that CBS (the parent company of Jackson's Epic label) threatened to pull all of its artist's videos off the station unless the Jackson videos were shown. Eventually, MTV capitulated and put "Billie Jean" into rotation, and it became known as the 'video that broke the color barrier.' It remains unclear what motivated MTV to play Jackson's videos, but what is clear is that the artist behind them did nothing less than dominate pop music in the early eighties and in the process revitalized the entire music industry.

Michael, Madonna, Prince and Bruce

THE KING OF POP

Michael Jackson (1958-) was no stranger to the pop music world when he released his first major solo album *Off the Wall* in 1978. When the Jackson 5 burst on to the charts in 1969 and 1970 with four number

1 singles in a row, it was clear that eleven-year-old Michael was the group's star. Michael started his solo career in 1971 with the release of the number 4 "Got to Be There," and reached number 1 in 1972 with "Ben," the title cut from his second LP. However, it wasn't until 1979 when twenty-one year old Michael hooked up with veteran producer **Quincy Jones** that his meteoric rise to the top began. Their first collaboration, *Off the Wall*, was a well crafted masterpiece of funk, disco-pop, and soul that sold seven million copies and spawned four Top Ten hits, including two platinum number 1s: "Don't Stop 'Til You Get Enough" and "Rock with You." But as impressive as those figures were, they paled when compared with those of his next album. *Thriller*, released in 1982, went on to become the best selling LP in history with an astounding *forty-five million* copies sold worldwide. It also yielded an unprecedented seven Top Ten singles out of its nine songs, including two number 1s, "Billie Jean" and "Beat It," both written by Michael. *Thriller* garnered eight Grammy Awards for Jackson, four for Jones, and stayed on the charts for ninety-one weeks, thirty-seven at number 1. The videos from the album were so successful that Jackson produced a documentary entitled *The Making of Michael Jackson's Thriller* that sold nearly half a million copies. Michael-mania had arrived.

Thriller was groundbreaking on several levels:

❑ The music is superbly produced, arranged, and impeccably recorded with state-of-the-art digital technology.

❑ There are a remarkable variety of songs, from heavy funk grooves ("Thriller") to heavy metal ("Beat It") to light pop ("The Girl Is Mine").

❑ He also brought in a strong supporting cast of guest artists, including Eddie Van Halen, who played a scorching solo on "Beat It"; Paul McCartney, who sang in duet with Michael on "The Girl Is Mine," a song he co-wrote; and horror movie veteran Vincent Price, who did a semi-comical rap on the title cut.

❑ Jackson's vocals are also perfect, ranging from breathless and high energy to fragile and poignant.

❑ Jackson did such a good job of connecting to nearly every segment of the record buying public that it became the first album in history to simultaneously top the singles and album charts in both R&B and pop categories.

❑ The music videos that accompanied "Beat It," "Billie Jean" and "Thriller" more or less revolutionized the genre, as Jackson made each of them into epic mini-dramas of Hollywood proportions. The "Thriller" video, in which Jackson leads a troupe of ghoulish dancers in late night choreography, is often rated as the best music video of all time.

Although *Thriller* is an excellent album, what helped put it into the stratosphere was the aura that surrounded Michael throughout most of 1983, which he created through his innovative music videos and an incredible performance on the national TV special *Motown 25*. During

Michael Jackson's *Thriller* album went on to become the best selling LP in history, selling forty-five million copies worldwide. AP/WIDE WORLD PHOTOS

his solo appearance on the NBC program, which aired on May 16, 1982, Michael sang and danced his way through "Billie Jean" with a variety of unbelievable break-dance moves and his now famous moonwalk while wearing a black fedora and one white sequined glove. Up to this point in time, many Americans had not yet heard *Thriller,* and many still had a vision of Michael as an eleven-year-old phenom. After that night, Jackson became a pop legend, and sales of *Thriller* went through the roof.

Thriller was to be the apex of Michael Jackson's career. After two number 1 multi-platinum LPs (1987's *Bad* and 1991's *Dangerous*), his personal life began to get very weird, to say the least. He bought a ranch in California and turned it into an amusement park and called it Neverland. He underwent several cosmetic surgeries to reshape and thin his nose. He was accused by some in the black community of undergoing treatments to lighten his skin, although he claimed that he had a disorder known as vitiligo, which destroys skin pigmentation. Most troubling were the 1993 accusations of molesting a thirteen-year-old boy that had been a frequent overnight visitor to Neverland, which resulted in an out of court settlement reported to be nearly twenty million dollars. By this time, "Wacko Jacko" (as the press began calling him) had a serious image problem in the tabloids. The last ten years have, in some respects, gone even worse for the aging King of Pop, which included two short marriages, the first to Elvis Presley's only daughter Lisa Marie, which lasted just nineteen months, and an unflattering yet authorized 'behind the scenes' documentary film in 2003.

THE MATERIAL GIRL

Like Michael Jackson, **Madonna** (Madonna Ciccone, 1958–) combined interesting dancing and choreography, dramatic visual artistry and strong post-disco dance grooves to become a pop dynamo. Since her self-titled debut album in 1983, more than thirty of her singles have reached the Top Forty, with eleven number 1s and five more hitting number 2. Every one of her thirteen albums has gone platinum, with five of them going to number 1. Madonna is also one of the most controversial pop figures since Elvis Presley, eliciting strong reactions to her up front eroticism and sexuality. She has managed to keep herself in the public eye for twenty years through an unwavering ambition and an iron fisted control over her career.

After starting out as a dancer, Madonna began to make an impression in New York's trendy club scene as a singer. By 1983 she had a contract with Sire Records (owned by Warner Entertainment) and released her first album *Madonna*, which included the number 10 hit "Borderline." Her next two albums, *Like a Virgin* and *True Blue* went to number 1 and spawned nine more Top Ten singles. The song "Like a Virgin" was a number 1 hit whose title alone embroiled her in controversy. By 1985 she was parlaying her pop success into a movie career, starring in *Desperately Seeking Susan* and eventually other films including *Shanghai Surprise* (with then husband Sean Penn), *Dick Tracy* (with then boyfriend Warren Beatty) and Andrew Lloyd Webber's *Evita* in 1996, for which her starring role as Evita Peron won a Golden Globe Award for Best Actress (Musical or Comedy).

Madonna has pushed the controversy button throughout her career:

❏ Her 1984 single, "Borderline," was about inter-racial love.

❏ In her 1986 single "Papa Don't Preach," a young unwed pregnant woman defiantly decides to keep her baby, against her father's wishes.

❏ In her video to "Open Your Heart" she is shown scantily clad on display at a peepshow before a crowd of men.

❏ In 1989, the music video of "Like a Prayer" featured burning crosses and an erotic black Jesus figure, which prompted Pepsi to cancel her lucrative endorsement deal and the Vatican to censure her.

❏ In 1991 she produced an X-rated documentary film entitled *Truth or Dare.*

❏ In 1992 she published the coffee table book *Sex,* which featured nude and S&M clothed photos of herself.

❏ In 1994 she engaged in a profanity-laden shouting match with the host on *The Late Show with David Letterman.*

❏ Her latest LP, 2003's *American Life* received mixed reviews, in part because Madonna, for the first time, has rapped on record and in part for the sometimes confessional and sometimes political nature of the songs. However, the reviews did not keep the album from hitting number 1 on the *Billboard* 200.

THE ARTIST FORMERLY KNOWN AS . . .

Prince (Prince Rogers Nelson, 1958–) has also invoked controversy during his career, most noticeably for his decision in 1993 to change his name to an unpronounceable symbol, prompting many to call him simply "The Artist Formerly Known As Prince (TAFKAP). But he is undeniably one of the most talented and commercially successful pop musicians of the last twenty years, producing ten platinum albums and thirty Top Forty singles, including five number 1s. He has been amazingly prolific, averaging roughly an album a year through the eighties and nineties. He also reportedly has hundreds of songs that have never been released in his vaults. Perhaps most remarkably, he has achieved his success on his own terms: remaining in his hometown of Minneapolis, starting his own Paisley Park recording studio and label, writing, self-producing, and playing many of the instruments on his recordings, and directing his own music videos.

After releasing his first two albums *For You* and *Prince* in 1978 and 1979, Prince in 1980 released his first masterpiece, *Dirty Mind,* an eclectic mix of funk, R&B, new wave and pop in which he played nearly every instrument. His fifth album, 1983's *1999* went triple platinum and paved the way for the album that would take Prince to the top of the pop world. 1984's *Purple Rain,* recorded with his touring band **the Revolution,** was the soundtrack LP to the feature length film of the same name that sold eleven million copies after staying at number 1 for twenty-four weeks. Prince not only starred in the semi-autobiographical movie, he wrote and produced all the songs, five of which hit the Top Twenty Five, with two ("When Doves Cry" and "Let's Go Crazy") hitting number 1.

Prince's music has absorbed a variety of influences, from funk, jazz, R&B, punk, hard rock, and disco. He followed *Purple Rain* with another number 1 album, the bizarre *Around the World in a Day,* but did not have another number 1 until 1989's *Batman,* the soundtrack to Tim Burton's film. During the nineties he released ten LPs, all of which went either gold or platinum. During this time he also had ten singles hit the Top Forty, including 1991s number 1 "Cream." Prince has also been active as a talent promoter in the careers of many up and coming artists, including percussionist Sheila E, Carmen Electra, the Time, and the female vocal trio Vanity 6.

THE BOSS

Bruce Springsteen (1949–) is the latest version of rock and roll's working class hero. A prolific writer of songs that tell romanticized stories of the underprivileged, downtrodden, and those who are somehow missing out on the American Dream, Springsteen has been compared to Bob Dylan and Woody Guthrie, and hailed as the savior of rock and roll. By casting himself as hard working, small town, and blue collar, Springsteen in many ways was the antithesis of the eighties superstar, although that is exactly what he became. However, by continuing to write relevant music that perfectly reflects our times and putting on lengthy, high-energy concerts, he has remained a vital and important rock and roll artist.

Born in Freehold, New Jersey to a bus driver and a secretary, Springsteen worked his way through a variety of local bands and as an aspiring folksinger in Greenwich Village before auditioning for Columbia Records' legendary John Hammond in 1972. After signing with Columbia, Springsteen released his debut album *Greetings from Asbury Park, N.J.* in 1973, which contained a combination of folk and R&B influences and had modest sales. Later that year, he released his second LP, *The Wild, the Innocent, and the E Street Shuffle,* which garnered rave reviews but little interest from buyers. Then, in 1974 while playing at a club in Cambridge, Massachusetts, critic Jon Landau (his future manager) heard him, and wrote in the local rag *The Real Paper:* "I saw rock & roll's future and its name is Bruce Springsteen." Springsteen responded with his harder-edged third album in the fall of 1975, *Born to Run,* which hit number 3, included his first Top Forty hit (the title track, number 23) and garnered cover stories from both *Time* and *Newsweek* magazines. Although his star dimmed somewhat for a few years in the wake of the punk, new wave, and disco crazes, Springsteen released two noteworthy albums that eventually went platinum, *Darkness on the Edge of Town* (1978) and *The River* (1980). In 1982, he released the dark and stripped down *Nebraska,* a collection of demos that he recorded at home with his four-track cassette recorder. Even

Bruce Springseen is the latest version of rock and roll's working class hero.
Courtesy Lincoln Journal Star Library

though the songs typically told well-developed stories, the album was demanding for his established audience to listen to, and a somewhat risky career move.

Springsteen finally rose to superstar status in 1984 with the release of *Born in the U.S.A.,* which sold fourteen million copies and yielded seven Top Ten hits from its twelve songs, including the platinum selling "Dancing in the Dark" (number 2). The album's title cut is a pained story of a Vietnam veteran who is unable to find a job or rebuild his life on returning home from war. Ironically, both political parties in the 1984 presidential election used the song as a patriotic rallying cry, disregarding the song's message and focusing only on the anthem-like sing along hook, *"Born in the USA!"* Springsteen wisely distanced himself from such boosterism. His follow up to *Born in the U.S.A.* was the intensely personal *Tunnel of Love* (1987), which went triple platinum despite its *Nebraska*-like stark and pessimistic tone. While his most political album, 1995's *The Ghost of Tom Joad,* condemned the growing divide between America's rich and poor, perhaps his most poignant was 2002's *The Rising,* a timely reflection on life written in the aftermath of the September 11, 2001 attacks on the World Trade Center.

Springsteen's music is riveted to rocks past. His band, the **E Street Band,** which he used exclusively in the studio and on tours from 1974 through 1989, is your basic sixties garage band-styled guitar-bass-drums-Hammond organ combo, with a nod to fifties R&B with the addition of the honking tenor saxophone of **Clarence Clemons.** Springsteen's lyric writing is clearly indebted to Bob Dylan and the sixties folk ethos. At times even his arrangements have an unmistakable Dylan-esque quality, with gruff vocals and country-ish harmonica playing. Although record sales have slowed for Springsteen in recent years, his popularity cuts across generational lines and he remains a top concert attraction. As this book goes to print, he is in the middle of the year long "Rising" tour that included a ten-night run at New Jersey's 55,000 seat Giants Stadium, a homecoming of sorts, where he set a record for the most tickets ever sold in a concert series at one venue—more than half a million.

Other 1980s Goings On

THE BAD NEWS

The eighties started off with one of the saddest events in the history of American music: the murder of John Lennon outside his New York City apartment on December 8, 1980. Lennon had more or less retired from music in 1976 to be a stay-at-home dad after the birth of his son Sean, but had returned to recording new material with his wife Yoko Ono in the summer of 1980. The resulting album, *Double Fantasy,* had entered the charts on December 6; its single release "(Just Like) Starting Over" had entered in early November at number 38. As he and Yoko walked home from a late night recording session, Lennon was gunned down by deranged fan Mark David Chapman. In the wake of his death, a world-wide ten-minute silent vigil was held on December 14 at 2:00 pm EST; on December 27, both *Double Fantasy* and "(Just Like) Starting Over" hit number 1 (where they stayed for eight and five weeks, respectively). For many, Lennon's death, along with the fallout from disco and punk, represented an ending of sorts to a confusing time, while leaving a great amount of uncertainty about the future of rock music.

THE PMRC

As America experienced a period of political conservatism marked by the presidency of Ronald Reagan (1981–1989), the watchdog group known as the Parents Music Resource Center (**PMRC**) was born in May 1985 to "to educate and inform parents of this alarming new trend . . . towards lyrics that are sexually explicit." The group also claimed that rock music glorified violence, drug use, suicide, and criminal activity. Formed by a group of 'Washington Wives' that included Susan Baker (wife of Secretary of the Treasury James Baker), Tipper Gore (wife of Sen. Al Gore of Tennessee), Peatsy Hollings (wife of Sen. Ernest Hollings of South Carolina), the PMRC immediately garnered considerable influence in the nation's capital and the backing of many religious and conservative political groups. On September 19, only four months after the PMRC's founding, the Senate Commerce, Technology and Transportation Committee began hearings to investigate the pornographic content of rock music.

The PMRC advocated the use of warning labels to inform parents as to the graphic nature of the lyrics contained in a record that were similar to the movie rating system: X for sexually explicit material, O for occult, V for violence, and so on. Among those who testified against the idea were Frank Zappa, Dee Snider of Twisted Sister, and country singer John Denver. Zappa was particularly articulate in his opening remarks, attempting to expose the group's efforts as a thinly veiled form of censorship. From his five-page long opening remarks are these two paragraphs:

> The PMRC proposal is an ill-conceived piece of nonsense which fails to deliver any real benefits to children, infringes the civil liberties of people who are not children, and promises to keep the courts busy for years, dealing with the interpretational and enforcemental problems inherent in the proposal's design.

And also:

> The establishment of a rating system, voluntary or otherwise, opens the door to an endless parade of Moral Quality Control Programs based on "Things Certain Christians Don't Like." What if the next bunch of Washington Wives demands a large yellow "J" on all material written or performed by Jews, in order to save helpless children from exposure to 'concealed Zionist doctrine'?

In spite of his testimony, the mere threat of government intervention prompted the RIAA (Recording Industry Association of America) on November 1, 1985 to ask its members to either affix a warning label or actually print the lyrics on the sleeve of the objectionable records. Over the next three years, forty-nine new albums (out of 7500 released by RIAA members) displayed a warning label. The PMRC has remained in existence, although it has lost considerable clout in recent years. And the warning labels still exist.

SCAM

Another depressing eighties incident was the **Milli Vanilli** scam from 1989, when it was revealed that the vocal duo of Rob Pilatus and Fabrice Morvan in fact did not sing on their own records or even at their concerts. After three number 1 hits in 1989 and a Grammy Award for Best New Artist, producer Frank Farian called a press conference in November 1990 to confirm that the swirling rumors that they in fact only lip-synched their songs were true. Five days later, the National Academy of Recording Arts and Sciences revoked their Grammy—the only time in history such an action has been taken. The fact that a hoax of such magnitude could be so successful in fooling everyone (including the Grammy voters) was a demonstration of how overly image conscious much of pop music had become in the MTV decade. Although Milli Vanilli were hardly the first group to misrepresent themselves to the public (see the Crystals and the Monkees, chapter 3), the public reaction against them was severe, ending both Pilatus and Morvan's careers. Pilatus later committed suicide in 1998.

CHARITY ROCK

On a more positive note, there was a flurry of charity events staged during the decade, ranging from "We Are the World," Live Aid, Sun City, and tours supporting Amnesty International. Modeled after the successful single "Do They Know It's Christmas" to assist famine relief in Ethiopia by the British group **Band Aid, "We Are the World"** was written by Michael Jackson and Lionel Ritchie to benefit the relief agency U.S.A. for Africa. A group of forty-five artists were assembled at A&M Studios in Hollywood on the night of January 28, 1985 under the supervision of producer Quincy Jones, who insisted that they "check their egos at the door." The song hit number 1 three weeks after its release, and eventually sold over seven million copies. The singers who participated in the recording included Michael Jackson, Lionel Ritchie, Stevie Wonder, Paul Simon, Bruce Springsteen, Madonna, Bob Dylan, Diana Ross, Cyndi Lauper, Ray Charles, Willie Nelson, Billy Joel, Smokey Robinson, and Harry Belafonte.

Live Aid, the simultaneous concerts held at London's Wembley Stadium and Philadelphia's JFK Stadium on July 13, 1985 was the largest staged event in history. Conceived by promoter **Bob Geldorf** (the brainchild behind Band Aid) to again assist famine relief in Ethiopia, the concerts lasted fourteen hours and featured a host of stars, including Paul McCartney, Eric Clapton, Elton John, and Mick Jagger, and were broadcast by fourteen satellites to 160 countries. Phil Collins performed twice—first in London, then in Philadelphia after hopping a Concorde for the trans-Atlantic flight. Ultimately the effort raised over $100 million.

Live Aid spawned a number of music benefit telethons, including the **Farm Aid** concerts spearheaded by Willie Nelson to benefit and draw attention to American farmers caught up in difficult economic times. The first Farm Aid concert was held in Champaign, Illinois on September 22, 1985 and featured Bob Dylan, Billy Joel, B. B. King, Loretta Lynn, Roy Orbison, Tom Petty, and others. Subsequent concerts have been held yearly at stadiums around the country.

WORLDBEAT

A **worldbeat** (or sometimes called **world music**) movement gained momentum in the eighties that saw many artists exploring musical influences from different cultures. One of the first and most successful endeavors was Paul Simon's *Graceland* LP from 1986. Much of the recording was done in South Africa using local musicians and singers. Simon experimented quite successfully with combining rock with influences as disparate as Zulu a cappella singing, South African **mbaqanga** music (street music that incorporates American doo wop and R&B influences), **zydeco** (Creole dance music of southwest Louisiana) and **conjunto** (small group accordion dance music native to Texas and northern Mexico). *Graceland* went on to win the 1986 Album of the Year Grammy Award, sell more than five million copies, and become a benchmark against which other such experiments were judged. **Peter Gabriel** (*Passion: Music for "The Last Temptation of Christ,* 1989), **Mickey Hart** (*Dafos,* 1989), **Ry Cooder** (*Talking Timbuktu,* 1994 with **Ali Farka Toure**), and **David Byrne** (*Rei Momo,* 1989) were among the rock musicians who experimented with worldbeat and brought a heightened global consciousness to rock. Some characteristics of Worldbeat and some key recordings are listed in Box 12–1.

Box 12-1 Worldbeat

Characteristics of Worldbeat
1. Musical influences from other cultures incorporated into rock music
2. Instruments from other cultures combined with traditional rock instruments
3. Musicians or singers from other cultures sometimes also participate

Key Worldbeat Recordings
❑ *Graceland*—Paul Simon 1986
❑ *Passion: Music for "The Last Temptation of Christ"*—Peter Gabriel 1989

Box 12-2 Eighties Alternative

Characteristics of Eighties Alternative
1. Umbrella term encompassing a wide variety of stylistic approaches with a decidedly independent attitude
2. Influences from punk, psychedelia, folk, and hard rock
3. Usually associated with more mature college audiences

Key Eighties Alternative Recordings
❑ "Radio Free Europe"—R.E.M., 1981
❑ *Daydream Nation*—Sonic Youth, 1988
❑ *BloodSugarSexMagik*—Red Hot Chili Peppers, 1991

Eighties Alternative, Metal and Other Pop Stars

THE UNDERGROUND SCENE

The eighties also saw the emergence of several 'underground' rock scenes in college towns such as Athens, Georgia, Seattle, Washington, Boston, Minneapolis, and Austin, Texas. Key to the development of these scenes were the large student populations, the bars and clubs that featured live music, and student-run college radio stations whose programming was free from corporate interference. It was from these circumstances that so-called **alternative rock** bands such as R.E.M., Sonic Youth, and the Replacements rose to prominence. Alternative rock is not so much a particular style as it is a spirit of independence from the major labels and mainstream styles. Alternative bands favored a garage band approach that incorporated influences from punk, psychedelic music, folk rock, and hard rock. Although these bands were off the radar screen at the beginning of the decade, by the end of the eighties they were capturing a large audience and laid the groundwork for a thriving alternative market in the nineties. Some characteristics of Alternative Rock and some key recordings are listed in Box 12-2.

Formed in 1980 in Athens, Georgia, **R.E.M. (Michael Stipe,** vocals; Bill Berry, drums; Peter Buck, guitar; Mike Mills, bass) sparked the alternative movement with their 1981 single release "Radio Free Europe" and slowly built a devoted following through their early recordings on I.R.S., such as 1983's *Murmur* and 1985's *Fables of the Reconstruction.* By the time they signed a $10 million, five-record deal with Warner and released the number 12 *Green* in 1988, they had become "America's Hippest Band," according to *Rolling Stone.* R.E.M.'s mixture of punk, jangly folk, and introspective vocals made them sound retro and progressive at the same time, and one of the most influential bands of the eighties. Their tenth album, 1991's *Out of Time* went quadruple platinum and produced two Top Ten hits, the gold record "Losing My Religion" (number 4) and "Shiny Happy People" (number 10). Two more platinum albums followed, the somber *Automatic for the People* and *Monster.*

Sonic Youth, formed in New York City in 1981, were fond of using feedback and alternative guitar tunings (sometimes achieved with screwdrivers or drumsticks wedged in between the strings and fret boards) in their early years, although they began to gravitate toward pop by decades end. During the late eighties, the band released three albums, *EVOL* (1986), *Sister* (1987), *Daydream Nation* (1988), that became enormously influential to the alternative musicians of the nineties. The **Replacements,** formed in 1980 in Minneapolis and fronted by **Paul Westerberg,** were critically lauded but received little in the way of commercial success. Part of their commercial failure was of their own doing: they developed a reputation for drunk and disorderly conduct on stage, which was confirmed during an appearance on *Saturday Night Live* in which Westerberg blurted out the "f" word. They broke up in 1991.

The **Red Hot Chili Peppers** are one of the most innovative and unique alternative bands to emerge from the nineties. Formed in 1983 by Fairfax High School (Los Angeles) classmates **Anthony Kiedis** (vocals), **Michael Balzary** (bass), **Jack Irons** (drums), and **Hillel Slovak** (guitar), the band originally called themselves Anthem School. Later that year, they began playing strip clubs along L.A.'s Sunset Strip and started to hone their high energy stage act, which occasionally included the gimmick of performing in only a strategically placed tube sock (which was *not* worn on either foot, by the way). Around this time they also changed their name to the Red Hot Chili Peppers, and Balzary began to call himself **Flea.**

The Chili Peppers have managed to capture the essence of punk while incorporating funk influences from George Clinton and Sly and the Family Stone (Clinton produced their second LP, 1985's *Freaky Styley*). In spite of a number of tragedies and personnel changes throughout the eighties and nineties, the band has forged ahead, breaking down musical barriers along the way. Their third album, *The Uplift Mofo Party Plan* (1987) was the first to chart (number 148) and contained their signature song "Party on Your Pussy." With the release of 1989's *Mother's Milk*, the Peppers were receiving airplay on MTV for their videos of their cover of Stevie Wonder's "Higher Ground" and "Knock Me Down," a tribute to former guitarist Slovak, who died from a heroin overdose in 1988. Their 1991 LP *BloodSugarSexMagik* is considered by many to be their best, and has been certified triple platinum.

Red Hot Chili Peppers

- ❏ Anthony Kiedis
- ❏ Michael Balzary
- ❏ Jack Irons
- ❏ Hillel Slovak

Other influential alternative bands from the eighties included **Hüsker Dü** (also from Minneapolis), **Fugazi,** the **Minutemen,** the **Butthole Surfers,** and **Mission of Burma.**

METAL IN THE EIGHTIES

Metal continued to be popular throughout the eighties, even as it evolved and subdivided into a number of splinters. A more commercially-oriented version known as **pop metal** emerged from bands like Van Halen (see chapter 9) and Britain's **Def Leppard,** who used keyboards and vocal harmonies with catchy pop hooks to make their sound more accessible to a wider audience. The strategy paid off as they racked up five platinum albums in the eighties and early nineties, including 1987's *Hysteria,* which sold eleven million copies and spawned four Top Ten singles. On New Year's Eve 1984, drummer **Rick Allen** lost his left arm in an auto accident, but was able to return to drumming with the band the following year with a specially designed electronic drum kit. Some characteristics of Pop Metal and some key recordings are listed in Box 12–3.

Also from Britain came a faster, harder strain that became known as the **New Wave of British Heavy Metal,** led by bands such as Judas Priest (see chapter 9), **Motorhead,** and **Iron Maiden,** whose five albums in the decade all achieved platinum status. As hardcore matured in the eighties, it evolved into a style known as **thrash** or **speed metal,** an extremely fast and technically demanding form whose ominous and angry edge drew great appeal from alienated suburban white teens and little critical or radio support. **Anthrax** (four gold albums in the eighties and nineties), **Megadeth** (three platinum LPs) and **Metallica** (four platinum LPs) were the most prominent in this genre. Metallica was the most influential metal band of the eighties, bringing a no nonsense approach to the genre through intricate compositions and incredibly tight instrumentals. Their 1988 album *. . . And Justice for All* went to number 6 without much in the way of radio support; 1991's *Metallica* hit number 1, selling eight million copies and staying on the charts for eighty-five weeks. In recent years, the band, led by drummer **Lars Ulrich,** took a leadership role in attacking the Internet file sharing service **Napster** in an attempt to prevent their music from being downloaded for free (see chapter 14). Although they ultimately dropped their lawsuit, Metallica was for a short while at the center of the file sharing

---

Box 12-3 Pop Metal

Characteristics of Pop Metal
1. More commercial pop oriented while retaining characteristics of metal
2. Use of vocal harmonies
3. Use of keyboards

Key Pop Metal Recordings
❏ *1984*—Van Halen, 1984
❏ *Hysteria*—Def Leppard, 1987

Box 12-4 Speed Metal

Characteristics of Speed Metal
1. Faster, darker and more intense update of metal
2. Technically demanding; virtuoso performers
3. Complex and difficult musical compositions

Key Speed Metal Recordings
❑ *Peace Sells . . . But Who's Buying?*—Megadeth 1986
❑ *. . . And Justice for All*—Metallica 1988

controversy that continues to this day. Some characteristics of Speed Metal and some key recordings are listed in Box 12-4.

TOPS IN POP

Finally, among the most commercially successful artists in the eighties were Ireland's **U2,** whose LP *The Joshua Tree* went quintuple platinum in 1987, produced two number 1 singles ("With or Without You," "I Still Haven't Found what I'm Looking For") and stayed in the Top Forty for over a year; and former Genesis drummer **Phil Collins,** whose 1985 LP *No Jacket Required* (number 1, seven million copies, two number 1 singles) won the Album of the Year Grammy. Also among the tops in eighties pop were Americans **Huey Lewis and the News** (twelve Top Ten hits, including three number 1s and three platinum selling albums); **Whitney Houston** (seven number 1 hits, and two multi-platinum albums—*Whitney Houston* and *Whitney* which stayed at number 1 for a combined twenty five weeks); and **Paula Abdul** (six number 1 singles between 1988 and 1991 and the seven million selling *Forever Your Girl* from 1989).

Chapter 12
Study Questions

1. Name four significant changes in technology in the music business in the eighties.

   _____

   _____

   _____

2. Describe the programming on MTV in its early years and some of the controversies surrounding it.

   _____

   _____

   _____

3. Describe some reasons why *Thriller* became the best selling album of all time.

   _____

   _____

   _____

4. Name four instances in which Madonna pushed herself into a position of controversy.

   _____

   _____

   _____

5. Name four ways in which Prince has carved out a unique and successful career.

   _____

   _____

   _____

   _____

   _____

6. Describe the influences on Bruce Springsteen's songwriting and E Street Band.

_____

_____

_____

_____

_____

7. What was the PMRC and what was its effect on rock?

_____

_____

_____

_____

_____

8. Who were some of the important performers of worldbeat and what techniques did they use in their music?

_____

_____

_____

_____

_____

9. Describe the sound of eighties alternative music and how it became popular.

_____

_____

_____

_____

10. What are some important differences between pop metal and speed metal?

_____

_____

_____

_____

Rap

Hip Hop Culture

The Origins of Hip Hop

Rap is the latest extension of the blues-jazz-R&B lineage of musical expressions that have emerged from the black cultural experience in America. ♪♫♫

Rap music is one part (along with break-dancing and graffiti art) of a cultural form known as **hip hop** that emerged in the South Bronx neighborhoods of New York City in the late seventies. **Rap** is the latest extension of the blues-jazz-R&B lineage of musical expressions that have emerged from the black cultural experience in America. Its most obvious musical connection to previous rock styles are funk (especially James Brown) and disco; however, rap is an entirely different animal altogether that continues to evolve and assimilate other musical influences. Because of the violent and graphic nature of the lyrics of much contemporary rap, the genre and its purveyors have been at the center of an enormous amount of controversy, more than any other style in rock's history. But a closer look at the origins of rap and its motivations reveal that perhaps not all of the anger and outrage directed toward it is warranted.

Hip hop has been described as the definitive cultural movement of this generation, and it is through rap music that its message has been transmitted to the American mainstream audience. In the years leading up to the emergence of rap, black youth culture was nearly invisible to the rest of the country, the exceptions consisting primarily of athletes and crime reports. However, black athletes in the sixties for the most part lived in a conservative sports climate, without a true cultural identity of their own, and often did not connect with the black youth of the streets. Rap has changed all of that. As Bakari Kitwana states in his authoritative book *The Hip Hop Generation:* "Because of rap, the voices, images, style, attitude, and language of young Blacks have become central in American culture, transcending geographical, social, and economic boundaries." Today, because of rap, hip hop is omni-present in national TV ads, fashion, movies and movie stars, and professional sports, particularly basketball. Rap lyrics have also articulated the issues that confront many young blacks, such as police brutality, unemployment, drugs, and gangs, in much the same way that civil rights leaders did in the previous generations.

Hip hop emerged in the mid to late seventies as a form of self expression for the largely black and Hispanic communities of the South Bronx in New York City, in an attempt to negotiate with their oppressive and dismal living conditions. Facing an economic crisis, New York City narrowly avoided bankruptcy in 1975, the same year that President Gerald Ford announced that he would veto any Congressional bill that included a bailout for the city (resulting in the famous *New York Daily News* headline "Ford to City: Drop Dead"). During this period, the Bronx had been devastated by the ravages of reduced federal funding, shifting and disappearing job opportunities, and the diminished availability of affordable housing. To further complicate matters, the Bronx had been literally cut in half in the sixties by the construction of the Cross Bronx Expressway, which destroyed more than 60,000 homes in stable neighborhoods and effectively isolated the southern half of the borough. The resulting infestation of slumlords and toxic waste dumps, increase of violent crime and loss of city services created an urban crisis that left the South Bronx in squalor. When a two-day citywide power outage occurred on July 13 and 14, 1977, hundreds of stores in the area were looted and vandalized, resulting in hundreds of millions of dollars in damage. After President Jimmy Carter made a highly publicized tour of the destruction, the South Bronx was characterized as a war zone in the media and through sensationalized films like *Fort Apache, The Bronx.*

THE BEGINNINGS OF RAP

In response to these sordid living conditions and the destruction of traditional community institutions such as neighborhood associations and community centers, residents of the area began to fashion their own cultural values and identities. By the late seventies, informal neighborhood groups called crews or posses began forming as a means of providing identity and support for their members. (This kind of group identity remains deeply rooted in hip hop culture, and references to **crews** or **posses** are frequent in rap recordings.) At parties and other social gatherings, it became fashionable for crews to display graffiti art, break-dancing moves, and play records as a way to gain notoriety and celebrity. In the earliest stages of the development of rap (around 1977), DJs such as Bronx native **Afrika Bambaataa** (Kevin Donovan) and two Caribbean expatriates, **Kool Herc** and **Grandmaster Flash** (Joseph Saddler) would spin records in innovative ways to create excitement. Kool Herc in particular was instrumental in developing the art of mixing smooth transitions between two turntables to feature the **break,** or the most danceable, instrumental sections of records. Kool Herc also began to recite rhymes to accompany his mixing, a technique he inherited from his native Jamaica, where it was called **toasting.** Grandmaster Flash is given credit for perfecting the practice of **scratching** or **back spinning,** to play a record back and forth quickly to create a scratching sound. Eventually, MCs (master of ceremonies) were added to take over most of the rhyming and vocal interactions, and began to attract the most attention from audiences. These were the earliest rappers. Some characteristics of Rap and some key recordings are listed in Box 13–1.

Grandmaster Flash is given credit for perfecting the practice of **scratching** or **back spinning,** to play a record back and forth quickly to create a scratching sound.

Box 13-1

Characteristics of Rap
1. Rhythmic and rhyming spoken lyrics with rhythmic accompaniment heavily influenced by funk and disco
2. Use of sampled sounds and pieces of existing songs that are repeated to create a minimalist, hypnotic effect
3. Early rap (old school) included the use of scratching and back spinning of turntables to create percussive effects
4. Two scenes developed by the late eighties on the East and West Coasts

Key Rap Recordings
- "Rapper's Delight"—the Sugar Hill Gang, 1979
- "The Message"—Grandmaster Flash and the Furious Five, 1982
- *Raising Hell*—Run-D.M.C., 1986
- *As Nasty As They Wanna Be*—2 Live Crew, 1989

Throughout this stage of development, rap was still pretty much contained to the Bronx, Harlem, and a few other neighborhoods in New York City. In September 1979, the outside world got its first glimpse of the new style when "Rapper's Delight" by the **Sugar Hill Gang** of **Sugar Hill Records** hit number 36 on the pop chart and eventually sold over a million copies. Sugar Hill Records was owned by Sylvia Robinson, a former R&B singer ("Pillow Talk," number 3, 1973) who had noticed how street MCs who added lyrics and chants to funk and disco records were becoming popular in New York City. To capitalize on the fad, in September 1979, she put together three New Jersey teens who recorded a rap over a rhythm track derived from Chic's early summer number 1 hit "Good Times." Not only did the song popularize the word 'rap,' but "Rapper's Delight" also alerted MCs and DJs to the commercial potential of the new style. Within the next few years, more rap singles—all on small, independent labels such as Sugar Hill—became big sellers, including "The Breaks" by **Kurtis Blow,** and Afrika Bambaataa and the Soul Sonic Force's "Planet Rock." This first generation of rappers performed what has become known as **old school rap,** most of which had themes of fun and partying. However, one record from this era that signaled a significant change of direction was Grandmaster Flash and the Furious Five's "The Message," from 1982. A graphic (and controversial) description of the harsh realities of ghetto life in the South Bronx, "The Message" was the first rap record to address social issues, and laid the groundwork for an essential part of rap's future development.

East Coast Rap

Walk This Way

Throughout the early eighties, rap expanded further into the pop charts, and its influence began to extend outside of the Bronx and into other urban areas such as Roxbury in Boston, the Fifth Ward in Houston, Overtown in Miami, and Watts and Compton in Los Angeles. In 1986 rap albums by two New York groups reached multiplatinum status, *Raising Hell* (number 3) by **Run-D.M.C.** and *Licensed to Ill* (number 1 for seven weeks) by the **Beastie Boys,** signaling a new level of commercial appeal of the music. *Licensed to Ill* was released by the independent **Def Jam Records,** the first important rap label. Run-D.M.C., consisting of three middle class and college-educated rappers (Run, aka **Joseph Simmons;** DMC, aka **Darryl McDaniels;** and Jam Master Jay, aka **Jason Mizell**) had already achieved the first gold rap album with 1984's *Run-D.M.C. Raising Hell* was propelled by an ingenious piece of marketing, a rap remake of Aerosmith's 1976 hit "Walk This Way," recorded with that band's Steve Tyler and Joe Perry. "Walk This Way" hit number 4 and sold over a million records to fans of both rap and metal, and its innovative video was the first of the genre to receive airplay on MTV. Run-D.M.C. had a harder edge than earlier rap groups, and featured an innovative vocal delivery: Simmons and McDaniels would often finish each other's lines instead of trading verses. The Beastie Boys, the first important white rap group, had a number 7 hit with "You've Got to Fight for Your Right to Party" from *Licensed to Ill.*

Other East Coast rappers also emerged during this time, including **Public Enemy, L.L. Cool J.** (Ladies Love Cool James), the female trio **Salt-n-Pepa, Queen Latifa,** and Miami's **2 Live Crew.** By this time rap was becoming more militant, aggressive, contentious, and controversial. One of the pioneers of what would eventually become known as gangsta rap was Philadelphia's **Schoolly D** (Jesse Weaver), whose 1986 release "PSK—What Does It Mean?," a narrative about a Philadelphia gang, is widely credited with inventing the style. In 1987, the Bronx's **Boogie Down Productions** (KRS-One and DJ Scott LaRock) released the classic *Criminal Minded,* an album that was also influential in gangsta rap's development. LaRock was shot to death later in the year in an eerie foreshadowing of rap's future violence.

CNN FOR BLACK CULTURE

In 1988, Public Enemy, led by rapper **Chuck D,** his sidekick Flavor Flav, and the Bomb Squad production team, released the controversial LP *It Takes a Nation to Hold Us Back,* which stepped up the rhetoric of black anger to levels above and beyond Schoolly D and BDP. Calling themselves the "prophets of rage," PE combined the politically charged rhymes of Chuck D with the Bomb Squad's heavily layered avant-garde rhythm tracks. Chuck D was also critical of the white controlled media (as related in 1988's "Don't Believe the Hype"), and called rap "CNN for black culture." PE has encountered more than its share of controversy, from 1988's volatile "Bring the Noise," to the statement by Professor Griff, the groups 'minister of information,' that Jews are responsible for "the majority of wickedness that goes on across the globe."

2 Live Crew's 1989 LP *As Nasty As They Wanna Be* became the first recording ever to be declared obscene by an American court, even though the group included a warning label on the cover and simultaneously released an edited version called *As Clean As They Wanna Be.* Led by founder **Luther Campbell,** the group's number 26 hit "Me So Horny" created a moral outrage that prompted evangelical Christian attorney Jack Thompson to file suit against Campbell. In 1990 a Broward County (Florida) judge declared the album to be legally obscene, making it illegal to sell, and in short order record retailers in Ft. Lauderdale and Huntsville, Alabama were arrested for selling it (both were prosecuted but acquitted). The band was also arrested for performing the songs in a Hollywood, Florida nightclub. Eventually *Nasty* sold more than two million copies (eight times as many as the clean version), a jury cleared 2 Live Crew after thirteen minutes of deliberation, and in 1992 the 11th U.S. Circuit Court of Appeals reversed the obscenity ruling. However, by that time 2 Live Crew had disbanded.

West Coast Rap

Gangsta Rap

Meanwhile, California was becoming a hotbed of rap development. Oakland's **M.C. Hammer** (Stanley Burrell) released the pop-accessible LP *Please Hammer Don't Hurt 'Em* in 1990 (containing the number 8 hit "U Can't Touch This" and two other Top Ten singles), which went on to sell ten million copies and become the bestselling rap album of all time. But other West Coast rappers, particularly those from the ghettos of Los Angeles, were turning up the threatening and menacing tone of gangsta rap to the boiling point. The West Coast gangsta rap that emerged in the nineties is among the most controversial and despised music ever produced. The main point of contention was the use of the first person accounting of vivid descriptions of violence, rage, and sexist degradation rather than the more passive third person used in previous rap narratives, such as "The Message." One of the first instances of the style on the West Coast came from **Ice T** (Tracy Morrow), who assumed the persona of hardened Los Angeles criminal in his 1986 record "6 'n the Mornin'." This and subsequent other Ice T recordings were criticized as glorifying violence, when in reality, the songs usually sent a not-so-subtle message that crime and violence don't pay. His newly formed group **Body Count** received national notoriety with the release of its self-titled debut album in 1992, which contained the track "Cop Killer." The song was denounced by police departments all over the country, as well as President George H. W. Bush, Vice President Dan Quayle, and the PMRC, and was ultimately dropped from the album by Time Warner, owner of Sire Records. In response, Ice T left the label. Some characteristics of Gangsta Rap some key recordings are listed in Box 13–2.

The controversy over gangsta rap escalated further with 1989's double platinum *Straight Outta Compton* by **NWA** (Niggaz with Attitude), a Los Angeles based group led by **Ice Cube** (O'Shea Jackson) and **Dr. Dre** (Andre Young). Although the album went multiplatinum, it incensed rap's detractors with its narratives of gang violence, drive-by shootings,

---

Box 13-2 Gangsta Rap

Characteristics of Gangsta Rap
1. Lyrics use first person accounting of gang related themes that include violence, rage and sexual degradation
2. Hard hitting, angry vocal delivery
3. Guns, sirens, and other urban sound effects often used

Key Gangsta Rap Recordings
❏ *Straight Outta Compton*—NWA, 1989
❏ "Cop Killer"—Body Count, 1992
❏ *The Chronic*—Dr. Dre, 1993
❏ "Hit 'Em Up"—2pac Shakur, 1996

and drug dealings in songs like "Gangsta Gangsta" and the title cut. The most offensive song, "Fuck tha Police" caused the FBI to send a "warning letter" to the groups label, Priority. Unlike Ice T's earlier recordings, the songs on *Straight Outta Compton* offer no social commentaries, but instead are vicious tirades directed toward women, the police, and the group's adversaries. Although NWA began to unravel in the early nineties, they had another smash hit with 1991's *Efil4zaggin (Niggaz 4 Life* spelled backwards), which hit number 1 two weeks after it's release and went platinum.

In 1992 Dr. Dre, along with producer Marion **"Suge" Knight,** started the independent label **Death Row,** which released Dre's landmark debut LP *The Chronic* in 1993. The album went triple platinum, hit number 3 on the charts, spawned two Top Ten singles, and introduced Dre's understudy, **Snoop Doggy Dog** (Calvin Broadus). Reviews of Snoop and his lazy drawl style of rapping were enthusiastic, which fueled excitement about his own forthcoming debut LP. However, while recording the album in August, Snoop and his bodyguard were arrested for the murder of a man they claimed was a stalker. When *Doggystyle* was finally released in November, the pent up anticipation resulted in it becoming the first debut album in history to enter the *Billboard* pop chart at number 1 (it eventually went quadruple platinum). After a lengthy trial in late 1995 and early 1996, Snoop was cleared of all charges. His second album, The *Doggfather* was released later that year. Snoop has since become a celebrity beyond the scope of rap, with his numerous movie and TV roles.

THE EAST COAST-WEST COAST RIVALRY

By the mid nineties, an ugly East Coast-West Coast rivalry began to develop that consumed the attention of the entire rap community and in the end turned violent and tragically lethal. It started in 1995 when Death Star's promising new artist **Tupac Shakur** (2pac) (1971–96) squared off against the **Notorious B.I.G.** (Christopher Wallace, formerly known as **Biggie Smalls**) (1972–97), who was signed to **Sean "Puffy" Combs'** (aka **Puff Daddy** or **P. Diddy**) New York based **Bad Boy** label. 2pac, the son of two members of the Black Panthers (a radical black power group from the sixties), was on a meteoric rise to stardom with the release of his first two albums *2pacalypse Now* (1991) and *Strictly 4 My N.I.G.G.A.Z.* (1993), and his appearances in several films, including the lead role in John Singleton's *Poetic Justice.* However, by the time his third album *Me Against the World* was released in March 1995, he was in prison on a sexual assault charge. While in prison, *Me Against the World* entered the charts at number 1, making 2pac the first recording artist in history to have a top rated album while incarcerated.

The feud between 2pac and the Notorious B.I.G. began after 2pac was shot five times and robbed of thousands of dollars of jewelry in an attack at a New York recording studio on November 30, 1994. While serving his jail term, 2pac implicated B.I.G., Combs, and two others for the

By the mid nineties, an ugly East Coast-West Coast rivalry began to develop that consumed the attention of the entire rap community and in the end turned violent and tragically lethal.

The death of Tupac Shakur (pictured here with producer Marion "Suge" Knight-right) stunned the entire rap community.
AP/WIDE WORLD PHOTOS

attack. One month after 2pac was released from prison in October 1995 (after Suge Knight posted a $1.4 million bond), his close friend Randy "Stretch" Walker was assassinated in gangland fashion—exactly one year to the day after 2pac's own shooting. Although there seemed to be a clear message in the murder, Shakur renewed his attacks on B.I.G.; soon the war of words grew to include not only Death Row and Bad Boy, but the entire West Coast and East Coast rap scenes. Things went from bad to worse with the release of 2pac's 1996 single "Hit 'Em Up," a malicious attack on his rival that included the boast that he had slept with B.I.G.'s estranged wife, Faith Evans. By this time, 2pac was at the top of the rap world: his latest LP *All Eyez on Me*—his debut on Death Row—had quickly shot to number 1 after its February release, eventually going quadruple platinum. Then, tragedy struck. On the night of September 7, 1996, after leaving the Mike Tyson-Bruce Seldon fight at the MGM Grand Hotel in Las Vegas, 2pac was shot four times by a drive-by shooter while riding in the passenger seat of Suge Knight's car on the Las Vegas strip. Although he was rushed to the University of Nevada Medical Center, 2pac died six days later. The murder stunned the entire rap community; thousands mourned his passing.

Suspicion began immediately that 2pac's murder was retaliation by the Notorious B.I.G. for 2pac's comments about Faith Evans. By this time, B.I.G. was every bit the star that 2pac had been; as one of Bad Boy's first clients, B.I.G.'s first LP, 1994's *Ready to Die* had risen to number 8 and contained the single "Big Poppa," which hit number 6 on the singles charts in January 1995. After his marriage to Faith Evans, B.I.G. helped turn Bad Boy into the predominant East Coast rap label by guiding the careers of Junior M.A.F.I.A., Total, and 112, and had one more Top Ten hit himself with 1995's "One More Chance/Stay with Me" (recorded with Method Man). He had also seen his share of personal turmoil, including a widely known affair with Junior M.A.F.I.A. member **Lil' Kim** that resulted in his estrangement from Evans, and a criminal mischief conviction that resulted from attacking two autograph seekers with a baseball bat.

THE AFTERMATH

Many had hoped that 2pac's murder would put an end to the bitter East/West rivalry, but there was one more tragic and unexpected twist to the plot. On March 9, 1997, as B.I.G. was leaving the Soul Train Music Awards party in Los Angeles, he too was shot when a vehicle pulled up alongside the car he was riding in and pumped 6–10 shots into it. Biggie's bodyguard rushed him to Cedars-Sinai Medical Center, but he was dead on arrival. Although conspiracy theorists believed that B.I.G.'s death was retribution for 2pac's and amid reports of LAPD corruption, neither case has been solved. The Notorious B.I.G.'s final album *Life after Death* was released within days of his death, and sold 700,000 copies in the first week and ten million within two years. It also spawned two number 1 singles that were both certified platinum, making B.I.G. the first entertainer in history to have two posthumous number 1 hits. 2pac's death has prompted somewhere in the vicinity of fifteen compilations and reissues. In 2002, filmmaker Nick Broomfield made a documentary of the tragic story entitled *Biggie and Tupac*.

With so much common talent and perspective to share, the murders of 2pac and the Notorious B.I.G. were tragic and unnecessary. While their music was difficult for many Middle Americans to listen to, it is important to remember that the stories that 2pac, B.I.G., NWA, and others related were not fictional ones. These artists did not invent the miserable conditions in the ghetto, the gang related warfare, or the drive-by shootings. Like the first blues singers from the Mississippi Delta that came nearly one hundred years before them, rappers are their generation's voice of the downtrodden and oppressed, of people who otherwise aren't being heard. When miserable living conditions exist for some Americans, like they did in the South Bronx in the seventies and still do in many urban areas, the results can have far reaching effects. As rock critic Mikal Gilmore states: "The America that we are making for others is ultimately the America we will make for ourselves. It will not be on the other side of town. It will be right outside our front door."

Chapter 13
Study Questions

1. Describe some of the reasons that rap emerged from the South Bronx in the late seventies.

   _____

   _____

   _____

2. What were some of the cultural entities that emerged from the depressing conditions in the South Bronx?

   _____

   _____

   _____

3. How was the creation of rap influenced by Jamaican culture?

   _____

   _____

   _____

4. What are some of the characteristics of old school rap?

   _____

   _____

   _____

   _____

5. What is the importance of Run-D.M.C.'s "Walk This Way"?

   _____

   _____

   _____

6. Why is "The Message" by Grandmaster Flash and "PSK—What Does It Mean?" by Schoolly D important?

_____

_____

_____

_____

_____

7. Describe some of the ways that Public Enemy and 2 Live Crew had an impact on the evolution of rap.

_____

_____

_____

_____

_____

8. How did gangsta rap differ from previous rap styles?

_____

_____

_____

_____

_____

9. In what ways did the East Coast-West Coast rivalry escalate?

_____

_____

_____

_____

10. In what ways is rap similar to the blues?

_____

_____

_____

_____

Rock Matures

The Changing Face of Rock

THE FUTURE

The nineties saw the unprecedented fragmentation of rock into a number of styles that catered to an increasingly splintered audience. Of course, this was a trend that had really started in the seventies, only to be interrupted for a few years by the temporary centering that MTV, Michael, Madonna, Prince, and Bruce had provided. Today in the 21st century, there are too many rock genres to be adequately covered by any one text, so this one will not attempt to be the first. However, in spite of so much interest in developing new ways to rock, one can almost sense that there is an uncertainty about the direction that the music is going in. One sign of this is an overabundance of music being produced that is rooted in nostalgia, such as the many hip hop soul vocal groups (copied after fifties doo wop), the so-called garage bands (sixties redux) and the continuing influence of punk (seventies). Artists from previous rock years also remain popular and in the news; many 'dinosaur' bands such as the Stones or Crosby, Stills, and Nash still tour to sellout audiences. Century-ending polls of the best "this" and most influential "that" were often dominated by the Beatles or other groups from the sixties; indeed, the Fab Four's 2000 release *The Beatles 1* quickly shot to the top of the charts. Are these signs that something is seriously lacking in modern rock, or simply that there are a lot of nostalgic baby boomers out there?

Of course, the Internet has had a dramatic impact on rock and roll as well. Many observers say that peer-to-peer Internet sites that allow users to download music for free are the culprits in the sharp decline of record sales in the past two years. While there is little doubt that this has had an effect, there may be other factors that have contributed to the downturn. Some believe that the menu offered up by the major labels is once again out of sync with the more in-tune music consumer. For instance, the 2001 Album of the Year Grammy Award went to a *bluegrass* album—the little publicized soundtrack to the film *O Brother, Where Art Thou?* To be sure, the LP is a great one, but could this be a sign that once again consumers are dying for something different than the bland, safe pop that is being thrown at them? If so, this isn't the first time that this has happened: the Swing Era died almost overnight for exactly the same reason. Rock and roll itself was born out of this scenario. But history has also shown that rock has had an uncanny ability to reinvent itself whenever things get too stale or too boring: one only has to think back to the Sex Pistols for an example. Certainly as we approach the fifty-year anniversary of the birth of rock and roll, the time is right for a new artist, group, or style to emerge and breathe new life into the music and the industry.

NIRVANA

The last time that occurred was in 1991, when **Nirvana** broke through to stardom with their seminal LP *Nevermind.* Seemingly coming out of

Nirvana, in an undated publicity photo. Left to right: Kurt Cobain, Dave Grohl, Krist Novoselic.
© Joe Giron/CORBIS

nowhere, soon after its release the album sold out its initial printing of 50,000 copies; by January 1992 it had knocked off Michael Jackson's highly touted *Dangerous* to become the number 1 album in America. It was a moment full of obvious symbolism: the King of Pop and his highly produced eighties electronic dance music was dethroned by a group wearing torn jeans and T-shirts, who were uncomfortable with stardom, and played music that eschewed glitz and glamour and embraced the do-it-yourself attitude of post punk alternative rock. *Nevermind* eventually was certified seven times platinum; although Jackson had one last number 1 album in 2001, he struggled through the nineties.

Nirvana's beginnings go back to 1987 and the tiny town of Aberdeen, Washington, 100 miles southwest of Seattle, where guitarist/vocalist/ songwriter **Kurt Cobain** (1967–1994) grew up. Cobain's early years could easily be described as miserable. At age eight, his parents divorced, forcing him to move back and forth from one set of relatives to another. Growing older, he grew increasingly sullen, resentful, and withdrawn. As an artistic youth who did not fit in with most people in the redneck logging town, Cobain was often beat up by other kids just because he was 'different,' including once for befriending an openly gay fellow student. But he found solace in music: first the Beatles, then metal, and finally punk. In 1987, around the time he turned twenty, Cobain and fellow Aberdonian **Krist Novoselic** (bass) formed what would eventually become Nirvana, moving to nearby Olympia to work the Olympia-Tacoma-Seattle bar circuit. While working its way through a series of drummers, the band signed with local independent label **Sub Pop** and recorded its first LP, *Bleach*, in the spring of 1989. *Bleach* was recorded for $606.17, contained twelve Cobain originals, and scored favorable reviews from the underground rock press. It also sold an impressive 35,000 copies. Shortly after recording *Bleach*, Nirvana finalized their lineup with the addition of drummer **Dave Grohl.**

TRAGEDY

During the summer of 1989, Nirvana recorded several song demos with producer Butch Vig, with the intention of shopping them around to major labels. After eventually signing with Geffen (DGC) for $287,000, they recorded *Nevermind* in the summer of 1991 and released it in September. Propelled by Cobain's brilliant songwriting, including the generational anthem "Smells Like Teen Spirit" (number 6, platinum) and the powerful and dynamic playing of Grohl and Novoselic, *Nevermind* hit the charts in early November and stayed there for fifty weeks. In February 1992, Cobain married singer **Courtney Love,** with whom he fathered a daughter. With a new family and his band the talk of the music world, one would think that Kurt Cobain's unhappy personal life was finally turning around.

However, Cobain was ill prepared to become the spokesman for his generation, and turned to heroin for comfort. In the last year of his life, there were no less than five incidents that were either suicide attempts or could be perceived as such, including three drug overdoses. The last of these occurred on March 18, 1994; twelve days later he checked into the Exodus Recovery Clinic in Los Angeles. On April 1, after telling security he was going out for some cigarettes, Cobain escaped from the clinic and disappeared. After several days of frantic searching by family and police, his body was discovered on April 8 at his home in Seattle, in the room above the garage. He had shot himself in the head with a 20-gauge shotgun four days earlier. His death was mourned by millions of fans, and he was eulogized by numerous tributes on radio and MTV in the weeks and months that followed.

Alternative Music in the Nineties

GRUNGE AND OTHER ALTERNATIVE MUSIC

In spite of Cobain's personal trauma, Nirvana had managed to finish their fourth album, *In Utero* in the summer of 1993, and posthumously released *MTV Unplugged in New York,* recorded from the TV special taped the previous year. Both LPs hit number 1 and went multi-platinum, and *Unplugged* won the 1995 Alternative Music Grammy Award. By this time Nirvana had succeeded in almost single-handedly returning the rock mainstream to a punk esthetic with an updated version of that style that became known as **grunge.** Grunge eschewed the virtuosic artistry and pretentiousness of metal; songs were often slow and plodding, and usually contain very little in the way of chord progressions. Choruses often are set apart from verses simply by start-stop dynamic contrasts. The style had evolved in the mid to late eighties in Seattle's thriving underground rock scene, with support from local radio stations, a prospering underground rock press, and the Sub Pop label, which had also signed local bands **Soundgarden, Mud Honey,** and **Alice in Chains.** Another local band, **Pearl Jam,** formed in 1990, was able to benefit from

Box 14-1 Grunge

Characteristics of Grunge
1. Punk influences, both in music and in attitude
2. Slow, plodding tempos
3. Simple chord progressions
4. Avoidance of virtuosity, pretension or posturing
5. Start-stop dynamics
6. Lyrics are often of dark and murky themes, sung in a plaintive, lamenting manner
7. Accompanying fashion included plaid flannel shirts, ripped jeans, stocking caps and mountain boots.

Key Grunge Recordings
- ❏ *Nevermind*—Nirvana, 1991
- ❏ *Ten*—Pearl Jam, 1991

the growing interest in the Seattle scene and signed with major label Epic. Their debut LP *Ten* sold seven million copies and stayed on the charts for 100 weeks. Some characteristics of Grunge and some key recordings are listed in Box 14-1.

Grunge gave a huge boost to the alternative music scene that had first appeared in the eighties. The most creative and inspired alternative bands from the nineties included **Phish, Radiohead,** the **Dave Matthews Band,** and **Beck.** Phish could be described as a Grateful Dead redux, with it's eclectic mix of bluegrass, country, folk, and rock and roll, all tied together with a whimsical sensibility. Like the Dead, Phish has put more effort into their live performances than their records and have become one of the top live attractions in rock. To capture the essence of their live performances on record, they have released an amazing twenty live albums since 2001. Radiohead formed in 1989 in Oxford, England, and first garnered attention in 1993 with the hit single "Creep" from their debut album *Pablo Honey.* Over the last ten years the band has maintained an iconoclastic approach to music, combining the best values of alternative rock (angst-ridden lyrics, post-punk attitudes, etc.) with an ear toward creating unusual and experimental electronic textures. Their breakthrough came in 1997 with the release of *OK Computer;* by 2000, their popularity had grown to the point that their fourth album *Kid A* debuted at number 1 on the U.S. charts.

The Dave Matthews Band, led by the transplanted South African guitarist/vocalist, has become one of rocks most popular alternative bands since their inception in the early nineties. Like many alternative bands, their initial success came by connecting with college audiences through non-stop touring. After self-releasing *Remember Two Things* in 1993, the band was able to sign with RCA and release *Under the Table & Dreaming* the following year. Helped in part by the hit single "What Would You Say," the album went quadruple platinum. In 1996, their single "So Much to Say" was awarded a Grammy, and since 1998 the band has released three number 1 albums and no less than six live LPs. The sound of the DMB combines pop oriented world beat and loose jam-band sensibilities with touches of country and folk.

Key Nineties Alternative Recordings

- ❏ *Under the Table & Dreaming*— Dave Matthews Band, 1994
- ❏ *OK Computer*— Radiohead, 1997
- ❏ *Odelay*—Beck, 1996

Beck (Beck Hansen) is perhaps the most inventive and original musician on today's scene. He is the son of Bibbe Hansen, a part of Andy Warhol's Factory scene in the sixties and the grandson of Al Hansen, an important figure in the New York art scene who is best known for helping launch the career of Yoko Ono. After trying his hand at acoustic blues, folk, and poetry, Beck made his first recordings in 1992; by 1994 he signed a lucrative contract with Geffen and released *Mellow Gold,* which hit number 13. Geffen also re-released the underground smash "Loser," which became a Hot 100 number 10 hit. "Loser" captures the essence of Beck's ability to create his own musical universe, combining bottleneck blues guitar, a hip hop beat, rap lyrics, and an infectious sing along hook. Subsequent albums Odelay (1996) and *Mutations* (1998) received Alternative Music Grammy Awards.

Other Nineties Goings On

Lollapalooza, Lilith Fair and Other Stuff

The emergence of grunge wasn't the only big news in rock in the nineties. In 1991 Billboard began using a new **SoundScan** technology to track record sales, instead of relying on informal reporting by record store employees or figures manipulated by record labels. The more accurate SoundScan reporting produced some interesting results, as some of the supposedly top sellers turned out to be not so hot, and a few one hit wonders appeared from out of nowhere. The poster child for this era could be country singer Billy Ray Cyrus, whose "Achy Breaky Heart" spent twenty-two weeks on the charts in 1992 before Cyrus disappeared from the radar screen. Country music in fact experienced a tremendous boom in the nineties, although it's market was still fragmented off to the side of the mainstream. **Garth Brooks** sold more than fifty million records in the nineties, and although he had seventeen number 1 country hits, only one single cracked the Hot 100 ("Lost in You," number 5, 1999). To be fair, Brooks has had an astonishing nine number 1 albums on the Billboard 200 since 1990, but his limited success with singles in the Hot 100 suggests that radio programming remains highly fragmented, with his singles only being played on country stations.

The nineties also saw a return to popularity of outdoor festivals. The first, **Lollapalooza,** began in 1991 as a one time, twenty-one day tour by seven alternative bands that was so successful that it became an annual summer event through 1997. It is also staging a comeback in the summer of 2003 as this book is being written. **Lilith Fair,** a sort of Lollapalooza for women artists, was started in 1997 by **Sarah McLachlan** and continued through 1999. Canadian singer/songwriter McLachlan has produced six albums since her debut in 1989, including 1993's platinum selling *Fumbling Toward Ecstasy.* She has also garnered three Grammys, including one for 1999's number 14 hit "I Will Remember You," recorded live at a Lilith Fair concert. Some of the best new emerging women in rock were featured on one or more Lilith Fairs, including McLachlan, **Fiona Apple, Shawn Colvin, Lauryn Hill,** and **Suzanne Vega.** Other women who made important debuts in the nineties included **Alanis Morrisette,** whose *Jagged Little Pill* was the best selling album of 1996, and the eclectic **Ani DiFranco,** whose 1997 LP *Living in Clip* went gold. **Woodstock** was re-enacted in both 1994 and 1999, and although 1994's event went smoothly, rioting and arson marred the latter festival.

The year 1999 was the "Year of Latin Music" as a number of Latino artists enjoyed commercial success. Leading the way was venerable rock stalwart Carlos Santana, whose album *Supernatural* won eight Grammy Awards. Other Latin artists with Top Ten hits in 1999 include **Marc Anthony, Christine Aguilera, Gloria Estefan, Jennifer Lopez,** and **Ricky Martin,** a former soap opera star whose self-titled album (his first in English) included the number 1 hit "Livin' La Vida Loca." Pop artists who hit the top of the charts in the nineties include divas **Mariah Carey, Celine Dion,** and Jackson family scion **Janet Jackson;** hip hop soul groups **TLC, Boyz II Men,** and **R. Kelly;** and teeny bopper sensations **Britney Spears,** the **Backstreet Boys,** and **'N Sync.** The 1995 single "One Sweet Day" by Mariah Carey and Boyz II Men stayed at number 1 for sixteen weeks, making it the number 1 hit in the history of the Billboard Hot 100.

THE CONTROVERSY CONTINUES

At the turn of the millennium, rock's newest lightning rod for controversy was white rapper **Eminem** (Marshall Mathers III) (1973–). With lyrics that include graphic depictions of violence and bizarre sexual exploits, misogyny, and homophobia, Eminem has drawn some of the harshest criticism of any rock artist in history, while simultaneously winning a legion of diehard fans. However, he has skillfully used this controversy to maintain a high media profile that has enabled him to extend his artistic grasp beyond music.

Mathers endured an impoverished and troubled childhood, shuffling back and forth between homes in Jefferson City, Missouri, and Detroit. After taking up rap at fourteen—initially using his initials M&M as a moniker—and working his way through a number of groups in Detroit, he made his first record in 1995 as a member of Soul Intent. His debut as a soloist, *Infinite,* followed in 1996, which received lukewarm revues. Around this time, Mathers created an alter ego named Slim Shady, through whom he began to

At the turn of the century rock's newest lightning rod for controversy was white rapper Eminem (Marshall Mathers III). AP/WIDE WORLD PHOTOS

comment on his own troubled personal life. He bitterly spoke of his girl-friend, who left him and barred him from seeing their child. He also related scathing stories of his mother, who was accused of physically and mentally abusing his younger brother (she later filed a lawsuit against her son, claiming that comments about her in his songs caused emotional distress and damage to her reputation). While his own personal life was beginning to disintegrate into drug and alcohol abuse (and a suicide attempt), Mathers released *The Slim Shady EP,* a breakthrough which drew his first positive reaction from the rap community.

After taking second place in the freestyle category at the 1997 Rap Olympics MC Battle in Los Angeles, a Mathers demo tape caught the attention of producer Dr. Dre. Within minutes of their first meeting (in which Dre was reportedly shocked to learn that Eminem was white), the two began recording "My Name Is," which led to Eminem's signing with Interscope in 1998. The song was later released as a single and included on 1999's *The Slim Shady LP,* which went triple platinum. By the time his third album was released in the summer of 2000, Eminem had become a phenom: *The Marshall Mathers LP* became the fastest selling rap album in history, selling nearly two million copies in its first week alone. With this album, Eminem drew his largest criticism to date, with it's homophobic overtones in "Kill You," and a graphic description of killing his wife in "Kim" (which caused her to attempt suicide and later divorce him). In the context of this controversy, Eminem surprised everyone by appearing at the 2000 Grammy Awards ceremony in a duet with the openly gay Elton John. In 2002 he appeared with generally good reviews in the film *8 Mile,* loosely based on his life, and continued to spark controversy by attacking Moby and Limp Bizkit in the song "Without Me." His latest release, 2002's *The Eminem Show* caused little uproar, suggesting that like many controversial rock personalities before him, Eminem's shock value has perhaps worn off somewhat.

Limp Bizkit, along with **Korn, Kid Rock,** and **Rage against the Machine** combined elements of metal and punk with rap, and drew their share of criticism for generally mean spirited and violence-prone lyrics.

The File Sharing Controversy

The Majors Rule—Or Do They?

As rock nears its 50th anniversary, the battle between the major labels and the small independents continues to wage. On the surface it would appear that the majors would have the upper hand. In the business climate of the nineties, mergers and takeovers have been the rule, with ever-larger companies gobbling each other up and ultimately being absorbed into large multi-national conglomerates. Industries such as broadcasting, banking, telecommunications, and oil have all experienced this trend. With soaring profits in the eighties and nineties due to the introduction of the compact disc, record labels became takeover targets. Today, ownership of nearly all the major labels is concentrated

The Five Conglomerates That Control the Music Industry Today

Vivendi Universal, based in Paris, owner of MCA, Decca, and Motown

EMI, based in London, owner of Capitol, Virgin, and Blue Note

AOL Time Warner, based in New York, owner of Warner, Atlantic, and Elektra

Sony, based in Tokyo, owner of Columbia and Epic

Bertelsmann Music Group, based in Gütersloh, Germany, owner of RCA and Arista

into the hands of five huge conglomerates, who have focused their attention on promoting fewer and fewer artists they know will sell millions of records. With unprecedented financial backing and control of the marketplace, the majors seemed well positioned to withstand any challenges they face. However, they are now involved in a fight for their very existence.

In 2001, shipments of CDs fell by 6% and sales by 10%, the first major sales slump since the early eighties. Record labels began laying off thousands of employees and severed the contracts of many artists to cut costs. (The most publicized case was that of Mariah Carey, who was paid $28 million by Virgin just so they could void her contract.) Although a stale economy certainly had some effect on sales (especially after the September 11 disaster), finger pointing began in earnest among artists, consumers, and the record companies as to who was to blame. Many artists feel that the long-term contracts they are forced to sign inhibit their artistic freedom, and have sought to become 'free agents,' similar to actors, who are not contractually bound to a studio for more than one movie. Consumers contend that they are buying less music because they don't like what is being offered. When the industry abandoned the less profitable CD single format, many buyers balked at having to pay $15 to $18 for an entire CD that often contained only two or three good tracks and a bunch of filler.

MP3, NAPSTER

For their part, the record labels, with the most at stake, have laid the blame for declining sales on the practice of Internet **file sharing.** File sharing became possible after the creation of the **MP3** (MPEG Audio Layer III) format by the Motion Pictures Experts Group in 1992. MP3 files are roughly 1/10 the size of standard CD audio tracks with virtually no loss of sonic quality, making them ideal for storage on computer hard drives. The format first gained widespread acceptance among consumers in 1997, when MP3.com went online offering 3,000 songs for free download. Within a year it became the most popular site on the World Wide Web, getting three million hits per month. (MP3 eventually developed into an online distribution service where small labels and independent artists sell their music for a fee.) In 1998, Diamond Rio introduced the first portable MP3 player, the PMP300, which effectively freed the MP3 from the confines of the computer. But the real file sharing controversy began in late 1999 when an eighteen-year-old college dropout named **Shawn Fanning** developed a new software program he called **Napster.**

Napster's ingenious setup allowed users to connect through the server's central site (Napster.com) and exchange MP3 files. Napster only contained *lists* of songs made available by its users; the actual MP3 files exist only on their personal computers and are never transferred into the Napster site. Using a powerful search engine and a **peer-to-peer protocol,** Napster was able to connect those seeking a specific song with those who had the song on their computer, allowing the first person to download the song directly from the second person's computer.

It only took about a month before the Recording Industry Association of America (RIAA) filed suit to stop Napster, claiming they are guilty of "contributory and vicarious copyright infringement." In its defense, Napster claimed that they were protected under the 1992 **Audio Home Recording Act,** which allows consumers to make personal copies of copyrighted material. It also claimed that its service is not unlike copying machines or VCRs, whose manufacturers are not held responsible for the potential illegal use by owners of their products. Nonetheless, at the preliminary hearing in March 2000, Judge Marilyn Hall Patel of the Federal Court in San Francisco ruled that Napster was in fact violating copyright laws. Although appeals would drag the case on for another two years, in the end Napster was shut down.

SUBPOENA CITY

Although the RIAA won the Napster case, the publicity surrounding it brought the whole file sharing issue to the national spotlight. Within months, it seemed that everyone was downloading music for free—Napster's connections went from one million to five million a month by July 2000. Another ISP, Gnutella, began operating in May 2000, using a decentralized form of the peer-to-peer protocol that seemingly made the company safe from legal suit. Soon after its appearance, the company publicly released the software's source code, and within weeks several other file-sharing sites popped up to cater to the increased demand by the public. Today, there is a dizzying array of sites available for downloading music, including Limewire, Morpheus, and Grokster.

But the RIAA has not given up the fight. Citing statistics that show that blank CDs outsold prerecorded CDs for the first time in 2001, together with the explosive popularity of home CD burners, the industry has dug its heels in for a prolonged fight to stamp out what they refer to as commercial piracy. Under the terms laid out by the 1998 **Digital Millennium Copyright Act** (DMCA), ISP's cannot be held liable for alleged copyright abuses by their users, but are required to turn over the names of those suspected of such. In the summer of 2003, the RIAA began serving subpoenas on hundreds of unsuspecting file sharers, with the threat of fines of up to $150,000 per song offered for illegal copy on

Using a powerful search engine and a **peer-to-peer protocol,** Napster was able to connect those seeking a specific song with those who had the song on their computer, allowing the first person to download the song directly from the second person's computer.

their computers. Whether these cases, which could eventually number in the thousands if not millions, ever go to court is anybody's guess. But it is clear by now that the RIAA, however self-righteous its motives may be, is attacking its own customers, a move that may ultimately be counterproductive. Consumers today have a wide choice of entertainment options open to them, including video games, DVDs, movies, instant messaging, and cell phones that feature text messaging, and digital cameras. Many may never return to their previous record buying habits. Many others are annoyed that the record industry is clinging to an outdated and inefficient business model rather than embracing new technology and responding to the desires of their customers.

To Hear the Future, Listen to the Past

As rock approaches its 50th anniversary, it is clear that there are some serious legal issues that need to be resolved. But rock will continue to negotiate the minefields of corporate interference, attempts at censorship, new technologies and changing consumer tastes to evolve in ways that we can only imagine today. And what will rock sound like in the future? It is clear that the best way to make guesses about what lies ahead is to look to the past. In its short time on earth, rock music has shown a remarkable ability to reshape, recombine, and reform the styles and sounds from its own heritage to construct new styles that will seem fresh to its ever-changing youngest and most ardent audience. While the new styles may sound somewhat familiar to those with a few years under their belt, the process is evolutionary nonetheless.

Rock musicians will continue to push the creative envelope, indies will continue to fight with the majors, and teenagers will continue to look for music that speaks to them in a way that no other form of communication can. And you can bet on this: rock music—that which was created by black R&B singers and Southern white cats, popularized by renegade DJs and independent record labels who connected it to their disaffected white teenage audience—will continue to be rebellious, independent, resentful of authority, and live by its own terms.

Chapter 14
Study Questions

1. In what ways is grunge different than heavy metal?

_____

_____

_____

_____

2. What are some of the reasons that Seattle was important to grunge?

_____

_____

_____

_____

3. Why did Kurt Cobain become a spokesman for his generation?

_____

_____

_____

_____

4. Describe some of the techniques and concepts that nineties alternative artists are using to evolve their music.

_____

_____

_____

5. Name three musical events from the nineties that made headlines.

_____

_____

_____

6. What are some of the controversies that Eminem has embroiled himself in?

_____

_____

_____

_____

7. Describe exactly what MPEG Audio Layer III is and why it is important to today's music business.

_____

_____

_____

_____

_____

8. Describe the tactics currently being used by the major labels to combat file sharing.

_____

_____

_____

_____

_____

9. What are some of the reasons that some artists, independent labels and consumers use in defense of file sharing?

_____

_____

_____

_____

10. How have recent copyright laws defined the debate over file sharing?

_____

_____

_____

_____

APPENDIX A

Music Synopses

Track

"THE WAY YOU LOOK TONIGHT"
(Jerome Kerns/Dorothy Fields), **Frank Sinatra**

This Tin Pan Alley standard, written for the 1936 film *Swing Time*, won an Oscar for composer Jerome Kern and lyricist Dorothy Fields. It is written in the 32 bar **standard song form**, which incorporates four 8-bar sections in an AABA configuration. Each A section ends with the title of the tune; interestingly, the B section, or bridge, ends with the line "My Foolish Heart", which Tin Pan Alley writers Ned Washington and Victor Young used as the title for their 1949 standard written for the movie of the same name.

"The Way You Look Tonight" was recorded on January 27, 1964 in Los Angeles when Sinatra was 48 years old and at the top of his form. Nelson Riddle, who would later go on to work with Linda Ronstadt and many others, wrote this outstanding arrangement. The backup orchestra is a standard jazz big band (trumpet, trombone, saxophone and rhythm sections) with an added string section, which makes its entrance at the end of the first A section (0:32). Notice also how the rhythm section plays a two-beat rhythm until the bridge (1:12), where it switches to a walking bass 4/4 rhythm. After playing through the entire tune once, the song repeats from the bridge (2:06), where the saxes briefly take the melody. For the last A (2:35), the song modulates up from the key of Eb to E.

Track

"HEY! BA-BA-RE-BOP"
(Lionel Hampton/Curly Hamner), **Lionel Hampton and his Orchestra**

Personnel: Lionel Hampton: vibes, vocal; Jimmy Nottingham, Joe Morris, Wendell Cully, Lamar Wright, Jr., Dave Page: trumpets; Booty Wood, Jimmy Wormick: trombones; Bobby Plater, Ben Kynard: alto saxes; Johnny Griffin: tenor sax; Milt Buckner: piano; Fred Radcliffe: drums; Charles Harris, Ted Sinclair: basses; Billy Mackel: guitar

Lionel Hampton first achieved fame as a member of the Benny Goodman Orchestra in 1936, when he and pianist Teddy Wilson broke the color barrier in jazz by becoming the first black musicians to play in a major white swing band. Hampton stayed with Goodman until 1940, when he formed his own big band, and scored one of the first ever R&B hits in 1942 with "Flying Home."

Written by Hampton and bandleader/drummer Curley Hamner, "Hey! Ba-Ba-Re-Bop" was recorded in Los Angeles on December 1, 1945. It is a 12 bar blues that starts with one chorus of piano solo by Milt Buckner. The first sung verse (0:21) is simply a call and response singing of the title between Hampton and the rest of the band. The second (0:43) and third verses (1:05) feature **stop time** in the first 4 bars. After a screaming trumpet solo (1:27) and a clarinet solo (1:48), both of which have horn riffs scored in the background, Hampton returns with a chorus of scat singing (2:33), and one more stop time verse (2:54) before the song comes to a close on a giant chord.

"ALL NIGHT LONG"

(Johnny Otis/Devonia Willams), **Johnny Otis and His Orchestra**

Personnel: Johnny Otis: vocal; Devonia Williams: piano; Pete Lewis: Guitar; Mario DeLagarde: ball; Leard Bell: drums; Walter Henry: alto sax; Hosea Sapp: trumpet

"All Night Long" was recorded in New York on March 19, 1951 and debuted on the *Billboard* R&B chart on August 25, eventually peaking at #6. The song marked the first recorded vocal by bandleader/drummer/vibraphonist Otis, who would later also sing on his biggest hit, 1958's million seller "Willie and the Hand Jive". The song is a perfect example of the jump band style of rhythm and blues, with its prominent boogie bass line and small two-piece horn section. It also contains an early reference to the word rock, as in "just grab your baby and rock/all Night Long" (incidentally, the song was written and recorded before Allen Freed named his radio show *The Moondog House Rock and Roll Party*). The lyrics to "all Night Long" tell the story of a group of guys who are bent on going out and having fun, eventually drawing the attention of the police. It is told in the same humorous fashion made popular by Louis Jordan in the forties.

"WHY DO FOOLS FALL IN LOVE"

(Herman Santiago/Jimmy Merchant), **Frankie Lymon and the Teenagers**

Personnel: Frankie Lymon, Jimmy Merchant, Herman Santiago, Joe Negroni, Sherman Garnes: vocals; Jimmy Wright: tenor sax; Jimmy Shirley: guitar; Al Hall: bass; Gene Brooks: drums
Produced by George Goldman
Highest chart position: #6, 1956; sixteen weeks on the Hot 100

The Teenagers, made up of five school buddies from New York, were the quintessential "unknowns discovered singing on the street corner" doo wop group. After another singer named Richard Barrett discovered them in 1955, the group signed with George Goldner's Gee records. At their first recording session, they performed "Why Do Fools Fall in Love," a song that Teenagers Herman Santiago and Jimmy Merchant co-wrote. However, Santiago, who was supposed to sing lead, had a cold, and the job was handed to Lymon. Subsequently he and producer Goldman were given writing credits for the song (this was later overturned by a federal judge in the early nineties). The song has been a Hot 100 hit four times, most recently in 1981 with Diana Ross's version.

"Why Do Fools Fall in Love" starts with Sherman Garnes' distinctive bass "Hey, doom-ma-ta-doom-ma" vocal before the rest of the group enters. The first verse of this AABA tune starts at 0:14 with Lymon's high, distinctive vocal pleading and the rest of the Teenagers singing backup parts. At 0:57, tenor sax man Jimmy Wright plays an invigorating solo (he was in fact the leader of the backup band on this recording), before the song repeats (starting at 1:20) in its entirety. At 2:03 there is a short tag to end the song.

Track 5

"SHINE, SHAVE, SHOWER"
(Lefty Frizzell/Jim Beck), **Lefty Frizzell**

Personnel: Lefty Frizzell: vocals, acoustic guitar; Norman Stevens: lead guitar; Jimmie Curtis: steel guitar; R. I. "Pee Wee" Stuart: fiddle; Madge Suttee: piano; Bobby Williamson: bass

"Shine, Shave, Shower" was recorded at Lefty Frizzell's first session at engineer Jim Beck's Dallas studio on July 25, 1950. Beck was well connected in music publishing circles, and it is probable that Frizzell gave him co-writing credit in exchange for pitching this and other originals to major label executives in Nashville. The contract that Beck secured for Frizzell with Columbia resulted in this session, in which Frizzell also recorded his first hit "If You've Got the Money, I've Got the Time." "Shine, Shave, Shower" was released as the B-side of "Look What Thoughts Will Do" in October 1950.

"Shine, Shave, Shower" tells the story of a man who is getting ready to go out on the town with his baby on Saturday night. After a quick solo vocal introduction by Frizzell, the verse starts at 0:09 with full band accompaniment. Another example of the AABA standard song form, Frizzell sings one full verse, which is followed at 0:49 by a verse that consists of a 16-bar guitar solo by Norman Stevens, and two 8-bar solos on fiddle and piano. At 1:25 Frizzell repeats the verse (without singing the bridge at 2:05, where a short guitar solo is inserted). At 2:24, a short tag finishes the song. Although "Shine, Shave, Shower" uses the traditional country instruments of fiddle and steel guitar, it does not include drums, which later honky tonk recordings did use.

Track 6

"CRAZY MAN CRAZY"
(Bill Haley), **Bill Haley and His Comets**

Personnel: Bill Haley: guitar, lead vocal; Danny Cedrone: lead guitar; Billy Williamson: steel guitar; Billy Guesack: drums; Marshall Lytle: bass; Johnny Grande: piano
Highest chart position: #15, 1953

When "Crazy Man Crazy" was recorded for Philadelphia's Essex label in late 1952, Bill Haley had just reformed his country western band the Saddlemen into a lean, mean rock and roll machine that he called the Comets. The song became the first rock and roll song in history to hit the pop charts in 1953, before Elvis Presley had even made his first demo recordings at Sun Records. The success of "Crazy Man Crazy" and other Haley recordings such as "Rock the Joint" led to his signing with Decca in 1954, with whom he had fourteen Top Forty records, including his 1955 smash "Rock Around the Clock."

"Crazy Man Crazy" starts with a wild drum intro by Billy Guesack (who was the Comets session drummer; their live drummer was Dick Richards) and Danny Cedrone's startling guitar glissando. At 0:05, Haley sings two choruses, which consist mostly of repeating the song title with Cedrone and steel guitarist Billy Williamson responding in call and response fashion. At 0:28, Haley sings one verse followed by one more chorus. At 0:51, the band chants "Go, Go, Go, Everybody" before Cedrone and Williamson play short but effective solos. At 1:26, two more choruses are sung, followed by the last verse (1:49), one more chorus (2:00), and one more chorus of "Go, Go, Go, Everybody" (2:12) before the track fades out amid screams and shouts. Also notice the driving slap bass playing of Marshall Lytle and Guesack's crackling snare drum that keep this song hopping from start to finish.

"TUTTI FRUTTI"

(Richard Penniman, Dorothy LaBostrie, Joe Lubin), **Little Richard**

Track 7

Personnel: Little Richard: piano, vocals; Alvin "Red" Tyler: bari sax; Lee Allen: tenor sax;
Earl Palmer: drums; Huey Smith: piano; Frank Fields: bass; guitarist unknown)
Produced by Bumps Blackwell and Art Rupe
Highest chart position: #17, 1956

The story of "Tutti Frutti" is one of the legends of early rock and roll. Signed by
Art Rupe's Specialty Records, Richard's first day of recording at J&M Studio
yielded nothing spectacular: four blues tunes. The next day, September 14, 1955,
the results were pretty much the same. Finally the band took a break at a nearby
club called the Drop. There, Richard sat down at the piano and belted out an
obscene version of what was to become "Tutti Frutti." Up to this point, Huey
"Piano" Smith had been playing piano on the session; after Richard took over on
the keys, he was able to cut loose with his explosive vocal style. It took just
three takes to come up with this jewel, after Dorothy LaBostrie was brought in
to clean up Richard's lyrics.

"Tutti Frutti" is a 12-bar blues that starts off with one of the most memorable
vocal chants in the history of rock and roll. Richard uses stop time throughout
the song, most often at the end of each verse, where he repeats the opening
line. After the fifth verse (1:19), tenor sax man Lee Allen cuts loose with a short
but intense solo. This recording shows off the tightly knit band of trumpeter
Dave Bartholomew, who "supervised" this and many other sessions at J&M in
the fifties (the title "producer" had not been invented at this time, although that
is essentially what Bartholomew's job was).

"SCHOOL DAY"

(Chuck Berry), **Chuck Berry**

Track 8

Personnel: Chuck Berry: guitar, vocal; Hubert Sumlin: guitar; Johnny Johnson: piano;
Willie Dixon: bass; Fred Below: drums)
Produced by Leonard Chess
Highest chart position: #3, 1957

Recorded at Chicago's Chess Studios on January 21, 1957, "School Day" was
Chuck Berry's third and highest charting record to date. With scorching guitar
work, an infectious shuffle beat and a great story line, it immediately connected
with teenagers. "The lyrics depict the way it was in my time. I had no idea what
was going on in the classes during the time I composed it, much less what's hap-
pening today. Recording the song with breaks in the rhythm was intended to
emphasize the jumps and changes I found in classes in high school compared to
the one room and one teacher I had in elementary school."

In this 12-bar blues, Berry makes excellent use of call and response between the
short vocal clips and double-stop guitar riffs. After four verses (by which time the
story's character has made it to 3 o'clock and the nearest juke joint) the singing
relents for one chorus to allow the guitar to come front and center in a signature
Berry solo (1:29). The legendary Chess rhythm section, which included Willie
Dixon on bass and Fred Below on drums, stays in a strong supporting role
throughout the recording. Berry had six more Top Forty hits after "School Day"
before he was arrested in late 1959 for violating the Mann Act.

Track

"GREAT BALLS OF FIRE"
(Otis Blackwell/Jack Hammer), **Jerry Lee Lewis**

Personnel: Jerry Lee Lewis: piano; Roland Janes: guitar; J. M. Van Eaton: drums; bassist unknown
Produced by Sam Phillips
Highest charting positions: #2 pop, #3 R&B, #1 country

"Great Balls of Fire" was recorded on October 8, 1957 at Sam Phillips' Sun Studio in Memphis. Phillips' studio was small, only eighteen by thirty-three feet, and typically musicians played so loud that the sound would become compressed in the tight quarters. The recorded result almost explodes out of the speaker cabinets. On top of this, Phillips often added his famous tape-delay echo to the voice, which can easily be heard on this recording.

Lewis had appeared on the nationally broadcast *Steve Allen Show* earlier in the year to promote his first smash single, "Whole Lot of Shakin' Going On." Both the hit and the TV appearance guaranteed that a record as electrifying and openly sexual as "Great Balls of Fire" would become a hit. The song was written in part by Otis Blackwell, who had seen Lewis on the Allen show (Blackwell had previously written "All Shook Up" and "Don't Be Cruel" for Elvis) and sent a demo to Phillips. In the moments leading up to the final take, Jerry Lee's own religious upbringing began to gnaw at his conscience. He launched into a lengthy diatribe (that Phillips recorded in its entirety) that concluded with, "Man, I got the devil in me! If I didn't have, I'd be a Christian!"

Track

"PEGGY SUE"
(Buddy Holly, Jerry Allison, Norman Petty), **Buddy Holly and the Crickets**

Personnel: Buddy Holly: guitar, vocals; Joe B. Mauldin: bass; Jerry Allison: drums
Produced by Norman Petty
Highest chart position: #3, 1957

"Peggy Sue" was recorded in June 1957 during three days of sessions at Norman Petty's Nor Va Jak Studio in Clovis, New Mexico. Immediately distinguishing the song are the relentless paradiddles played on the tom toms by drummer Jerry Allison, an unusual departure from the standard backbeat snare of rock and roll. With slim instrumentation of guitar, bass and drums (the Crickets' rhythm guitarist Niki Sullivan is not used here), "Peggy Sue" relies heavily on Holly's hiccupping vocals to get his message of love across. Notice how Holly changes his voice in the third verse (1:05) to that of an adolescent. He also plays a fine chordal guitar solo at 1:24.

Although producer Petty added his name to the writing credits (a common practice in those days), he also reportedly came up with the idea for the interesting chord change in the chorus behind the "Pretty, pretty, pretty, pretty Peggy Sue" line, first heard at 0:49.

"ON BROADWAY"

(Jerry Leiber/Mike Stoller/Cynthia Weill/Barry Mann), **the Drifters**

Track 11

Personnel: Rudy Lewis: lead vocal; Johnny Moore: tenor vocal; Charlie Thomas: tenor vocal; Gene Pearson: baritone vocal; Johnny Terry: bass vocal; Phil Spector: guitar solo; other musicians and singers unidentified
Produced by Jerry Leiber and Mike Stoller
Highest chart position: #9, 1963

"On Broadway" was the twelfth Top Forty hit for the Drifters in a four-year period. Notable in the Leiber/Stoller production of this record are the percussion instruments (including castanets and timpani), vibes, rhythm guitar playing a propulsive *chunk-chunk-chunk-chunk*, string section and female backup singers, brass section, and Phil Spector's memorable twangy guitar solo. Recorded January 22, 1963 in New York City.

"HE'S SO FINE"

(Ronnie Mack), **the Chiffons**

Track 12

Personnel: Judy Craig, Barbara Lee, Patricia Bennett, Sylvia Peterson: vocals; background instrumentals: the Tokens
Produced by the Tokens
Highest charting position: #1, 1963

The Chiffons were four chums from the Bronx who would often sing together in the school lunchroom. In late 1962, they were heard by songwriter Ronnie Mack, who asked them to record a few songs that he had written. No one was interested until the members of the Tokens ("The Lion Sleeps Tonight", #1, 1961) heard the demo and financed their own recording of "He's So Fine", playing the rhythm instruments themselves. After signing the Chiffons to the small Laurie label, the song was released and went to #1 on March 30, 1963.

"He's So Fine" is the quintessential girl group song about longing for the attention of a perfect boy ("I don't know how I'm gonna do it/But I'm gonna make him mine"). The high point of the song comes at 1:19, when, over a stop time rhythm, the Chiffons sing, "I just can't wait, I just can't wait, to be held in his arms." But the most distinctive characteristic of the song is the background chant "Doo lang, doo lang, doo lang," which is the only harmony background (accompanied by bass and drums) in the first eight bars of the tune. The song received additional publicity in 1976 when the estate of Ronnie Mack (who died right after the song went gold) sued George Harrison for plagiarism over his song "My Sweet Lord" and won.

Track

13

"MISERLOU"
(Tauber/Wise/Rubanis/Leeds), **Dick Dale and the Del-tones**

Personnel: Dick Dale: electric guitar; other musicians unknown

Dick Dale's third release, "Miserlou" was his most intense to date, and although none of his recordings ever hit the charts, he was nonetheless the creator of the surf style. His concerts by the time of its May 1962 release were drawing thousands of fans, who watched him play his guitar left-handed (without re-stringing it, as Hendrix would later do) and often upside down and backwards (Dale later claimed that a young Hendrix often came to hear him play at the Rendezvous Ballroom in Del Ray, California). Dale also introduced a portable device, developed by Fender Instruments, which provided a reverberation effect that made his guitar sound as if it was actually underwater, intensifying the effect of his glissandos to capture the sound of waves crashing down. In 1994 "Miserlou" became the title song for Quentin Tarantino's Blockbuster movie "Pulp Fiction" and reached cult classic status.

The song starts with Dale's unique (at the time) single-note staccato picking technique that was borrowed from the bouzouki and mandolin music of his native Lebanon (in fact, "Miserlou" was a Greek pop hit from the 1940s). Throughout the song, there are three guitar parts: the melody, the rhythmic *chu-chunk, chunk* which comes in on beat two of each measure, and the constant root-fifth double picking that became a defining characteristic of surf music. Dale's glissandos can be heard throughout (the first at 0:24); he also deftly switches back and forth between playing the songs melody in the lowest octave (at the beginning), to a higher octave (0:26) to add variety.

Track

14

"THE LITTLE OLD LADY (FROM PASADENA)"
(Don Altfeld/Roger Christian), **Jan and Dean**

Personnel: Jan Berry, Dean Torrence: vocals; the Honeys: backup vocals; other musicians unknown
Highest chart position: #3, 1964

"The Little Old Lady (from Pasadena)" was written in part by friend and former football teammate from University High School in West Los Angeles, Don Altfeld (Don's father was also president of the Jan and Dean fan club). It was inspired by an actual granny, Kathrine Milner (who was actually from Oxnard, California!) It became the groups tenth Top Forty hit and their seventh Gold Record.

Jan and Dean often worked with Brian Wilson (Torrence actually sang lead, uncredited, on the Beach Boys 1966 hit "Barbara Ann"), and his influence is heard throughout "The Little Old Lady (from Pasadena)." The opening acappella vocal harmonies sound as if they actually were the Beach Boys singing, as do the background "oo –wee-oo" vocals that enter at 0:29. Other interesting touches reminiscent of the Beach Boys include the use of the harmonica as the solo instrument at 1:29, and the key changes at 1:28 and 2:06. Also of interest, Marilyn Rovell, one of the members of the backup vocal group the Honeys, married Brian Wilson in 1964. Of course, the songs lyrics were also right sown surf alley, with an interesting twist: a granny who "can't keep her foot off the accelerator."

"PRETTY BOY FLOYD"
(Woody Guthrie), **Woody Guthrie**

Track 15

Personnel: Woody Guthrie: vocal and guitar)
Written and recorded in March 1939

During his life, Woody Guthrie wrote a number of epic ballads about outlaws, often celebrating them as populist heroes that, like Robin Hood, stole from the rich and gave to the poor. "Pretty Boy Floyd" is just such a tale, about the real life bank robber Charles Floyd. After growing up in the dust bowl years on a small farm in Oklahoma, Floyd decided that the only way to get ahead in life was through robbery. As a young man, Floyd moved from payroll robbery to robbing small banks throughout the Midwest. Living in Kansas City during the corrupt years of the Pendergast administration, Floyd made connections with organized crime elements and learned to use a machine gun. As his reputation grew and federal agents began pursuing him, he hid out in the backwoods, protected by the locals, who viewed him as a folk hero. He was eventually killed by FBI agents in an open Ohio farm field.

Guthrie's song captures the essence of Floyd the folk hero with lines such as, "Well, you say that I'm an outlaw/You say that I'm a thief/Here's a Christmas dinner/For the families on relief." It is sung with Guthrie's characteristic 'talking blues' style that became so influential to Bob Dylan and other folk artists. It is also performed in the traditional folk style, with only acoustic guitar accompaniment.

"HOUSE OF THE RISING SUN"
(traditional), **Joan Baez**

Track 16

Personnel: Joan Baez: guitar, vocals

Ten of the thirteen songs on Joan Baez's self-titled debut album were traditional folk songs, including "House of the Rising Sun," one of the most recorded songs in history. Other artists that have put their own versions on record include Bob Dylan, Duane Eddy, the Everly Brothers, Woody Guthrie, Nina Simone and the Ventures. The most famous version of course, is that of the Animals, whose 1964 record hit #1 and convinced Bob Dylan that the worlds of folk and rock didn't have to be mutually exclusive. The song is a mournful tale of a whorehouse in New Orleans, and includes the admonition by the singer to "Go tell my baby sister/Don't do what I have done/Go shun that house in New Orleans/They call the Rising Sun." Baez's rendition is unadorned, performed in the same way that she would in a coffeehouse, showcasing her angel-like voice.

Track

"A HARD RAIN'S A-GONNA FALL"
(Bob Dylan), **Bob Dylan**

Personnel: Bob Dylan: guitar, vocals
Produced by John Hammond
Released May 27, 1963

From Dylan's second album *The Freewheelin' Bob Dylan*, "A Hard Rain's A-Gonna Fall" was written in the fall of 1962 during the Cuban Missile Crisis. In September, Soviet missiles were discovered on Cuba, just ninety miles from the coast of Florida. Over the next several weeks, President John F. Kennedy and Soviet Premier Nikita Khrushchev faced off in a potentially deadly diplomatic stand off that brought America and the Soviet Union to the brink of nuclear war and the possible destruction of the entire world. By the time Khrushchev announced on October 28 that the missiles would be dismantled, Dylan had managed to perfectly capture (as he would do time and again) the anxieties of the era and paint a bleak picture of a post nuclear holocaust scenario. The song was an immediate sensation in the coffee shops and clubs in the Greenwich Village folk scene and helped establish Dylan as the voice of his generation.

Track

"PAPA'S GOT A BRAND NEW BAG, PT. I"
(James Brown), **James Brown**

Personnel: James Brown: vocal; Joe Dupars, Ron Tooley, Levi Rasbury: trumpets; Wilmer Milton: trombone; Nat Jones: alto sax; Maceo Parker: tenor and baritone saxes; St. Clair Pinckney, Eldee Williams, Al "Brisco" Clark: tenor saxes; Nat Jones: organ; Jimmy Nolen: guitar; Sam Thomas or Bernard Odum: bass; Melvin Parker: drums
Highest chart position: #8, 1965

As James Brown's first Top Ten hit, "Papa's Got a Brand New Bag, Pt. 1" marked the singer's emergence into mainstream crossover success. The song was recorded in February 1965 at Arthur Studios in Charlotte, North Carolina in less than an hour after a long bus ride on the way to a gig, a common practice for Brown's band at the time. "Pt. 1" is a shortened, sped up version of the original master, "Papa's Got a Brand New Bag, Pts. 1, 2, & 3", in which Maceo Parker takes solos on both tenor and baritone saxophones on an extended bridge vamp. The song itself was based on a line that Brown ad libbed at an earlier performance.

"Papa's Got a Brand New Bag, Pt. 1" is a 12-bar blues with an 8-bar vamp inserted after the second verse (0:48) and the fourth verse (1:48). Notice how throughout the song the guitar, bass, and horns all play in a very short, staccato fashion, essentially making them sound almost as if they are percussion instruments rather than melodic. The repetitive nature of the parts played by the rhythm section instruments is a clear harbinger of the coming soul movement of the seventies. Of course, the most distinguishing characteristic of the song is Jimmy Nolen's stiletto-like guitar riff after the hook is sung.

"YOU KEEP ME HANGING ON"

(Brian Holland/Lamont Dozier/Eddie Holland), **the Supremes**

Track 19

Personnel: Diana Ross, Mary Wilson, Florence Ballard: vocals; the Funk Brothers: rhythm section
Produced by Holland/Dozier/Holland
Highest chart position: #1, 1966

As their eighth #1 hit in a little over two years, "You Keep Me Hanging On" represented a change of direction toward a harder rock sound for the Supremes. Gone are the richly orchestrated strings and horns, leaving the hard driving Funk Brothers rhythm section to propel the song. Guitarist Robert White's Morse code-like guitar riff continues throughout the entire song except for the bridges. Two staples of all Holland/Dozier/Holland productions are also present: the relentless emphasis on the backbeat (by the snare drums, rhythm guitar and tambourine), and the funky, percolating bass of James Jamerson.

"You Keep Me Hanging On" was recorded at Motown's Snakepit studio on June 30, 1966 and hit the charts on October 29 at #68. In three weeks it was the #1 song in the country, where it stayed for two weeks. The Supremes next two records would also hit #1, ending a remarkable run of ten #1 records out of the thirteen released since July, 1964.

"SOUL MAN"

(Isaac Hayes/David Porter), **Sam and Dave**

Track 20

Personnel: Sam Moore, Dave Prater: vocals; Isaac Hayes: piano; Steve Cropper: guitar; Donald "Duck" Dunn: bass; Al Jackson, Jr.: drums; Wayne Jackson: trumpet; Andrew Love: tenor sax
Produced by Isaac Hayes and David Porter
Highest chart position: #2, 1967

"Soul Man" was the highest charting hit for Sam and Dave, but stalled at #2 for three weeks in the fall of 1967 and never quite made it to the top. Recorded on August 10, it featured Stax Records two session groups – Booker T. and the MG's and the Memphis Horns – although Booker T. Jones himself was away at college and missed the session. "Soul Man" did manage to hit #1 on the R&B charts for seven weeks, and over the years has become a soul anthem that has transcended its time and place to become a part of American culture.

There are a number of ingredients that work together to make "Soul Man" so irresistible. First, the simple but punchy beat laid down by drummer Jackson, bassist Dunn and guitarist Cropper is one of the most infectious dance beats ever recorded. Cropper's opening riff and the five-note lick in each chorus (that draws a "Play it, Steve!" from the singers) are among the most memorable in rock. Sam and Dave are quite simply on fire, soul evangelists who sing the praises of their manhood ("I learned how to love, before I could eat!"), sometimes harmonizing, sometimes going back and forth in call and response fashion. And then there are the powerful Memphis Horns, who add just the right punch without getting in the way. The song was redone and featured in the 1978 movie *Blues Brothers*, sung by Dan Ackroyd and John Belushi.

"THANK YOU (FALETTINME BE MICE ELF AGIN)"
(Sylvester Stewart), **Sly and the Family Stone**

Personnel: Sylvester "Sly Stone" Stewart: vocals, keyboards; Larry Graham: bass; Freddie Stone: guitar; Rosie Stone: piano, vocals; Gregg Errico: drums; Cynthia Robinson: trumpet; Jerry Martini: saxophone
Highest chart position: #1, 1970

Sly Stone's multi-ethnic, multi-gender band produced some of the most commercially successful funk of the seventies, with "Thank You ("Thank You (Falettinme Be Mice Elf Agin)" becoming his second #1 hit in February 1970. The song is built around a simple one chord, one bar pattern played by bassist Graham, guitarist Freddie Stone and drummer Errico that the band departs from only twice, for short interludes at 1:12 and 2:16. Group vocal chants are used throughout the entire song.

"Thank You ("Thank You (Falettinme Be Mice Elf Agin)" is an anthem to individual freedom, and the triumph of turning away from the violence of the streets. It came at a time when Sly Stone was under pressure to "align himself with the voices of despair and nihilism", according to David Kapralik, who wrote an article on the singer for *Rolling Stone* in 1971. Despite continuing to write songs with positive messages that resonated with both black and white youth, the pressure of fame and fortune proved to be enough for twenty-five year old Sly to develop a cocaine habit that would hamper him throughout the seventies.

"GET UP, STAND UP"
(Bob Marley/Peter Tosh), **Peter Tosh**

Personnel: Peter Tosh: vocals, guitar, keyboards; Sly Dunbar: drums; Earl Lindo: keyboards; Bunny Wailers: background vocals; Robbie Shakespeare: bass; Al Anderson: guitar; Carlie Barrett: drums; Harold Butler: clavinet; Tyrone Downie: keyboards; Karl Pitterson: guitar; Skully: percussion; Abdul Wall: guitar
Produced by Peter Tosh
Recorded at Randy's Studio 17, Kingston, Jamaica

"Get Up, Stand Up" is the opening track from *Equal Rights*, the 1977 album that launched Peter Tosh (real name: Peter MacIntosh) to star status that rivaled his former band mate Bob Marley. It is also one of the most political reggae albums from either artist, with songs that protest the policies of South Africa ("Apartheid"), rally against Babylon oppressors ("Downpresser Man"), and preach of African unity ("Africa"). Of course, "Get Up, Stand Up," a rallying cry to take action against the system (co-written with Marley), is the most political of all. On "Get Up, Stand Up," Tosh sings with clear, impassioned vocals, while backed by the powerful rhythm section anchored by Sly Dunbar and Carlie Barrett on drums and Robbie Shakespeare on bass.

REFERENCES

Altschuler, Glenn C.: *All Shook Up: How Rock and Roll Changed America;* Oxford University Press, New York, 2003

AMG All Music Guide

Barkley, Elizabeth F.: *Crossroads: Popular Music in America;* Prentice Hall, Inc, Upper Saddle River, New Jersey, 2003

Bronson, Fred: *The Billboard Book of Number One Hits;* Billboard Publications, New York, 1992

Christgau, Robert: *Any Way You Choose It: Rock and Other Pop Music 1967–1973;* Penguin Books, Baltimore, MD, 1973

Cogan, Jim and Clark, William: *Temples of Sound: Inside the Great Recording Studios;* Chronicle Books, San Francisco, 2003

Cohodas, Nadine: *Spinning Blues Into Gold: The Chess Brothers and the Legendary Chess Records;* St. Martin's Press, St. Martin's Press, New York, 2000

Curtis, Jim: *Rock Eras: Interpretations of Music and Society, 1954–1984;* Bowling Green State University Press, 1987

Davis, Francis: *The History of the Blues;* Hyperion Books, New York, 1995

Davis, Stephen: *Hammer of the Gods: The Led Zeppelin Saga;* Ballantine Books, 1985

Escott, Colin with Hawkins, Martin: *Good Rockin' Tonight: Sun Records and the Birth of Rock 'n' Roll;* St. Martins Press, New York, 1991

Fong-Torres, Ben: *The Hits Just Keep on Coming: The History of Top 40 Radio;* Miller Freeman Books, San Francisco, 1998

Friedlander, Paul: *Rock & Roll: A Social History;* Westview Press, Boulder, CO, 1996

Gaines, Steven: *Heroes and Villains: The True Story of the Beach Boys;* Da Capo Press, New York, 1995

Garofalo, Reebee: *Rockin' Out: Popular Music in the USA;* Prentice Hall, Inc, Upper Saddle River, New Jersey, 2002

Gillett, Charlie: *The Sound of the City: The Rise of Rock and Roll;* Outerbridge & Dienstfrey, New York, 1970

Gilmore, Mikal: *Night Beat: A Shadow History of Rock and Roll;* Doubleday, New York, 1998

Guralnick, Peter: *Last Train to Memphis: The Rise and Fall of Elvis Presley;* Little, Brown and Company, Boston, 1994

Guralnick, Peter: *Sweet Soul Music: Rhythm and Blues and the Southern Dream of Freedom;* Back Bay Books, Boston, 1986

Harry, Bill: *The Ultimate Beatles Encyclopedia;* MJF Books, New York, 1992

Hertsgaard, Mark: *A Day in the Life: The Music and Artistry of the Beatles;* Delacorte Press, 1995

Holm-Hudson, Kevin: *Progressive Rock Reconsidered;* Routledge, New York, 2002

Kitwana, Bakari: *The Hip Hop Generation: Young Blacks and the Crisis in African-American Culture;* Basic Civitas Books, New York, 2002

Konow, David: *Bang Your Head: The Rise and Fall of Heavy Metal;* Three Rivers Press, New York, 2002

Kostelanetz, Richard: *The Frank Zappa Companion: Four Decades of Commentary;* Schirmer Books, New York, 1997

Laing, Dave: *One Chord Wonders: Power and Meaning in Punk Rock;* Open University Press, Milton Keynes, U.K., 1985

Lomax. Alan: *The Land Where the Blues Began;* New Press, New York, 1993

Norman, Philip: *Shout, The Beatles in Their Generation;* Fireside Books, New York, 1981

Palmer, Robert: *Dancing in the Street: A Rock and Roll History;* BBC Books, London, 1996

Romanowski, Patricia and George-Warren, Holly: *The New Rolling Stone Encyclopedia of Rock & Roll;* Fireside, New York, 1995

Rose, Tricia: *Black Noise: Rap Music and Black Culture in Contemporary America;* Wesleyan University Press, Hanover, 1994

Schaefer, G. W. Sandy; Smith, Donald S.; Shellans, Michael J.: *Here to Stay: Rock and Roll through the '70s;* GILA Publishing Co., 2001

Shelton, Robert: *No Direction Home: The Life and Music of Bob Dylan;* Ballantine Books, New York, 1986

Snyder, Randall: *An Outline History of Rock and Roll;* Kendall/Hunt, Dubuque, IA, 2001

Sounes, Howard: *Down the Highway: The Life of Bob Dylan;* Grove Press, New York, 2001

Starr, Larry and Waterman, Christopher: *American Popular Music: From Minstrelsy to MTV;* Oxford University Press, New York, 2003

Stuessy, Joe and Lipscomb, Scott: *Rock and Roll, It's History and Stylistic Development;* Prentice Hall, Inc, Upper Saddle River, New Jersey, 2003

Thompson, Dave: *Never Fade Away: The Kurt Cobain Story;* St. Martin's, 1994

Ward, Ed; Stokes, Geoffrey, and Tucker, Ken: *Rock of Ages: The History of Rock and Roll;* Prentice Hall, Inc, Englewood Cliffs, New Jersey, 1986

Whitburn, Joel: *The Billboard Book of Top 40 Albums;* Billboard Publications, New York, 1995

Whitburn, Joel: *The Billboard Book of Top 40 Hits;* Billboard Publications, New York, 1996

White, Armond: *Rebel For the Hell of It: The Life of Tupac Shakur;* Thunder's Mouth Press, New York, 1997

Wicke, Peter: *Rock Music: Culture, aesthetics and sociology;* Cambridge University Press, New York, 1987

INDEX

A

AAB lyric form, 7
Abbey Road, 120-121
Abdul, Paula, 252
Abramson, Herb, 24
acid rock (psychedelic rock). *See* San
    Francisco acid rock
Aerosmith, 189-190, 258
African Americans. *See also* soul music
    Brown, James, as spokesman for, 90
    funk and, 204
    pop artists' career decline in, 202
    rock and roll's roots influenced
        by, 2, 7-14
Aguilera, Christine, 273
Air Supply, 178
Albin, Peter, 143
Aldon Music, 55-56, 93
Alexander, J.W., 91
Alice Cooper, 188-189
Alice in Chains, 270
"All You Need Is Love," 119
Allen, Lee, 35
Allen, Rick, 251
Allen, Steve, 33, 53
Allen, Woody, 165
Allison, Jerry, 43
Allman, Duane, 153, 175-176
Allman, Greg, 175-176
The Allman Brothers Band, 153,
    174-176
The Almanac Singers, 73
Alpert, Herb, 65
Altamont, 125-126, 160
alternative rock, 269
    characteristics/key recordings
        of, 249
    nineties in, 270-273
The Amboy Dukes, 137, 191
American Bandstand, 42, 52-54,
    61, 163
amplifier, 61
The Anchor, 226
Anderson, Ian, 195
Anderson, Jon, 194
Anderson, Pink, 193

Anderson, Signe, 141
Andrews, Sam, 143
the Animals, 56, 131, 151, 167
Anka, Paul, 43, 51
Anthem School, 250
Anthony, Marc, 273
Anthony, Michael, 190
Anthrax, 191, 251
Apple, Fiona, 273
The Archies, 67
Are You Experienced?, 154, 171-172
Armstrong, Louis, 3, 9
art rock, 191
    characteristics of, 192
    important bands in, 193-195
    key recordings of, 192
The Artist Formerly Known As,
    243-244
Asher, Tony, 63
Ashford and Simpson, 94-95
Ashford, Nicholas, 94
Ashford, Rosalind, 99
Atkins, Chet, 32, 44
Atkins, Cholly, 93
Atlanta Rhythm Section, 176
Atlantic Records, 13
Audio Home Recording Act, 276
Autry, Gene, 16
Avalon ballroom, 138, 143
Avalon, Frankie, 51-52, 60
Avalone, Francis. *See* Avalon, Frankie
Avory, Mick, 123, 131
Axton, Estelle, 100-103
Axton, Packy, 101
Ayler, Albert, 224

B

The B52's, 230
Bach, J.S., 191
Bacharach, Burt, 65-66
Bacharach/David, 65-66
back spinning, 257
The Backstreet Boys, 273
Bad Boy, 261-263
Baez, Joan, 14, 74-75, 77-78, 80, 146
Baker, Ginger, 152, 155

Baker, James, 246
Baker, Susan, 246
Baldry, Long John, 197
Balin, Marty, 138, 140-141
ballads, 14
Ballard, Florence, 99
Ballard, Hank, 12-13
Balzary, Michael, 250
Bambaataa, Afrika, 257-258
Band Aid, 248
Band of Gypsys, 156
The Band, 79-81, 146, 171-172
Bangs, Lester, 182
Banks, Peter, 194
bar blues band style, 11
The Bar-Kays, 103-104
Barrett, Aston, 212
Barrett, Carlton, 212
Barrett, Syd, 193
Barry, Jeff, 56, 58-59
Bartholomew, Dave, 35
the Basement Tapes, 80, 171
Basie, Count, 9, 210
Bates, Norman, 226
BBC. *See* British Broadcasting
    Corporation
BDP, 259
The Beach Boys, 14, 44, 57, 60, *62,*
    62-64
Beard, Annette, 99
The Beastie Boys, 258-259
beat writers, 77
Beatlemania, 115
Beatles for Sale, 117
The Beatles, 37, 39, 41, 44, 53, 57, 60,
    63, 66, 105, 114-115, *116,*
    126-127, 160, 186, 191-192, 215,
    221, 226, 268-269
    aftermath of, 121-122
    "All You Need Is Love," TV appear-
        ance by, 119
    American arrival of, 110, 116
    best selling single of, 119
    breakup of, 120-121
    drugs and, 79, 117-118, 137
    Dylan and, 79, 81, 117
    The Ed Sullivan Show with, 116